SAP PRESS e-books

Print or e-book, Kindle or iPad, workplace or airplane: Choose where and how to read your SAP PRESS books! You can now get all our titles as e-books, too:

- By download and online access
- For all popular devices
- And, of course, DRM-free

Convinced? Then go to www.sap-press.com and get your e-book today.

SAP PRESS is a joint initiative of SAP and Rheinwerk Publishing. The know-how offered by SAP specialists combined with the expertise of Rheinwerk Publishing offers the reader expert books in the field. SAP PRESS features first-hand information and expert advice, and provides useful skills for professional decision-making.

SAP PRESS offers a variety of books on technical and business-related topics for the SAP user. For further information, please visit our website: *www.sap-press.com*.

Janet Salmon, Michel Haesendonckx
SAP S/4HANA Finance: The Reference Guide to What's New
2019, 505 pages, hardcover and e-book
www.sap-press.com/4838

Stoil Jotev
Configuring SAP S/4HANA Finance
2019, 756 pages, hardcover and e-book
www.sap-press.com/4857

Anup Maheshwari
Implementing SAP S/4HANA Finance: System Conversion Guide (3rd Edition)
2020, 632 pages, hardcover and e-book
www.sap-press.com/5058

Mehta, Aijaz, Duncan, Parikh
SAP S/4HANA Finance: An Introduction
2019, 397 pages, hardcover and e-book
www.sap-press.com/4784

Peter Jones, Charles Soper
Implementing SAP Business Planning and Consolidation (3rd Edition)
2018, 965 pages, hardcover and e-book
www.sap-press.com/4600

Eric Ryan, Thiagu Bala, Satyendra Raghav,
Azharuddin Mohammed

Group Reporting with SAP S/4HANA®

Rheinwerk
Publishing

Editor Megan Fuerst
Acquisitions Editor Emily Nicholls
Copyeditor Julie McNamee
Cover Design Graham Geary
Photo Credit Shutterstock.com: 26258740/© Rich Lindie
Layout Design Vera Brauner
Production Graham Geary
Typesetting III-satz, Husby (Germany)
Printed and bound in the United States of America, on paper from sustainable sources

ISBN 978-1-4932-1999-5
© 2021 by Rheinwerk Publishing, Inc., Boston (MA)
1st edition 2021

Library of Congress Cataloging-in-Publication Data
Library of Congress Cataloging-in-Publication Data
Names: Ryan, Eric, author. | Bala, Thiagu, author. | Raghav, Satyendra,
    author. | Mohammed, Azharuddin, author.
Title: Group reporting with SAP S/4HANA / Eric Ryan, Thiagu Bala,
    Satyendra Raghav, Azharuddin Mohammed.
Description: 1st edition. | Bonn ; Boston : Rheinwerk Publishing, 2020. |
    Includes index.
Identifiers: LCCN 2020036129 (print) | LCCN 2020036130 (ebook) | ISBN
    9781493219995 (hardcover) | ISBN 9781493220007 (ebook)
Subjects: LCSH: Financial statements--Data processing. | Accounting--Data
    processing. | SAP HANA (Electronic resource)
Classification: LCC HF5681.B2 R88 2020 (print) | LCC HF5681.B2 (ebook) |
    DDC 657/.32028553--dc23
LC record available at https://lccn.loc.gov/2020036129
LC ebook record available at https://lccn.loc.gov/2020036130

Contents at a Glance

1	Introduction to Consolidation	17
2	Group Reporting Architecture and Components	31
3	Master Data	69
4	Transaction Data	121
5	Currency Translation	175
6	Intercompany Elimination	215
7	Consolidation of Investments	257
8	Consolidation Entries	283
9	Matrix Consolidation	299
10	Financial Close	313
11	Consolidation Reporting	323
12	Conclusion	357

Dear Reader,

Have you ever seen the painting *A Sunday on La Grande Jatte* by Georges Seurat? Think dots. Thousands of dots.

Growing up near Chicago, I was lucky enough to pay frequent visits to The Art Institute of Chicago, where this famous painting has long been a fixture. (Perhaps you remember that scene in *Ferris Bueller's Day Off*?) It's an impressive example of pointillism, a technique where the artist carefully places dots of various colors that combine in the eye of the viewer to create a cohesive image. In the case of this painting, the disparate dots blend to form a peaceful scene of Parisian park-goers on the riverbank.

Why was I reminded of this painting while editing the book in your hands? When organizations report on their month-and year-end finances, they must consolidate data of many different types from many different locations—an even grander scale than thousands of dots on a canvas. Group reporting allows companies to develop a cohesive view of their consolidated finances. In this book, you'll get the expert guidance you need to create such a masterpiece with SAP S/4HANA. There is art in finance, after all!

What did you think about *Group Reporting with SAP S/4HANA*? Your comments and suggestions are the most useful tools to help us make our books the best they can be. Please feel free to contact me and share any praise or criticism you may have.

Thank you for purchasing a book from SAP PRESS!

Megan Fuerst
Editor, SAP PRESS

meganf@rheinwerk-publishing.com
www.sap-press.com
Rheinwerk Publishing · Boston, MA

Contents

Preface 13

1 Introduction to Consolidation   17

1.1 **Financial Consolidation Basics** 17
    1.1.1 Consolidation Steps 18
    1.1.2 Consolidation Concepts 20

1.2 **Why Consolidate Financials Data?** 22
    1.2.1 International Financial Reporting Standards 22
    1.2.2 Generally Accepted Accounting Principles 23

1.3 **Evolution of Consolidation with SAP Solutions** 23
    1.3.1 Financial Accounting: Legal Consolidation 24
    1.3.2 Enterprise Controlling: Consolidation System 24
    1.3.3 SAP Strategic Enterprise Management: Business Consolidation System 25
    1.3.4 SAP Business Planning and Consolidation 26
    1.3.5 Real-Time Consolidation in SAP S/4HANA 28
    1.3.6 Group Reporting with SAP S/4HANA 29

1.4 **Summary** 30

2 Group Reporting Architecture and Components   31

2.1 **SAP S/4HANA Finance** 31
    2.1.1 Architecture 32
    2.1.2 SAP Fiori 34

2.2 **Group Reporting** 37
    2.2.1 Technical Architecture 37
    2.2.2 Finance Analytics 38
    2.2.3 Predelivered Content 48

2.3 **Summary** 68

3   Master Data   69

3.1   Global Settings 69

3.2   Group Reporting Master Data 72

    3.2.1   Consolidation Entities 72

    3.2.2   Financial Statement Items 79

    3.2.3   Financial Statement Item Attributes and Hierarchies 83

    3.2.4   Breakdown Categories 92

    3.2.5   Subitem Categories and Subitems 93

    3.2.6   Consolidation Fields (Additional Fields) 100

    3.2.7   Consolidation Versions 103

    3.2.8   Document Types 107

3.3   Selections 118

3.4   Summary 120

4   Transaction Data   121

4.1   What Is the Data Monitor? 121

    4.1.1   Layout 122

    4.1.2   Task 123

4.2   Configuring the Data Monitor 124

4.3   Integrating Transaction Data 130

    4.3.1   Universal Ledger 131

    4.3.2   Flexible Upload 133

    4.3.3   API Integration (Cloud Only) 138

4.4   Plan Data Integration 139

4.5   Balance Carryforward 140

    4.5.1   Setting Up Balance Carryforward 140

    4.5.2   Executing and Validating the Balance Carryforward 145

4.6   Calculation of Net Income 147

4.7   Data Validation 152

    4.7.1   Validation Rules 152

    4.7.2   Validation Methods 156

    4.7.3   Import/Export Validation Settings 160

    4.7.4   Reported Data Validation 161

    4.7.5   Standardized Data Validation 163

4.8   Journal Entries 164

	4.8.1	Group Journal Entries	164
	4.8.2	General Journal Entries	167
	4.8.3	Release Universal Journal Task	170
	4.8.4	Validate Universal Journal Task	171
4.9	**Summary**		172

5   Currency Translation   175

5.1	**What Is Currency Translation?**		175
	5.1.1	Currency Translation Basics	176
	5.1.2	Currency Translation in SAP S/4HANA	179
5.2	**Configuring Currency Translation**		181
	5.2.1	Exchange Rate Types	181
	5.2.2	Exchange Rate Indicators	191
	5.2.3	Currency Translation Methods	194
	5.2.4	Consolidation Unit Method Assignment	201
	5.2.5	Financial Statement Item Currency Translation Attribute	202
5.3	**Translating Reported Currency**		206
	5.3.1	Execution in the Data Monitor	206
	5.3.2	Validating the Execution	207
	5.3.3	Reporting	207
5.4	**Summary**		213

6   Intercompany Elimination   215

6.1	**What Is Intercompany Elimination?**		216
	6.1.1	Reporting and Financial Statements	216
	6.1.2	Sales and COGS Elimination	219
	6.1.3	Inventory Elimination	220
	6.1.4	Expense Elimination	221
6.2	**What Is the Consolidation Monitor?**		222
	6.2.1	Layout	223
	6.2.2	Tasks	224
6.3	**Configuring the Consolidation Monitor**		227
	6.3.1	Reclassification Methods	227
	6.3.2	Tasks and Task Groups	233
	6.3.3	Defining Document Types	237

6.4 **Configuring Intercompany Elimination** 240
    6.4.1 Business Rules 240
    6.4.2 Predefined Configurations 248

6.5 **Eliminating Intercompany Transactions** 249
    6.5.1 Execution in the Consolidation Monitor 249
    6.5.2 Validating Eliminations and Reclassifications 251
    6.5.3 Reporting 253

6.6 **Summary** 255

7   Consolidation of Investments   257

7.1 **What Is Consolidation of Investments?** 258
    7.1.1 Rule-Based Consolidation of Investments 258
    7.1.2 Activity-Based Consolidation of Investments 262

7.2 **Configuring Consolidation of Investments** 264
    7.2.1 Reviewing Consolidation Methods 264
    7.2.2 Configuring Consolidation Groups 269
    7.2.3 Modifying Predefined Configuration 271

7.3 **Running Equity Pickup** 279
    7.3.1 Execution in the Consolidation Monitor 279
    7.3.2 Validating Consolidation of Investments 280
    7.3.3 Reporting 281

7.4 **Summary** 282

8   Consolidation Entries   283

8.1 **Common Consolidation Entries** 283

8.2 **Journal Entry Template** 285
    8.2.1 Getting Started 286
    8.2.2 Configuring the Journal Entry Template 288
    8.2.3 Making Consolidation Entries 291

8.3 **Summary** 297

9 Matrix Consolidation

9.1	What Is Matrix Consolidation?	299
9.2	Configuring Matrix Consolidation	300
	9.2.1 Parameters and Master Data	301
	9.2.2 Business Rules	302
9.3	Running Matrix Consolidation	305
	9.3.1 Managing Global Accounting Hierarchies	305
	9.3.2 Reporting	307
9.4	Summary	311

10 Financial Close

10.1	Ledger Close	313
10.2	Group Close	316
	10.2.1 Period-End Close	316
	10.2.2 Dependencies on Ledger Close	319
	10.2.3 Continuous Accounting Using Group Reporting	319
10.3	Summary	321

11 Consolidation Reporting

11.1	Predefined Reports	323
	11.1.1 Local (Preconsolidation) Reports	323
	11.1.2 Group (Consolidated) Reports	324
11.2	Drill-Through to Transaction Data	326
11.3	Data Analysis Using Reporting Rules	328
11.4	Additional Reporting Tools	333
	11.4.1 SAP Analysis for Microsoft Office	333
	11.4.2 SAP Analytics Cloud	342
	11.4.3 SAP Fiori	350
11.5	Summary	355

12 Conclusion

357

12.1 **Book Summary** 357

12.2 **Considerations for Your Group Reporting Journey** 358

12.3 **Five Key Takeaways** 360

The Authors 363

Index 365

Preface

With the release of SAP S/4HANA Finance for group reporting, organizations are presented with a unique opportunity to use technology to enable their external reporting and consolidation processes. Further, with the introduction of group reporting, organizations can transform into intelligent enterprises that use innovative technology to efficiently and effectively close the books while making informed decisions using accurate, real-time data.

As you read through this book, we'll introduce you to the consolidation process, which is the unique architecture that group reporting uses to deliver value to organizations around the world, and we'll explore the wide world of consolidated reporting.

Objective of This Book

Many finance organizations in companies around the world are faced with the same challenges. How do I close my books faster? How do I avoid manual activities such as data reconciliation and manual journal entries? What is my reporting strategy to deliver insightful, meaningful information in a timely fashion? For those companies on the SAP S/4HANA journey, they need to consider the role a consolidation tool plays in their journey, specifically, group reporting, SAP's strategic consolidation solution that seeks to deliver a faster close and reliable, reconciled data that can be delivered to management in near real time.

This book is intended to be a guide for those seeking a deeper understanding of the consolidation process and how group reporting enables the process to create an intelligent enterprise. More specifically, this book illustrates the consolidation process in great detail and includes the following:

- A comprehensive overview of group reporting architecture, including the data model, integration with SAP S/4HANA, and support for reporting.
- A deep dive into group reporting configuration, including global settings necessary for successful implementation and specific master data elements.
- An exploration into the nuances of integrating financial data for consolidation across key consolidation activities: balance carryforward, currency translation, consolidation of investments, and financial reporting.
- An in-depth look at new functionality provided by the tool, including matrix consolidation and local and group close.

Target Audience

This book is intended for business users, technology consultants, and functional consultants who want to better understand the role that group reporting plays in financial consolidations. This book will be useful for those who are part of a finance organization and have an interest in learning more about financial consolidations or who are looking for a reference as they embark on their implementation journey. From consultants, IT professionals, business users, and others, there is something for everyone in the pages within.

IT professionals, for example, will reference this book during their company's global group reporting project implementation. It will help them understand what to expect during the implementation process, provided a deeper understanding of the consolidation process, and offer some tips and tricks in maintaining the solution going forward.

For IT or business consultants, this book will act as a guide during their implementation journey and be a helpful reference during the entire project lifecycle. Further, it will become an indispensable reference document during the build and testing phases of the project.

Business users and management professionals may choose to read this book in a variety of ways. If group reporting was just implemented, this would be an excellent reference guide. Further, those business users who are not familiar with SAP nomenclature and terminology will find this book easy to understand and digest as they get familiar with the SAP terminology. If group reporting is about to be deployed or in the process of being implemented, business users may find this a helpful reference during the implementation journey, specifically during the design phase across each consolidation activity and during the testing phase as business users put their "hands on the keyboard" for the first time and get started with the tool.

How to Read This Book

This book can be read in many ways but is intended to be read sequentially, starting with an introduction to consolidation all the way through each of the detailed activities that are part of the consolidation process. This book's structure is made up of the following chapters:

- **Chapter 1: Introduction to Consolidation**
  In Chapter 1, we introduce consolidation, the motivations behind it, and how consolidation solutions have evolved at SAP.
- **Chapter 2: Group Reporting Architecture and Components**
  The journey of the book continues with Chapter 2, which details the data model advances with SAP's newest suite. This chapter covers the new on-premise and cloud

architecture of SAP S/4HANA, and it then focuses on the technical architecture and the available components that support group reporting specifically.

- **Chapter 3: Master Data**
  In Chapter 3, we dive into group reporting configuration and its dependency on certain global settings and a set of specific master data elements. This chapter explains how to configure each master data element with step-by-step instructions and screenshots.

- **Chapter 4: Transaction Data**
  Chapter 4 teaches the different approaches to integrating financial transaction data for consolidation. It focuses on how to configure both the Data Monitor and its tasks, including plan data integration, balance carryforward, calculation of net income, data validation, and journal entries.

- **Chapter 5: Currency Translation**
  Chapter 5 discusses the currency translation activity and dives into its configuration, including the methods and method assignments. It ends with instructions on executing, testing, and reporting on currency translation in the Data Monitor.

- **Chapter 6: Intercompany Elimination**
  Chapter 6 focuses on intercompany elimination using the Consolidation Monitor. It gives step-by-step instructions for configuring the Consolidation Monitor and intercompany elimination, as well as eliminating intercompany transactions.

- **Chapter 7: Consolidation of Investments**
  Chapter 7 moves on to consolidation of investments, which is an accounting method used for managing investments when an investing company doesn't control the entity that it has ownership in. This chapter explains the consolidation of investments process and discusses the initial and subsequent accounting entries required over the life of an equity investment. It then gives step-by-step instructions for configuring consolidation of investments and running the equity pickup process through reporting.

- **Chapter 8: Consolidation Entries**
  Chapter 8 highlights the common consolidation entries. It explains how the journal entry template is configured and then populated with consolidation entries.

- **Chapter 9: Matrix Consolidation**
  Chapter 9 explains matrix consolidation, including how to configure and execute it via the Consolidation Monitor. This is something new for group reporting in release 1909.

- **Chapter 10: Financial Close**
  Chapter 10 walks through the typical ledger and group close processes that accounting and finance teams perform each month. It introduces the continuous accounting concept that facilitates a faster close.

- **Chapter 11: Consolidation Reporting**

  Chapter 11 focuses on big-picture reporting: the reporting architecture used as part of group reporting; predefined reports, including local and group reports; drill-through functionality with examples; and available reporting tools.

- **Chapter 12: Conclusion**

  Chapter 12 reflects on the content covered in the book, outlines a few considerations for group reporting projects, and identifies five key takeaways.

Now, let's dive in to our first chapter to begin our journey with consolidation and SAP.

Chapter 1
Introduction to Consolidation

We'll start our journey through SAP S/4HANA Finance for group reporting with consolidation basics and detail how consolidation functionality has evolved over the years with SAP.

One of the most critical steps for any company is closing its financial books. As part of this financial process, companies with many business units will combine financial data from several business units within one single entity to report all business units together. This process is commonly referred to as *financial consolidation*. We'll explore further details regarding financial consolidations, regulations associated with consolidation, and the history of consolidation with SAP in this chapter.

1.1 Financial Consolidation Basics

In financial accounting, consolidated financial statements provide a comprehensive view of the financial position of both the parent company and its subsidiaries, rather than one company's standalone position. In consolidated accounting, the information from a parent company and its subsidiaries is treated as though it comes from a single entity. Figure 1.1 is an example consolidation entity structure with a parent and each of its children. The example used is a fictional soda company with Natural Soda Parent Company as the parent and its subsidiaries in North America and the United Kingdom. Further, you'll see Natural Soda Bottling is only 80% owned by Natural Soda NA, while Natural Soda UK is a minority owner in Natural Soda Iceland at only 40%. The consolidation entity structure is also commonly referred to as the ownership structure.

There are primarily two types of consolidation:

- **Legal consolidation**
  Performed due to the legal requirement of submitting financial statements to legal and statutory authorities. This consolidation is typically performed following Generally Accepted Accounting Principles (GAAP) or International Financial Reporting Standards (IFRS).
- **Management consolidation**
  Performed due to management requrements to understand the management view of the profit and loss (P&L) statement, balance sheet, and cash flow statement.

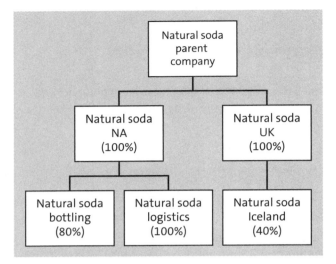

Figure 1.1 Example Consolidation Entity Structure

In both types of consolidation, activities fall into four main buckets:

- Data preparation
- Preconsolidation activities, including balance carryforward, manual journal entries, and so on
- Postconsolidation activities, including currency translation, intercompany elimations, and consolidation of investments
- Reporting and analysis

In the following sections, we'll unpack the main process steps that fall within these four buckets, before exploring key consolidation concepts.

1.1.1   Consolidation Steps

Figure 1.2 walks through the standard consolidation process steps, starting with data collection:

1. **Data collection**
   Data is collected from multiple sources, including but not limited to other general ledgers, flat file uploads, or a central repository.

2. **Balance carryforward**
   The ending balance from the prior fiscal year is carried forward to the beginning balance of the current fiscal year for all balance sheet accounts.

3. **Currency translation**
   Local currency is converted to one or more group currencies in accordance with accounting principles.

4. **Retained earnings reclass**

All activities that impact the income statement are completed so net income can be calculated for the corporate group. This activity closes out the income statement by transferring the balance of the income summary, net income, to the retained earnings account.

5. **Intercompany elimination**

All intercompany transactions should be eliminated at a parent level company to avoid double counting of transactions.

6. **Journal entries**

Post-elimination journal entries are made in the form of topside adjustments usually at the request of finance during the month-end close.

7. **Reporting**

Finance and accounting will want to run the P&L report, balance sheet report, trial balance report, and cash flow statement each month. Other specific operational reports may also be requested, for example, a specific segment P&L statement.

8. **Lock period**

After the revenue accounts, expense accounts, income summary, and dividend accounts are closed out, the period can be locked, which doesn't allow any further financial transactions to occur for the period. For instance, if you've just closed the month of June, period 6, after it's locked, no further entries are allowed to be posted for June.

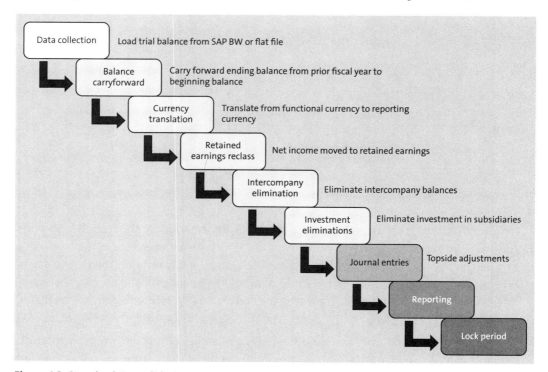

Figure 1.2 Standard Consolidation Process Steps

1.1.2   Consolidation Concepts

The four main concepts that are the lifeblood of consolidations—currency translation, intercompany eliminations, investment eliminations, and ownership—define how and where certain eliminations take place, as defined by the ownership group structure.

To start, *currency translation* is executed, translating all local currencies to the defined group currencies. Even if the company is a single currency company, and therefore doesn't need to translate, its usually a leading practice to configure currency translation and translate your currency, even if your local currency is the same as your group.

Following currency translation, the next fundamental consolidation concept is *intercompany elimination*, which refers to the process of "eliminating" transactions that occur between companies included in the preparation of consolidated accounts. It's also commonly referred to as the removal of transactions that occur between companies included in the consolidation group.

In Figure 1.3, you can see a sample parent company with transactions between both of its subsidiaries, along with the transactions that occur from subsidiary to subsidiary. During the process of performing intercompany eliminations, all intercompany transactions occurring under the umbrella of the parent, as illustrated here, must be eliminated to avoid double counting.

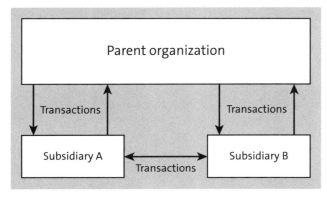

Figure 1.3 Example: Intercompany Eliminations

Next, *ownership* refers to the storage of specific information for the consolidation process. For example, ownership information will include maintenance of the ownership percentage of entities, consolidation methods, and specific rollup of data using a hierarchical view of the information for legal or management consolidations. Data stored here will be used to perform intercompany and ownership interest elimination entries.

The majority of corporations performing financial consolidations own multiple legal subsidiaries. In addition, a corporation may have a wide variety of ownership interests and complex ownership relationships that require specific month-end accounting activities.

The ownership structure (shown earlier in Figure 1.1) is also stored within the group reporting application to support intercompany eliminations and consolidation of investments. Both of these activities in the consolidation process require a reference to an ownership structure.

> **Note**
>
> Chapter 3 will discuss some of the settings required to capture ownership data for use in the entire consolidation process.

Finally, *consolidation of investments* is the step in the consolidation process to elimi-nate equity ownership in consolidation units that belong to the consolidation group (defined in ownership). Consolidation of investments eliminates the parent's invest-ment with its proportionate share in the stockholder's equity of the subsidiary. In doing so, the following investment elimination methods are available:

- **Purchase method**
  Typically used when an investor owns over 50% of the investee's shares. The pur-chase method is usually the method used by companies following GAAP for owner-ship of over 50%.

  The assets of the investee are added to the balance sheet of the investor at the fair market value price. Liabilities of the investee are subtracted from the fair value of the assets, and the amount paid by the investor over the net book value of the investee's assets and liabilities is goodwill. Goodwill is kept on the balance sheet and amortized annually.

- **Equity method**
  Typically used when a company holds 20% to 50% ownership of another company's stock, which is considered to be a significant influence in the investee. Under the equity method, the initial investment will be recorded at the historical cost, and adjustments are made to investment value as the investor's ownership position changes, including percentage ownership in net income, loss, and dividend payouts.

  For example, Company XYZ buys 10,000 shares of Company ABC at $15 a share. Company A would record the cost of the investment at cost, that is, $150,000. As profit or income is derived from the investment, it would change the value of the investment over time, proportionate to the investor's shares in the investee. This is known as "equity pickup."

  Unlike the purchase method, the equity method doesn't have an elimination to per-form as part of consolidation. Rather, the investor simply reports its proportionate share of the investee's equity at cost of the investment.

- **Proportional consolidation method**
  Specific to a joint venture, the proportional consolidation method records the assets and liabilities of a joint venture on a company's balance sheet in direct proportion to the percentage of ownership a company has in the venture. Let's look at an example.

From our example before, if Company XYZ has 60% controlling interest in Company ABC, Company XYZ would record the investment in Company ABC as 60% of its assets, liabilities, revenues, and expenses. If Company XYZ has revenues of $20 million and Company ABC has revenues of $10 million, Company XYZ would have total revenue of $26 million.

1.2   Why Consolidate Financials Data?

Consolidation of financial statements allows companies to report the aggregate reporting results of separate business units and separate legal entities. The Financial Accounting Standards Board (FASB) defines consolidated financial statement reporting as "reporting of an entity structured with a parent company and subsidiaries."

The amount of ownership the parent company has in the subsidiary is usually the driver behind whether a company chooses to file a consolidated financial statement, which may offer other advantages as well. Ownership of 50% or more in another company is the common definition of a subsidiary and allows the parent company to include it in a consolidated financial statement.

A company may account for its subsidiary ownership using the cost method or the equity method should it choose not to produce consolidated financial statements. The cost method is used when a company's investment doesn't have significant control or influence in the company being invested in, generally less than 20%. On the other hand, the equity method is generally used when the investment contains a more significant stake, usually between 20% and 50% ownership stake.

When a company produces a set of financial results, it's required to follow a set of financial reporting and accounting standards that vary from country by country. In this section, we'll dig into two sets of standards that are commonly used around the world:

- International Financial Reporting Standards (IFRS)
- Generally Accepted Accounting Principles (GAAP)

1.2.1   International Financial Reporting Standards

The international set of accounting standards are referred to as the International Financial Reporting Standards (IFRS). The purpose of IFRS is to have a commonly defined accounting language to be understood from company to company around the world. The International Accounting Standards Board (IASB) is an independent standard setting body responsible for promoting the use and application of IFRS.

IFRS is the standard for companies in the European Union and many other countries, but not in the United States. IFRS differs from GAAP in that IFRS is based on principles, meaning it has broad guidelines that are more easily followed.

While there are many differences between IFRS and GAAP, one main difference is in the handling of inventory. IFRS doesn't allow the use of last in, first out (LIFO) inventory accounting methods, whereas GAAP allows for it. IFRS permits use of inventory reversals whereas GAAP doesn't.

IFRS has a few principles defined for presenting and preparing consolidated financial statements. Specific consolidation principles to be followed can be found in IFRS 10 at *www.iasplus.com/en/standards/ifrs/ifrs10*. The principles are straightforward, including requiring any parent entities that have a controlling stake in other entities to therefore present consolidated financial statements. From an IFRS perspective, the concept of control is important to define consolidated financial statements of a group in which the parent and its subsidiaries consolidate their assets, liabilities, equity, income, and expenses, and cash flows into a single entity.

The investor/investee relationship is important to consolidations as determined by control. IFRS 10:7 defines an investor having control of an investee if the investor has all of the following: power over the investee, ability to use its power, and the right to returns in dealing with the investee. If all three of these conditions are met, the investor has control of the investee.

1.2.2   Generally Accepted Accounting Principles

Generally Accepted Accounting Principles (GAAP) is the common set of accepted accounting principles, standards, and procedures that companies must adhere to when preparing and assembling their financial statements. In the United States, the FASB defines the financial reporting practices, which are organized within the framework of GAAP.

GAAP require companies to eliminate intercompany transactions from their consolidated financial statements. In other words, they remove any movement of revenue, expenses, asset, liability, or equity from one entity to another within the same group to avoid double counting at the consolidated entity level. For more information on specific GAAP rules that must be followed, review the FASB Accounting Standards Codification (ASC) 323 and ASC 810.

1.3   Evolution of Consolidation with SAP Solutions

Since SAP launched SAP R/3 in 1992, it has tried to provide a technical solution to support financial consolidations. Technology has evolved since then, and SAP's underlying architecture has taken advantage of those technology innovations. Figure 1.4 shows how these solutions have evolved from SAP R/3.

What used to be a month-end accounting process following the closing of the books is now something that can be run in near real time throughout the month.

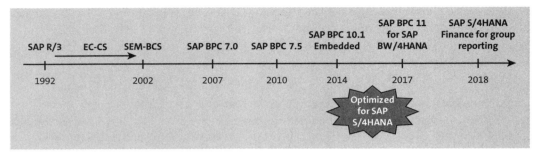

Figure 1.4 Timeline of SAP Consolidation Solutions

In the following sections, we'll explore the evolution of consolidation with different SAP solutions, including each of their features and, for some, a look into their architecture. This will help you understand how we've arrived at SAP S/4HANA group reporting, the most innovative consolidation solution yet.

1.3.1   Financial Accounting: Legal Consolidation

SAP's initial consolidation tool was a subcomponent of the overall Financial Accounting (FI) module supported as part of SAP R/3, officially launched in 1992. It gave companies the ability to consolidate their financial statements through the use of transaction codes but lacked any built-in web interface or business process functionality. It was maintained by the IT organization and required a deep knowledge of SAP R/3 to configure and use it. The core features included with Financial Accounting – Legal Consolidation (FI-LC) were as follows:

- Visibility was provided into underlying financial transactions with the ability to aggregate trial balances from multiple companies.
- The key dependency was that all companies in the group were on the common data platform; if not, significant integration and mapping to a single chart of accounts was required.

1.3.2   Enterprise Controlling: Consolidation System

When SAP introduced a complete architecture change from SAP R/3 to SAP ERP 6.0, Enterprise Controlling – Consolidation System (EC-CS) was also introduced as part of SAP ERP 6.0. Upon its release, there would be two common ways to consolidate financials, either using EC-CS or using a custom reporting solution on SAP Business Warehouse (SAP BW).

EC-CS allowed companies to consolidate multiple entities (i.e., company codes) directly within the ledger. EC-CS has similar features that exist in today's consolidation tools, but it was based on SAP BW technology rather than in-memory computing, which is used in SAP S/4HANA. Additionally, the tool wasn't as intuitive for business users. Instead, to configure and execute a consolidation in EC-CS, one had to have a deep understanding of transaction codes to make master data changes and to monitor consolidation tasks. While EC-CS did offer both a Data Monitor and Consolidation Monitor, they were GUI-based and not web-based tools as they are today.

To summarize, the following core features were included in EC-CS:

- Accounting document principles and logs for transparency into transactions and reconciliation activities
- Process monitor to actively manage execution of the consolidation process, identifying those processes that aren't started, in progress, completed, and failed
- Automatic consolidation of investments and intercompany eliminations

1.3.3   SAP Strategic Enterprise Management: Business Consolidation System

SAP released the SAP BW version of SAP Strategic Enterprise Management – Business Consolidation System (SEM-BCS) in 2002. SAP SEM offered customers the ability to perform comprehensive simulations and scenario analysis, saving valuable time and modeling effort in the process. BCS offered customers a breadth of flexibility in that it was customer definable with strong integration to SAP BW. For example, customers could define their own consolidation units whether they were entities or profit centers. This allowed for flexibility in performing management consolidations, something SAP Business Planning and Consolidation (SAP BPC) and Real-Time Consolidation (RTC) didn't offer. However, this new feature is part of SAP HANA Finance for group reporting as of release 1909, called matrix consolidations. We'll explore this feature in Chapter 9.

Other common features in SEM-BCS are as follows:

- **Data collection**
  Online data entry, flexible uploads, or loads from an InfoProvider (either SAP BusinessObjects Business Intelligence [SAP BusinessObjects BI] or a connected SAP system) are allowed. Data isn't real time and must be interfaced or loaded to be consumed in consolidations.
- **Flexible hierarchies**
  Hierarchies can be created for nearly any characteristic from financial master data to specific consolidation dimensions.
- **Versioning**
  Versioning allows execution of different consolidations for different types of data (actuals or budget) or to run different what-if scenarios and simulations.
- **Standard consolidation tasks**
  Currency translation intercompany eliminations, consolidation of investments, and balance carryforward can be run.

- **Reporting**
  SAP BusinessObjects BI reporting is used to analyze financial data with some preconfigured SAP BusinessObjects BI content.

1.3.4   SAP Business Planning and Consolidation

In 2007, SAP acquired OutlookSoft as a strategic acquisition to extend its depth beyond core enterprise resource planning (ERP) software and into the world of corporate performance management with a focus on planning, budgeting, forecasting, and consolidations. OutlookSoft's largest product was renamed SAP Business Planning and Consolidation (SAP BPC).

SAP BPC has been around for more than 10 years and remains, to this day, a very reliable product that was SAP's first attempt at a tool that could largely be managed by the business user. At the time of acquisition, OutlookSoft ran on a Microsoft platform, which meant very little maintenance and support. However, as the tool matured, SAP soon integrated SAP BPC with SAP NetWeaver, which allows the tool to run on SAP BW technology.

To date, there are multiple versions of SAP BPC, as follows:

- **SAP BPC 10.1, version for SAP NetWeaver**
  Commonly referred to as classic SAP BPC, this version is an extension of existing SAP BPC software that can be used for both planning and consolidation solutions. Additionally, data must be loaded to the SAP BPC cube either from SAP BW or from external systems, such as flat files. And, finally, SAP BPC 10.1 uses both SAP BW and SAP BPC systems for security configuration as users are created in the SAP BW system and granted permissions for objects and data in SAP BPC.

- **SAP BPC 10.1, version for SAP NetWeaver, embedded on SAP HANA**
  SAP BPC 10.1, embedded, is for planning only, and the embedded consolidation tool is group reporting. As a result, there is no transfer of data to the SAP BPC cube, rather it uses the SAP BW system and its objects directly. On the security front, most features are configured in SAP BW directly.

- **SAP BPC optimized for SAP S/4HANA**
  SAP BPC optimized for SAP S/4HANA eliminates data replication and leverages the real-time access to both transaction and master data in SAP S/4HANA. Additionally, it runs exclusively on the SAP S/4HANA Finance system and doesn't require a separate SAP BW system or replication of transactional or master data.

- **SAP BPC, version for Microsoft**
  This business planning, reporting, and consolidation solution built on Microsoft SQL Server technology is designed to be flexible and maintained by the business versus being maintained, historically, by IT.

While we're not going to go into details on each version in this book, we'll point out the key features that are unique to the SAP BPC product.

Before looking at the features, it's worth taking a peek at a high-level conceptual architecture feeding information from SAP ERP into SAP BW and then into SAP BPC. As you can see in Figure 1.5, data is moved between SAP ERP, SAP BW, and SAP BPC, which is no longer the case when using group reporting. Additionally, SAP BW and SAP BPC both have to be modeled to consume the information for use in consolidation and thus financial reporting. SAP BPC would have specific consolidation models defined to consume data from the source systems, in this case, SAP ERP, but you could also have flat files feeding SAP BPC as well.

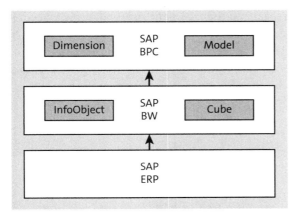

Figure 1.5 Classic SAP BPC Conceptual Architecture

Standard SAP BPC 10.1 is a planning, consolidation, and reporting solution based on SAP BW technology that includes the following features:

- **Users**
  SAP BPC is designed to be used and maintained by finance (business) users with minimal maintenance required.

- **Data collection**
  Integrations need to be built between SAP BW and SAP BPC through interfaces, which means there is no real-time access to data.

- **Data modeling**
  Modeling occurs through the web client instead of using SAP GUI.

- **Scripting**
  Scripting is written with Script Logic only.

- **Standard consolidation tasks**
  Currency translation, intercompany eliminations, consolidation of investments, and balance carryforward can be run.

- **Reporting**
  Enterprise Performance Management (EPM) is the Excel-based add-in used for executing packages, data inputs, and reporting.

1.3.5   Real-Time Consolidation in SAP S/4HANA

In 2016, Real-Time Consolidation (RTC) was introduced as part of the 1610 SAP S/4HANA release. Prior to release of SAP S/4HANA, SAP didn't have a fully integrated planning and consolidation tool within the SAP HANA suite of tools. In summary, RTC was intended to be the next-generation consolidation tool that offered integration between SAP S/4HANA and SAP BPC by allowing direct access to the Universal Journal and leveraging the consolidation capabilities offered by SAP BPC.

Figure 1.6 illustrates the RTC architecture as part of the RTC release 1610 FSP 01. As you can see, RTC allows users to perform legal and management consolidations and contains two tables in the SAP HANA database: table ACDOCA, the Universal Journal, which contains all financial line item documents, and table ACDOCC, the consolidation journal, which is an extension of table ACDOCA. All planning and consolidations take place within SAP S/4HANA, and users can consume all information from SAP HANA via the frontend tools of SAP Fiori, SAP Analysis for Microsoft Office, Design Studio, and the SAP BPC web console.

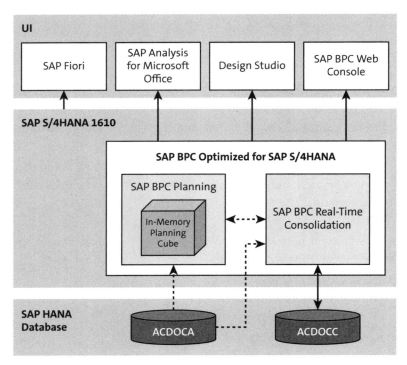

Figure 1.6 Real-Time Consolidation Architecture

RTC includes the following features:

- Integrated, common master data across RTC and SAP S/4HANA, eliminating the need to perform dual maintenance and addressing inconsistent data

- Requires use of group chart of accounts to facilitate aggregation of operational chart of accounts
- No longer needs to replicate and load data as the Universal Journal can be accessed in real time for consolidation
- Option to use SAP S/4HANA to perform currency translation in the Universal Journal prior to the consolidation process starting or executing within SAP BPC itself
- Ability to execute preliminary consolidation on actuals, supporting finance's desire to execute a continuous close throughout the month or simulate a certain business scenario
- Continued use of the web client to update business rules, Consolidation Monitor, and ownership structures
- Reporting performed in SAP Analysis for Microsoft Office, the newest version of the Excel add-in tool

While RTC did offer SAP's first integrated consolidation solution supporting "real time" consolidations, it had some architectural challenges that required a change to the long-term solution that SAP would support on its road map:

- Performance memory challenges were reoccurring with RTC due to the fact that the number of records could increase dramatically given the ability to map any field from table ACDOCA to table ACDOCC (the consolidation table). Additionally, the currency translation code wasn't optimized, requiring increased attention to the application of new SAP Notes.
- Master data also faced some issues, including missing descriptions in the Consolidation Monitor and reverse sign functionality.
- Only one key figure could be used in the consolidation model, and it can be a challenging concept for business users to understand that they can only use one group amount. Certainly, this could be mitigated, but it required some customization.

That long-term solution would be SAP S/4HANA Finance for group reporting.

1.3.6   Group Reporting with SAP S/4HANA

SAP S/4HANA Finance for group reporting version 1909 combines the best of all existing consolidation solutions into one solution that customers can deploy either on-premise or in the cloud. In a nutshell, this is the next-generation consolidation solution integrated in the SAP S/4HANA platform that offers native integration with accounting, planning, and reporting.

We'll certainly dig into all the features and technical details of the tool further in the book, but we see the following group reporting 1909 features as differentiators for the product:

- **Continuous accounting**
  Efficient, tactical approach to managing the accounting cycle more strategically. With a simplified architecture and full data integration, group reporting supports accounting's goal of moving toward continuous accounting through the following:
  - A unified reporting framework for both local and group currencies
  - Leverage of all the details of SAP S/4HANA where applicable
- **Group reporting platform**
  Ability to report consolidated actuals in near or real time. Consolidated reporting of financials is made easy through a simplified group reporting platform that has the following:
  - The capability to consolidate actuals, plan, and different one-off simulations or what-if scenarios
  - Full integration with SAP Analytics Cloud and application programming interfaces (APIs) to ingest or extract data
  - Ability to run and execute all standard consolidation tasks, including currency translation, intercompany elimination, and investment consolidation
- **Engineered for the cloud**
  Capable of cloud portability and use on a cloud architecture. The next generation of consolidation solutions will be built on the cloud, but group reporting is architected in a way that can be supported on premise while also being cloud portable with the following:
  - Dedicated cloud releases that offer the latest product innovations to consumers quickly
  - Integrated reporting capability with SAP Analytics Cloud and SAP Analysis for Microsoft Office

We'll dig into the details of all the exciting new features group reporting has to offer throughout the rest of the book.

1.4   Summary

In this chapter, we provided an overview of the consolidations process with a focus on intercompany eliminations, ownership, and investment consolidation. We also explored some relevant regulations related to consolidations while gaining an understanding of both GAAP and IFRS. Then we took a brief look at the history of consolidation in SAP, from its start as FI-LC on SAP R/3 to the next-generation tool SAP offers today, group reporting.

In the next chapter, we'll take a look under the hood to understand the power behind group reporting's on-premise and cloud architecture.

Chapter 2

Group Reporting Architecture and Components

Now that you have an understanding of consolidation with SAP, let's see how this works in SAP S/4HANA. In this chapter, we'll discuss the architecture that underlies group reporting in SAP S/4HANA.

SAP S/4HANA includes numerous data model improvements that have facilitated the arrival of SAP's newest consolidation solution, SAP S/4HANA Finance for group reporting. This chapter covers the modern architecture of SAP S/4HANA and then focuses on the technical architecture and data model that underlies group reporting specifically.

In the following sections, we'll explain the different reporting tool options, such as SAP Fiori, SAP Analysis for Microsoft Office, and SAP BusinessObjects Business Intelligence (SAP BusinessObjects BI), as well as the architecture of embedded analytics and the semantic layer of the reporting layer, core data services (CDS), and virtual data models (VDMs) within SAP S/4HANA. We'll explore the key features of different reporting tools and a sample decision tree to select the reporting tool to meet your requirements. We'll also provide an overview of the predelivered SAP Fiori apps.

2.1 SAP S/4HANA Finance

Over the years, growth in transactional databases and other data sources, as well as their associated systems, have complicated enterprise applications and infrastructure. Information is flooding into business, pushing data volumes through the roof. The world creates 2.5 quintillion bytes of data every day, and it's expected to grow even more in upcoming years. The massive growth of structured data is challenging enough and has complicated and impeded many organizations' ability to meet the needs of their business, whether that is timely access to analytics, the ability to absorb new business models, or being able to create unique, streamlined business processes. These shifts are making companies go through digital journeys, such as transforming business models, reengineering business processes, and reimagining work.

In this section, we'll explain the architecture and describe the three different types of SAP Fiori apps (analytical, transactional, and fact sheet).

2.1.1   Architecture

SAP S/4HANA serves as the digital platform for innovation and business process automation by reimaging the business processes and user experience (UX) as a harmonized single source of truth. SAP S/4HANA is built on the advanced in-memory computing platform (SAP HANA). SAP simplified the architecture by using the Universal Journal (table ACODCA) to drive one standard view of financial data for both financial accounting and controlling to help ensure enterprise-wide consistency to minimize reconciliation.

Figure 2.1 shows the SAP S/4HANA architecture and the different types of SAP Fiori apps. Following are the SAP S/4HANA architecture components:

- **SAP Fiori apps**

  SAP Fiori is a new UX for SAP software and applications. It provides a set of applications that are used in regular business functions such as work approvals, financial apps, calculation apps, and various self-service apps. SAP has developed SAP Fiori apps based on SAPUI5.

- **Analytical apps**

  Analytical apps provide role-based, real-time information about business operations. Analytical apps integrate the power of SAP HANA with SAP Business Suite to provide real-time information from a large volume of data in the frontend web browser.

- **Fact sheet apps**

  Fact sheet apps enable the business to drill down to the key information and contextual information in business operations. In SAP Fiori tiles, you can drill down to further details. It also allows you to navigate from one fact sheet to all its related fact sheets. Fact sheets also allow you to navigate to transactional apps to run SAP transactions. A few fact sheets also provide an integration option of geographical maps. You can call fact sheets from SAP Fiori launchpad search results, or from other fact sheet, transactional, or analytical apps.

  Fact sheets only run on the SAP HANA database and require an ABAP stack, and they can't be ported to SAP HANA Live two-tier architecture.

- **SAP Gateway**

  SAP Gateway offers development and generation tools to create OData services to a variety of client development tools. It establishes a connection between SAP Business Suite data and target clients, platforms, and programming framework.

  SAP Gateway is an open standards-based framework that developers can use to connect non-SAP applications to SAP applications more efficiently. It's also used to connect to and access SAP applications from mobile devices.

  SAP S/4HANA uses SAP Gateway and OData services to bring business data to compelling SAP Fiori apps.

- **Transactional logic**
  In transactional logic, additional logic can be applied to enhance the CDS views. Customers generally implement further checks, set default values, or create mappings in combination with custom fields in the logic. Additional joins and aggregations can be applied in the transactional logic.

- **Analytical engine**
  The analytical engine is used to evaluate and execute analytical queries at runtime. All the analytical tools consume CDS views, which make up the VDM of SAP S/4HANA. To use CDS views of type analytical queries, you must set up the analytical engine.

- **Enterprise search**
  Enterprise search is a search solution that provides unified, comprehensive, and secure real-time access to organizational data, which enables users to search for structured data (business objects) and allows direct access to the associated applications and actions. With SAP S/4HANA Cloud, users can use the powerful search bar and interact with the tool by using natural language.

- **CDS views**
  CDS views are built on existing database tables and views to provide an efficient method of data modeling. With CDS, data models are defined and consumed on the database rather than on the application server. CDS also offers capabilities beyond the traditional data modeling tools, including support for conceptual modeling and relationship definitions, built-in functions, and extensions.

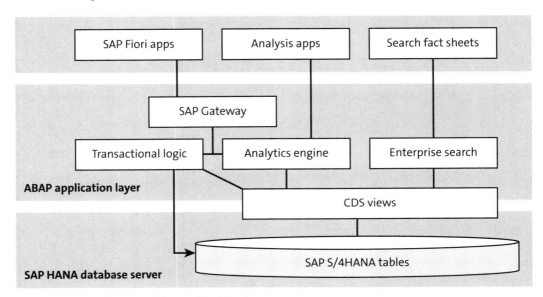

Figure 2.1 SAP S/4HANA High-Level Architecture

2.1.2   SAP Fiori

SAP's UX has come a long way from the early green screens of SAP R1. The legacy of SAP's tool was more focused on speed and performance, but customer experience is the new digital standard. SAP's next-generation UI, SAP Fiori, is built using HTML5/SAPUI5 mobile and OData services. SAP Fiori launchpad is the home page that is role-based for each user and has built-in advanced search capabilities to locate a document or master data records. Each SAP Fiori app is embedded in a tile and grouped together based on the user role. SAP Fiori apps can run on any device, including smartphones, tablets, laptops, and desktops. Each SAP Fiori app encloses the SAP transactions used by customers within SAP S/4HANA to render a fresh and modern UI to accomplish their tasks quickly and effortlessly. Whether working on a transaction or doing analytics, the user will have the same look and feel.

Figure 2.2 shows a standard purchase order, and Figure 2.3 shows the transition into the new SAP Fiori report, including key performance indicator (KPI) evaluations ❶, drill-downs ❷, and visualizations ❸.

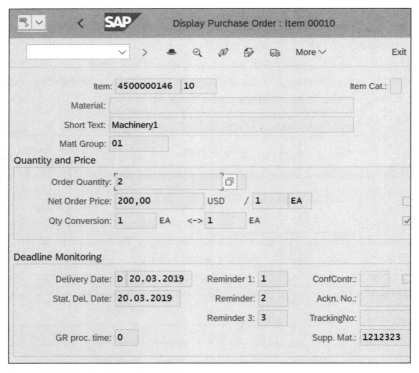

Figure 2.2 Standard Purchase Order

Figure 2.3 SAP UI Journey (SAP Fiori)

SAP Fiori apps provide tailored information for respective business roles. The role-based design enhances the overall UX with modern usability based on mobile principle with a high level of productivity, state-of-the-art performance, seamless interaction, and consistency across multiple devices.

Figure 2.4 shows the conceptual view of SAP Fiori's design and technology. The **Concept** section indicates that SAP Fiori is a role-based application with quick responsiveness supporting multiple devices and form factors but still simple and effective for the business. The design components enable faster decision-making for the business.

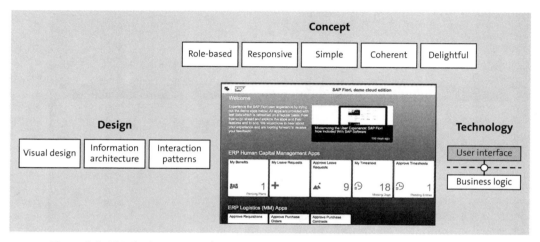

Figure 2.4 SAP Fiori Conceptual Overview

The SAP Fiori catalog is a set of related SAP Fiori apps that are combined into a catalog. IT administrators can assign SAP Fiori apps to a catalog. Several predelivered catalogs are available for consolidation (consolidation process, consolidation data preparation, period preparation, etc.). Groups are assigned to roles, and roles are assigned to users from Transaction SU01. Users can access an SAP Fiori app from the group or use the app search bar to find the application.

More than 400 SAP Fiori apps are predelivered in version 1909, and the apps are categorized into the following three types:

- **Transactional**
  Transactional apps are primarily used to execute business transactional tasks and represent simplified views and interaction with existing business processes and solutions.

- **Analytical**
  Analytical apps query the business data from SAP S/4HANA based on the user role and pull both the characteristics and key figures and present them in the SAP Fiori app. Analytical apps run on an ABAP/SAP HANA database and use VDMs.

- **Fact sheet**
  Fact sheet apps display contextual information and key facts about central objects used in business operations and help the users navigate from one fact sheet to its related fact sheets.

2.2   Group Reporting

In this section, we'll focus on the following areas: technical architecture, the key features of group reporting, different options to load data into group reporting, and usage of different analytics tools. We'll also cover the various reporting tools available to consume group reporting data.

2.2.1   Technical Architecture

Group reporting can be deployed as an on-premise solution on SAP S/4HANA Finance release 1809 or above and SAP S/4HANA Cloud. Group reporting is a unified financial consolidation and reporting solution with integrated and group data for greater transparency and analysis.

Group reporting includes the following key features:

- Continuous close
- Shared master data between transactional and consolidation solutions
- Several predelivered contents
- Matrix consolidation using several dimensions
- Support for multiple subgroup currencies
- Support for additional and custom dimensions (customer, profit center, etc.)
- Real-time data access
- On-the-fly drilldown to transaction data
- Currency translations using both cumulative and periodic balances

Figure 2.5 shows the overall group reporting architecture for both on-premise and cloud architectures. The identity provider is the Identity Authentication service to allow the users to access SAP Cloud Platform using various authentication types, such as form-based/Security Assertion Markup Language (SAML). The SAP S/4HANA Cloud SDK provides an access layer for application developers to consume the data models and data for developers. It provides a rich set of out-of-the-box libraries such as Java libraries, JavaScript libraries, and project templates that can be used to connect the SAP S/4HANA or SAP S/4HANA Cloud systems. The presentation layer has all the SAP Fiori apps (data load apps, data collection apps, etc.) for the users to execute the consolidation process and reports.

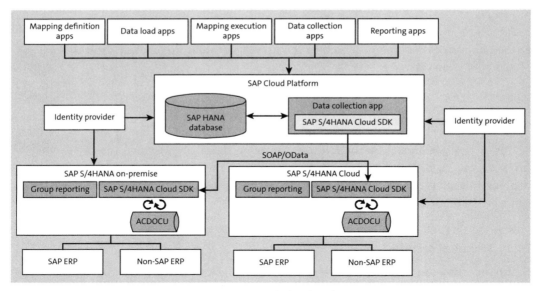

Figure 2.5 Group Reporting On-Premise and Cloud Architecture

The first step in the consolidation process is collecting the data from the subsidiaries and the parent company. Group reporting supports several data gathering methods:

- **Integrated approach**
  The consolidation solution can read the data in real time from the operational system SAP S/4HANA Universal Journal. Instead of deleting and reloading the data, the system can do incremental data loads. If the source system is a Central Finance implementation of SAP S/4HANA, then the data can be replicated in near real time into group reporting with extract, transform, load (ETL) capabilities using SAP Landscape Transformation Replication Server.

- **API**
  You might often see that the subsidiaries' transactional environment is on a non-SAP system, and the consolidation engine provides built-in APIs to load the data from non-SAP systems (only on SAP S/4HANA Cloud).

- **File upload**
  Group reporting also provides a standard interface to upload Excel and flat files.

- **Manual process**
  Predefined manual data entry forms are also available for the local accountants to publish their data, and these forms can also be custom built based on the dimension structure.

2.2.2   Finance Analytics

In the traditional reporting environment, the operational data (e.g., sales orders, invoice documents, account payables [AP], etc.) is extracted from the source system and loaded into the reporting system on predetermined frequencies for analytics. When transaction and analytics are separated, the business decisions are limited because the transactional and reporting data is often out of sync, and the analysis becomes meaningless.

In this section, we'll discuss SAP S/4HANA embedded analytics, as well as how CDS views and several SAP reporting solutions can be used for analysis, including a decision tree for deciding when to use them.

Embedded Analytics

Figure 2.6 shows the embedded architecture and how SAP S/4HANA brings both the transactions and analytics together into a single seamless platform. The presentation layer (SAP Fiori and analytics tools) is the entry point for users to access the transactions and reports. All the business logic for transactions is embedded in the application layer, but all calculations are pushed down to the database layer. The database layer has the physical storage of data in physical tables such as table ACDOCA, table ACDOCP, and so on.

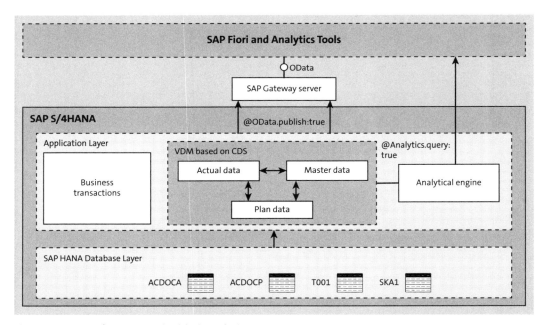

Figure 2.6 SAP S/4HANA Embedded Analytics

SAP S/4HANA embedded analytics empower business users to do analytics in real time on live transaction data in a single platform. It comes with a predefined set of VDMs to enable business users to make timely business decisions and provide actionable insights from the data.

Core Data Services

CDS is a semantically rich, data-persistent model in SAP S/4HANA on live transaction data. There are two types of CDS views: one using the ABAP application layer, and another built directly on top of native SAP HANA.

VDMs are built using ABAP CDS views. There are several physical tables in SAP S/4HANA, and it's challenging for business users to remember the names and field definitions of the tables and the relationship between tables. The VDMs are analytical models built on top of CDS by applying more filters and organizing the data, making it easier for business users to access them. The VDM serves as a data source to the target reporting application such as SAP Fiori, SAP BusinessObjects Web Intelligence, SAP Analysis for Microsoft Office, and so on.

The Query Browser (see Figure 2.7) is an SAP Fiori app available to explore standard CDS views and VDMs provided by SAP and custom CDS views created by customers. The Query Browser supports several search options to find a view, view name, field name, or application name.

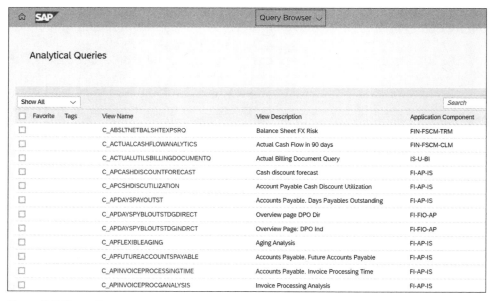

Figure 2.7 Query Browser

The Query Browser includes the following features:

- Search VDM views for components
- Mark views as favorites
- Group, sort, and filter views
- Personalize views
- Download a list of views to Excel

Several reporting tools are available for group reporting, and selecting the right report development tool is an integral part of the tactical approach to reporting that can help save the implementation team's time and expenses.

SAP Analytics Cloud

SAP Analytics Cloud is a next-generation software-as-a-service (SaaS) solution that enables business users to discover, plan, predict, perform on-the-fly what-if analysis, and collaborate, all within the same platform.

Figure 2.8 shows several possible ways to present the information in a dashboard using different types of charts, dropdowns, and filters.

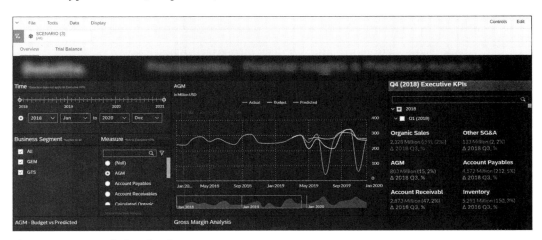

Figure 2.8 SAP Analytics Cloud

SAP Analytics Cloud includes the following key features:

- Design, visualize, and create management reports
- Personalized home page and predelivered consolidation stories
- Built-in automatic insights with smart assist to reveal key influencers
- Predictive forecasting using visual guidance
- Bidirectional data flow to group reporting with real-time simulations and what-if analysis
- Simple and intuitive data entry capabilities to group reporting
- Seamless data flow between SAP and non-SAP source systems
- Top-down or bottom-up variance analysis reporting

SAP Analytics Cloud comes with several data connectivity options. These include cloud data sources such as SAP Cloud Platform, SAP S/4HANA Cloud, SAP SuccessFactors, and SAP Ariba. SAP data sources include SAP Universe, SAP HANA, SAP Business Warehouse (SAP BW), SAP BW/4HANA, and SAP S/4HANA. You can also connect to outside non-SAP solutions via SAP HANA smart data integration (SDI) with SAP Cloud Platform, including Apache Hive, Amazon Web Services (AWS), SAP Adaptive Server Enterprise (SAP ASE), SAP IQ, OData, SAP MaxDB, and more. Finally, social media sources, such as Facebook, Google, and Twitter, can also connect via SDI.

SAP Analysis for Microsoft Office

SAP Analysis for Microsoft Office is a multidimensional online analytical processing (OLAP) data analysis tool to filter data, manipulate data, identify trends, and integrate with Excel and PowerPoint as an add-in. SAP Analysis for Microsoft Office provides guided navigation, data visualization, and flexible hierarchy drilldown options and fulfills the requirements of information consumers, business analysts, and superusers.

SAP Analysis for Microsoft Office includes the following key features:

- Analyze large data sets to uncover deep business insights
- Discover, compare, and forecast business drivers in Excel
- Share discoveries by embedding data analytics into PowerPoint presentations
- Boost analyst efficiency with content reuse and real-time query responses
- Speed data analysis with in-memory computing technology
- Insert SAP Business Explorer (SAP BEx) query results directly into your presentations
- Export current analysis from Excel
- Get easy access to data hierarchies
- Sync with other SAP BusinessObjects clients
- Live PowerPoint presentations
- Simple drag-and-drop tools to filter, drill down into, slice and dice, and replace data
- Analyze data from different sources such as SAP BW, SAP BW/4HANA, and SAP S/4HANA
- Tight integration with both Excel and PowerPoint

When is SAP Analysis for Microsoft Office the right analysis tool to use? Some of the typical user requirements from the finance user community that can be fulfilled by using SAP Analysis for Microsoft Office are as follows:

- Create calculations using Excel formulas and the data retrieved from the data model.
- Create a hierarchy on a flat dimension for which a hierarchy doesn't exist in the source query.
- Use the precalculated SAP Analysis for Microsoft Office functions to create a new measure on the report (e.g., moving average, percentage contribution, etc.).
- Create highly formatted financial statements to print (profit & loss [P&L], balance sheet).

- Report on aggregated data but with the flexibility to drill down to line items based on the source field definition and then again navigate to the actual postings in the source system.

- Modify existing reports ad hoc to add more dimensions or to report on dimension attributes (properties). For example, the report will have a customer as a dimension, but the user needs to add the address, city, and zip code to the report and save it as a local report or publish it on the server.

- Create a workbook for user-created what-if scenarios with each tab displaying one scenario.

- Perform on-the-fly currency translation for all the measures on the report.

- Perform conditional formatting based on a set of predetermined threshold values to highlight essential values or unexpected results in the report.

- Create a report from several data sources and link the common dimension (e.g., filter a report sourced from two data sources with the same company code member filter).

Figure 2.9 shows a sample P&L report displayed using SAP Analysis for Microsoft Office.

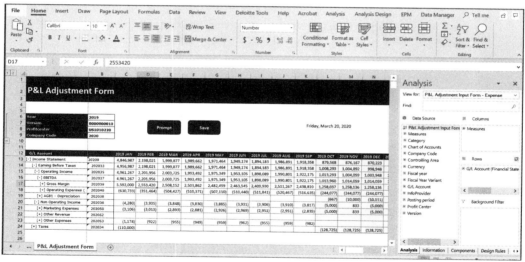

Figure 2.9 Sample SAP Analysis for Microsoft Office Report

In Figure 2.10, you can see how SAP Analysis for Microsoft Office can connect to several types of data sources: CDS, VDMs, SAP BEx queries, and CompositeProviders. The CompositeProvider can merge data from SAP BW and SAP HANA views using several join operations. The virtual data provider can combine data from different models in real-time without physically storing the data. Virtual data providers can also be used within the CompositeProvider.

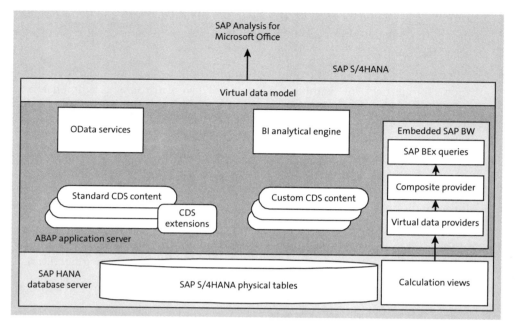

Figure 2.10 Reporting Architecture with Connectivity Options to SAP Analysis for Microsoft Office

SAP BusinessObjects Web Intelligence

SAP BusinessObjects Web Intelligence is a state-of-the-art ad hoc query, reporting, and analytical tool with features to filter, drill, pivot, create a visualization, publish and distribute reports. You can launch SAP BusinessObjects Web Intelligence from the SAP BusinessObjects BI launchpad within the SAP BusinessObjects BI portal. Alternatively, you can also install an SAP BusinessObjects Web Intelligence Microsoft desktop version on your PC or laptop and launch the local version.

Figure 2.11 shows a sample SAP BusinessObjects Web Intelligence report for pricing materials with valid start and end dates.

SAP BusinessObjects Web Intelligence includes the following key features:

- Powerful ad hoc reporting
- Easy-to-use interface for end-user reporting
- Business-friendly and simplified "semantic layer" to hide the complexity
- Self-service reporting and analysis
- Simple UI with enhanced productivity
- Combine data from SAP and non-SAP data in a single report
- A rich repeatable framework of features
- Powerful visualizations
- Report publishing and sharing

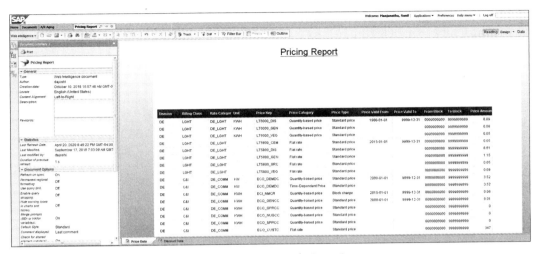

Figure 2.11 SAP BusinessObjects Web Intelligence Sample Report

Decision Tree for Group Reporting Tools

We've provided insights into many reporting tools in the previous sections. We'll combine all the information and criteria to provide a simplified decision tree that can be used to select a tool based on your requirements. However, the decision tree is to provide you with a simplistic approach, and other reporting tools can also be used to meet your requirements. Figure 2.12 shows a simple decision tree to guide users to select the appropriate reporting tool. In a nutshell, you start navigating the decision tree based on your user requirements to choose the reporting tool that best suits your needs.

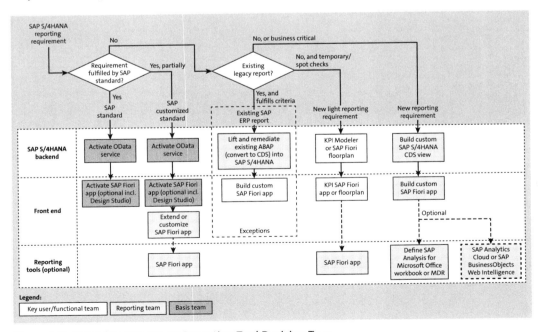

Figure 2.12 SAP S/4HANA Group Reporting Tool Decision Tree

The comparison shown in Table 2.1 shows various business scenarios and each tool's capability to handle it to help you decide which tool is best suited to fulfill a specific analytics or reporting requirement.

	SAP Fiori (Custom SAPUI5)	SAP Analysis for Microsoft Office	SAP Business-Objects Web Intelligence	SAP Analytics Cloud	Comment
Data visuali-zation	Mostly sup-ported	Somewhat supported	Mostly sup-ported	Fully sup-ported	SAP Fiori can provide the desired dash-boards, but requires development. SAP Ana-lytics Cloud provides extensive data visual-izations and data exploration capabili-ties.
Self-service reporting	Not sup-ported	Fully sup-ported	Fully sup-ported	Mostly sup-ported	SAP Analysis for Micro-soft Office provides self-service reporting with less training. SAP Analytics Cloud allows data scientists and superusers to build their own dashboards.
Parame-terized and dynamic layout	Fully sup-ported	Fully sup-ported	Mostly sup-ported	Somewhat supported	SAP Analysis for Micro-soft Office provides users with a large amount of flexibility.
Highly format-ted reporting	Not sup-ported	Somewhat supported	Mostly sup-ported	Somewhat supported	SAP Analysis for Micro-soft Office provides intuitively formatted reports, which can be exported in multiple formats. SAP Analytics Cloud provides a can-vas page for pixel-exact reporting, and respon-sive pages can be used (in the mobile app as well).

Table 2.1 Group Reporting Analytics Tool Comparison

	SAP Fiori (Custom SAPUI5)	SAP Analysis for Microsoft Office	SAP Business-Objects Web Intelligence	SAP Analytics Cloud	Comment
Mobile reporting	Somewhat supported	Not supported	Somewhat supported	Somewhat supported	SAP Fiori requires high development customization and security verification. SAP Analytics Cloud supports mobile functionality.
Hierarchical capabilities	Mostly supported	Mostly supported	Mostly supported	Mostly supported	All tools support SAP HANA hierarchies.
Capability to show high data volumes	Minimal support	Fully supported	Mostly supported	Somewhat supported	SAP BusinessObjects Web Intelligence can show large tables, but only with proxy (paging) functionality. SAP Analysis for Microsoft Office can fetch large tables and make them directly available.
Alerts available	Fully supported	Not supported	Fully supported	Mostly supported	SAP Fiori and SAP Analytics Cloud can provide notifications/popups.
Schedule reports	Minimal support	Somewhat supported	Fully supported	Not supported	SAP Analysis for Microsoft Office requires business objects server to schedule reports. SAP Fiori requires coding.
Operational reporting	Fully supported	Minimal support	Somewhat supported	Minimal support	SAP Fiori provides a seamless integration and UX.
Report jump functionality	Mostly supported	Somewhat supported	Fully supported	Somewhat supported	SAP Fiori requires coding. SAP Analysis for Microsoft Office functionality is accessed by two clicks instead of one. SAP Analytics Cloud provides jump functionality natively.

Table 2.1 Group Reporting Analytics Tool Comparison (Cont.)

	SAP Fiori (Custom SAPUI5)	SAP Analysis for Microsoft Office	SAP Business-Objects Web Intelligence	SAP Analytics Cloud	Comment
Separate server required	No	No*	Yes	Yes	*SAP Analysis for Microsoft Office requires a business objects server for broadcasting/scheduling functionality and storing preformatted workbooks.
Dashboard visualizations	Mostly supported	Somewhat supported	Fully supported	Fully supported	SAP Fiori requires coding.
Custom development effort	High	Low	Low	Medium	SAP Fiori requires extensive development efforts for OData services, custom SAPUI5, and underlying CDS views or calculation view annotations

Table 2.1 Group Reporting Analytics Tool Comparison (Cont.)

2.2.3   Predelivered Content

The predelivered content encompasses a wide range of predefined analytical and consolidation SAP Fiori apps. This predefined content can significantly help to reduce the time and effort required to set up and implement the consolidation process from preparing the data to executing the consolidation reports. However, even with all its benefits, the delivered content might not fulfill all your requirements, and you should always check and validate whether you can use the standard app as it is, or whether it would make more sense to use it as a template to create your own custom app or enhance the standard content.

The predelivered apps are grouped into the following seven categories:

- **Period Preparation**
- **Consolidation Data Collection**
- **Consolidation Master Data**
- **Consolidation Settings**
- **Consolidation Master Data**
- **Group Reports**
- **Consolidation Process**

We'll walk through the most relevant apps and content found in these categories in the following sections.

Data Monitor

The Data Monitor is an SAP Fiori app that allows users to run the activities to prepare data before running consolidations and eliminations, and each activity is called a task. The Data Monitor displays the consolidation unit hierarchy in the rows and configured tasks in the columns. Most of the tasks can be used as is, and some of them you might need to configure. We'll get into the details of the configuration in Chapter 4.

Figure 2.13 shows the **Consolidation Data Preparation** tab and the app to launch the Data Monitor.

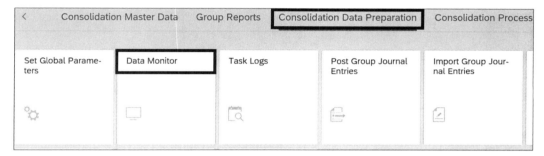

Figure 2.13 Accessing the Data Monitor SAP Fiori App

Figure 2.14 shows all the tasks that you can execute from the Data Monitor app (currency translation, calculate net income, balance carryforward, data validation, etc.).

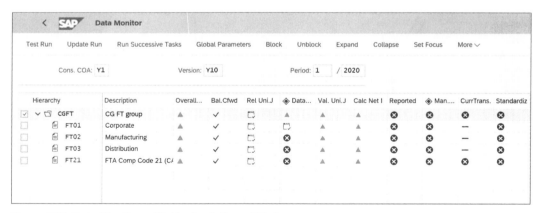

Figure 2.14 Data Monitor with the Predelivered Tasks

Table 2.2 shows all the available Data Monitor tasks with the task ID.

Sequence ID	Task ID	Description	Document Type
1	1010	Balance carryforward	N/A
2	1015	Release Universal Journal	0F
3	1020	Data collection	00, 01, 02
4	1050	Validation of Universal Journal	N/A
5	1030	Calculate net income	N/A
6	1080	Reported data validation	N/A
7	1095	Manual posting	11–19
8	1100	Currency translation	N/A
9	1130	Preparation for consolidation group changes	N/A
10	1180	Standardized data validation	N/A

Table 2.2 All the Standard Out-of-the-Box Data Monitor Tasks

Maintain Exchange Rates

Group reporting uses the SAP S/4HANA table TCURR for the currency translation and provides several flexible methods for currency translation, which we'll explain in detailed step-by-step instructions in Chapter 4. In this section, we'll show you the standard SAP Fiori apps you can leverage to maintain the exchange rates. You have to enter the exchange rates into table TCURR.

Figure 2.15 shows the structure of table TCURR and the field definitions.

Field	Key	Initi...	Data element	Data Type	Length	Decima...	Coordinate	Short Description
MANDT	✓	✓	MANDT	CLNT	3	0	0	Client
KURST	✓	✓	KURST_CURR	CHAR	4	0	0	Exchange rate type
FCURR	✓	✓	FCURR_CURR	CUKY	5	0	0	From currency
TCURR	✓	✓	TCURR_CURR	CUKY	5	0	0	To-currency
GDATU	✓	✓	GDATU_INV	CHAR	8	0	0	Date As of Which the Exchange Rate Is Effective
UKURS		✓	UKURS_CURR	DEC	9	5	0	Exchange Rate
FFACT		✓	FFACT_CURR	DEC	9	0	0	Ratio for the "from" currency units
TFACT		✓	TFACT_CURR	DEC	9	0	0	Ratio for the "to" currency units

Figure 2.15 Table TCURR Currency Exchange Rates Table Structure

Figure 2.16 shows the **Period Preparation** tab and the tiles for the two delivered SAP Fiori apps to load exchange rates:

- **Import Foreign Exchange Rates**
  The group reporting administrator can use the Import Foreign Exchange Rates app to import foreign exchange rates into the tool and use them in the currency translation process.

- **Currency Exchange Rates**
  The group reporting administrator can view, create, or delete exchange rates, as well as update the validity periods for the exchange rates.

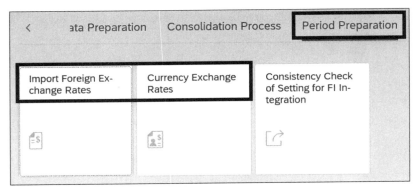

Figure 2.16 Tiles for the Predelivered SAP Fiori Apps to Load Exchange Rates

Consistency Check

Consistency Check of Setting for FI Integration is an SAP Fiori app that allows you to check for the data integration for the period you want to execute the consolidation process. The recommendation is to run the validation check process as part of your data preparation activities for the consolidation. You need to select six mandatory parameters (**Dimension** – **Profit Center**, **Company Code**, **Version**, **Consolidation Chart of Accounts**, **Ledger**, and **Fiscal Year**).

Figure 2.17 shows the **Period Preparation** tab and the corresponding tile to launch the data consistency app.

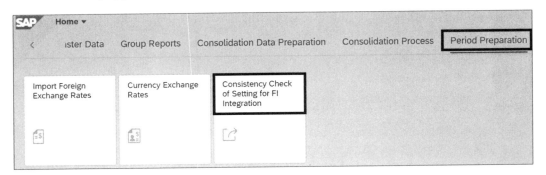

Figure 2.17 Data Consistency Check

After you execute the app, it will list all the data mapping and integration errors. Figure 2.18 shows a few examples of the most common errors.

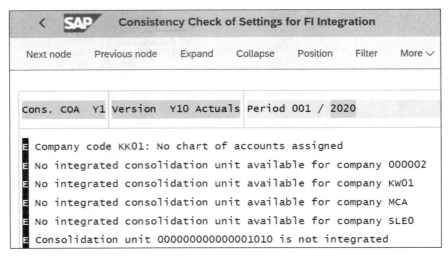

Figure 2.18 Consistency Check App Errors

Common consistency check errors include the following:

- No chart of accounts assigned. The company code within the consolidation group isn't assigned to a chart of accounts
- No integrated consolidation unit available. The company code isn't assigned or mapped to a consolidation unit.
- Other common errors are exchange rate not available, and period is closed for posting.

Copy Total Records

During your consolidation process, you might run into several scenarios where you may need to copy different data sets:

- Period-end financial data
- Elimination entries
- Consolidation entries
- Copy from one version to another version

For example, you can copy one version to another version and use the copied data set to serve as the basis of additional consolidation simulation. However, the SAP Fiori app has a lot more flexibility in copying a subset of data. You can copy the data either using manual file upload or using the Copy Totals Records app shown in Figure 2.19.

The Copy Total Records app provides several selection parameters to copy the data within the consolidation data model.

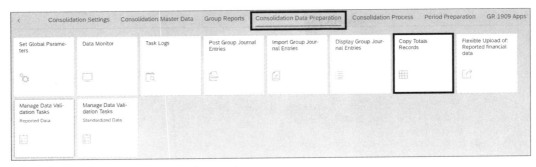

Figure 2.19 Copy Total (Transaction) Records

The Copy Totals Records SAP Fiori app has several groups of parameters for the copy function, as shown in Figure 2.20 (mandatory parameters are marked with *):

- **Organizational units**
  In this section, you can select the **Dimension**, the **Consolidation Group**, and the **Consolidation Unit**. You can only copy the data within the same consolidation group.

- **Posting level**
  In this section, you can select one or more types of data you want to copy: financial, elimination, or consolidation data sets.

- **Settings**
  In this section, you can select the source and target for version, fiscal year, and period. You also have the option to restrict to copy yearly, semi-annual, quarterly, or monthly data.

- **Further settings**
  In this section, you can add more filter criteria for the copy, chart of accounts, financial statement (FS) item, transaction currency, document type, and so on.

- **Technical settings**
  In this section, you can select the consolidation process to log the copy function to track all the records copied using the function. The test run is beneficial to check for consistency before copying the data set.

  The **Delete target data first** and **Cumulative** options should be used with caution. The SAP Fiori app will show a warning if there is data that exists in the target period. Still, if you continue with the execution, the delete target data will permanently delete the data from the target, and there is no option to retrieve it. Cumulative settings will add the transactions to the existing target period, so if you're copying the data twice with the setting checked, the postings will be doubled.

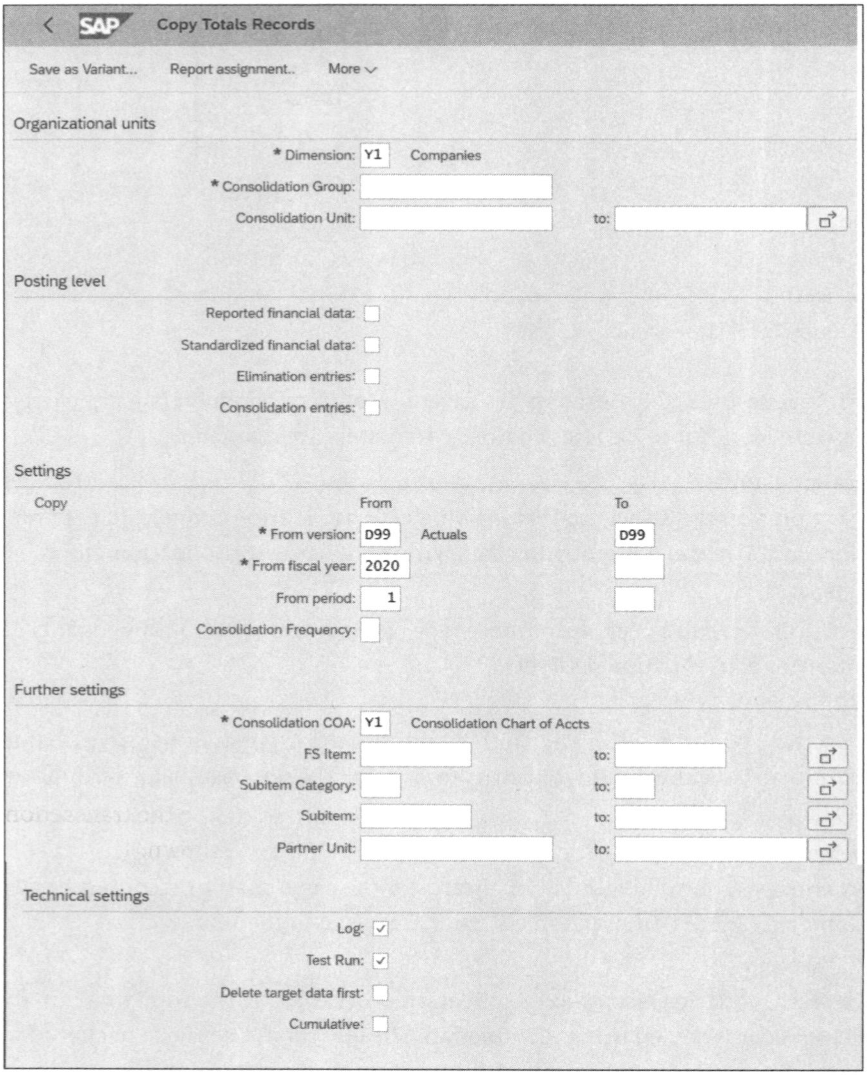

Figure 2.20 Copy Total Records Parameters

Task Logs

The month-end close process in the consolidation tool process requires several steps, such as preparing data preparation, collecting and loading the data, executing the currency translation, posting manual or automated journal entries, and so on. Depending on the type of process, each step will be performed by one or more users. Capturing the log of all changes to the data is critical because it's required for auditing the process. The system captures all the application activities in detail, and Task Logs is a powerful reporting SAP Fiori app to retrieve the system log. Figure 2.21 shows the Task Logs app with a wide range of fields to filter the application logs.

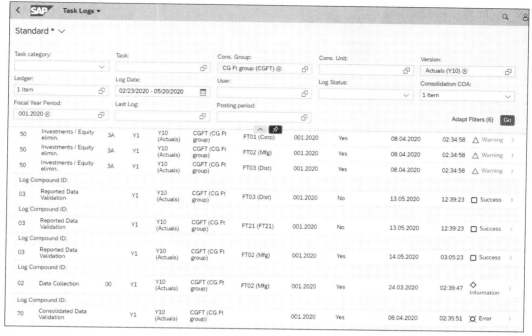

Figure 2.21 Task Logs App

After you enter the data selections and execute the app, a detailed task log header with more than 20 fields will be displayed. You can click the **View Setting** icon to show or hide any field. Furthermore, you can click on the **Header** log to get into the transaction level log details. In Figure 2.22, a sample currency translation log is shown.

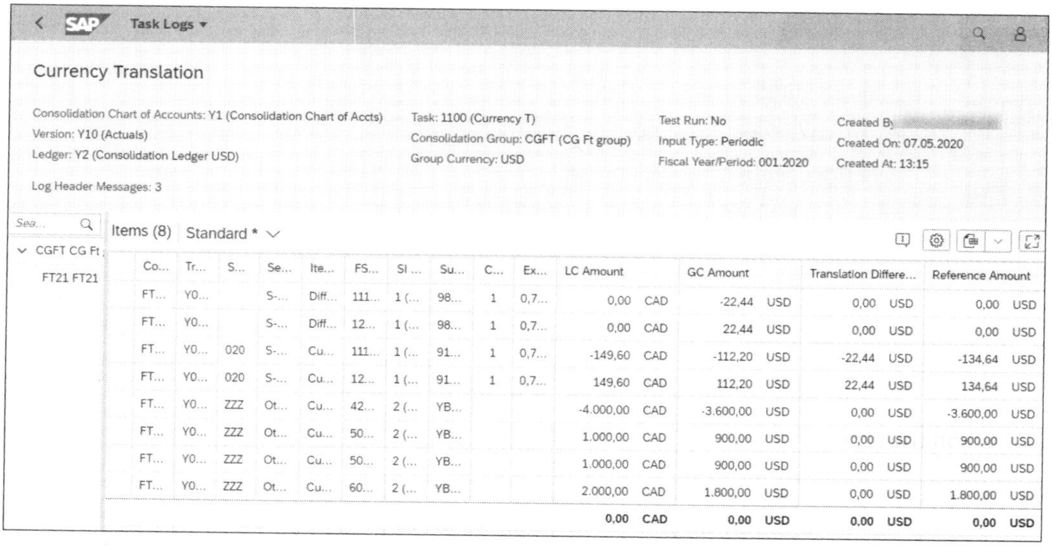

Figure 2.22 Task Log: Currency Translation Detail Log

Import Journal Entries

Although you've loaded the financial data through a flat file or data released from table ACDOCA, there are still several reasons to upload journal entries. As a group accountant, you might have seen data inconsistency for a few consolidation units (company codes). The local accountant can send the journal entries for the accounts in question to adjust the financial statement imbalances and close the period. The Import Group Journal Entries SAP Fiori app, whose tile is shown in Figure 2.23, allows users to post several journal entries by a simple upload process.

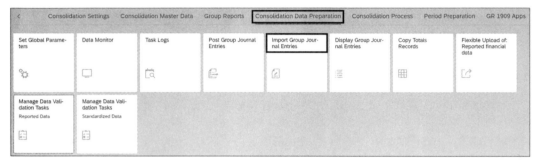

Figure 2.23 Import Group Journal Entries App Tile

The user can download one of three SAP-delivered templates to upload the entries:

- **Unit-Dependent Adjustments**
  - Post adjustment entries to the reported financial data.
  - Post document types 01–19.
  - After the file upload, the **Data Collection** task status will be updated in the Data Monitor, and the **Manual Posting** task status will be updated in the Consolidation Monitor.

- **Two-Sided Elimination**
  - Post two-sided adjustment to eliminate entries for consolidation unit pairs.
  - Post document types 21 and 22.
  - After the file upload, the **Data Collection** task status will be updated in the Data Monitor, and the **Manual Elimination** task status will be updated in the Consolidation Monitor.

- **Group-Dependent Adjustment**
  - Post consolidation entries to eliminate entries that represent elimination postings that are explicitly dependent on consolidation groups, for example, consolidation of investments.
  - Post document types 31, 32, and 39.
  - After the file upload, the **Data Collection** task status will be updated in the Data Monitor, and the **Manual Elimination** task status will be updated in the Consolidation Monitor.

The import template files have two sections, **Header** and **Line Item**. The header contains the information about the journal entry itself, such as the document type and whether it's a manual correction to the posted data or two-sided elimination entries.

Table 2.3 shows the file format with field length to upload the journal entries. You have to populate all fields except remarks, which is an optional field.

Field Name	Length	Description
Journal Entry ID	10	A unique identifier for the journal entry, e.g., 101
Document Type	2	01–19, 21, 22, 31, 32, or 39
Consolidation Chart of Account	2	Chart of account ID, e.g., Y1
Consolidation Version	3	Budget, plan, or actual, e.g., Y10
Fiscal Year	4	Fiscal year to post the data, e.g., 2020
Posting Period	3	Posting period, e.g., 001
Consolidation Unit	18	Legal entity to post the journal entry
Remarks	50	Comments to the journal entry

Table 2.3 Journal Entry Upload Template File Format

The **Line Item** section of the file has the fields to capture the amount of the journal entry in both local and group currency and the FS item. Each line item should have a unique ID within the **Journal Entry ID** in the **Header** section. The data is uploaded first from the app, the user can check and validate if the records are in the correct format, and the master data is checked for referential integrity. After the information is verified, the user can post the journal entries.

Post Group Journal Entries

Although you can mass upload the journal entries, the Post Journal Entries app is the most common method for manual posting. There are several functions available within the app:

- **Copy**
  You can enter the selection criteria and apply the filter to pick a journal entry, copy both the **Header** (general data) and the line items, and then update the fields to post it. After you copy the entry, the check function in the **General Data** section validates the posting for data integrity and balance checks.

- **Reverse**
  You can reverse a journal entry posting.

- **Delete**

  You can delete only the templates using the function, but the journal entries can only be reversed.

- **Create**

  You can create a draft (template) of the most commonly used journal entry to use it later or for every period. The template can also be shared with other users by using the **Share** link within the app.

Figure 2.24 shows the SAP Fiori app with the standard view to post the journal entry.

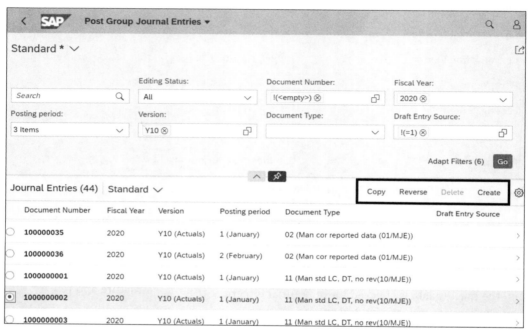

Figure 2.24 Post Group Journal Entries

After you post the journal entries, you can view the posted data from the same app. However, from a security design perspective, the app might be restricted to a business role such as an accountant. Therefore, the Display Group Journal Entries app can be assigned to a broader user group.

Mass Reversal

You can use the Mass Reversal app to reverse several entries at the same time based on the selection criteria, as shown in Figure 2.25. After the entries are displayed on the app, click **Reverse** on the top of the toolbar or **Refresh** at the bottom.

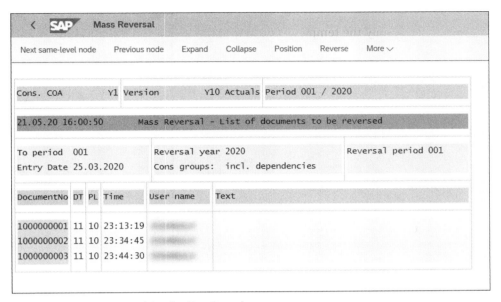

Figure 2.25 Mass Reversal Application Sample

Manage Group Structure

SAP S/4HANA Finance for group reporting has a large number of master data elements to perform the consolidation logic. A trading partner is a legal entity and is called a consolidation unit in group reporting and assigned to a consolidation group for consolidation. The eliminations are performed on pairs of trading partners within a consolidation group, but specific accounts aren't eliminated.

A consolidation unit is the smallest element in a corporate group structure and represents legal subsidiaries. SAP S/4HANA companies are linked to consolidation units on a one-to-one basis. The SAP S/4HANA company ID must equal the consolidation unit ID. The consolidation units can be assigned to the consolidation group using the Manage Group Structure SAP Fiori app, and it has two views: group and unit.

Figure 2.26 shows the **Group View**. You can click the **Assign** button to select the consolidation units to assign to the group.

The following three fields should be selected for you to manage the consolidation group structure:

- **Consolidation Version**
  Select the consolidation version to assign the units.

- **Consolidation Group**
  Select the consolidation group to assign the units.

- **Fiscal Year and Period**
  Enter the period you want the consolidation unit to be assigned to the group.

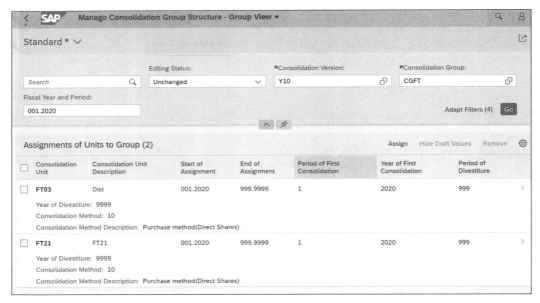

Figure 2.26 Manage Consolidation Group

Mapping Financial Statement Items and General Ledger Accounts

The FS item will be used instead of the account dimension (used in older SAP Business Planning and Consolidation [SAP BPC] versions) for consolidation purposes in group reporting. FS items will be maintained with all SAP S/4HANA general ledger accounts. FS items can be mapped one to one or one to many with SAP S/4HANA general ledger accounts, and the mapping should be assigned to a consolidation version and effective periods, and they form the foundation for the group chart of accounts.

Figure 2.27 shows the different apps to assign, map, and import the FS items:

- **Define FS Items**
  Define a new FS item and assign it to a consolidation chart of accounts.

- **Assign FS Items Mappings**
  Assign the consolidation chart of accounts to the general ledger chart of accounts.

- **Map FS Items with G/L Accounts**
  Map general ledger accounts to FS items, one to one or many to one.

- **Import FS Item Mappings**
  You can download the predelivered template (Y1 – COA) from the app with or without the master data. When you're mapping the operational chart of accounts to the group chart of accounts for the first time, it's a lot easier to download the template and update than to add and update them manually.

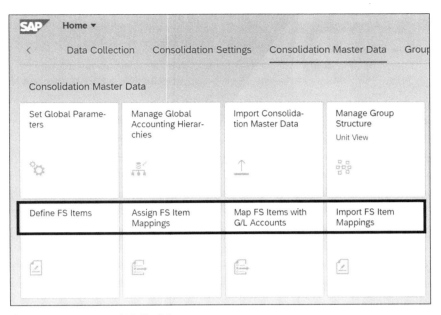

Figure 2.27 FS Items SAP Fiori Apps

The FS item hierarchies shown in Table 2.4 are predelivered.

Item Hierarchy	Description	Remarks
BS	Balance sheet	All items belong to balance sheets.
PL	P&L statement	All items belong to P&L statements.
BS_PL	Balance sheet and P&L	All items belong to the balance sheet and P&L statement.
ST	Statistical FS items	All items are needed for posting the group shares of individual investee units.
X1	Statement of equity	All items belong to the statement of changes in equity.
X2	Statement of cash flow	All items belong to the cash flow statement (indirect method).
X3	Statement of comprehensive income	All items belong to the statement of comprehensive income.
X4	P&L statement by function of expense	All items belong to P&L statements by the function of expense.

Table 2.4 Standard Predelivered Hierarchies List to Execute Consolidation Process and for Reporting

Item Hierarchy	Description	Remarks
X5	Intercompany reconciliation	All items belong to intercompany reconciliation reports. The statistical FS items stand for the respective reconciliation cases.
X6	Currency translation – reserve	This hierarchy contains investment and equity items.

Table 2.4 Standard Predelivered Hierarchies List to Execute Consolidation Process and for Reporting (Cont.)

Predefined Master Data

SAP has predelivered two subitem categories to split your transaction records further using subitems, which are also predelivered and assigned by default to either transactional or functional categories. There are too many to list them all, but Table 2.5 shows a few samples.

Subitem Category	Subitem	Sample Delivered Subitem Master Data	Total Delivered
Transactional	Transaction type	170-Transfers, 220-Depreciation, 140-Retirements	20
Functional	Functional area	Sales and distribution, marketing, administration	5

Table 2.5 Predelivered Subitem Categories to Classify the Transaction Records

The reported financial data can be procured from many data sources, such as a direct pull from table ACDOCA or an upload through the Data Monitor. During the process, there are so many entries that will be created in table ACDOCU (manual journal entries, reconciliation entries, etc.). Document types are used to categorize and to differentiate the data records in the consolidation model.

There are 41 document types predelivered, but each document type can only be used with the assigned business applications. Table 2.6 shows all the predelivered document types and the associated consolidation process within which you can use them.

Business Application	Document Type
Reported financial data	00, 03, 05, 06, 07
Manual posting in Data Monitor	01, 02, 04, 11–19, 1A, 1B, 1C10, 1P
Reclassification in Data Monitor	01, 02, 04, 11–19, 1A, 1B, 1C10, 1P

Table 2.6 Predelivered Document Types

Business Application	Document Type
Manual Posting in Consolidation Monitor	21, 22, 2E, 2F–2H, 2O, 2P, 31–33, 38, 39, 3A, 3B, 3Z
Reclassification in Consolidation Monitor	21, 22, 2E, 2F–2H, 2O, 2P, 31–33, 38, 39, 3A, 3B, 3Z

Table 2.6 Predelivered Document Types (Cont.)

In addition to the predefined content master data, SAP has also provided a standard chart of accounts (Y1) and versions (actuals – Y10, Y20; budget – YB).

Consolidation Monitor

Financial consolidation is the collective process through which assets, liabilities, revenues, and expenses of related entities are combined for companies to perform external group reporting of financials.

The following critical tasks are executed with the Consolidation Monitor:

- Eliminate intercompany balances (receivables and payables).
- Eliminate investment in subsidiaries.
- Consolidate investments.
- Perform equity pick-up.
- Make other manual adjustments.

The delivered Consolidation Monitor SAP Fiori app has all these tasks available as standard content.

Table 2.7 shows all the standard consolidation tasks available within group reporting that you can monitor from the app.

Task ID	Description	Assigned Method	Document Types
2011	IC Elim. Sales	S2010	2E
2021	IC Elim. Other Income/Expense	S2020	2F
2031	Dividends Elimination	S2030	2H
2041	IC Elim. Balance Sheet	S2040	2G
2100	Investments/Equity Elimin.	S2100	3A
2060	Auto Recl. PL30 No Reversed GC	-	30
2180	Total Divestiture	S2180	3Z

Table 2.7 Predelivered Consolidation Tasks

Task ID	Description	Assigned Method	Document Types
S190	Cust Reclass, PL10(LC)	-	10
S191	Cust Reclass, PL10(GC)	-	1P
S290	Cust Reclass, PL20(GC)	-	20
S291	Cust Reclass, PL20(GC)	-	2P

Table 2.7 Predelivered Consolidation Tasks (Cont.)

All the tasks shown in the Consolidation Monitor (see Figure 2.28) can be executed at the individual consolidation group level or in parallel.

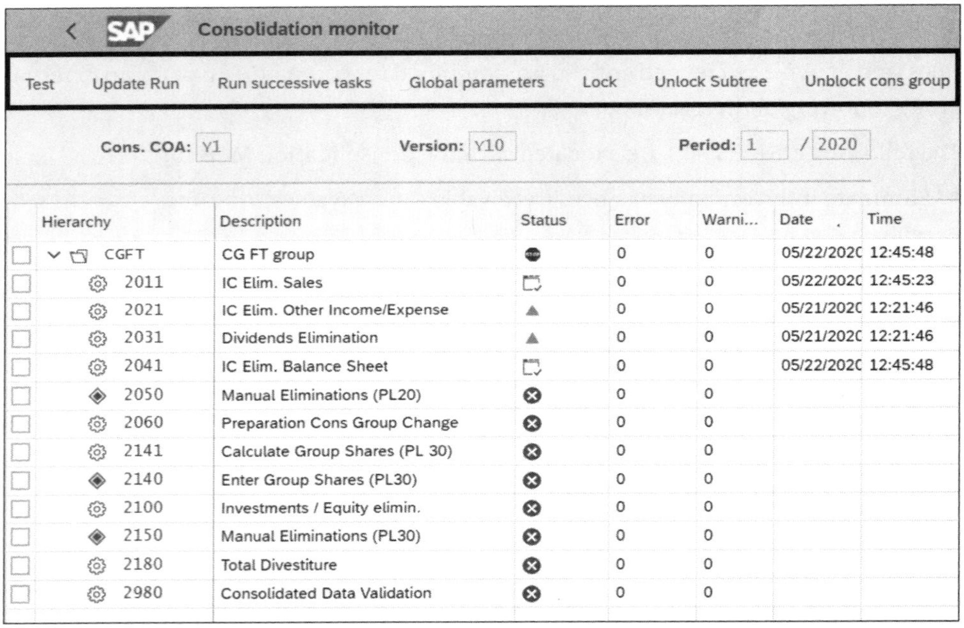

Figure 2.28 Consolidation Monitor

The key options shown at the top of the screen are as follows:

- **Test**
  Execute a test run without updating the data in the consolidation model.

- **Update Run**
  Execute the task and update the entries in the consolidation model.

- **Run successive tasks**
  Execute all the tasks in sequential order, and the system will continue with the next step, only if the previous task is successful.

- **Global parameters**
  Prompt to select the fiscal year, period, consolidation chart of accounts, and consolidation ledger.

- **Lock**
  Lock the period after month-end close.

- **Unlock Subtree**
  Unlock a subgroup if you have multiple consolidation groups.

- **Unblock cons group**
  Unlock the consolidation group, only if the period is open.

We'll discuss the Consolidation Monitor on a more detailed level in Chapter 6.

Group Data Analysis

No single report can satisfy or meet all the reporting requirements for both legal and management consolidation, not for any organization or an individual user. It's very common for the user group to have their unique requirements. Group Data Analysis is a new SAP Fiori app from the 1909 release that supports a wide range of reporting options to turn the information from the consolidation model to the desired outcome.

In a scenario, the corporate controller may want to analyze the P&L and balance sheet with the consolidation groups in a hierarchical view. However, the local accountant wants to report the same data, but in a flat structure, by viewing them by consolidation units. Financial planning and analysis (FP&A) users want to view the data with profit centers and segments. These are common user requirements, and the app can meet all the requirements without having to build a canned report.

The app supports the following three different views:

- **Group consolidation view**
  The consolidation group is a flat list of the assigned consolidation units with group-dependent attributes such as consolidation method, acquisition date, and divestiture date. The assignment and attribute definitions are made by using the **Manage Consolidation Group Structure – Group View (New)** or the **Manage Consolidation Group Structure – Unit View (New)** within the Group Data Analysis app.

- **Hierarchical consolidation view**
  This view is based on the hierarchies of consolidation units, profit centers, and segments that are maintained in the Manage Global Accounting Hierarchies app.

- **Combined view**
  When generating a report for consolidated data, you can get a combined view by specifying both the consolidation group and any relevant hierarchies.

Figure 2.29 shows a simple hierarchical view report, but the report can be enhanced using reporting rules.

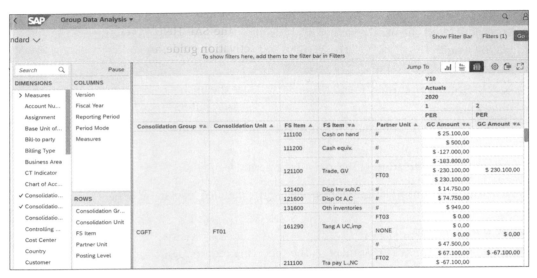

Figure 2.29 Group Data Analysis

SAP had predelivered five reporting rule hierarchies, and they can be used in the Group Data Analysis app, as shown in Table 2.8. Chapter 11 will show an example report to use a reporting item hierarchy.

Reporting Item Hierarchy ID	Name	Description
X1	Statement of Equity	All reporting items belong to the statement of changes in equity.
X2	Cash Flow Statement	All reporting items belong to the cash flow statement (indirect method).
X3	Statement of Comprehensive Income	All reporting items belong to the statement of comprehensive income.
X4	P&L Function by Expense	All reporting items belong to the P&L statement by function by expenses.
X5	Interunit Reconciliation	All reporting FS items belong to interunit reconciliation reports. Each reporting item is standard for a reconciliation type, e.g., income and expense.

Table 2.8 Predelivered Reporting Rule Hierarchies

Best Practices and Reinstalling Business Content

SAP has best practices for group reporting and recommends installing the best practices to get the baseline configuration. You can install the best practices from the IMG, execute Transaction CXE9N, and click **Install SAP Best Practices Content**.

As a prerequisite, update the best practice content to the latest version and apply all corrections before starting the activation. Refer to the SAP Help Portal at *http://s-prs.co/v515100*, navigate to the SAP Best Practices activation guide, and follow the steps to activate scope item – 1SG (Group Reporting).

After you install the best practices, you can't initialize the business content, so the recommended approach is to install the best practices in a sandbox environment and validate the feasibility of the features to meet your requirements.

Authorization

SAP delivers standard roles and business catalog templates with group reporting security content (role, catalogs, authorization objects). You can use the predelivered content as a reference to set up your security roles (SAP Fiori and backend roles) based on functional and security design to meet the business requirements.

Table 2.9 shows the business roles that can be assigned to users. The standard roles can also be copied to create your security role.

No.	Business Role	Description	Business Catalogs
1	SAP_BR_GL_ACCOUNTANT_GRP	General Ledger Accountant – Group Reporting	6
2	SAP_BR_GRP_ACCOUNTANT	Group Accountant	11
3	SAP_BR_ADMINISTRATOR_GRP	Administrator – Group Reporting	11
4	SAP_BR_EXTERNAL_AUDITOR_GRP	External Auditor – Group Reporting	10
5	SAP_BR_BUSINESS_ANALYST_GRP	Business Analyst – Group Reporting	2

Table 2.9 Predelivered Security Roles

Table 2.10 shows the business catalogs in which the SAP Fiori apps are grouped together based on the consolidation process. For example, the consolidation master data catalog will be assigned the group reporting administrator to load the master data, whereas the business users might have access only to the consolidation group reports catalog.

No.	Business Catalog	Description
1	SAP_FIN_BCG_CCON_ADMIN	Consolidation – Master Data
2	SAP_FIN_BCG_CCON_MASTDATA	Consolidation – Financial Consolidation for Local Accountants
3	SAP_FIN_BCG_CONS_LOCAL	Consolidation – Group Reports

Table 2.10 Predelivered Business Catalogs (SAP Fiori App Groups)

No.	Business Catalog	Description
4	SAP_FIN_BCG_CCON_DATAPRE	Consolidation – Data Preparation
5	SAP_FIN_BCG_CCON_LC_REPORT	Consolidation – Local Reports
6	SAP_FIN_BCG_CCON_REPORT	Consolidation – Group Reports

Table 2.10 Predelivered Business Catalogs (SAP Fiori App Groups) (Cont.)

2.3   Summary

In this chapter, you learned about SAP S/4HANA and the reporting architecture. We also reviewed several reporting tools and the connectivity options available for group reporting and how to select the tool with the decision criteria. The chapter also provided a high-level overview of most of the predelivered content, including SAP Fiori apps. We'll continue our journey exploring the configuration and setup of the consolidation and learn how to fulfill your reporting requirements.

In the next chapter, we'll cover the steps involved in master data configuration.

Chapter 3
Master Data

This chapter will cover the master data and configuration settings required for SAP S/4HANA Finance for group reporting. The chapter will provide information regarding standard delivered content integrated with SAP S/4HANA as the source and configuration of master data settings for external sources as well.

Master data, or metadata, as it's called in certain solutions, serves as a basic and core component of the implementation. These configurations provide the basis to develop the process rules and scope of the consolidation model. In this chapter, we'll go through each master data element as required in group reporting and discuss how to configure each of them during an implementation.

Group reporting with SAP S/4HANA requires one-time settings that influence the overall design of the solution. The subsequent section contains information about what each of these settings are and what significance they have in the overall design. We'll then cover the group reporting master data objects, such as consolidation units, financial statement (FS) items, breakdown categories, subitem categories, versions, and document types, and describe each of them within the context of SAP-delivered content.

3.1 Global Settings

Group reporting is an integral part of SAP S/4HANA Finance, and similar to other financial modules, it needs to be set up as Customizing in the SAP Implementation Guide (IMG). Figure 3.1 shows the group reporting Customizing menu in the overall IMG structure. The **SAP S/4HANA for Group Reporting** node consists of various subsections for configurations and master data for consolidations. Transaction CXE9N is used frequently to provide direct access and a cleaner view of group reporting-specific Customizing tasks without actually navigating the entire IMG menu.

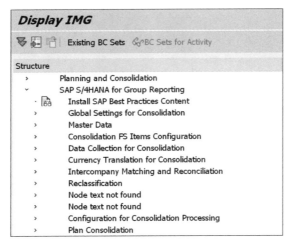

Figure 3.1 IMG for SAP S/4HANA Group Reporting

For the initial setup, going to **SAP S/4HANA for Group Reporting • Global Settings for Consolidation • Initialize Settings** generates standard settings that are mandatory for group reporting configuration when customers don't want to use the standard SAP Best Practices content delivered by SAP. As shown in Figure 3.2, consolidation can be executed in two modes: select **Test Run** to simulate the execution in test mode, or deselect it to fill the tables with initial settings.

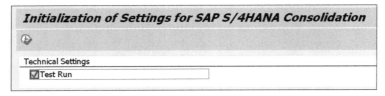

Figure 3.2 Initialization Settings

With new group reporting, even for setting up the initial configuration, global parameters have to be set. To do this, execute Transaction CXGP, or go to the SAP Fiori Set Global Parameters app. You can also navigate to **SAP S/4HANA for Group Reporting • Global Settings for Consolidation • Check Global System Settings** in the IMG. After you arrive, you can validate or update the following options:

- **Global parameters**
  Parameters apply to all further steps of the consolidation process, setting the context or scope and have to be set as shown in Figure 3.3:
  - **Cons Group/Cons Unit**
    Optional fields to set the consolidation group and unit.
  - **Version**
    Sets of financial data undergoing consolidations such as actuals or budget. A more

detailed explanation of versions and their significance in configuration is given in Section 3.2.7.

- **Fiscal year/Period**
  Time period identifying the consolidation period.

- **Ledger**
  Used for storing alternate group currencies required for consolidations. Based on consolidation ledger reporting, the currencies might be the same or different from accounting ledgers at the source.

- **Cons. COA**
  Group reporting chart of accounts and superordinate characteristics of FS item in group reporting. As part of standard business content, SAP provides **Y10** as the chart of accounts.

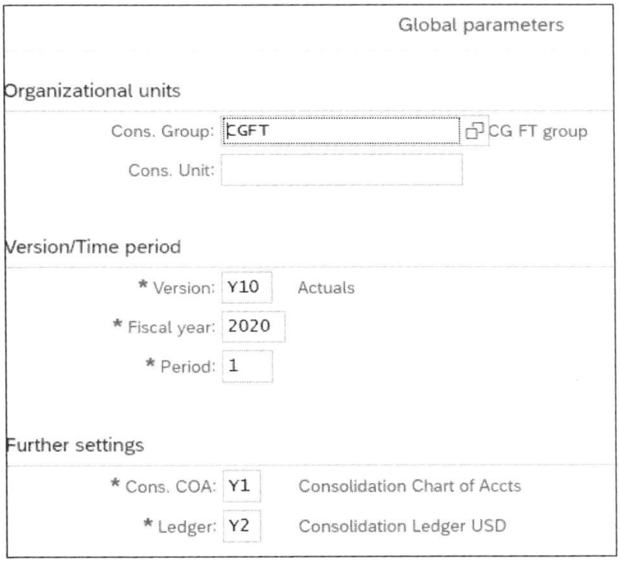

Figure 3.3 Setting Global Parameters

- **From Year for LIs in SAP S/4HANA**
  Sets the fiscal year starting when the group reporting table ACDOCU updates the data. It's an initial setting and can't be updated once saved.

- **From Year for New Group Report Logic**
  Provides a starting year for the new group reporting logic to be effective. The logic contains various delivered functions that support consolidations.

- **Reclassification: Selection Object in Trigger**
  If selected, allows the use of selection objects supporting complex combinations. If not selected, the trigger and/or percentage setting is specified in individual methods.

- **Validation in SAP S/4HANA Consolidation**
  Uses group reporting validation functions. If not selected, the system uses the conventional (Enterprise Controlling – Consolidation System [EC-CS]) validations.

- **Breakdown Category (Selection Object in Maximum Selection)**
  Provides the flexibility of using selection objects for complex criteria based on breakdown categories.

- **Currency Translation (Selection Object in Method)**
  Allows the use of a selection object for complex selection. If not selected, the source data region becomes specific to the method.

- **FS Role Attribute**
  Used during the configuration of automatic postings of items such as net income or deferred taxes.

3.2   Group Reporting Master Data

Master data configuration in the IMG consists of all consolidation-specific master data used in group reporting. Customization includes changing or defining consolidation ledgers for multicurrency consolidation requirements. SAP-delivered content provides two standard consolidation ledgers (Y1 for EUR and Y2 for USD group currency). Customer requirements can drive the creation of multiple ledgers depending on the requirement names, and the use of "C<#>" provides the customer with identifiable consolidation ledgers in the system.

Another master data field is the consolidation type dimension, which is mandatory and preselected in the system. Only one consolidation type dimension (Y1) is predelivered as standard by SAP and can't be modified in configuration. The following sections provide details about data configuration for consolidation models.

3.2.1   Consolidation Entities

All consolidation models have one of the most sought characteristics in data, the *entity dimension*. This dimension depicts the legal entities of an organizational structure and forms the basis of all fundamental processing within consolidations. Group reporting identifies the consolidation unit as a legal entity equivalent to a company code in SAP S/4HANA. In this section, we'll walk through consolidation units and consolidation groups.

Consolidation Units

Consolidation units are set up in group reporting and integrate automatically to an existing SAP S/4HANA company. A consolidation unit isn't integrated if it doesn't have a corresponding company in the SAP S/4HANA source.

With new group reporting, consolidation units are configured using standard SAP Fiori tiles, as shown in Figure 3.4. Use Transactions CX1M/CX1N/CX1O in SAP GUI for creating/modifying/displaying new units.

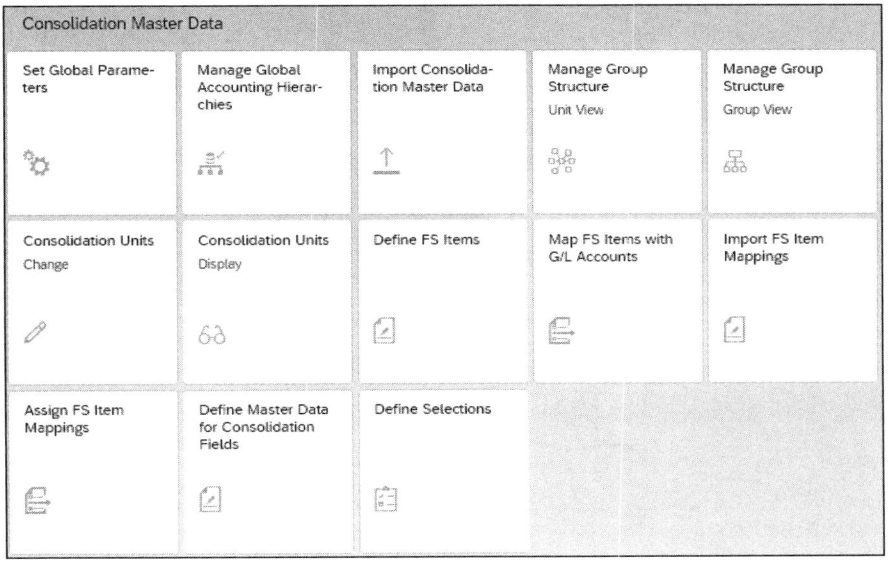

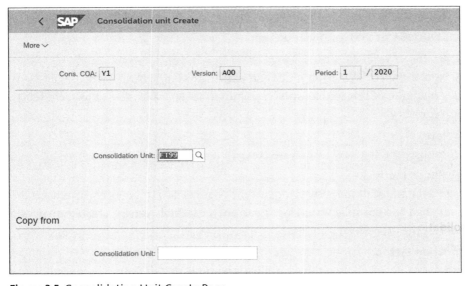

Figure 3.4 SAP Fiori App Interface for Master Data

When you select the **Consolidation Units** tile to open the **Consolidation unit Create** page (see Figure 3.5), the subsequent screen with tabs grouping various attributes appears, as shown in Figure 3.6.

Figure 3.5 Consolidation Unit Create Page

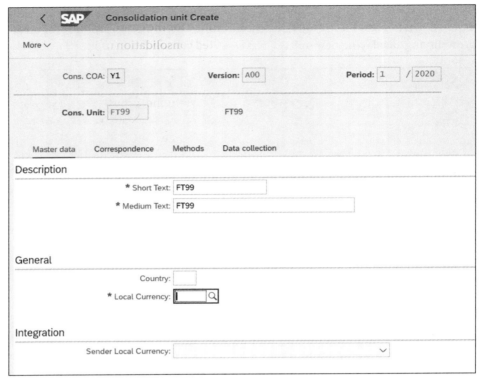

Figure 3.6 Consolidation Unit Attributes

The following consolidation unit attributes in group reporting are available for various tasks to work properly during data collection for the consolidation process:

- **Local Currency**
  Local currency of the consolidation unit.

- **Integration**
  Relevant if the consolidation unit is an existing SAP S/4HANA company and provides mapping of the source Universal Journal table (table ACDOCA) to table ACDOCU (local currency).

- **Tax Rate**
  Percentage used to calculate deferred taxes automatically.

- **Translation Method**
  Assigns the translation method for currency conversion if the local currency is different than the consolidation ledger currency. Methods can be created or reused based on the predelivered content.

- **Validation Method**
  Automatically picked up if the consolidation unit is part of the set in the validation methods.

- **Data Transfer Method**

  Provides one of the delivered options of data source for the consolidation unit. Read from Universal Document is the option for integrated consolidation units for real-time integration.

- **Entry in Group Currency**

  Used for filling the transaction currency field with the group currency when selected.

- **Fiscal Year Variant**

  Provides the fiscal year variant identifier of the SAP S/4HANA company for sourcing the data from the Universal Journal.

- **Effect. Year of Read from Univ. Document**

  Provides the *starting from* year for the data to populate table ACDOCU from the SAP S/4HANA source.

Figure 3.7 shows the input template used to upload the master data for consolidation units in group reporting. This standard template can be filled in for bulk uploads with all the attributes in a single line to reduce the deployment time after the master data moves across the SAP landscape.

This standard template is downloaded with or without existing master data using the SAP Fiori Import Consolidation Master Data app. Choose **Actions • Download Master Data • Download** to download the file containing the master data. The template downloaded can be modified to update new consolidation units and can be uploaded using the **Upload** button, as shown in Figure 3.8.

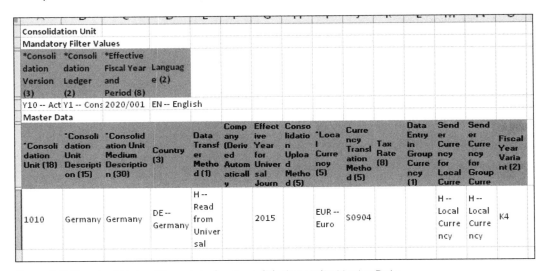

Figure 3.7 Standard Upload Template for Consolidation Units Master Data

Name	Upload Errors	To Be Checked	Checked Successfully	Checked with Warnings	Checked with Errors	Imported		
Consolidation Group Structure	0	11	5	0	0	1	Actions ∨	>
Consolidation Unit	0	0	0	0	16	22	Actions ∨	>

Figure 3.8 Import Consolidation Unit Master Data: Upload Button

Consolidation Groups

Consolidation units configured in the system are set together based on the holding entity and subsidiary relationship in an ownership-based hierarchy. This structure created for consolidation of entities is called a *consolidation group*.

You can use Transaction CX1P/CX1Q/CX1R in SAP GUI for creating/modifying/displaying new groups or the SAP Fiori Consolidation Groups Create & Change app.

Figure 3.9 and Figure 3.10 provide the input screens for a new consolidation group creation. After the you click the **Consolidation Groups Create & Change** tile to open the app, the initial screen in Figure 3.9 is shown. Enter a **Consolidation Group**, and click on **More • Consolidation Group • Create** to create a new group.

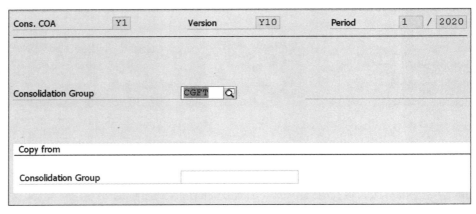

Figure 3.9 Consolidation Group: Create

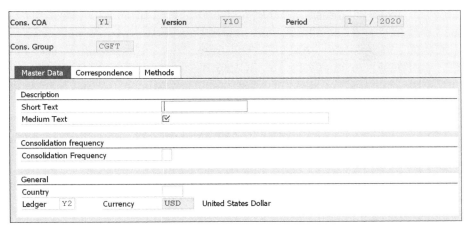

Figure 3.10 Attributes for Consolidation Group

While creating the consolidation groups, the following attributes are available:

- **Consolidation Frequency**
  This option sets the frequency for preparing the financial statements based on preset intervals.

- **Country**
  This field sets the country for information purposes only.

- **Ledger**
  This field specifies the ledger for reporting in ledger/group currency.

- **Methods**
  Similar to consolidation units, validation methods are assigned to consolidation groups under the **Methods** tab.

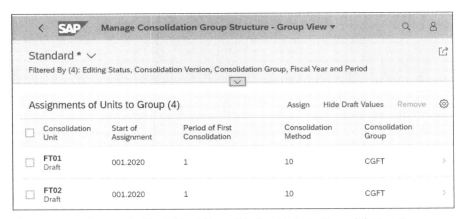

Figure 3.11 Assignment of Individual Consolidation Units to Consolidation Groups

Maintain the consolidation group structure by adding individual consolidation units using the SAP Fiori Manage Group Structure: Group View app, as shown in Figure 3.11, or using the bulk upload method via the SAP Fiori Import Consolidation Master Data app, as shown in Figure 3.12. Adding individual entities is a time-consuming activity. Updates using bulk uploads with standard file formats makes the changes easier and faster for any ongoing maintenance. The file upload provides an overall view of all entities with attributes in a group as compared to individual maintenance that is prone to manual errors.

	Consolidation Group	Consolidation Unit	Con...	Start of Assig...	Period ...	Consolidation Me...
☐	CG0	1010	Y10	001.2015	999	10
☐	CG0	1710	Y10	001.2015	999	10
☐	CG2	1010	Y10	001.2015	999	10
☐	CG2	1710	Y10	001.2015	999	10
☐	CG3	S3000	Y10	001.2015	999	00

Figure 3.12 Mass Assignments Using the Standard Import Template

The following attributes are required when assigning the consolidation units to consolidation groups and are critical in consolidation processing:

- **Start of Assignment**
  This is the year/period the consolidation unit was introduced into the group.

- **Period/Year of First Consolidation**
  This is the year/period of the first consolidation, which can be greater than or equal to the start of assignment.

- **Consolidation Method**
  This is the accounting technique of consolidations (parent, purchase, or equity method).

- **Consolidation Version**
  This is the version the consolidation unit is dependent on if specified in special versions.

- **End of Assignment**
  This is the year/period the consolidation unit was removed from the group.

- **First Consolidation at End of Period**
  When selected in the group structure, first consolidation considers all reported data from all prior periods, including the first period.

- **Period/Year of Divestiture**
  This is the year/period of the last consolidation; however, the consolidation unit can be removed from the group only in the first period of the subsequent year of divestiture.

- **Divestiture at Beginning of Period**
  When selected in the group structure, the last consolidation reverses the total records of all prior periods.

In addition to these assignment properties, a few more key points should be considered for consolidation groups and consolidation unit assignments and can prove useful during an implementation:

- The consolidation group hierarchies are means of master data maintenance and tasks execution; they aren't meant for hierarchy reporting purposes.

- You can create multiple consolidation group hierarchies in one dimension; for example, there may be a need for a legal and regional hierarchy.

- A consolidation unit can belong to different consolidation groups, and a given consolidation group can belong to different hierarchies.

- The assignment of consolidation units to consolidation groups is neither a dimensional hierarchy nor is it used for rollup.

- Consolidation group currency is determined by the currency of the ledger assigned to the group.

- A parent unit can be specified for the consolidation group, and each group has one consolidation unit assigned as parent.

- Multiple levels of groups should not have the same ledger assignment in a version for consistency in group currency assignments.

- An assigned consolidation unit in a group can be removed, but the system doesn't perform a consistency check with transaction data and can thereby cause inconsistencies after the unit is removed.

3.2.2 Financial Statement Items

FS items represent the account dimension as in any other consolidation tool. After consolidation units, this is the second fundamental characteristic and sets the basis for consolidation tasks, such as currency translations, eliminations, and investment consolidations. FS items and hierarchies derive the financial statements and are useful in reporting. Each FS item has associated attributes that categorize and define the nature of the FS item. They help classify the FS items to allow consolidation tasks to run based on the requirements at various stages of the process.

FS items use a superordinate characteristic consolidation chart of accounts similar to SAP S/4HANA, which uses a local chart of accounts at the operational level for financial statements. As part of SAP Best Practices content delivered by SAP, Y1 is the predefined consolidation chart of accounts to use. A consolidation chart of accounts specifies the length of the FS items.

Although custom consolidation charts of accounts can be created if the delivered chart of accounts doesn't fulfill your requirements, there are other configurations that should be customized after a new chart of accounts is created. Use IMG menu **SAP S/4HANA for Group Reporting • Master Data • Define Consolidation Chart of Accounts • Create Con Chart of Accounts** or Transaction CX10 for creating a new chart of accounts. Figure 3.13 shows the screen to create a new chart of accounts. Provide a meaningful **Description** and length of FS item IDs to create a new consolidation chart of accounts.

Consolidation Chart of Accounts Create

Consolidation COA	Y2
General	
Description	Consolidation CoA
Output length of FS items	10

Figure 3.13 New Chart of Accounts Creation

Now that we've seen how a chart of accounts is set up in the system and what its significance is, creating FS items is the next step in the configuration.

With group reporting, FS items are created with properties as explained earlier. Figure 3.14 shows the import template used for creating new FS items. The column headers are aligned in a way to provide an easy all-headers view, although the headers are in a single row. The template provides a file interface that allows FS items to be created in mass with ease. Each column represents an attribute that is to be defined for an FS item, and multiple rows define master data IDs that are to be created.

Financial Statement Item							
Mandatory Filter Values							
*Consolidation Language (2)							
Master Data							
*Financial Statement Item (10)	*FS Item Description (15)	FS Item Medium Description (50)	FS Item Long Description (250)	*FS Item Type (10)	Breakdown Category (4)	Is Blocked Against Posting (1)	
Is Consolidation Item (1)	Carry Forward Balances (For Statistical FS Items)	FS Item Role (30)	Data Collection Selection (30)	Currency Translation Selection (30)	Elimination Selection (30)	Cash Flow Selection (30)	
Scope Selection (30)	Other Selection (30)	Elimination Target (10)	Non-Controlling Interest Target (10)	Planning Target (10)	Link Title (255)	Link URL (1333)	

Figure 3.14 FS Items: Master Data Standard Import Template

You can also create individual FS items one at a time with the SAP Fiori Define FS Items app, as shown in Figure 3.15. Values must be provided for the following properties:

- **Financial Statement Item**
  Sets the unique ID with length less than or equal to that specified while defining the consolidation chart of accounts.

- **Consolidation Chart of Accounts**
  Sets the consolidation chart of accounts the account is assigned to.

- **FS Item Type**
  Defines the nature of FS item such as balance sheet or income statement account. There are six types to choose from:
  - **INC** for income
  - **EXP** for expenses
  - **AST** for assets
  - **LEQ** for liabilities
  - **STAT** for nonfinancial statement items
  - **REPT** reporting specific items

- **Breakdown Category**
  Sets the additional check through a specific breakdown category on the FS item to ensure correctness and consistency in transaction data. For example, a partner unit mandatory breakdown category can be set to intercompany accounts. This ensures no transaction data without a partner unit is in the system, and incorrect records are identified before the elimination process is triggered.

- **Is Blocked Against Posting**
  Allows FS items to be locked for any data entry.

- **Is Consolidation Item**
  Identifies items in consolidation statements.

- **FS Item Role**
  Used in configuration of automatic postings and determines item where the posting needs to happen. FS item and FS item role are mapped one to one.

- **Data Collection**
  Helps in grouping FS items in data entry reports for flexible reporting.

- **Currency Translation**
  Allows a currency translation method associated with the FS item, which is used in identifying the currency translations attribute and subsequently a method to run during consolidation.

- **Elimination (Selection)**
  Allows an elimination method specific to an FS item, which is used in eliminations processing during consolidation.

- **Cash Flow**
  Allows the selection of cash flow-specific FS items for reporting rules.

- **Scope**
  Allows additional selection for specifying the scope of FS items, which can be used to identify whether an item is relevant for actuals, plan, or both.

- **Other**
  Can be used for custom selections defined per customer needs. (We'll discuss how new attributes values can be added in Section 3.2.3.)

- **Elimination (Target)**
  Used for specifying the offset account for eliminations rules.

- **Non-Controlling Interest**
  Used for specifying the noncontrolling interest (NCI) or minority interest target for consolidation of investment rules.

- **Planning**
  Used for specifying the target planning FS items in case they have to be used in planning via other tools, such as SAP Analytics Cloud.

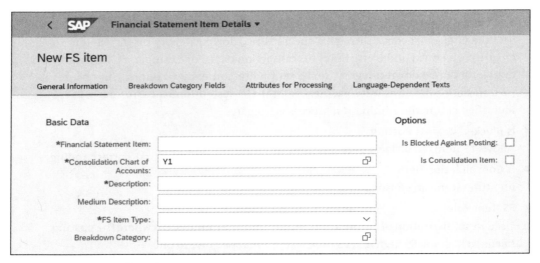

Figure 3.15 Define FS Items App

In addition to these properties, the following key points should be considered when it comes to FS items:

- Alphanumeric characters, underscores, and hyphens are allowed for FS item IDs.
- Consolidation charts of accounts are transportable using the standard SAP transport framework, which involves capturing objects in transport requests to move across the SAP landscape of development to production deployments.

- FS item master data needs to be updated individually in each target system and can't be transported.
- Usage of a standard upload template is recommended in each system to reduce errors. The template can be downloaded using standard the SAP Fiori Import Consolidation Master Data app.
- Reporting items used in reporting rules need to be configured as REPT type FS items in the master data.
- If the customer decides to create a custom chart of accounts for consolidation, the following configuration items also require an update:
  - Breakdown categories
  - FS items
  - FS item hierarchies
  - Selections
  - FS item mapping
  - FS items for automatic postings
  - Validation rules
  - Currency translation settings
  - Reclassification settings
  - Consolidation of investments
  - Reporting items

3.2.3   Financial Statement Item Attributes and Hierarchies

This section provides details regarding the processing attributes and corresponding value set for each FS item for performing consolidation-specific tasks. Attributes provide a systematic grouping of FS items and support the configuration. Hierarchies, on the other hand, support financial reporting and are primarily used for setting up a parent-child relationship for financial statements. Hierarchies and attributes are used for setting up reporting rules in group reporting for more intuitive and flexible reporting needs.

Attributes

Use IMG menu path **SAP S/4HANA for Group Reporting • Consolidation FS Item Configuration • FS Item Attribute • Values Attribute • Attribute Value** or Transaction CX8ITAVC for creating new attribute values. Figure 3.16 shows the screen to create new attribute values for selected attributes.

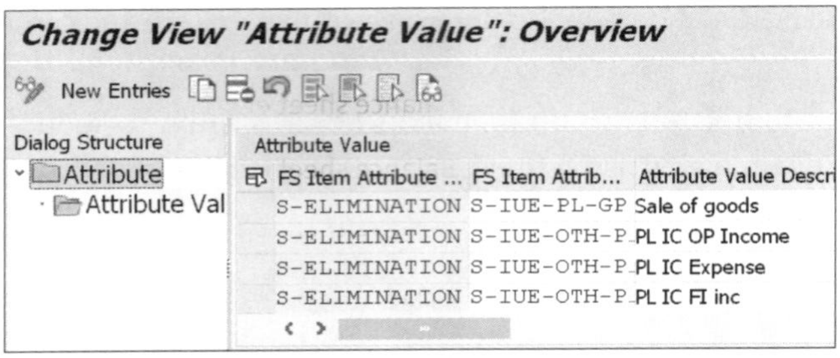

Figure 3.16 FS Item Attribute Values Maintenance

New entries can be created by selecting **New Entries** for any customer needs. Table 3.1 provides the selection attribute list as part of delivered SAP Best Practices configuration.

Attribute Name	Value Description	Usage
S-ELIMINATION	Elimination	Intercompany eliminations
S-CURRENCY-TRANSLATION	Currency translation	Currency translations
S-ROLE	FS item roles	Automatic postings
S-DATA-COLLECTION	Data collection	Data entry layout reports
S-CASH-FLOW	Cash flow	Cash flow rules
S-SCOPE	Scope	Data context
S-CUSTOMER-SPECIFIC	Customer-specific	Other custom requirement

Table 3.1 FS Item Attributes

Each of these attributes have attribute values predelivered as part of the business content. In the **Dialog Structure**, select **Attribute** and then choose **Attribute Values** to see the values. Table 3.2 lists a predelivered content sample for each of the attributes. You can choose to reuse the delivered attributes and their values, or you can create your own attributes depending on your requirements.

Attribute Value Name	Value Description	Usage
	S-ELIMINATION	
S-IUE-PL-GP	Sale of Goods	Profit and loss (P&L) eliminations
S-IUE-OTH-PL-INC	PL IC OP Income	P&L eliminations
S-IUE-OTH-PL-EXP	PL IC Expense	P&L eliminations
S-IUE-DIV	Dividends	P&L eliminations

Table 3.2 FS Item Attribute Values

Attribute Value Name	Value Description	Usage
S-IUE-BS-AR	IC Trade Receivable	Balance sheet eliminations
S-IUE-BS-AP	IC Trade Payables	Balance sheet eliminations
S-IUE-BS-OR-C	IC Other Receivable Current	Balance sheet eliminations
S-IUE-BS-OP-C	IC Other Payable Current	Balance sheet eliminations
S-IUE-BS-DIV-REC	BS Dividends Receivables	Balance sheet eliminations
S-IUE-BS-DIV-PAY	BS Dividends Payables	Balance sheet eliminations
S-IUE-BS-DER	IC Derivatives, Current	Balance sheet eliminations
S-COI-INV	Investments	Consolidation of investments
S-COI-OCI	Other Compr. Income	Consolidation of investments
S-COI-RET-EARN	Retained Earnings	Consolidation of investments
	S-CURRENCY-TRANSLATION	
S-CT-BS-CLO	B/S Items: Closing Rate	Balance sheet translations
S-CT-BS-HIST	B/S Items: Historical Conversion	Balance sheet translations
S-CT-BS-HIST-OPE	B/S Items: Hist Conv, OPE	Balance sheet translations
S-CT-PL-AVG	P&L Items - Average Rate	P&L translations
S-CT-ANI-BS	Net Income	Balance sheet translations
S-CT-NCI-NI	NCI-Net Income	Balance sheet translations
S-CT-ANI-PL	Net Income/Loss	P&L translations
	S-ROLE	
S-ANI-BS	Annual Net Income: B/S	FS items for automatic postings
S-ANI-PL	Annual Net Income: P&L	FS items for automatic postings
S-DEF-TAX-AST	Deferred Tax: Assets	FS items for automatic postings
S-DEF-TAX-LIA	Deferred Tax: Liabilities	FS items for automatic postings
S-DEF-TAX-PL	Deferred Tax: Expense	FS items for automatic postings
S-CT-DIFF	C/T Difference	Foreign exchange translations
S-CT-ROUND-PL	C/T Rounding Diff: P&L	Foreign exchange translations
S-RETAINED-EARNING	Retained Earning	Reclassifications
S-PERCENTAGE-GS	Percentage (%) – Group Share	Reclassifications

Table 3.2 FS Item Attribute Values (Cont.)

Attribute Value Name	Value Description	Usage
	S-DATA-COLLECTION	
S-A-CASH	Cash and Cash Equivalents	Report layouts
S-A-TRADE-OTH-REC	Trade and Other Current Receivables	Report layouts
S-A-CUR-TAX	Current Tax Assets	Report layouts
S-A-OTH-CUR	Other Current Assets	Report layouts
S-A-INVENTORIES	Inventories	Report layouts
S-L-TRADE-OTH-PAY	Trade and Other Current Payables	Report layouts
S-L-CUR-TAX	Current Tax Liabilities	Report layouts
S-L-OTH-CUR	Other Current Liabilities	Report layouts
S-E-ISSUED-CAP	Issued Capital	Report layouts
S-E-SHARE-PREMIUM	Share Premium	Report layouts
S-E-RETAIN-EARNINGS	Retained Earnings	Report layouts
S-P-REVENUE	Revenue	Report layouts
S-P-COS	Changes in Inventory/COS	Report layouts
S-P-OTH-OP-INC	Other Operating Income	Report layouts
	S-CASH-FLOW	
S-CF-AMT-A1	Amortization Intangible Assets	Reporting rules
S-CF-BAL-L1	Balancing Accnt: Bal.sheet	Reporting rules
S-CF-BP-A1	Clearing: Bargain Purchase	Reporting rules
S-CF-CASH-A1	Cash and Cash Equivalents	Reporting rules
S-CF-CASH-L1	Bank Overdrafts	Reporting rules
	S-SCOPE	
S-ACTUALS	Actuals FS Item	Report layouts
S-PLANNING	Planning FS Item	Report layouts
S-ALL	FS Item Used Both	Report layouts

Table 3.2 FS Item Attribute Values (Cont.)

Hierarchies

FS item hierarchies are set up using the SAP Fiori Manage Global Accounting Hierarchies app. This SAP Fiori app supports the creation of multiple consolidation-specific hierarchies such as FS items, reporting items, consolidation units, and subitems, and it has a built-in standard interface for direct consumption of master data from SAP S/4HANA. This app serves as a unified interface for both group reporting and SAP S/4HANA.

As part of predelivered SAP Best Practices content, Table 3.3 provides the details of hierarchies for group reporting.

ID	Description	Type	Purpose
BS	Balance Sheet	FS item	All balance sheet items
PL	P&L	FS item	All P&L items
BS_PL	Balance Sheet and P&L	FS item	Balance sheet and P&L combined
X1	Statement of Equity	Reporting item	Statement of changes in equity
X2	Statement of Cash Flow	Reporting item	Indirect method-based cash flow statement
X3	Statement of Comprehensive Inc	Reporting item	Statement of comprehensive income
X4	P&L By Function of Exp	Reporting item	Standard report for P&L
X5	IC Reconciliation	Reporting item	Intercompany reconciliation for analysis
X6	Currency Translation Reserves	FS item	Investment and equity analysis
ST	Statistical FS Items	FS item	Items pertaining to group shares postings

Table 3.3 Delivered Standard Hierarchies

All reporting item hierarchies are runtime hierarchies and don't store values in the database. The reporting rules definitions are maintained using Transaction FINCS_RRULE.

> **Note**
> Hierarchies can be created manually in the SAP Fiori Manage Global Accounting Hierarchies app or can be uploaded using an Excel template.

While SAP delivers preconfigured hierarchies for FS items and reporting items that are specific to delivered content, hierarchies for all others must be created based on your requirements. The following types of hierarchies are consolidation-relevant in group reporting:

- Document type
- FS item
- Posting level
- Profit center
- Reporting item
- Segment
- Subitem
- Consolidation unit

Because the app is also used to create hierarchies for SAP S/4HANA characteristics, not all the hierarchy types will be discussed in this section to confine the scope to group reporting usage. These delivered hierarchies aren't always necessary, so the requirement can be turned off in Customizing. Section 3.2.6 covers the master data aspects for turning hierarchies on or off for relevant characteristics.

To add a new hierarchy in the Manage Global Accounting Hierarchies app, click the **+** symbol, as shown in Figure 3.17, and provide the following inputs in the available fields, as shown in Figure 3.18:

- **Type**
  Type of hierarchy. Choose from those listed in Figure 3.17.
- **Hierarchy ID**
  An alphanumeric unique identifier.
- **Hierarchy Description**
  Description of the hierarchy.
- **Superordinate characteristic**
  Compounding characteristic of the **Hierarchy ID**; for example, an FS item type hierarchy would require a group chart of accounts as a mandatory input.
- **Valid From/To**
  Validity date range for time-dependent hierarchies.
- **Note**
  A descriptive optional note for the hierarchy.

As shown in Figure 3.18, the **Create New Hierarchy** screen can differ depending on the **Hierarchy Type** that you pick. Different types require different superordinate characteristics or options.

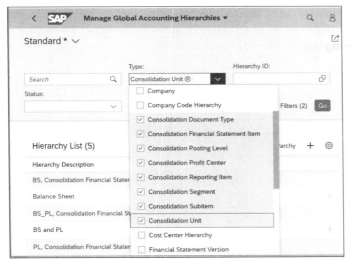

Figure 3.17 Delivered Hierarchies Specific to Consolidations

Figure 3.18 Options When Creating New Hierarchies

After a new hierarchy is created, new members or nodes can be added to the hierarchy to create the structure. You can update the structure and add members or nodes under the **Nodes** section in the **Timeframe** tab, as shown in Figure 3.19.

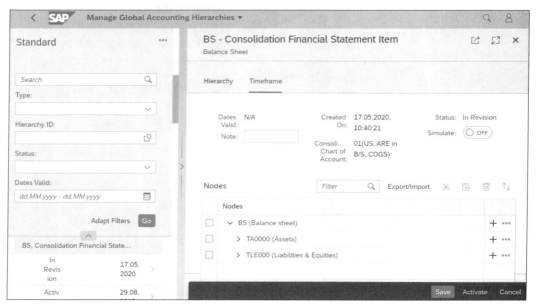

Figure 3.19 Hierarchy Edit Options

A new member in the hierarchy is created by adding individual members/nodes using either the **Fast Entry** or **Import Nodes** buttons (accessed by clicking …) in the Manage Global Accounting Hierarchies app to import an existing node from an existing hierarchy, as shown in Figure 3.20.

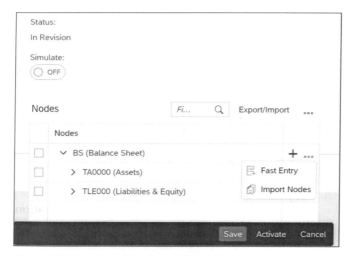

Figure 3.20 Creating Members of the Hierarchy

Another built-in option, **Export/Import**, as shown earlier in Figure 3.19, should be used to maintain the hierarchy in bulk. The option enables you to automatically create an upload template file, which can be saved to a local folder. Downloaded templates should be updated with new members of the hierarchy based on the requirements and imported using the same **Export/Import** option. The import template, as shown in Figure 3.21, requires input in the following mandatory fields for a successful upload:

- **Type**
  Can be the root, a node, or a member; one hierarchy has only one **Root** member.

- **ID**
  Member ID.

- **Parent ID**
  Parent ID of the member specified in the **ID** column.

A	B	C	D	E	F
Consolidation Financial Statement Item					
Hierarchy ID:	BS				
Valid from:	00.00.0000				
Valid to:	00.00.0000				
Consolidation Chart of Accounts:	01				
Consolidation Financial Statement Item	**Level**	**Type**	**ID**	**Description**	**Parent ID**
|- BS (Balance sheet)	1	Root	BS	Balance sheet	
|- TA0000 (Assets)	2	Node	TA0000	Assets	BS
|- TLE000 (Liabilities & Equities)	2	Node	TLE000	Liabilities & Equities	BS

Figure 3.21 Sample of a Hierarchy Upload Template

In addition, the following key points should be considered when it comes to hierarchies:

- Hierarchies are used in group reporting for matrix eliminations (eliminations based on hierarchies) for management consolidations.
- Variables for hierarchies are available automatically in reports.
- Hierarchies can be imported from SAP S/4HANA for dimensions such as profit center for synchronization.
- Nodes within hierarchies can also be used in selections for flexible maintenance.
- Nodes are also available for use in reporting rules for dynamic reporting items.
- A hierarchy can be in the following statuses:
  - **Draft**: A hierarchy is created and is only saved but not activated even once. Hierarchies in **Draft** status can be deleted.
  - **In Revision**: An active version of a hierarchy already exists, and the configuration and the reports will use the last active version.
  - **Active**: A version of the hierarchy is available for reporting in SAP Analysis for Microsoft Office and SAP Fiori reports.

3.2.4   Breakdown Categories

Standard group reporting provides a control using breakdowns on subassignments within transaction data. Breakdown categories act as gatekeeper controls to maintain data consistency within consolidations. A typical example for breakdown categories is keeping balance sheet accounts consistent with a transaction type to capture the activity. These transaction types are then used as identifiers in the carryforward process where relevant transactions from the prior year are moved to the opening period of the current year. Each FS item is associated with a category to enforce the control.

SAP provides standard breakdown categories or you can create custom categories to meet any specific requirements.

Use Transaction CX1I4 or the SAP Fiori Display Breakdown Categories app to display/ create breakdown categories. You can also follow IMG path **SAP S/4HANA for Group Reporting • Master Data • Define Breakdown Categories**. For creating a new breakdown category, click the SAP Fiori **Display Breakdown Categories** tile to arrive at the screen shown in Figure 3.22, where you can define characteristics.

Breakdown Cat.	1A00	TT915		
Characteristic	Break.Type	Text	Fixed val.	Max. Selection
Period of Acq.	0	breakdown		
Partner Unit		No breakdown		
Trans.currency		No breakdown		
Unit of measure		No breakdown		
Subitem Categor.	3	Required break.	1	
Subitem	2	Required break.		S-BC-TT-01
Acquis. Year	0	No breakdown		

Figure 3.22 Breakdown Category Characteristics

The following **Characteristic** fields are required for creating new breakdown categories and have to be marked as mandatory or optional with a constant value or selection entry:

- **Period of Acq.**
  Period of acquisition for historical exchange rates based on the posting date.

- **Partner Unit**
  Trading partner that can be a valid member of master data if specified as the default value.

- **Trans. currency**
  Transaction currency for future releases.

- **Unit of measure**
  Measurement unit for quantities.

- **Subitem Category**
  Categories for subitems, either transaction type for balance sheet or functional area for P&L.

- **Subitem**
  Subitem value based on the **Subitem Category**.
- **Acquis. Year**
  Acquisition year, in relation to the acquisition period.

In the **Break.Type** entry field on the screen shown in Figure 3.22, for each characteristic field, only a predefined list of values is permitted that defines the behavior of the characteristic. These values are listed in Table 3.4 with their significance.

Value	Purpose
0	Breakdown not required
1	Breakdown optional/blank value allowed
2	Breakdown required/if blank set default
3	Breakdown required/no blanks, default allowed
4	Breakdown required/no blanks, no default value allowed

Table 3.4 Breakdown Types

In addition, the following key points should be considered when it comes to breakdown categories:

- Breakdown categories are assigned to FS items.
- Assignment of breakdown categories isn't dependent on parameters such as version, time, or ledger.
- If there are changes to the breakdown categories assignment to an FS item, the SAP Fiori Check Correct Breakdowns of Transaction Data app needs to be executed to check and correct the subassignments.
- For a breakdown categories update, the system prompts for a consistency check automatically; however, the task might be needed for different versions if there is a dependency.

3.2.5   Subitem Categories and Subitems

The purpose of a subitem category is to classify the subassignments of FS items. Categories such as transaction types (category type 1) and functional areas (category type 2) are predelivered as content. Transaction type or movement type are also common in other consolidation solutions and are associated with balance sheet accounts, for example. As another example, subitem 900 of category 1 is associated with the opening balances of a balance sheet FS item in group reporting.

Table 3.5 provides the predelivered subitems in group reporting.

Subitem Category	Description	ID	Subitem Description	Subitem for Balance Carryforward	Subitem for Acquisition	Subitem for Divestiture
1	Transaction type	900	Opening balance	900	901	998
1	Transaction type	901	Incoming units	900	901	998
1	Transaction type	902	Consolidation method change (old)	900	901	998
1	Transaction type	903	Consolidation method change (new)	900	901	998
1	Transaction type	904	Equity method rate change	900	901	998
1	Transaction type	906	Dividends	900	901	998
1	Transaction type	909	Change in accounting policies	900	901	998
1	Transaction type	915	Net variation	900	901	998
1	Transaction type	920	Increase/purchase	900	901	998
1	Transaction type	925	Increase in depreciation	900	901	998
1	Transaction type	930	Decrease/disposal	900	901	998
1	Transaction type	935	Decrease in depreciation	900	901	998

Table 3.5 Delivered Subitems in Group Reporting

Subitem Category	Description	ID	Subitem Description	Subitem for Balance Carryforward	Subitem for Acquisition	Subitem for Divestiture
1	Transaction type	940	Capital increase/decrease	900	901	998
1	Transaction type	950	Reclassification	900	901	998
1	Transaction type	955	Fair value	900	901	998
1	Transaction type	970	Internal merger	900	901	998
1	Transaction type	980	Currency translation adjust.	900	901	998
1	Transaction type	992	Change in ownership interest	900	901	998
1	Transaction type	998	Outgoing units	900	901	998
2	Functional area	YB10	Sales revenue	N/A	N/A	N/A
2	Functional area	YB15	Sales discounts and allow	N/A	N/A	N/A
2	Functional area	YB20	Cost of goods sold	N/A	N/A	N/A
2	Functional area	YB25	Consulting/services	N/A	N/A	N/A
2	Functional area	YB30	Sales and distribution	N/A	N/A	N/A
2	Functional area	YB35	Marketing	N/A	N/A	N/A
2	Functional area	YB40	Administration	N/A	N/A	N/A

Table 3.5 Delivered Subitems in Group Reporting (Cont.)

Subitem Category	Description	ID	Subitem Description	Subitem for Balance Carryforward	Subitem for Acquisition	Subitem for Divestiture
2	Functional area	YB50	Research & development	N/A	N/A	N/A
2	Functional area	YB70	Other gains	N/A	N/A	N/A
2	Functional area	YB75	Other expenses	N/A	N/A	N/A
2	Functional area	YB77	Gain from investments	N/A	N/A	N/A
2	Functional area	YB79	Gain from shares & loans	N/A	N/A	N/A
2	Functional area	YB81	Interest & similar gains	N/A	N/A	N/A
2	Functional area	YB83	Amort.curr. Fin.assets;sec	N/A	N/A	N/A
2	Functional area	YB85	Interest & similar costs	N/A	N/A	N/A
2	Functional area	YB87	Extraordinary gain	N/A	N/A	N/A
2	Functional area	YB89	Extraordinary expense	N/A	N/A	N/A
2	Functional area	YB90	Taxes from income and rev	N/A	N/A	N/A
2	Functional area	YB98	Other taxes	N/A	N/A	N/A
2	Functional area	YB99	Dummy functional area	N/A	N/A	N/A

Table 3.5 Delivered Subitems in Group Reporting (Cont.)

Subitem Category	Description	ID	Subitem Description	Subitem for Balance Carryforward	Subitem for Acquisition	Subitem for Divestiture
2	Functional area	YD20	IC difference - operating	N/A	N/A	N/A
2	Functional area	YD70	IC difference - financial	N/A	N/A	N/A

Table 3.5 Delivered Subitems in Group Reporting (Cont.)

As explained in the previous section, breakdown categories use the subitem category and subitems extensively to help with setting controls. These then allow for document-level enrichment for further processes in consolidations. In an integrated data scenario where the data source is SAP S/4HANA, the subitem field is mapped automatically with the relevant field of the SAP S/4HANA accounting document.

Use Transaction CX1S4 or the SAP Fiori Import Master Data for Consolidation Fields app to create subitems. You can also follow IMG path **SAP S/4HANA for Group Reporting • Master Data • Define Subitem Categories and Subitems**.

Using the menu path, you'll see the screen shown in Figure 3.23. New customer-specific subitems are created after clicking on the **Create** icon/button with the following mandatory fields, as shown in Figure 3.24:

- **Subitem**
  Unique member ID.
- **Medium Text**
  Description of the subitem defined.
- **Carry forward to subitem**
  Opening balance subitem identifier. During the carryforward process the defined subitem will be carried forward to the one mentioned in the field.
- **Retire./divest.subitem**
  Subitem identifier for any outgoing units.
- **Acquisition subitem**
  Subitem identifier for newly acquired units.
- **No Posting/Entry**
  Doesn't allow any manual postings to the defined member.

Maintain SI cat/SI: Change

Hierarchy	Descript.
∨ 📂 SubItemCat	
› 📁 1	Transaction Types
∨ 📂 2	Functional areas
· 📄 0001	Sales and Distribution
· 📄 0002	Marketing
· 📄 0003	Administration
· 📄 0004	Research and development
· 📄 0005	Production
· 📄 9999	Dummy FM (check assignme...
· 📄 YB10	Sales Revenue
· 📄 YB15	Sales discounts and allow
· 📄 YB20	Cost of goods sold

Figure 3.23 Subitem Categories

Subitem Category	1	Transaction Types
Properties		
Subitem	218	
Medium Text	Proceed LT Debt	
Selected subitems		
Carry forward to subitem	218	
Retire./divest.subitem	901	
Acquisition subitem	998	
☐ No Posting/Entry		

Figure 3.24 New Subitem Creation for Subitem Category 1

Figure 3.23 and Figure 3.24 show the screens used to create new subitems using SAP GUI. Alternatively, you can use standard SAP Fiori apps for mass upload of multiple subitems, as shown in Figure 3.25.

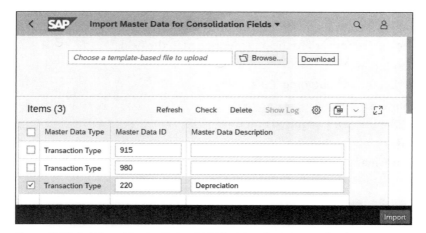

Figure 3.25 Subitem Master Data: SAP Fiori App for Mass Upload

A standard template is available for download and reuse using the **Download** option in the app, leading to the **Download Template** screen shown in Figure 3.26. In the **Master Data Type Selection** dropdown, choose from the following options:

- **Account Number**
- **Chart of Accounts**
- **Controlling Area**
- **Cost Center**
- **Functional Area**
- **Profit Center**
- **Segment for Segmental Reporting**
- **Transaction Type**

In Figure 3.26, **Transaction Type** is selected. **Data Selection** provides the option of downloading with or without existing master data from system for easy reference. Clicking **Download** then downloads the template onto the local system. Open the downloaded Microsoft Excel template as shown in Figure 3.27 with the member details to include the new member ID.

You can upload the template into the Import Master Data for Consolidation Fields app shown earlier in Figure 3.25 by clicking the **Browse** option. Choose the desired member, and click **Import** to create a new member.

Figure 3.26 Download Template: With Existing Master Data

Import Master Data			
*Master Data Type	*Master Data ID	Superordinate Field Va	Description
FinancialTransactionType	\<Transaction Type, max. 3 characters>		

Figure 3.27 Transaction Type: Master Data Import Template

In addition, the following key points should be considered when it comes to subitems:

- Default values for subitems can be defined for missing information in the accounting document in group reporting.

- Subitems are used in selections that support consolidation tasks such as currency translations and eliminations.
- Subitems are used in balance sheet reporting and cash flow reporting.
- Subitems can be aligned in hierarchies for reporting purposes.
- The transaction type and functional area subitem categories are integrated with SAP S/4HANA master data; however, group reporting-specific subitems can be created.
- General ledger consolidation transaction types in SAP S/4HANA need to be synchronized with group reporting transaction types.

3.2.6   Consolidation Fields (Additional Fields)

This section covers any additional master data requirements in consolidations. As a standard interface provided within group reporting, any additional characteristics that might be required in consolidation processes are configured here using this configuration setting in the IMG. There are additional attributes that can be set for each of the characteristics to control behavior during the process, for example, profit center and cost center customer group. Multiple configuration options are available, as shown in Figure 3.28, for new master data that we'll describe in this section.

Use Transaction FINCS_ADDLFLD_SEL_U or IMG path **SAP S/4HANA for Group Reporting • Master Data • Define Consolidation Master Data Fields** to customize additional master data, arriving at the screen shown in Figure 3.28.

Change View "Configuration of Additional Char

Configuration of Additional Characteristics

Field Name	Enable Inputs	Enable Maste...	Enable Hierarchy
BusinessArea	☐	☐	☐
PartnerCostCen.	☐	☐	☐
PartnerBusines.	☐	☐	☐
PartnerCompany	☐	☐	☐
CustomerSuppli.	☐	☐	☐
ProfitCenter	☑	☑	☑
Segment	☑	☑	☑
CostCenter	☑	☑	☐
FunctionalArea	☑	☑	☐

Figure 3.28 Additional Master Data Configuration

To provide a context for each additional master data option that is enabled or disabled, its impact on various features is shown in Figure 3.29.

The following options can be enabled for each field:

- **Master Data Possible**
  If selected, the characteristic is available in table ACDOCU.

- **Hierarchy Possible**
  If selected, the characteristic is available for hierarchies in SAP S/4HANA.

- **Hierarchy Elimination Possible**
  If selected, enables eliminations for matrix or management consolidation, typically for profit center and segment characteristics.

- **Clearing Inputs in BCF Possible**
  If selected, the characteristic is considered for clearing during the balance carryforward.

- **Superordinate Field**
  Compounding characteristic of the **Field Name** specified.

- **Reference Field**
  If specified, the field uses the master data of the reference field; typical examples are partner characteristics.

- **Enable Inputs**
  If selected, the field is available in group journal templates.

- **Enable Master Data**
  Members in group journals are validated against the master data of the characteristic; this works in tandem with **Enable Inputs**.

- **Enable Hierarchy**
  Works with the **Hierarchy Possible** option as described previously for enabling the reporting hierarchies in the analysis reports in group reporting.

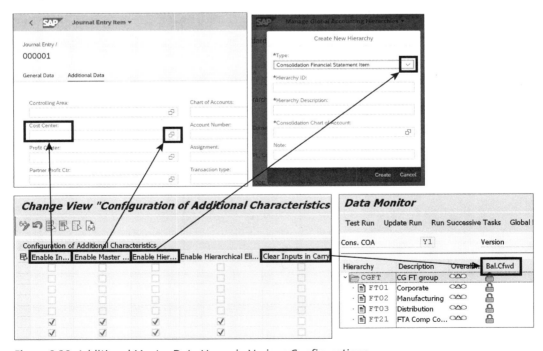

Figure 3.29 Additional Master Data Usage in Various Configurations

- **Enable Hierarchy Eliminations**
  Enables dynamic eliminations using the hierarchies for management or matrix consolidation purposes. Each enabled field creates a virtual dimension in the group reporting consolidation reports (SAP Fiori Group Data Analysis app) in runtime.
- **Clear Inputs in Carry.**
  Works with the prior **Clearing Inputs in BCF Possible** selection field to allow clearing of fields in the opening period during balance carryforward.

You can also use the standard SAP Fiori Define Master Data for Consolidation Fields app to define and maintain additional master data as specified in Customizing. Use the standard SAP Fiori Manage Global Accounting Hierarchies app to maintain hierarchies for the additional master data.

Figure 3.30 shows the SAP Fiori Define Master Data for Consolidation Fields app for master data maintenance. Characteristics that have master data enabled in Customizing appear in the app and provide the following additional information:

- **Consolidation Master Data Records**
  Provides the information on total group reporting-specific members for consolidation usage only.
- **Accounting Master Data Records**
  Provides the information on the member count as in SAP S/4HANA general ledger master data tables.
- **Link**
  Provides a link to manage member hierarchies if enabled in Customizing for the characteristic.

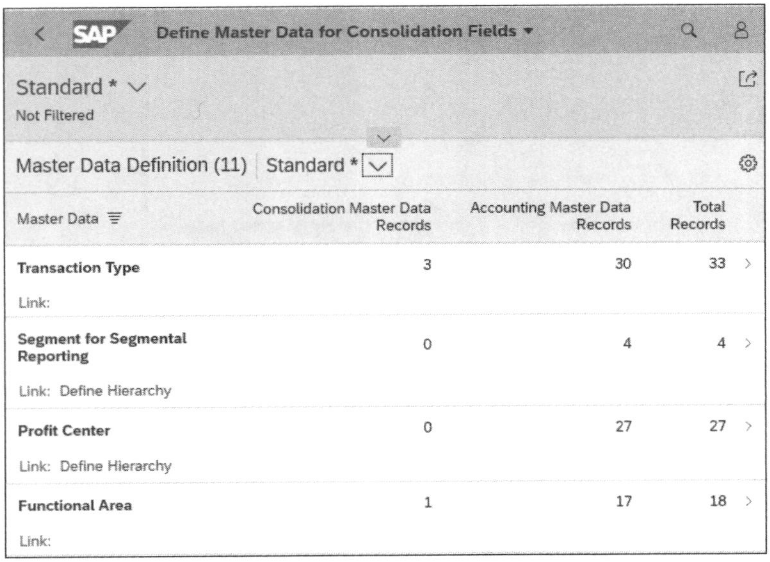

Master Data ≡	Consolidation Master Data Records	Accounting Master Data Records	Total Records	
Transaction Type	3	30	33	>
Link:				
Segment for Segmental Reporting	0	4	4	>
Link: Define Hierarchy				
Profit Center	0	27	27	>
Link: Define Hierarchy				
Functional Area	1	17	18	>
Link:				

Figure 3.30 SAP Fiori: Define Master Data for Consolidation Fields App

The following key points should be considered when it comes to additional master data configuration:

- Additional master data is allowed; however, you must consider the performance implications while selecting granular characteristics such as assignment number.

- Certain additional characteristics, when enabled, don't participate in consolidation tasks such as retained earnings calculations, so additional customization must be considered for including them.

- User-defined fields aren't yet supported for additional master data. The selection list to choose from is predelivered.

3.2.7   Consolidation Versions

Another dimension that is very common in consolidation is the category, or *version*, as it's called in group reporting. The primary purpose of the version dimension is to separate the data sets based on their nature. Version identifies the data set and the configuration rule set applicable to the data. It reduces configuration replication for simulation scenarios or various reporting scenarios as needed. Version also drives the access control to restrict the users viewing and manipulating the data during the consolidation process.

To emphasize the dual nature of the version dimension as mentioned earlier, group reporting has a data version that identifies the data set in use for consolidations and subsequently results in the processing of the same data set to generate financial statements. For example, actual, plan, and forecast are usual categorizations of data and might have a different rule set depending upon the requirements.

Group reporting also considers an object's version, and different versions of the same object are used for supporting the configuration for increasing usability across various scenarios. For example, to maintain consistency, a single FS item version can be set in the assignment across multiple data versions. This ensures easy maintenance and consistency across all data versions.

As part of the standard content delivered by SAP, multiple versions are available—for actuals data Y10 (actuals), Y12 (actuals and budget rates), and Y20 (actuals 2nd GC)—to provide a standard version providing results in a different group currency. For plan data, there are versions YB# (for budget) and YF# (for forecast). Based on your requirements, new versions can be created and customized.

Use Transaction CXDCPV or IMG path **SAP S/4HANA for Group Reporting • Master Data • Create Version from Reference Version** to create a new version. Figure 3.31 provides information regarding how a new version has been created using the standard delivered version as reference template. **Dimension** should be set to Y1 as the default, **Template Version** can be Y10 from where the copy would happen, and **Target Version** is the new version to be created. It's particularly useful to test the creation by enabling the **Test Run** feature before clicking the **Execute** button.

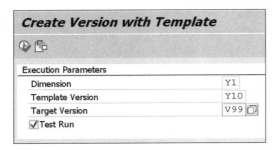

Figure 3.31 Version Creation with Delivered Content Y10 Reference

You can also use Transaction CXB1 or IMG path **SAP S/4HANA for Group Reporting • Master Data • Define Versions** for updating the attributes of the new created version, as shown in Figure 3.32, for the configuration. Specific details regarding each of these fields are as follows:

- **Version for Plan Data**
  This option sets the version for plan-specific data. The system automatically uses the planning table as the source (table ACDOCP) as opposed to Universal Journal (table ACDOCA) when the option isn't selected.

- **Source Category**
  This works in conjunction with **Version for Plan Data**. The category specified in this field is the source category in the planning table.

- **Source Ledger**
  This works in conjunction with **Version for Plan Data**. The ledger specified in this property is the source ledger in the planning table.

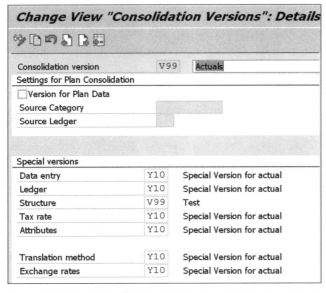

Figure 3.32 Updating the Special Versions for the New Version

Before proceeding further with other fields, it's important to understand the concept of *special versions* in group reporting, as they play an important role in the version configuration. Special versions allow the consolidation object and rule sets to be reused without having to reconfigure them individually for each new version. Figure 3.33 shows the relationship of a special version with the consolidation version and the Customizing object. Each task, when triggered within a consolidation version, refers to the object and rule set version (special version) as defined in the consolidation version definition and creates results in the consolidation version.

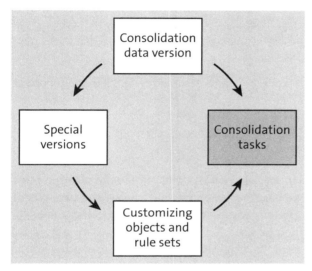

Figure 3.33 Special Versions Relationship in Group Reporting

Each consolidation version has the following special version fields (shown previously in Figure 3.32) to support the existing settings reusability:

- **Data entry**
  This field allows the use of object versions for the data transfer method, upload methods, and validation methods to consolidation units within the current consolidation version.

- **Ledger**
  This field allows the use of object versions for ledger and group currency assignments to consolidation groups.

- **Structure**
  This field allows the use of object versions for the consolidation group structure and the corresponding consolidation units within each group structure, including the relevant settings such as the consolidation method.

- **Tax rate**
  This field allows the tax rate assignment reusability for the current version.

- **Attributes**
  This field is valid for group reporting for SAP S/4HANA Cloud only and mostly should be set to the delivered **Y10** special version.

- **Translation method**
  This field allows the assignment of currency translation methods to consolidation units.

- **Exchange rates**
  This field allows the assignment of exchange rates to exchange rate indicators.

- **Reclassifications**
  This field allows the usage of object versions for assigning methods and document types to reclassification tasks.

- **Reporting Rules**
  This field allows the object version of reporting rules to be assigned to the reporting rule variant.

- **FS Group Items**
  This field allows the object version of FS items to be assigned to general ledger account mapping.

Figure 3.34 shows the relation of each special version in reference to the corresponding task for more clarity on the concept. For **Translation method,** the system uses **V99** as the special version. Currency translation method customizations specific to version V99 in Transaction CXD1 would then be used for the currency translation method. Another example is the Assignment of Financial Statement Items app, which uses the **FS Group Items** version (**Y10**), in this case, for mapping the consolidation chart of accounts with the general ledger chart of account.

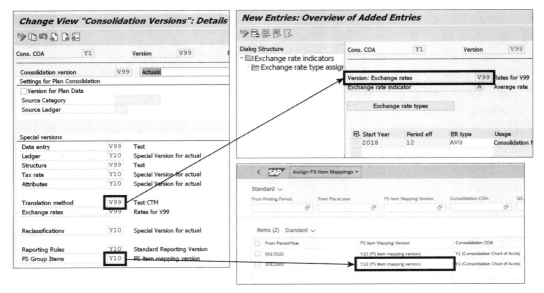

Figure 3.34 Configuration References with Special Version Assignment

As an added functionality, at the bottom of the screen of Transaction CXB1, the **Task Versions** option enables you to view only tasks that have been assigned with special versions. As an example, if **Translation method** is assigned with special version **V99**, this and all other special versions are set to **Y10** as default. This entry **V99** would be available in the **Task Versions** list.

New special versions are created using the same consolidation version screen, which is accessed by clicking the **Create** button located beside each special version and then clicking the **New Entries** button, as shown in Figure 3.35. Enter an ID in the **Version** field and a **Description** for the new special version, and click the **Save** button/icon.

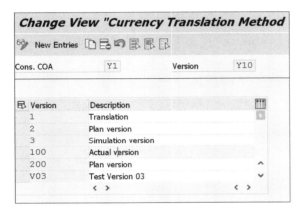

Figure 3.35 Creation of a Special Version

The following key points should be considered when it comes to consolidation versions:

- Versions once created can't be deleted.
- The consolidation version can allow simulations such as various exchange rates on consolidated financial statements using the special versions.
- Versions can be used to prepare statements and reports in multiple statutory accounting such as US GAAP or local GAAP.

3.2.8 Document Types

Group reporting supports a detailed trace of the data footprint during consolidation. With the use of document types, right from the data acquisition to top-side journal entries, a data trail is maintained for postings made during the entire consolidation process. Similar to the concept of the SAP S/4HANA document type, the entries that are posted to group reporting also have a type associated based on the nature of the posting.

Each document type is further associated with a posting level. Posting levels categorize data as reported data, standardized data, and consolidated data in group reporting, depending on the nature of selected data. Posting levels in conjunction with document types are jointly called the audit trail dimension. Posting levels are prebuilt in the system and can't be enhanced or added to the delivered list.

Table 3.6 provides the built-in posting levels. Table 3.7 provides the data categorization and delivered document types associated with the posting levels.

Posting Level	Activity	Data Level
<Blank>	Accounting data released from table ACDOCA or table ACDOCP	Consolidation unit
0C	Corrections to accounting data	Consolidation unit
00	File upload, loaded data based on application programming interface (API)	Consolidation unit
01	Correction to reported data carried forward to 00	Consolidation unit
10	Adjustments to reported data	Consolidation unit
0T	Rounding from currency translation	Consolidation unit
20	Eliminations	Consolidation unit + partner
30	Consolidations activities	Consolidation group
02	Reported data consolidation group change	Consolidation group; consolidation unit
12	Standardized data consolidation group change	Consolidation group; consolidation unit
22	Consolidated data consolidation group change	Consolidation group; consolidation unit

Table 3.6 Posting Levels for Data Source Identification

Data			Posting Levels	Delivered Document Types
Consolidated	Standardized	Reported	▪ <Blank>: Accounting data ▪ 00: Reported data ▪ 01: Corrections ▪ 0C: Corrections	▪ 0F ▪ 00; 03; 05–07; 0A–0E; 0G ▪ 02 ▪ 01; 04
			▪ 10: Adjustments ▪ 0T: Rounding ▪ 20: Eliminations	▪ 11–14; 17–19; 1A–1C; 1O–1P ▪ All ▪ 21; 22; 2E–2H
			▪ 30: Consolidations ▪ 02; 12; 22: Preparations of changes to consolidation group	▪ 30; 32–33; 3A–3B; 38–39; 3Z ▪ 0Z; 1Z; 2Z

Table 3.7 Posting Level and Data Categorizations in Group Reporting

The standard document types delivered as part of SAP Best Practices content are shown in Table 3.8.

ID	Description (Posting Level/Type)	Balance Check Values	Currency/ Quantity	Deferred Tax	Appli-cation	Reversal
00	Upload reported data (00/UPL)	2	LC/GC		B	
01	Man cor univ journal (0C/MJE)	0	LC/GC		9	
02	Man cor reported data (01/MJE)	0	LC		9	Next period/ not next fiscal year
03	Man input reported dat (00/MDC)	2	LC/GC		A	
04	Man input correct uj (0C/MDC)	0	LC/GC		A	
05	Annual net income (00/AUT)	2	LC/GC		C	
06	Rounding (00/AUT)	2	LC/GC		D	
07	External reported dat (00/API)	2	LC/GC		E	
0F	Realtime from FI (0F/INT)	0	TC/LC/GC/QTY		9	
0T	Currency trans (0T/AUT)	2	GC		8	
0Z	Prep group changes (02/AUT)	0	GC		9	
11	Man std LC, DT, no rev (10/MJE)	0	LC	DR/CR	9	
12	Man std LC, DT, rev (10/MJE)	0	LC	DR/CR	9	Next period
13	Man std LC, no DT/ rev (10/MJE)	0	LC		9	
16	Man std GC, DT, no rev (10/MJE)	0	LC/GC	DR/CR	9	
17	Man std GC, DT, rev (10/MJE)	0	LC/GC	DR/CR	9	Next period

Table 3.8 Delivered Document Types

ID	Description (Posting Level/Type)	Balance Check Values	Currency/ Quantity	Deferred Tax	Appli- cation	Reversal
18	Man std GC, no DT/ rev (10/MJE)	0	LC/GC		9	
19	Man std GC, rev, no DT (10/MJE)	0	LC/GC		9	Next period
1A	Aut std LC, DT, rev (10/AUT)	0	LC	DR/CR	7	Next period
1B	Aut std LC, rev, no DT(10/AUT)	0	LC		7	Next period
1C	Aut std GC, no DT/ rev (10/AUT)	0	GC		7	
1O	Aut std LC, DT, no rev (10/AUT)	0	LC	DR/CR	7	
1P	Aut std GC, DT, no rev (10/AUT)	0	GC	DR/CR	7	
1Z	Prep group changes (12/AUT)	0	GC		9	
21	Man elim cor, rev (20/MJE)		GC		1	Next period
22	Man elim cor, no rev (20/MJE)		GC		1	Not next fiscal year
2E	IC elim gross profit (20/AUT)	0	GC		7	Next period/ not next fiscal year
2F	IC elim other inc& exp (20/AUT)	0	GC		7	Next period/ not next fiscal year
2G	IC elim balance sheet (20/AUT)	0	GC		7	Next period
2H	IC elim dividends (20/AUT)	0	GC		7	Next period/ not next fiscal year
2O	Aut elim cust 1 (20/AUT)	0	GC		7	Next period/ not next fiscal year
2P	Aut elim cust 2 (20/AUT)	0	GC		7	Next period/ not next fiscal year

Table 3.8 Delivered Document Types (Cont.)

ID	Description (Posting Level/Type)	Balance Check Values	Currency/ Quantity	Deferred Tax	Appli- cation	Reversal
2Z	Prep group changes (22/AUT)		GC		9	
30	Aut reclass cust (30/AUT)		GC		7	
31	Man cons adj, rev (30/MJE)		GC		9	Next period/ not next fiscal year
32	Man cons adj, no rev (30/MJE)		GC		9	
39	Group shares (30/MJE)	2	GC/QTY		9	
3A	Invest, equity elim (30/AUT)	0	GC		7	
3Z	Total divestiture (30/AUT)	0	GC		7	
14	Man std LC, rev, no DT (10/MJE)	0	LC	DR/CR	9	Next period
33	Man Col adj, no rev (30/MJE)	0	GC		6	
3B	Auto Col adj. (30/AUT)	0	GC		6	
38	Group shares (30/AUT)	2	QTY		F	
0A	C/I control data (00/MDC)	2	TC/LC/GC/ QTY		A	
0C	Mapping from import (00/MDC)	2	TC/LC/GC/ QTY		E	
0D	Mapping from accounting (00/MDC)	2	TC/LC/GC/ QTY		E	
0E	Form data (00/MDC)	2	TC/LC/GC/ QTY		E	
0G	C/I control data (00/MDC)	2	TC/LC/GC/ QTY		E	

Table 3.8 Delivered Document Types (Cont.)

ID	Description (Posting Level/Type)	Balance Check Values	Currency/ Quantity	Deferred Tax	Appli-cation	Reversal
0B	C/I control data (00/UPL)	2	TC/LC/GC/ QTY		B	
0Z	Prep group changes (02/AUT)	0	GC		9	

Legend

Balance check values:

- 0: Error when balance not equal to zero
- 1: Warning when balance not equal to zero
- 2: No balance check

Application values:

- 1: Elimination of payables and receivables
- 7: Reclassification
- 8: Currency translation
- 9: Other
- A: Online data entry
- B: Flexible upload
- C: Net profit calculation
- D: Rounding
- F: Posting of group shares

System abbreviations:

- TC: Transaction currency
- DR/CR: Debit/credit
- MJE: Manual journal entry
- MDC: Manual data collection
- UPL: Upload
- C/I: Consolidation of investments
- LC: Local currency
- GC: Group currency
- Man: Manual
- Aut: Automatic

Table 3.8 Delivered Document Types (Cont.)

Use Transaction CXE1 or IMG path **SAP S/4HANA for Group Reporting • Master Data • Define Document Types** to create a new document type. You can also use Transaction CX53 or IMG path **SAP S/4HANA for Group Reporting • Master Data • Edit Number Range Intervals for Posting** for setting the number ranges for document types.

In addition to the document types specified previously, you can follow the menu path mentioned earlier and shown in Figure 3.36. For any additional custom document types defined in the system per your requirements, click **New Entries**. The following field inputs are required in the subsequent screen, as shown in Figure 3.37:

- **Document Type**
  Enter the two-digit alphanumeric ID for the document type.

- **Posting Level**
  Assign an existing posting level to the document type.

- **Balance check**
  If selected, the debit amount must be equal to the credit amount.

- **Bus.application**
  Specify the type of activity the document type refers to by choosing from the existing standard list of entries.

- **Translate to Group Currency**
  If selected, the transaction currency is converted to the group currency.

- **Posting**
  Choose the type of posting, which can be either of the following:
  - **Manual**: Document type is only used for manual postings.
  - **Automatic**: Document type is used for automatic postings such as eliminations.

- **Currencies**
  Post amounts in relevant currency, which can be any of the following options:
  - **Post in transaction currency**: Post in transaction currency.
  - **Post in local currency**: Post in local currency.
  - **Post in group currency:** Post in group currency
  - **Post quantities**: Post quantities with or without currency; a unit of measure is mandatory for posting a quantity.

- **Deferred Income Taxes**
  Automatically calculate the deferred income tax, which can be either of the following options:
  - **Credit deferred tax**: Automatically credits the deferred tax during the posting.
  - **Debit deferred taxes**: Automatically debits the deferred tax during the posting.

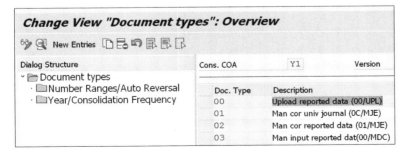

Figure 3.36 Document Type Creation

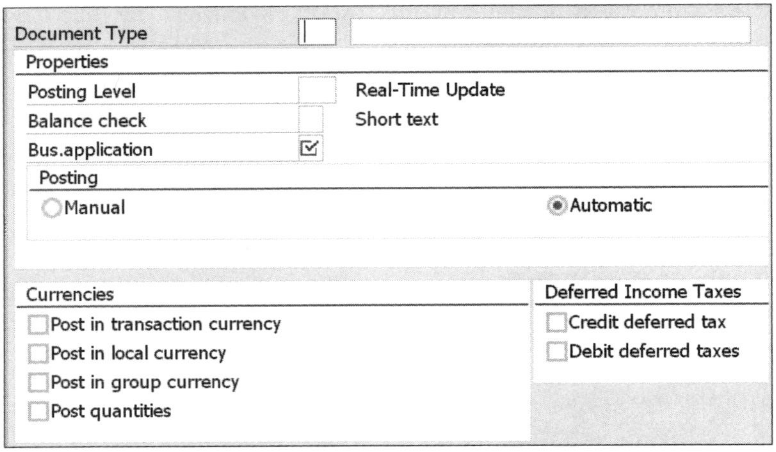

Figure 3.37 Custom Document Type Creation

In addition to these field values, each document type has two additional settings to be configured under **Number Ranges/Auto Reversal** and **Year/Consolidation Frequency** in the **Dialog Structure**. These settings define how the document will be posted and if there are any reverse postings in the subsequent period for each consolidation version (see Figure 3.38):

- **Number range**
  Number that identifies the number range for the number assignment. Figure 3.39 shows the number ranges as defined in the system and the current document number status.
- **Auto reversal**
  Posts a reversal document of the current posting in the subsequent period automatically. A reversal is created and posted at the same time when the current document is posted. Closing period reversals are done in the opening period of the new year.

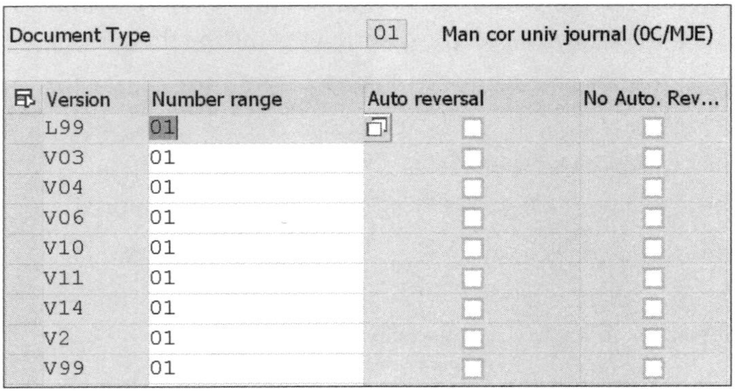

Document Type 01 Man cor univ journal (0C/MJE)

Version	Number range	Auto reversal	No Auto. Rev...
L99	01	☐	☐
V03	01	☐	☐
V04	01	☐	☐
V06	01	☐	☐
V10	01	☐	☐
V11	01	☐	☐
V14	01	☐	☐
V2	01	☐	☐
V99	01	☐	☐

Figure 3.38 Version-Specific Document Type Setting for Reversal

- **Consolidation Frequency**

  Depending on the consolidation frequency (monthly, yearly, etc.), the reversal entry is posted per the frequency.

- **No Auto. Reversal in Next FY**

  When selected, this setting doesn't reverse post in the next period when the period falls in the next year.

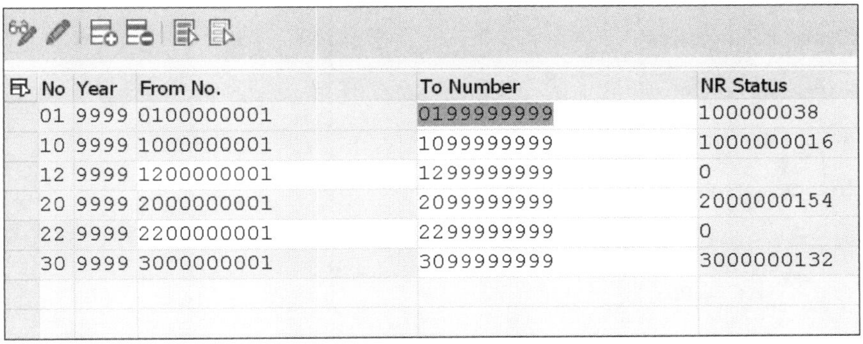

No	Year	From No.	To Number	NR Status
01	9999	0100000001	0199999999	100000038
10	9999	1000000001	1099999999	1000000016
12	9999	1200000001	1299999999	0
20	9999	2000000001	2099999999	2000000154
22	9999	2200000001	2299999999	0
30	9999	3000000001	3099999999	3000000132

Figure 3.39 Document Type Number Ranges

After you're done with configuring document types, the document types are associated with the reclassification methods and tasks. Reclassification methods contain the sequence of rules that consist of a triggering account set, a source combination, a destination combination, and rule-specific settings for customization. A detailed explanation of reclassification methods is provided in Chapter 6. Each method is then associated with a task to be run within the overall consolidation process.

Table 3.9 provides the details regarding each of these tasks.

Task	Description	Document Type
	Data Monitor	
1015	**Release Universal Journal**	0F
1020	**Data Collection**	00, 05, 07, etc.
1030	**Calc Net Income**	05 or others based on the source document type
1100	**Currency Translation**	Multiple based on the source document type
S190	**Cust Reclass, PL10(LC)**	1O
S191	**Cust Reclass, PL10(GC)**	1P

Table 3.9 Document Type Assignments to Tasks

Task	Description	Document Type
	Consolidation Monitor	
2011	IC Elim. Sales	2E
2021	IC Elim. Other Income/Expense	2F
2031	Dividends Elimination	2H
2041	IC Elim. Balance Sheet	2G
2100	Investments/Equity Elimin.	3A
2160	Auto Recl. PL30 No Reversed GC	30
2180	Total Divestiture	3Z
S290	Cust Reclass, PL20(GC)	2O
S291	Cust Reclass, PL20(GC)	2P

Table 3.9 Document Type Assignments to Tasks (Cont.)

Tasks beginning with "S###" are custom tasks that can be used for specific customer requirements. Each task can set version- and year-specific document types in the configuration.

In group reporting, the tasks are assigned to a monitor to help combine similar activities during the consolidation process, and activity/tasks are assigned with a document type when configuring the monitors. In relation to the information in Table 3.9, Figure 3.40 provides a view of the Data Monitor, and Figure 3.41 shows the Consolidation Monitor. Detailed explanations of the Data Monitor and the Consolidation Monitor are given in Chapter 4 and Chapter 6, respectively.

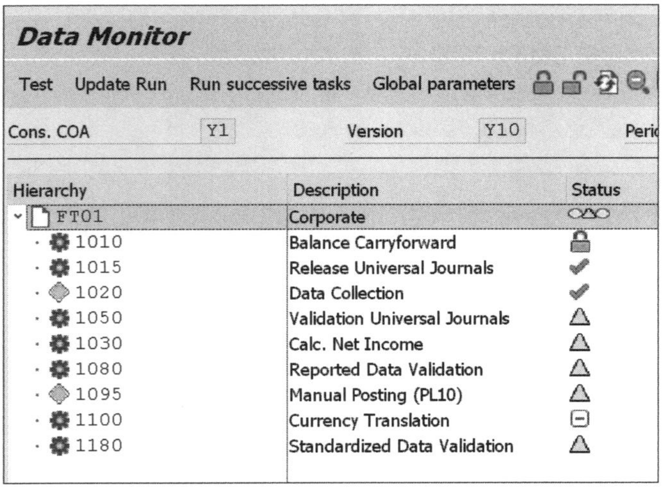

Figure 3.40 Document Type for Data Monitor

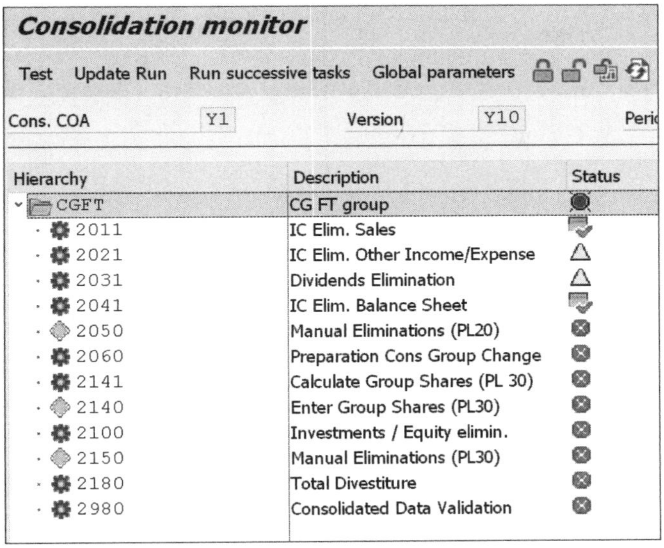

Figure 3.41 Document Type for Consolidation Monitor

Even though document types are created using an IMG path, there are dedicated SAP GUI transactions to help navigate directly to the create or change screens, as listed in Table 3.10.

Transaction	Activity
CXER	Define Document Types for Reported Financial Data
CXEG	Define Document Types for Manual Posting in Data Monitor
CXEH	Define Document Types for Reclassification in Data Monitor
CXEJ	Define Document Types for Manual Posting in Consolidation Monitor
CXEK	Define Document Types for Reclassification in Consolidation Monitor

Table 3.10 Additional Transactions for Creating Document Types

The following key points should be considered when it comes to document types:

- Document types are used in conjunction with posting levels.
- Posting levels and document types together provide a data footprint during the entire process of consolidations in group reporting.
- Posting levels are built in and can't be updated or added with new values. Document types are configurable and flexible to allow the addition of new members.
- Document types identify the source and type of data.
- Tasks in group reporting are associated with document types and are version and period dependent.

- A number range is associated with document types, and customers can create their own number ranges.
- Document types drive the nature of posting if it has to be reversed in a subsequent period.

3.3   Selections

While configuring the process steps, it's critical to create a group of master data members to be able to execute tasks on a very specific subset or pick only a selected data set for processing. Selections in group reporting prove very useful in filtering the members for such requirements and provide reuse capability without having to recreate the set for their own tasks. Selections can be used in settings related to reclassifications methods, validation rules, breakdown categories, and so on. You can use the SAP Fiori Define Selections app to create the new selections, as shown in Figure 3.42.

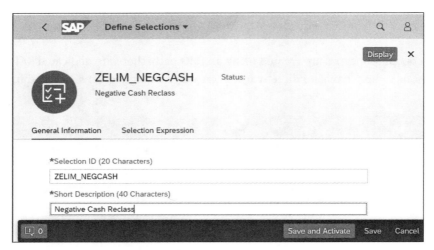

Figure 3.42 Creating a New Selection

A new selection can be created by defining the following fields:

- **Selection ID**
  Enter an ID with a maximum length of 20 characters.
- **Short Description**
  Enter a meaningful description.
- **Selection Expression**
  Make additional selections, including the following:
  - **Field:** Select the master data type, for example, FS item, consolidation units, and so on. The type also provides additional selections of value, hierarchy node, or attribute.

- **Operator:** Choose values such as **Include** or **Exclude** to specify values.
- **Value:** Enter the value of selected master data type.
- **Selection Condition Details:** Provide an informative SQL code, which is helpful when deciphering whether the system uses an AND/OR operator when using the same master data in conditions as shown in Figure 3.43. The code generated is as follows:

```
WHERE ((CONSOLIDATIONUNIT = 'FT01'
    OR CONSOLIDATIONUNIT = 'FT21')
    AND NOT (CONSOLIDATIONUNIT = 'FT02'))
```

- **Set to Inactive**
  A selection can be saved in one of three statuses: **Draft**, **Active**, and **Inactive**. Only active versions are used in configuration. Once active, selections can be deactivated to the inactive state if they aren't being used in configuration.

- **Copy**
  Copy existing selections to new ones and modify them per your needs.

- **Mass activation**
  Schedule background jobs to activate selections in a batch.

- **Show Value List**
  Display the filtered values that meet the selection conditions criteria.

- **Show Where-Used List**
  Show IDs and descriptions of the configuration methods that use the chosen selection after the selection is active and in use.

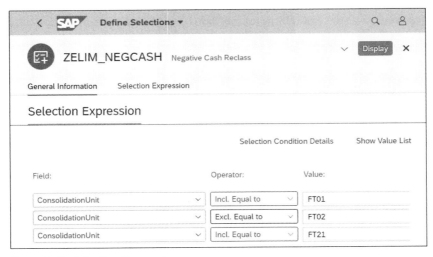

Figure 3.43 Selection Expression

The following key points should be considered when it comes to selections:

- Selections allow multiple filters to be used for the same field for more flexibility.
- Hierarchy nodes are allowed in selections to make the grouping more dynamic at runtime.
- Hierarchies with time dependency are also allowed with a valid from/to time frame.
- Compounded characteristics are allowed for selection and are also mandatory for master data types that have superordinate fields; for example, a general ledger account is compounded with a chart of accounts and must be specified with a value in the selection expression.
- Use of wildcards is supported for cases using the Like operator, for example, FinancialStatement Like 2*.
- Custom fields are supported if defined.

3.4   Summary

This chapter helped you understand the global settings and their significance in the overall consolidation process setup. You've also become familiar with the concept of master data in group reporting, consolidation groups, and how the legal entities are set up with their attributes in consolidation groups. You should now be able to set up hierarchies for various dimensions, such as FS items for reporting, as well as understand how additional master data fields can be enhanced for activating the hierarchies. You should now be able to work with consolidation versions and document types and understand how consolidation tasks work on a selection-based data set within the process.

In the next chapter, we'll shift gears from master data configuration to transaction data configuration.

Chapter 4
Transaction Data

Now that you understand how to set up global parameters and master data specific to SAP S/4HANA group reporting, let's see how to prepare data for consolidations. In this chapter, we'll discuss various Data Monitor tasks that will help you understand the complete process of data collection and preparation for consolidations.

Data collection is one of the critical steps in the corporate close process. It involves collecting data of legal subsidiaries from the Universal Journal in SAP S/4HANA, including manual entries and file uploads. To validate entity data and ensure the data quality, data can also be imported into consolidation table ACDOCU. In addition, you can carry forward year-end balances, roll your net income into retained earnings, and translate the trial balance from the local currency to the group currency.

In this chapter, you'll learn how to set up the Data Monitor and the different ways to integrate financial transaction data for consolidation. We'll also discuss some core data collection concepts such as balance carryforward, calculating net income, journal entries, and data validations.

4.1 What Is the Data Monitor?

The Data Monitor layout lists consolidation units, their groups, and various tasks that to perform on them. This layout also enables you to update the global parameters if required. The purpose of the Data Monitor is to consume the financial data of each consolidation unit and perform various tasks before the financial data is consolidated at a consolidated group level. All the Data Monitor tasks are predefined and ready to use. Each task must be configured and sequenced in the order of execution in the process. You'll open the period and execute the tasks on the consolidation units. After the task is successfully executed, you need to block the task and move to the next task. However, data collection tasks and manual posting tasks can be blocked even without being executed.

The Data Monitor can be accessed using both the SAP Implementation Guide (IMG) via Transaction CXCD and SAP Fiori. In the following sections, we'll take a look at both the layout and the tasks that are available.

4.1.1   Layout

Figure 4.1 shows the Data Monitor layout in SAP Fiori, which is where you can perform all the tasks before you execute consolidations.

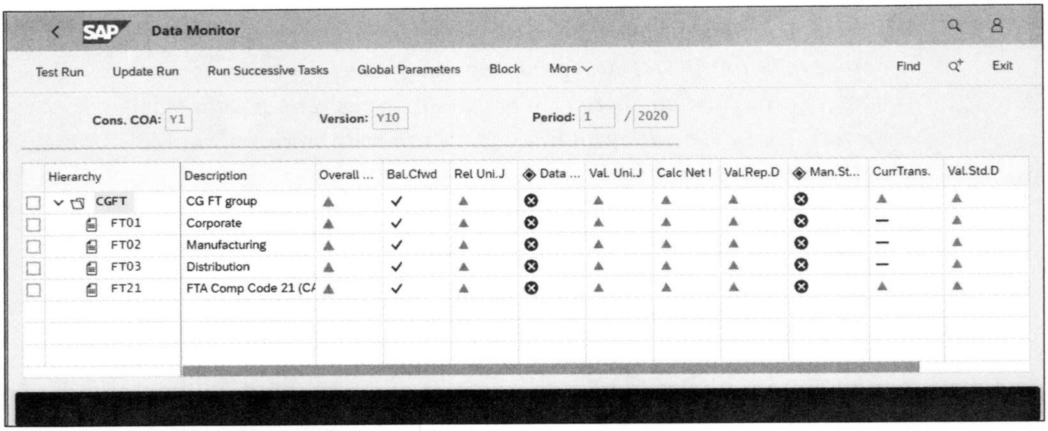

Figure 4.1 Data Monitor Layout

The Data Monitor displays the consolidation group and its units, tasks, and statuses, which means you can run tasks on both the consolidation units and the groups. In addition, you can double-click each status symbol and check the task status. Table 4.1 shows the various task statuses in the Data Monitor; all tasks start out in the **Initial Stage** status.

Task Status	Description
✓	Error free
▲	Incomplete
▭	Initial stage
⊗	Not applicable

Table 4.1 Task Statuses

The Data Monitor displays the organizational units under whatever consolidation group is entered in global settings. You can right-click on the group and see the units that make up that group and check the details related to master data and configuration, such as currency translation, data transfer methods, and so on. The following additional options are available to use in the Data Monitor:

- **Test Run**
  Allows you to simulate the task.

- **Update Run**
  Allows you to change the task status and generate documents.

- **Run Successive Tasks**
  Allows you to run multiple tasks at the same time.

- **Run Successive Tasks w/o Stop**
  Allows you to run multiple tasks at the same time but doesn't stop at milestone tasks.

- **Data and Consolidation Monitor**
  Allows you to run both Data Monitor and Consolidation Monitor at the same time.

- **Save User Layout**
  Allows you to save the layout and retain it when you log off and log back in.

4.1.2   Task

The Data Monitor contains several tasks that can be configured. The following tasks are displayed:

- **Balance carryforward**
  This task is used to update opening balances of the balance sheet.

- **Release Universal Journal**
  This task enables you to release organizational units reported as financial data from the Universal Journal prior to using the data for consolidation purposes.

- **Data collection**
  This task enables you to flexibly upload the reported financial data as well as post group journal entries to correct the reported financial data.

- **Validation of Universal Journal**
  This task enables you to validate the Universal Journal and identify if there are any missing or incorrect subassignments for financial statement (FS) items.

- **Calculate net income**
  This task enables you to calculate and post net income to the derived FS item in the balance sheet and profit and loss (P&L) statement.

- **Reported data validation**
  This task enables you to validate the reported financial data of a consolidation unit in its local currency per the assigned validation method to that consolidation unit.

- **Manual posting**
  This task enables you to manually post group journal entries to make any adjustments to the reported data.

- **Currency translation**
  This task enables you to translate the data of local companies that is in local currency to group currency so that you can use the data for consolidations.

- **Preparation for consolidation group changes**
  This task enables you to adjust the data when a new consolidation unit is acquired or divested from a consolidation group during the fiscal year so that the data during

the time period when the consolidation unit is part of the consolidation group is populated in group financial statements.

- **Standardized data validation**
  This task enables you to validate the financial data of a consolidation unit in its group currency per the assigned validation method of that consolidation unit.

4.2   Configuring the Data Monitor

In this section, you'll learn how to configure the Data Monitor and all the tasks that can be run from the monitor, how to assign them to a standard task group, and how to assign the task group to a dimension.

Table 4.2 lists all the tasks that the Data Monitor can have. In later sections, we'll cover each task in detail.

Task ID	Description	Document Types
1010	Balance Carry Forward	-
1015	Release Universal Journal	0F
1020	Data Collection	00, 01, 02
1030	Calculation of Net Income	-
1050	Validation of Universal Journal	-
1080	Validation of Reported Data (LC)	-
1095	Manual Posting (PL10)	11–14, 16–19
1100	Currency Translation	Original doc types
1130	Preparation for Consolidation Group Change	0Z, 1Z
1180	Validation of Standardized Data (GC)	-

Table 4.2 Data Monitor Tasks

All the tasks to be executed in the Data Monitor needs to be assigned to a task group. The following are initial activities you need to perform while configuring the Data Monitor:

- Check the predefined task groups, and create one if necessary.
- Assign the tasks to a task group.
- Identify the tasks that need to be blocked after execution.
- Identify the tasks that are potential milestones.
- Determine the predecessor for each task.

Because tasks are sets of processes that are required to be executed successfully to prepare for and perform consolidations, you'll encounter tasks in both the Data Monitor and the Consolidation Monitor.

Let's start by defining a task. To do so, execute Transaction CXE9N, and go to **Data Collection for Consolidation • Define Task** to see the screen shown in Figure 4.2. By default, the screen contains a list of standard Data Monitor tasks, but you can always add a new task by selecting the **New Entries** button, which is highlighted in Figure 4.2. Select a **Task**, **Task category**, **Short Text**, and **Medium Text**, and then click the **Save** button.

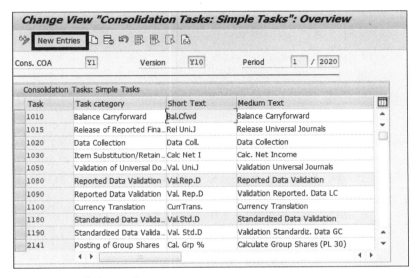

Figure 4.2 Defining Tasks

When you've defined all the tasks, move on to the next step in which you assign tasks to task groups.

Figure 4.3 shows the predelivered task groups for the Data Monitor and the Consolidation Monitor, which contain the tasks that need to be executed before you perform consolidations. In this section, we'll describe **S10: Standard Data monitor**. You can also create a new **Task group** and assign the tasks per your requirements. To access predefined task groups, execute Transaction CXE9N, select **Configuration for Consolidation Processing**, and then select **Define Task Group**. S10 contains all the tasks that you'll perform in the Data Monitor.

Next, go to **Task groups • Assign tasks to task group**, as shown in Figure 4.4, which shows the assignment of tasks to a task group. A task group can't exist without tasks (in this case, we're using the standard content delivered by SAP). All the tasks are assigned to the standard Data Monitor task group (**S10**), which means you can now proceed with the next steps in the configuration.

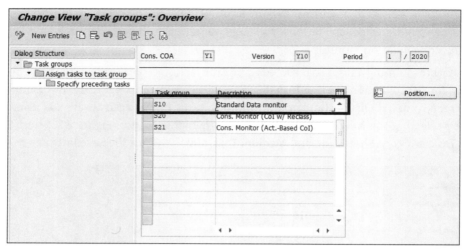

Figure 4.3 Defining Task Groups

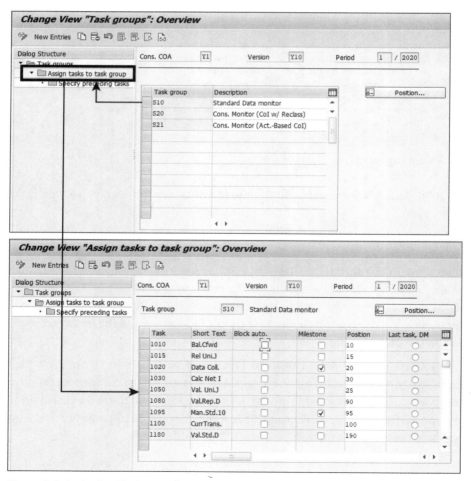

Figure 4.4 Assigning Task to Task Groups

Let's look into the details of the task settings for a deeper understanding of the Data Monitor tasks:

- **Task and Short Text**
  These fields provide the basic details of a task. The preceding example uses SAP-delivered tasks, but you can create custom tasks and assign them to your task group.

- **Block auto.**
  Checking this box blocks any task automatically after it's successfully executed; however, a task can also be blocked explicitly from the Data Monitor.

- **Milestone**
  This setting stops the consolidation process, which is very helpful especially during the automated execution of Data Monitor tasks. When you select a task as a **Milestone** task, you're instructing the system to stop the process after that task is executed. Data collection and manual postings are default milestone tasks.

- **Position**
  Checking this box indicates the position of certain tasks in the Data Monitor based on their numeric values in ascending order.

- **Last task, DM**
  This is a mandatory task in the Data Monitor that indicates the last task to be executed in the Data Monitor in order to execute the Consolidation Monitor without any errors.

Click **Save** when you're done.

You can also create a custom task group per the requirement by selecting the **New Entries** button in the **Change View "Assign tasks to task group": Overview** screen. To access it, execute Transaction CXE9N, select **Configuration for Consolidation Processing**, and enter the **Task, Short Text, Block auto., Milestone, Position**, and **Last Task, DM**, as shown in Figure 4.5.

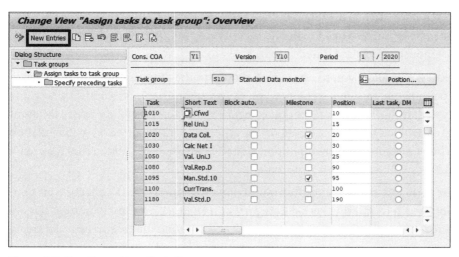

Figure 4.5 Creating a New Task Group

When a new task group is created, you need to assign it to a consolidation dimension. Assignment of task groups is version dependent by default, and it also signifies the period in which a task is effective. The period category gives you the ability to control when a task can be used. The Data Monitor task group and Consolidation Monitor task group contain the corresponding task groups that are used in the Data Monitor and Consolidation Monitor for a version. Figure 4.6 shows the details of the assignment. To access the screen, execute Transaction CXE9N, open **Configuration For Consolidation Processing**, and select **Assign Task Group To Dimension**.

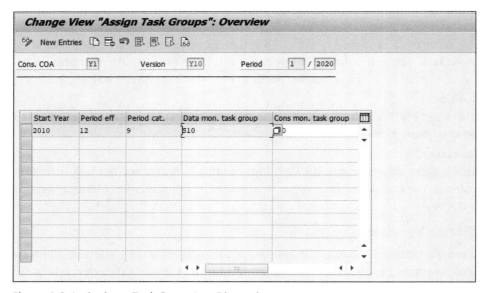

Figure 4.6 Assigning a Task Group to a Dimension

To assign the Data Monitor task group to the dimension for this example, you enter "S10" in the **Data mon. task group** field. After the task group is assigned to a consolidation dimension, you also need to define period categories per your requirements. Figure 4.7 demonstrates a predefined scenario.

Period categories allow you to assign task groups to the dimensions in different periods. Depending on your requirements, you can group the periods in a fiscal year using period categories. Furthermore, period categories give you the ability to use different data entry profiles in different periods for entering data reported by consolidation units. You can create your own period categories for each period, quarter year, half year, and year end, or per your requirements.

To access **Period Categories**, execute Transaction CXE9N, open **Data Collection for Consolidation**, and select **Define Period Categories.** In Figure 4.7, the period categories are defined for year-end, quarter-end, and period-end consolidations. You can also create additional period categories by clicking the **New Entries** button and entering the following fields (right side of Figure 4.7):

- **Period Type**
  Group accounting periods that have the same data collection requirements for consolidations.

- **Description**
  Enter a text description of the period type/period category.

- **Formula**
  Enter the period values here in which a period type is used.

Click **Save** when you're done.

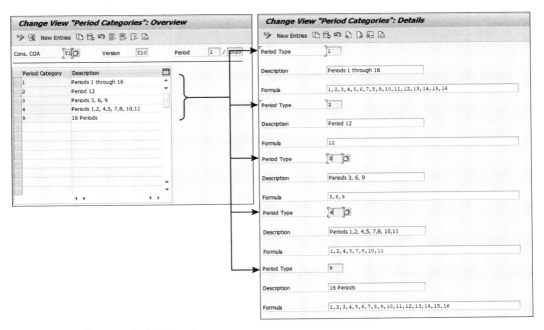

Figure 4.7 Defining Period Categories

In Figure 4.8, the predecessor tasks and task sequencing are shown, which acts as a checklist during the close process. Execution of a task isn't dependent on its preceeding task; however, the preceeding tasks must be executed and blocked so that a task can run successfully. After all the tasks are executed and blocked, the Data Monitor execution is complete. To assign the preceeding tasks, execute Transaction CXE9N, open **Configuration for Consolidation Processing**, and select **Assign tasks to task group** to see all the tasks that you've assigned to the Data Monitor. These tasks can be arranged per your requirements by selecting a task and clicking on **Specify preceding tasks** to select the task that you want to be the predecessor of the selected task.

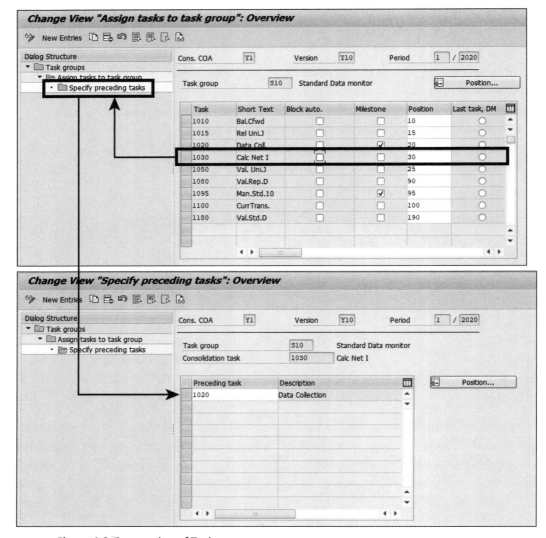

Figure 4.8 Sequencing of Tasks

4.3   Integrating Transaction Data

In this section, we'll discuss the integration of data between the Universal Journal and SAP S/4HANA Finance for group reporting, which is a key step in data preparation for the consolidation process. You need to ensure that any new postings in table ACDOCA are released to group reporting as well as ensure that no unwanted data is getting into group reporting. We'll also discuss the usage of flexible upload option to upload data to group reporting from any other source other than table ACDOCA before we conclude with an interesting feature of SAP S/4HANA Finance for group reporting, release 1909, which is to import reported financial data of consolidation units using an application programming interface (API).

4.3.1   Universal Ledger

In this section, we'll discuss data loads into SAP S/4HANA Finance for group reporting. At the consolidated group level, this data resides in table ACDOCU. We'll discuss the release Universal Journal task concepts, with which data can be loaded into table ACDOCU so that it can be consumed for consolidations.

Table ACDOCU contains consolidated data and data from other source systems that can be consumed in SAP Analytics Cloud, which enables you to run consolidations on plan data at the group level.

To execute consolidations, you need to release the reported financial data from table ACDOCA. The data release can be done multiple times in the current period. The best practice is to release data for consolidation purposes after locking the accounting period; otherwise, it's highly likely that additional data will be posted if the accounting period is open. If you fail to push it to table ACDOCU during the current period, then your financials won't include that data set.

The following are prerequisites for the release Universal Journal task:

1. Make sure that the period for which you're trying to release the data is open. To do so, select **More • Edit**, and then click on the **Select Display Period Info** option from the Data Monitor (refer to Figure 4.1).

2. All the consolidation units that will be consolidated must have the data transfer method set as **Read from Universal Document** and must have the effective year defined so that you can release the data starting that year. To access these settings, run the SAP Fiori Consolidation Units – Change View app (see Figure 4.9), enter the company code for which you need to maintain the data transfer method ("FT01", for this example), and press ⎡Enter⎤. In the **Data collection** tab, select the data transfer method as **Read from Universal Document**, select the effective year, and save.

3. Assign the FS items mappings, which we covered in Chapter 3.

Figure 4.9 shows what the **Data collection** tab for a consolidation unit looks like. You also need to make sure that the period is open before releasing the Universal Journal. To do that in the Data Monitor screen, click on **More • Edit**, and then choose **Display Period Info**, which provides the **Period information** screen where you can see if the period is open or closed (see upper-left portion of Figure 4.9).

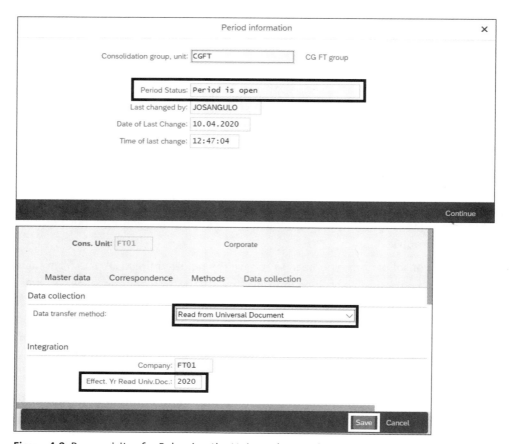

Figure 4.9 Prerequisites for Releasing the Universal Journal

Now let's discuss executing the release Universal Journal task. This task is run from the Data Monitor, as shown in Figure 4.10. To execute the task, right-click on the task, and select **Update**. The **Release Reported Financial Data** screen appears, where you can release the reported financial data in the following ways:

- **Reported Financial Data (Totals)**
  Release the data for the current period.

- **Reported Financial Data (Differences)**
  Release any new data and review the prior release and the delta for the current period.

- **Data from Prior Periods Without Release**
  Check the reported financial data from prior periods without releasing.

Make your selection, and click the **Save** icon. When you arrive at the **Release of Reported Financial Data for Consolidation** screen, click **Continue**. You'll receive a success message when you're done, which indicates that you've released the reported financial data and it's ready for consolidations.

At this point, you've completed the execution of the release Universal Journal task, so you can block the task and move on to the next task.

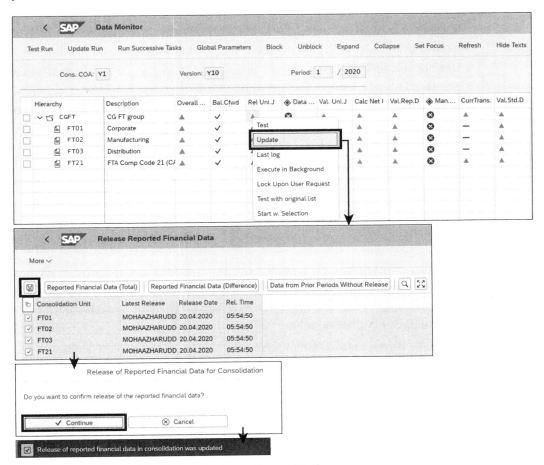

Figure 4.10 Execution of the Release Universal Journal Task

4.3.2   Flexible Upload

SAP S/4HANA Finance for group reporting offers a powerful feature called *flexible upload*, which is used to upload reported financial data into table ACDOCU. You can flexibly upload data in different versions, currencies, formats, and data types, depending on the upload methods. You can execute flexible upload via the Data Monitor or the SAP Fiori Flexible Upload of Reported Financial Data app. This feature is extremely helpful if you have a requirement to upload data of a non-SAP consolidation unit or if you need test data. You must ensure that the period is open before performing a flexible upload, and you must unblock the data collection task for all the periods for the consolidation units.

Figure 4.11 shows the **Consolidation Units** app in SAP Fiori under the **Consolidation Master Data** section. This is the most critical step before you trigger the flexible upload. Here, you need to assign the following methods:

- **Data transfer method**
  You can choose either of the following:
  - **Flexible upload**: Upload flat files to table ACDOCU. This option is widely used when a consolidation unit doesn't report its financials using SAP S/4HANA.
  - **Read from universal document**: Specify that a consolidation unit's data has been read from universal document table ACDOCA in SAP S/4HANA, which is the source. This option is used when a consolidation unit reports its financials in SAP S/4HANA.

- **Upload method**
  You can choose one from the following options. These are predefined, but you can always create an upload method and use it:
  - **CS01 (Flexible Upload to EC-CS)**: This method was used in Enterprise Controlling – Consolidation System (EC-CS) but doesn't have any application in group reporting.
  - **CS02 (Flex.Upload ECS-CS w/StdgEntr)**: This method was used in EC-CS but doesn't have any application in group reporting.
  - **SRD1 (File Driven Upload Mthd (tab))**: You choose this method when you have a file that has a tab as a delimiter.
  - **SRD2 (File Driven Upload Mthd (;))**: You choose this method when you have a file that has a semicolon as a delimiter.

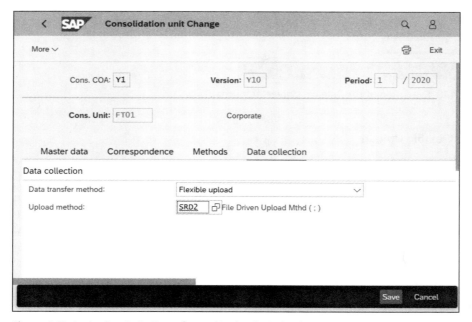

Figure 4.11 Assigning Data Transfer and Upload Methods

Now let's look into preparing the file that you want to upload per your flexible upload requirements. Figure 4.12 shows the template that you use for the flexible upload.

The two methods SRD1 and SRD2 are special file-driven methods and must be used as follows:

- **P**
  Defines that this is a header row.

- **PERIODICAL**
  X represents periodic, and blank represents year-to-date (YTD).

- **UPDATEMODE**
  1 represents **Delete all**, and **2** represents **Overwrite** mode.

- **NSEP**
  1 represents the number format "1,000.00", and **2** represents "1.000,00".

- **D**
  Defines that this is a data row.

Define the data rows as needed for the different input fields. All available input fields are shown in Figure 4.12.

This attached file can be used when uploading data using the methods SRD1 or SRD2. Make sure that you save the file as a *.csv* file with the delimiter ";" (method SRD2) or as a *.txt* file with a tab delimiter (method SRD1).

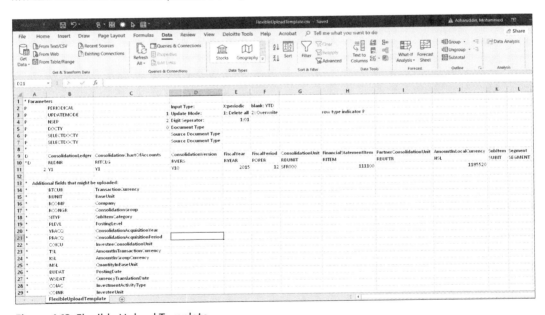

Figure 4.12 Flexible Upload Template

> **Note**
>
> Changing the upload method definition isn't supported. The structure of the data entry file should follow the method definition. Use methods SRD1 or SRD2 and the respective parameters in the upload file to control the behavior of the file import.

Now let's discuss how you can execute the flexible upload task. Flexible upload can be executed via the Data Monitor as well as by using the SAP Fiori Flexible Upload: Reported Financial Data app.

You must execute the following steps to perform a flexible upload through the Data Monitor, as shown in Figure 4.13:

1. Launch the Data Monitor.
2. Select the relevant task of the consolidation unit for which you want to collect data. Alternatively, you can also select the consolidation group to collect data for all consolidation units included in this group at the same time.
3. Right click, and select **Update**.
4. Click on the **Flexible upload** option.
5. Upload the file, and click the **Execute** button.

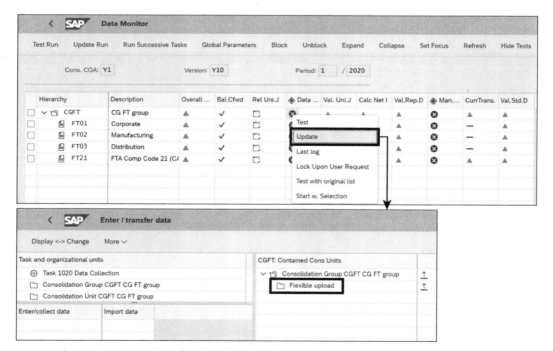

Figure 4.13 Execution of a Flexible Upload Using the Data Monitor

Next, let's review the execution steps when you perform a flexible upload through the Flexible Upload of Reported Financial Data app instead. Follow these steps, as shown in Figure 4.14:

1. Select the **Flexible Upload of: Reported financial data** tile from the **Consolidation Data Preparation** section of the SAP Fiori launchpad.

2. Enter the **Upload method**.

3. Enter the **Physical file name**.

4. Click the **Execute** button.

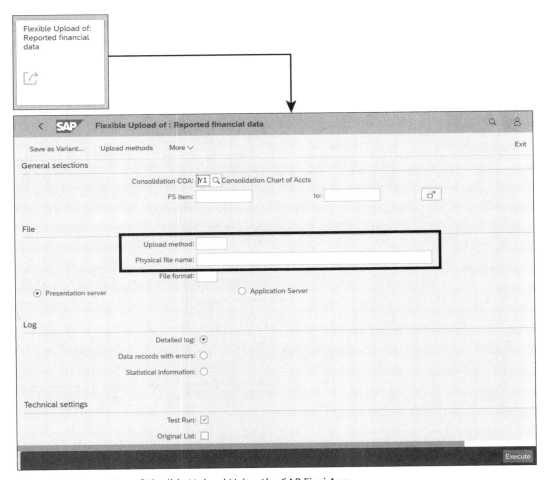

Figure 4.14 Execution of Flexible Upload Using the SAP Fiori App

After the execution is successful, you can check the detailed log for results and block the task (see Section 4.7 for more information). After you click the **Execute** button, the task log screen appears, where you can see the data of a consolidation unit uploaded via flexible upload.

4.3.3   API Integration (Cloud Only)

In the previous sections, we've covered different ways to upload reported financial data into Universal Journal consolidation journal entries (table ACDOCU). Apart from using the data collection task in the Data Monitor and executing the Flexible Upload of Reported Financial Data app, you can also call the following API services:

- **Reported Financial Data for Group Reporting – Bulk Import and Update**
  The purpose of this API is to import the bulk reported financial data of multiple consolidation units into SAP S/4HANA Cloud. It also verifies the data collection requirements, such as whether the period and data collection tasks are open for the required consolidation units, and verifies the mandatory values and relevant master data on the imported data. Finally, it identifies whether the data is YTD or periodic and makes all the required updates after the data is imported.

- **Reported Financial Data for Group Reporting – Receive Confirmation**
  The purpose of this API is to receive the status if the import of the reported financial data is successful or if any data contains errors and requires re-import after correction.

Next, you can map the logical port with the business system for reported data APIs. The two API services are published for SAP S/4HANA Cloud, but you can use them in the SAP S/4HANA environment if you set up the connection in Customizing for SAP S/4HANA for group reporting. Before you set up any connections, you need to create a logical port in service-oriented architecture (SOA) management for API services, which can be accessed using Transaction SOAMANAGER (typically done by the Basis team).

Figure 4.15 depicts the navigation and options for setting up the connections for APIs. To access, you need to execute Transaction CXE9N, open **Data Collection for Consolidation**, and select the **Map Logical Port with Business System for Reported Data API** option.

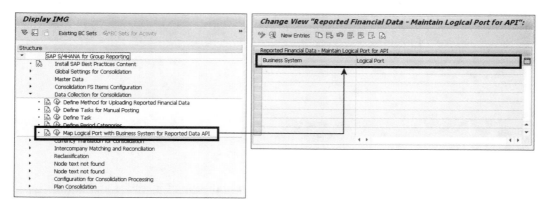

Figure 4.15 Setting Up the Connection for the Inbound and Outbound API Services

Enter the following:

- **Business System**
  Enter the system name for the inbound Reported Financial Data for Group Reporting – Bulk Import and Update API. The business system is also helpful in delivering back the status confirmation to the source.

- **Logical Port**
  Enter the ID of the logical port that you created in SOA management.

Click **Save** after entering the details to finish the mapping.

4.4 Plan Data Integration

Performing consolidations on plan data is another important feature of SAP S/4HANA Finance for group reporting. In this section, we'll discuss the integration of SAP Analytics Cloud and SAP S/4HANA Finance for group reporting and the steps involved in consolidating the plan data.

One of the main reasons that you would consolidate plan data is to compare the plan data and actual data on a periodic or YTD basis.

The following activities are achieved through this integration, as shown in Figure 4.16:

- Establish a connection between SAP S/4HANA and SAP Analytics Cloud.
- Transfer data from the Universal Journal entry line items (table ACDOCA) to SAP Analytics Cloud.
- Enable the planning process in SAP Analytics Cloud using the unconsolidated data that is transferred from table ACDOCA.

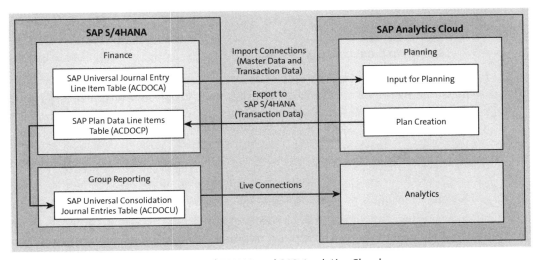

Figure 4.16 Integration between SAP S/4HANA and SAP Analytics Cloud

- Use SAP Analytics Cloud planning features, such as value-based drivers and spread (taking values from higher levels and spreading them to lower levels), to derive the plan data from the data that has been imported from table ACDOCA, which can then be used to populate the predelivered plan version.
- Export the planned transaction data to the plan data line items (table ACDOCP) to perform consolidations.
- Enable the Universal Journal consolidation journal entries table (table ACDOCU) to read data from the plan data line items (table ACDOCP) for group reporting purposes.

For more information on SAP Analytics Cloud integration, see Chapter 11, Section 11.4.2.

4.5   Balance Carryforward

Balance carryforward is one of the key activities of year-end close. It involves carrying forward account balances into the new fiscal year. SAP S/4HANA for group reporting has a predefined business rule that helps you achieve the carryforward. When you run balance carryforward, the system pulls the balances of relevant FS items from the previous fiscal year to the current fiscal year (i.e., opening balances in your balance sheet for the current year). The balance carryforward is a mandatory task for period 001 of each year in the Data Monitor. You also run balance carryforward in financial accounting prior to running it in group reporting so that the prior year balances are carried forward at both the local and group levels.

In this section, we'll discuss setting up balance carryforward in SAP S/4HANA Finance for group reporting in detail, then look into the execution of this task in the Data Monitor, and finally validate the results.

4.5.1   Setting Up Balance Carryforward

In this section, we focus on the step-by-step configuration of the balance carryforward business rule. Before we move on to any further steps, you need to ensure that the prior year is closed, and the period in which you're about to run the balance carryforward is open. Basically, you're carrying forward the year-end balances stored in FS items from the previous year to the current year, and the system allows you to carry forward the balances based on the FS item type property. You can relate this to the account type in earlier versions of SAP consolidation tools. At the end of the year, for the financial data of consolidation units in SAP S/4HANA, the system will reclass the net income to retained earnings, which is a balance sheet account. After this is done, you have your final ending balance sheet, which you carry forward. Balance carryforward writes data to period 000 in table ACDOCU. If the previous year's data changes, then you need to run the balance carryforward again. For this reason, the FS item property is crucial.

Financial Statement Items

Figure 4.17 shows the FS items and their corresponding FS item types. To access this screen, in SAP Fiori, under the **Consolidation Master Data** section, select the **Define FS Items** tile, choose **Consolidation COA**, and click **GO**. The following **FS Item Type** options are displayed:

- **Asset (AST)**
  This FS item type is carried forward by default.
- **Liabilities and Equity (LEQ)**
  This FS item type is carried forward by default.
- **Income/Expense (INC/EXP)**
  These FS item types aren't carried forward by default.

Balance carryforward keeps the original document type. Only document types of posting level 01 are carried forward to a document type of posting level 00.

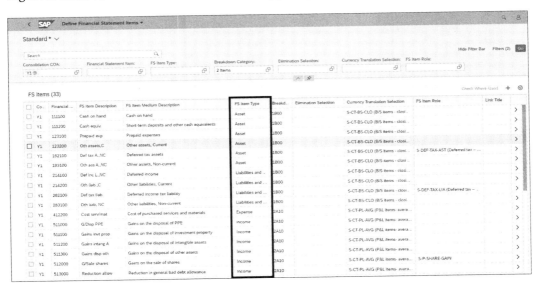

Figure 4.17 Defining FS Item Types

One of the most important steps in the configuration of the balance carryforward is setting up the FS items that need to be carried forward. Here, we'll discuss an SAP-defined scenario, which will help you understand how to set up the FS items that are to be carried forward. To do so, execute Transaction CXE9N in SAP GUI, go to **Consolidation FS Items Configuration**, and select the **Specify FS Items to be Carried Forward** option.

> **Note**
> Remember that FS items are carried forward in both local currency and group currency.

Figure 4.18 shows you the default SAP-delivered configuration for specifying which FS items need to be carried forward. You can always click on **New Entries** and do any custom configurations required. Apart from specifying the FS items to be carried forward, you also specify the subitem category and subitem for each FS item. You can relate subitems to transaction types/flow dimensions in earlier versions of SAP consolidation tools, which was covered in Chapter 3. The **Change View "Items to be Carried Forward:" Overview** screen on the left side of Figure 4.18 shows you all the FS items that are configured to be carried forward. Select an FS item and click on **Details** (magnifying glass icon) to see the details of the FS item that you want to be carried forward:

- FS item 317000 is the current year retained earnings controlling share.
- FS item 319000 is the current year retained earnings clearing FS item.
- FS item 321150 is the current year retained earnings noncontrolling share.

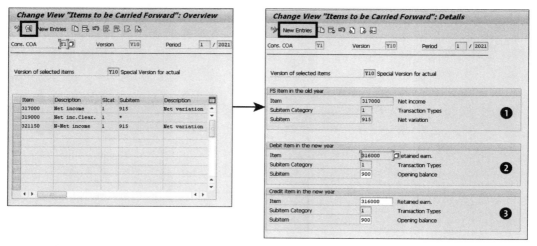

Figure 4.18 Define FS Items to be Carried Forward

Now let's look into **Change View "Items to be Carried Forward": Details** screen, shown on the right side of Figure 4.18, which describes the details of those FS items:

❶ FS item 317000 represents the annual net income in the prior year balance sheet, which reflects the net income/loss from FS item 799999 in the P&L statement.

❷ When you execute the balance carryforward, the amount recorded on the FS item annual net income (317000) of the previous year is carried forward to the FS item retained earnings (316000) of the current year, if the balance is a debit balance.

❸ When you execute the balance carryforward, the amount recorded on the FS item annual net income (317000) of the previous year is carried forward to the FS item retained earnings (316000) of the current year, if the balance is a credit balance.

If a requirement calls for having your own retained earning accounts or FS items, you can select **New Entries** and select FS items and subitems so that the net income is carried forward to the retained earnings, based on the FS items selected.

General Ledger Accounts

So far, we've covered setting up the FS items to perform balance carryforward. Now, let's discuss the general ledger accounts that need to be carried forward. Every general ledger account in SAP S/4HANA has a corresponding FS item in group reporting. In other words, the balances associated with a general ledger account will eventually be reflected in FS items, which requires the general ledger account to be updated while you set up the balance carryforward.

Figure 4.19 demonstrates an SAP predefined setting. To access this screen, execute Transaction CXE9N in SAP GUI, choose **Consolidation FS Items Configuration**, and select the **Specify Account Numbers to Be Carried Forward** option.

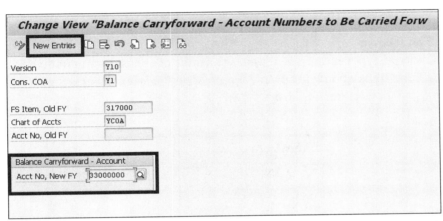

Figure 4.19 Defining the General Ledger Accounts That Need to Be Carried Forward

For the FS item annual net income 317000 in the prior year, the general ledger account 3300000 is used during balance carryforward as the target general ledger account in the current year. This general ledger account also needs to be mapped to retained earnings FS item 316000 in the current year so that the net income matches the retained earnings. However, this is SAP-delivered configuration; if you need to configure the general ledger accounts per your own requirement, you click **New Entries** and add the required general ledger accounts.

Subitems and Subitem Categories

Now let's look into the last setting that you need to configure before you're ready to kick off the balance carryforward business rule from the Data Monitor in SAP S/4HANA Finance for group reporting.

While discussing the details of FS items that need to be carried forward in previous sections, we came across subitems and subitem categories that need to be specified. To do this, execute Transaction CXE9N, expand **Master Data**, and select **Define Subitem Categories and Subitems**.

You'll see the predelivered content. In balance carryforward, you're concerned only about subitem category **Transaction Types**, as shown on the left side of Figure 4.20. Transaction type **915** is a net variation used for net income (profit/loss). When you select it, you further encounter the following subitems, as shown on the right side of Figure 4.20:

- **Carry forward to subitem**
  The ending balances are written to transaction type 900 when balance carryforward is run.

- **Retire./divest.subitem**
  This transaction type captures the flow of divesting a subsidiary in transaction type 998 from transaction type 915 in the current period and compares it with the ongoing operations of the subsidiary.

- **Acquisition subitem**
  This transaction type captures the flow of acquisition of a subsidiary in transaction type 901 from transaction type 915 in the current period and compares it with the ongoing operations of the subsidiary.

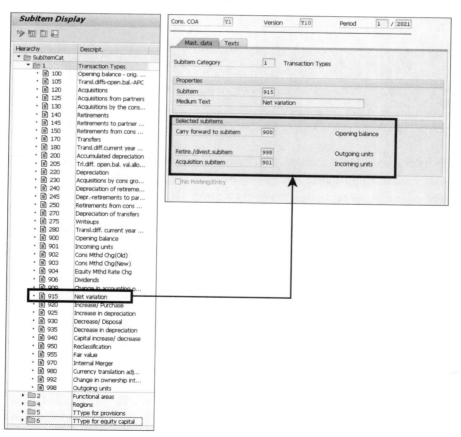

Figure 4.20 Define Subitem Categories and Their Subitems

You can always click on the transaction type and choose any transaction type you want per your requirements.

The system is now set up to allow you to run the balance carryforward. Let's now move on to executing the balance carryforward via the Data Monitor and validating the results.

4.5.2   Executing and Validating the Balance Carryforward

Now that the configuration of balance carryforward is complete, you can execute the business rule and review the results. You should also keep in mind that the prior year should be closed. If the prior year isn't closed and you ran the balance carryforward anyway, you need to run the rule again after the books are closed for the prior year to make sure that you're not missing any transactions. But the best practice is to run the balance carryforward after the prior year is closed. You also should make sure that the period in which the balance carryforward is about to run is open. You can validate this by selecting **More • Edit** from the upper-right corner of the Data Monitor screen and clicking **Display Period Info**.

You run the balance carryforward in the Data Monitor, as shown in Figure 4.21. You can run the balance carryforward for a group or for a consolidation unit by right-clicking the **Bal.Cfwd** task for the group or consolidation unit and clicking **Update**. You should see a green checkmark if the balance carryforward has run without any errors. You can also select the other options as needed:

- **Test**
  This option checks the readiness of the task.

- **Last log**
  This option provides you with the details of the log that was generated the last time the task was executed.

- **Execute in Background**
  This option provides you the flexibility of running a task in the background while performing other duties.

- **Start w. Selection**
  Similar to global settings, this option enables you to select details such as consolidation unit, consolidation group, version, and so on.

- **Test with original list**
  This option gives you the details of the first time the task was executed.

- **Lock Upon User Request**
  This option enables you to lock the task.

- **Block**
  After you successfully complete this task, you'll block the task before moving on to the next task, so that no one can rerun this task, which could be a Sarbanes-Oxley (SOX) Act violation.

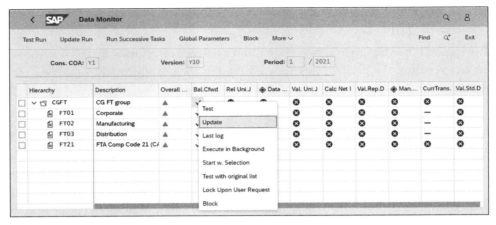

Figure 4.21 Executing Balance Carryforward

Figure 4.22 provides you the output of the balance carryforward task, showing the following:

❶ The 2020 balances are carried forward to 2021.

❷ The 915 subitem, which is the net variation in 2020, is copied to the 900 subitem, which is the opening balance for 2021.

❸ The ending balances of balance sheet FS items for 2020 are successfully carried forward to the opening balances of the balance sheet FS items for 2021.

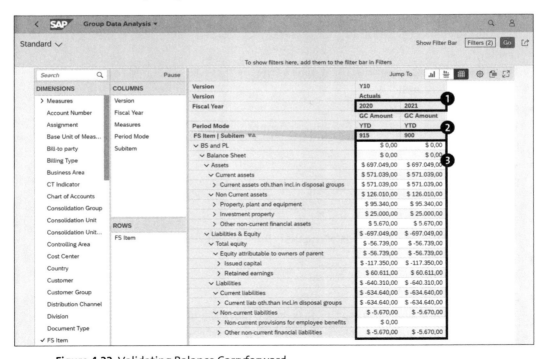

Figure 4.22 Validating Balance Carryforward

You should now be able to configure and run the balance carryforward task in the Data Monitor as one of the first steps in preparing for consolidation. We'll now move on to other tasks of the Data Monitor and gain more in-depth understanding of data collection in SAP S/4HANA Finance for group reporting.

4.6 Calculation of Net Income

In this section, we discuss how to calculate net income in SAP S/4HANA Finance for group reporting. We'll review the predelivered content, and then discuss how to calculate net income and validate the results. Before we jump into any configuration, you need to understand what net income is and how it's calculated in general. Net income is the net earnings of a company, which is calculated as total sales minus total expenses (expenses include cost of goods sold [COGS], selling expenses, general and administrative expenses, operating expenses, depreciation, interest, taxes, etc.). This number appears on a company's P&L statement and indicates the company's profitability and how a company is performing based on revenue and expenses of a consolidation unit.

Calc.Net Income is a mandatory task in the Data Monitor. With this task, FS item **Net Income/Loss** (P&L) in the reported data will be calculated and recorded (without any document number) to FS item **Net Income** (balance statement). To enable this, you need to configure the FS items to enable automatic postings, which can be done in SAP GUI by executing Transaction CXE9N, expanding **Consolidation FS Items Configuration**, and selecting **Specify Selected FS Items for Automatic Postings**.

The items are defined as selected FS items for the calculation of retained earnings and automated deferred tax calculation. They include annual net income (balance statement), annual net income (income statement), deferred tax asset and liability, and deferred tax expense.

Figure 4.23 shows setting up the balance sheet annual net income FS items that the system will use to post financial statement imbalances in the **ANI, B/S** tab. Figure 4.24 shows setting up the P&L annual net income FS items that the system will use to post financial statement imbalances in the **ANI, I/S** tab. The system calculates the imbalance and then posts an automatic balancing adjustment depending on how the retained earnings are set up.

The SAP system calculates the imbalance and then posts an automatic balancing adjustment. The automatic adjustment is dependent on how retained earnings are treated:

- When stating the appropriation of retained earnings at the end of the income statement, an adjustment to retained earnings occurs.
- When stating the appropriation of retained earnings in the balance sheet, an adjustment to annual net income occurs.

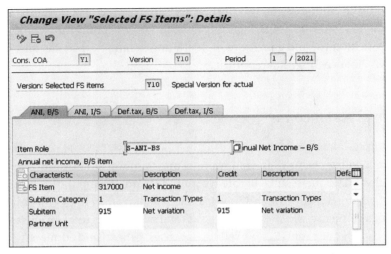

Figure 4.23 Specifying FS Items for Automatic Postings: ANI, B/S Tab

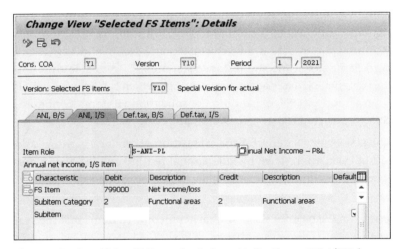

Figure 4.24 Specifying FS Items for Automatic Postings: ANI, I/S Tab

> **Note**
>
> The items you specify are dependent on the consolidated chart of accounts and the consolidation version.

For automatic entries, you need to feed the system the details of the FS items. In the previous two steps, you specified the FS items that you want the system to use to post financial statement imbalances. Table 4.3 shows an example related to net income calculation.

Balance Sheet			P&L Statement	
Total assets	100,000		Total revenue	(50,000)
Total liabilities	(75,000)		Total expenses	25,000
Net income	(25,000)		Net income	25,000

Table 4.3 An Example of Net Income Calculation

In the balance sheet, you derive net income based on the following formula:

Asset = Liabilities+ Equity + Net income

In P&L statements, you derive net income based on the following formula:

Revenue + Expense = Net income

You define the selected FS items for automatic posting of deferred taxes by navigating to the **Def.tax, B/S** tab (upper part of Figure 4.25) where you can specify your tax asset and tax liability FS items that are part of the balance sheet, as well as specify the **Transaction Type**. The lower part of Figure 4.25 shows the **Def.tax, I/S** tab where you specify the income statement FS items and, as this is related to the income statement, you use **Functional area** as the subitem rather than **Transaction Type**.

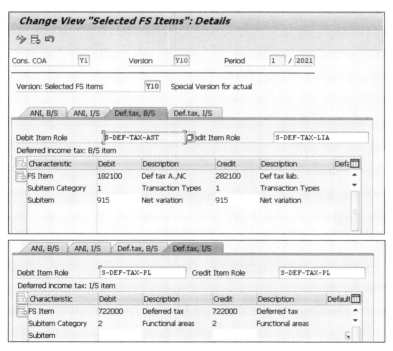

Figure 4.25 Specifying FS Items for Automatic Postings: Deferred Tax Balance Sheet and Income Statement

The taxes of all consolidation unit financial statements should be aligned with the group's earnings. However, there can be differences due to consolidation activities. Deferred taxes should be limited to balance temporary differences in earnings rather than balancing the tax expenses that are too high or too low in the future periods.

Here the deferred tax asset (182100) is balanced out with deferred income tax liability (282100) on the balance sheet, and the deferred tax (722000) is credited/debited on the income statement accordingly.

You can specify items by selecting the item role. If this is required for items, you must also specify subitems. **Item Role/Debit Item Role/Credit Item Role** is a FS item attribute that you need to specify here, which must have already been created while defining the FS items, as covered in Chapter 3. You can review the FS item roles for each FS item by accessing SAP Fiori and selecting the **Define FS Items** tile under **Consolidation Master Data** to open the app, as shown in Figure 4.26. An FS item role is an attribute that you use for automatic posting, for example, rolling your net income into retained earnings. Generally speaking, there is one-to-one mapping for FS item and FS item role.

Wherever its applicable, you can enhance the FS item role with subassignments. Figure 4.26 shows you the item roles that are maintained for FS items, which in turn are used in the net income calculation.

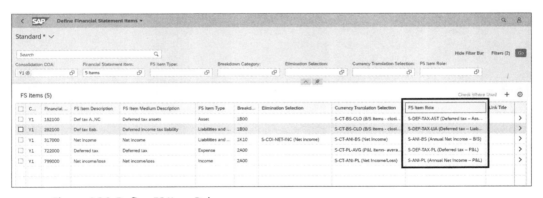

Figure 4.26 Define FS Item Roles

Now that you've configured the net income calculation task, you can execute the task in the Data Monitor. To do so, access SAP Fiori, and select the **Data Monitor** tile under **Consolidation Data Preparation**. Figure 4.27 shows you the execution process in Data Monitor. Click the **Update** option.

With the task configured and executed, it's now time to validate the results via the **Group Data Analysis** tile under **Group Reports**. Figure 4.28 shows that the system has posted the balances to the balance sheet annual net income FS items as well as P&L annual net income FS items.

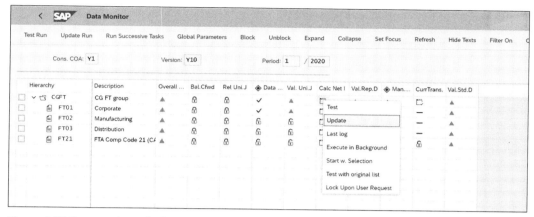

Figure 4.27 Execute the Calculate Net Income Task

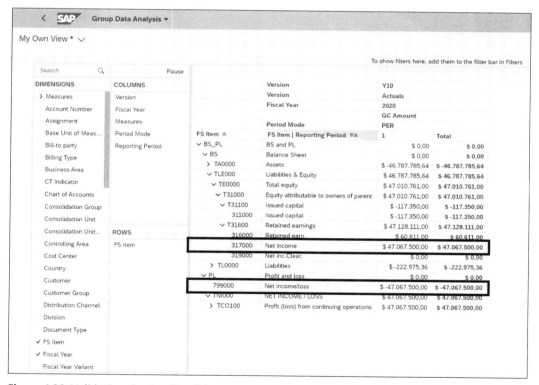

Figure 4.28 Validating the Results of the Net Income Calculation Task

With this, you've completed the setup and execution of the calculate net income task in the Data Monitor.

4.7   Data Validation

In this section, we'll discuss data validation, including SAP predelivered content to enable data validation such as validation rules and validation methods, and then run the tasks in the Data Monitor. Data validation is one of the key steps in the data collection stage of consolidations. Using this step, you determine the data quality, which is essential for the consolidation process.

Data validation is performed on reported, standardized, and consolidated data. In this section, we'll provide extensive coverage of reported and standardized data validations. We'll discuss consolidated data validation in coming chapters. While setting up the Data Monitor for this discussion, we've assigned the data validation tasks 1080 – Validate Reported Data and 1180 – Validated Standardized Data to Task Group S10, which is the Data Monitor.

Let's get started with discussing validation rules and assigning these rules to methods, and then move on to execution of the validation tasks in the Data Monitor.

4.7.1   Validation Rules

Validation rules are applied to data, for example, to make sure that the balance sheet is balanced in the consolidation – data collection process. By defining a rule, you're telling the system the validations that need to be performed. A rule can be a condition or expression; in this example, the rule will be a condition, which is *Assets = Liabilities + Equity*. You can relate this to controls that are defined in the Controls Monitor in earlier versions of SAP consolidation tools such as SAP Business Planning and Consolidation (SAP BPC). Let's discuss the predelivered validation rules and their configuration.

Figure 4.29 shows the SAP Fiori Data Validation app, which can be accessed by selecting the **Define Validation Rule** tile under **Consolidation Settings**. This app lists the SAP-delivered validation rules and allows you to create your own rules per the requirement. You have three main options on this screen:

- **Adapt Filters**
  Filter the validation rules by their statuses (**Draft**, **Active**, and **Inactive**).

- **Create Rule**
  Create a new rule, which we'll go over in detail.

- **Mass Activation**
  Activate multiple rules at the same time.

You can also export the rules to a spreadsheet with the help of the **Export** icon next to the **Mass Activation** option.

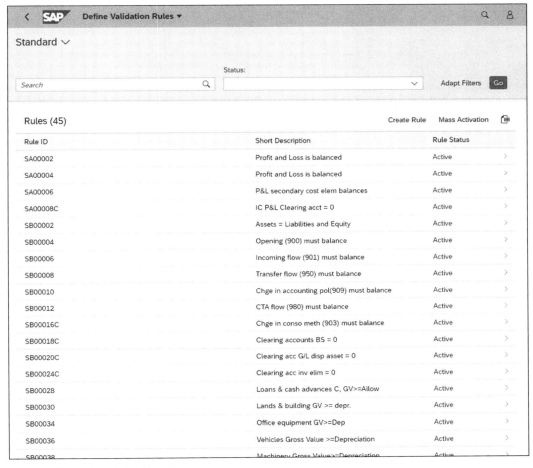

Figure 4.29 Define Validation Rules

Let's look at an example by clicking **Create Rule** to arrive at the screen shown in Figure 4.30. Here we're setting up a rule to validate if the balance sheet is balanced. You do it by updating the **Rule Expression** with a formula.

Let's look at the example in the figure, which is a classic balance sheet equation: *Assets = Liabilities + Equity*. The portion left of the "=" operator in this example is **Left Formula**, and the portion to the right of the operator is **Right Formula**.

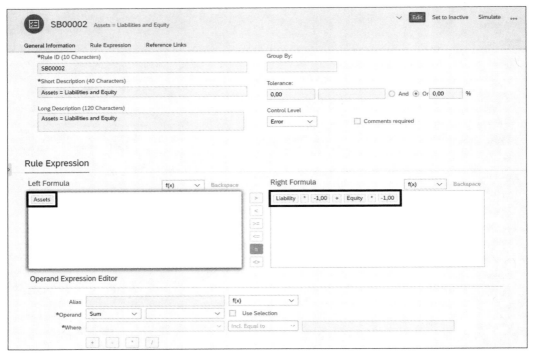

Figure 4.30 An Example of a Predefined Validation Rule

Sometimes, during an implementation, the predelivered rules might not be sufficient, so you need to create new validation rules to help with the requirement. To create a new rule, select **Create Rule** from the **Define Validations Rule** screen. The new rule will require you to enter basic information about the rule that you're creating in the **General Information** tab, as shown in Figure 4.31:

- **Rule ID**
  Enter the ID for the new rule you're creating; this is a mandatory field.

- **Short Description**
  Enter a description (short) for the new rule you're creating; this is a mandatory field.

- **Long Description**
  Enter a description (long); this is an optional field.

- **Group By**
  Group and organize your data based on dimensions such as company code, partner unit, and so on in the output screen (the Manage Data Validation Task app).

- **Tolerance**
  Set the threshold that is permitted when the rule is executed.

- **Control Level**
  Tell the system to alert you via an error/warning/information if the validation fails.

- **Comments required**
  Check this if you need any comments that would provide you more information on the validations in the Manage Data Validation app.

Figure 4.31 Creating a New Rule: General Information

Figure 4.32 shows the next step in creating a new validation rule, which is configuring a **Rule Expression**. This is where you specify the formulas and validation criteria. Per your requirements, you derive a formula and define the rule.

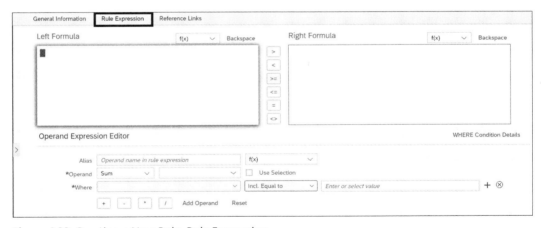

Figure 4.32 Creating a New Rule: Rule Expression

The following fields must be completed:

- **Left Formula/Right Formula**
  Based on your requirement, you derive a formula and configure it in the left and right formulas with an operator in between. For example, to set up validation rules for suspense accounts to be zero, the left formula must contain the corresponding FS item, and the right formula contains "0" with an operator "=" in the middle.

- **Operand**

  Here you specify the attribute based on which the formula is executed. You have four operands: **Amount**, **Quantity**, **Sum**, and **Number**.

- **Where**

  Here you specify where the values are coming from. Select the dimension, selection logic, and member. If you specify these details, the rule will be run only for that one dimension, logic, and member.

Finally, you'll update any references in the **Reference Links** tab, and save the new validation rule, as shown in Figure 4.33.

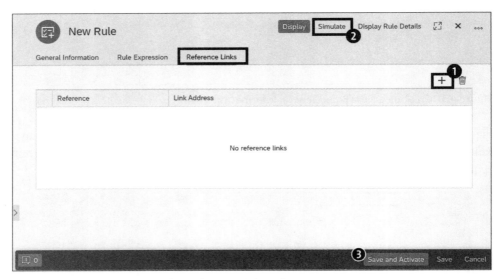

Figure 4.33 Creating a New Rule: Reference Links Tab

The following actions can be taken:

❶ Add (+)

This step is optional, but if you need to add a reference, click the **+** button.

❷ Display/Simulate

Before saving, you can check and simulate the validation rule by clicking the **Display** or **Simulate** buttons.

❸ Save and Activate

You finish the configuration of the new validation rule by clicking this button.

4.7.2 Validation Methods

Now that you have a good understanding of the validation rules, we'll move on to discuss the data validation method that is predefined for the Data Monitor and review how to create a new data validation method if required.

Data validation methods are collections of data validation rules that are required to perform a set of data validations on the collected data for consolidations. The validation method SRD1 is an SAP predelivered method that contains all the predefined rules.

Figure 4.34 shows the SAP Fiori Data Validations Methods app where you can access the data validation methods. To access this app, select the **Data Validation Methods** tile under **Consolidation Settings**.

Figure 4.34 Data Validation Methods App

In this screen, you can see the predelivered content as of now, but if you create any custom data validation methods, they would show up here. The two predelivered data validation methods are as follows:

- **SRD1**
  This data validation method for collected data while preparing for consolidations is linked to the Data Monitor.

- **SCD1**
  This data validation method for consolidated data while performing consolidations is linked to the Consolidation Monitor.

A validation method contains a group of validation rules that you want to perform on the data. Figure 4.35 shows the **SRD1** predelivered configuration in the SAP Fiori Define Validation Methods app.

In this example, the default rule group, **Totals Validation**, contains rule groups **P&L**, **Balance Sheet**, and **Consistency**. When you're creating your own validation methods, you would add a new group under **Totals Validation**. As you can see, this validation method contains validation rules that are divided into groups per the nature of those rules.

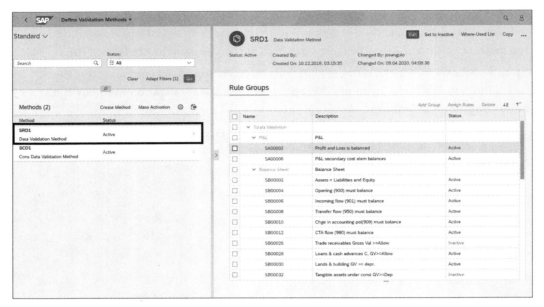

Figure 4.35 Predelivered Data Validation Method

These SAP-delivered validation rules won't always meet your needs, so you can use a new validation rule to create a new validation method by clicking **Create Method**. Figure 4.36 shows the following fields to complete in the **New Validation Method** screen:

❶ **Method ID**

This is a mandatory field by which a method is recognized. This is used in method assignments, which we'll cover in the coming sections.

❷ **Add Group**

You need to add a group to hold the validation rules.

❸ **Assign Rules**

This is the most important step in creating a new validation method as this is where you assign the validation rules. Figure 4.37 shows the screen that pops up when you try to assign rules. Select the rules that you want to use in the group, and click **OK**. You can create as many groups as required and assign rules to them.

❹ **Save and Activate**

After you've completed the preceding three steps, you can save the method and activate it to start using it in the Data Monitor.

You need to assign the validation method to a consolidation unit so that the data validations can be performed on the reported data of the consolidation unit. Refer to Section 4.3.2 for more information.

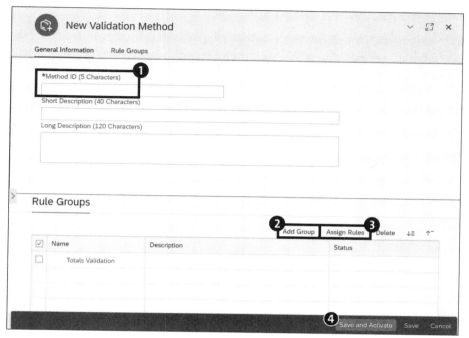

Figure 4.36 Creating a New Validation Rule

Rule	Long Description	Created By	Created On	Changed By	Changed On
	analysed TO DELETE				
SB00148 Chge impair on invest/subsid TO DELETE	Changes in impairment on investments in subsidiaries should be analysed TO DELETE		03.09.2018, 11:30:41		03.09.2018, 11:32:03
SB00024C Clearing acc inv elim = 0	Clearing accounts for investment of subsidiaries elimination must equal 0		03.09.2018, 11:30:41		03.09.2018, 11:32:01
SB00020C Clearing acc G/L disp asset = 0	Clearing accounts for internal Gain/loss on disp of assets should equal 0		03.09.2018, 11:30:41		03.09.2018, 11:31:58
SB00018C Clearing accounts BS = 0	Clearing accounts for intercompany elimination - BS should equal 0		03.09.2018, 11:30:41		03.09.2018, 11:32:15
SB00016C Chge in conso meth (903) must balance	The Change in consolidation method (new 903) must balance		03.09.2018, 11:30:41		03.09.2018, 11:31:54
SA00008C IC P&L Clearing acct = 0	Clearing accounts for intercompany elimination - P&L must equal 0		03.09.2018, 11:30:41		03.09.2018, 11:32:13
SA00004 Profit and Loss is balanced	Profit and Loss is balanced		03.09.2018, 11:30:41		03.09.2018, 11:31:01

Figure 4.37 Assigning Validation Rules to a Method

4.7.3   Import/Export Validation Settings

The SAP Fiori Import/Export Validation Settings app is used to import and export validation rules and methods. This app is very useful especially when you've validated all your validation rules and methods in lower environments and imported them in the higher environments. To access this app in SAP Fiori, choose **Consolidation Settings** and select the **Import/Export Validation Settings** tile. Figure 4.38 shows you the details of the app.

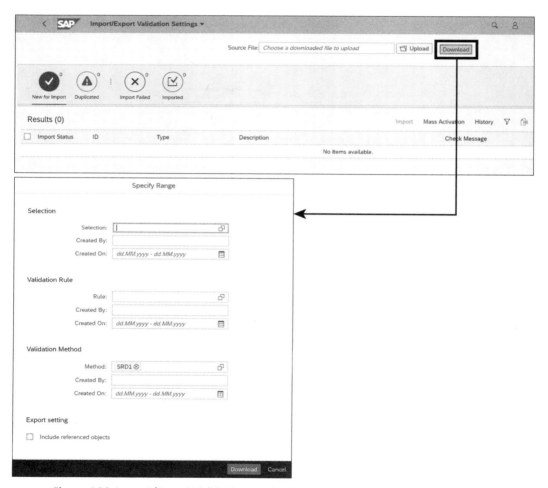

Figure 4.38 Import/Export Validation Settings App

Using this app, you can export your specified selections, validation rules, and methods to a spreadsheet by choosing the **Download** option. In the **Specify Range** popup, you can import any selections, rules, and methods exported from another system and then click the **Download** button. If there are any duplicate items, only the draft versions of existing items are overwritten because all the imported items have an initial **Draft** status.

The **Mass Activation** button can be used to activate the existing rules, methods, or selections that are in **Draft** status from the import activity.

4.7.4   Reported Data Validation

In previous sections, you've defined the validation rules and the validation methods and assigned the validation method to your consolidation unit. In this section, we discuss the execution of reported data validation task. By executing this task, you validate the reported financial data in the local currency according to the validation method you assigned to respective consolidation units.

Figure 4.39 shows the execution of the Data Monitor task **Val.Rep.D** (click the **Update** button).

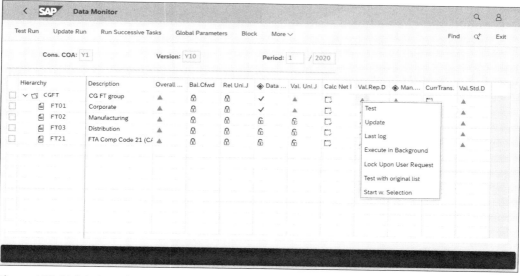

Figure 4.39 Validation of Reported Data Task

After the **Val.Rep.D** task is executed, you're redirected to the Manage Data Validation Tasks app, as shown in Figure 4.40. With this app, you can run reported data validation for the specified fiscal period and consolidation unit by entering details at the top of the screen and check the validation result by clicking **Go** with one row for each consolidation unit.

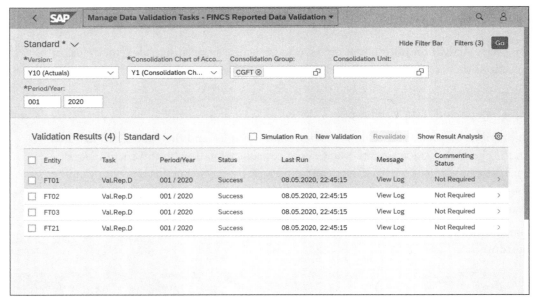

Figure 4.40 Manage Data Validation Tasks App: Reported Data

Figure 4.41 gives you the details of the preceding validation results. By clicking on any row in Figure 4.40, you'll access the corresponding consolidation detailed validation results.

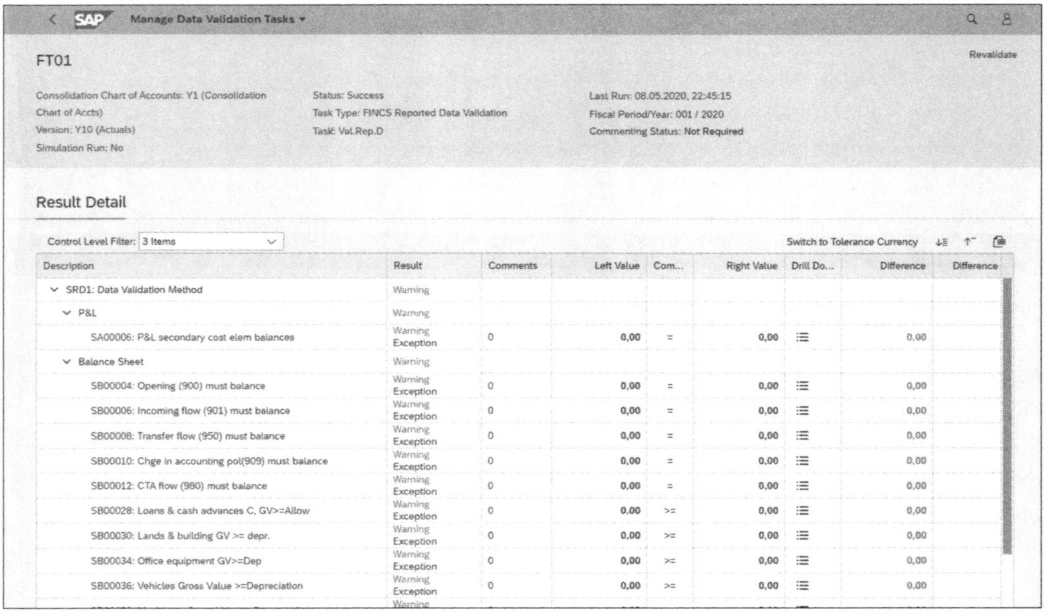

Figure 4.41 Detailed Task Log: Reported Data Validation

4.7.5 Standardized Data Validation

In this section, we discuss the execution of the reported data validation task. By executing this task, you validate the reported financial data in the local currency according to the validation method you assigned to the respective consolidation units.

Figure 4.42 shows the execution of Data Monitor task **Val.Std.D** using the **Update** button.

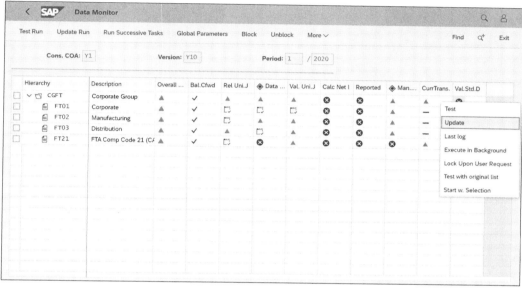

Figure 4.42 Execution of Standardized Data Validation Task

After the **Val.Std.D** task is executed, you're redirected to the Manage Data Validation Tasks app, as shown in Figure 4.43. With this app, you can run reported data validation for the specified fiscal period and consolidation unit and check the validation result with one row for each consolidation unit.

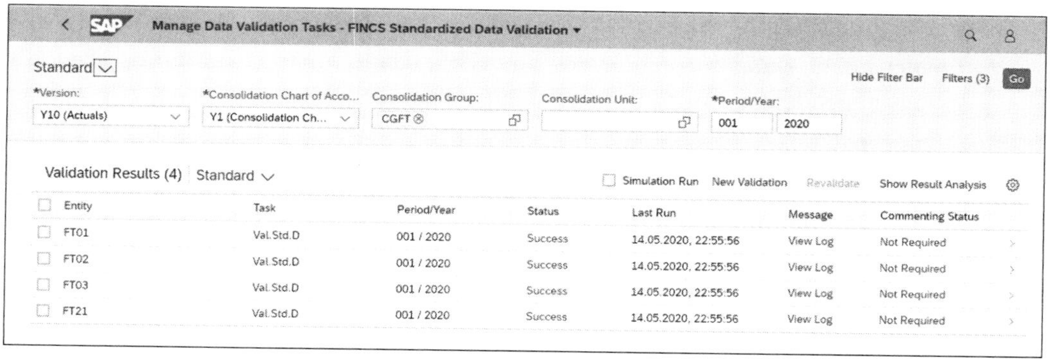

Figure 4.43 Manage Data Validation Tasks App: Standardized Data

Figure 4.44 gives you the details of the preceding validation results. By clicking on any row shown in Figure 4.43, you'll access the corresponding consolidation detailed validation results.

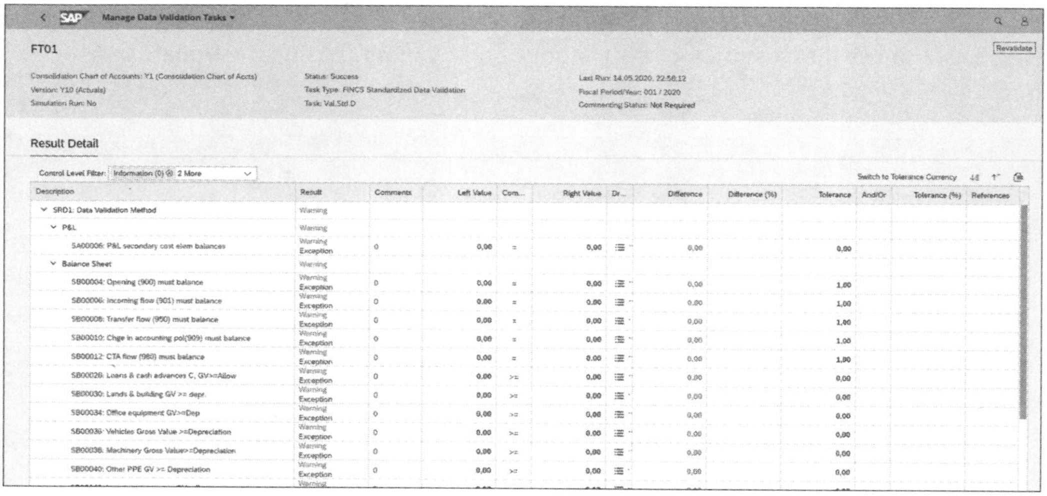

Figure 4.44 Detailed Task Log: Standardized Data Validation

4.8   Journal Entries

Group journal entries are the consolidation-specific journal entries you post to correct, standardize, or consolidate reported financial data to the requirements of the group. In the posting, you use different document types to fulfill these purposes.

This section describes the three apps available for posting, importing, and displaying group journal entries.

4.8.1   Group Journal Entries

The SAP Fiori Import Group Journal Entries app is helpful in adjusting the reported financial data, standardizing entries, and consolidation entries at a group level. It's mainly dependent on the following posting types:

- **Unit-dependent adjustments**
  Posting adjustments to reported financial data.
- **Two-sided elimination**
  Posting two-sided elimination entries for a consolidation unit and partner unit.
- **Group-dependent adjustments**
  Posting group elimination entries.

Within the Import Group Journal Entries app, you can download the template by clicking the **Download Template** button, as shown in Figure 4.45.

Figure 4.45 Import Group Journal Entries

While downloading the template, you need to choose the appropriate template based on the data you're uploading. Figure 4.46 shows you the different types of templates available, and Table 4.4 lists the details that will help you select an appropriate template.

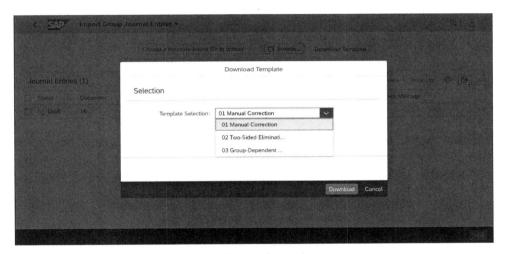

Figure 4.46 Import Group Journal Entry: Types of Templates

Template	Document Type	Posting Level
01	01: Manual correction of Universal Journal	0C
01	02: Manual correction of reported data	01
01	11: Manual standardizing in local currency, deferred tax, no automatic reversal in the subsequent period	10
01	12: Manual standardizing in local currency, deferred tax, automatic reversal	10
01	13: Manual standardizing in local currency, no deferred tax or automatic reversal	10

Table 4.4 Template Details for Selection

Template	Document Type	Posting Level
01	14: Manual standardizing in local currency, no deferred tax, automatic reversal	10
01	16: Manual standardizing in group currency, deferred tax, no automatic reversal	10
01	17: Manual standardizing in group currency, deferred tax, automatic reversal	10
01	18: Manual standardizing in group currency, no deferred tax or automatic reversal	10
01	19: Manual standardizing in group currency, no deferred tax, automatic reversal	10
02	21: Manual elimination correction, automatic reversal	20
02	22: Manual elimination correction, no automatic reversal	20
03	31: Manual consolidation adjustments, automatic reversal	30
03	32: Manual consolidation adjustments, no automatic reversal	30
03	39: Group shares	30

Table 4.4 Template Details for Selection (Cont.)

Figure 4.47 is an example of a posted manual correction journal entry. All the fields with asterisks are mandatory; you need to complete these fields and upload the journal entry back to the system as described next.

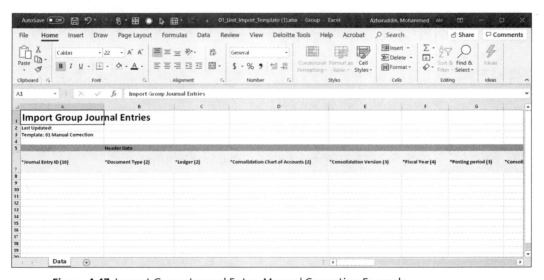

Figure 4.47 Import Group Journal Entry: Manual Correction Example

Now that you've imported the group journal entry, you can post it. This can also be done using the same Import Group Journal Entries app. Figure 4.48 shows the following steps to perform:

❶ **Browse**
Browse for the file that was downloaded in an earlier step, with information about the journal entry.

❷ **Check**
Check whether the journal entry has any errors before you proceed to post.

❸ **Post**
Click this button to make your adjustments in the system.

Figure 4.49 shows you what a successfully posted group journal entry will look like.

Figure 4.48 Import Group Journal Entry: Manual Correction Draft

Figure 4.49 Import Group Journal Entry: Successful Manual Correction Post

4.8.2   General Journal Entries

General journal entries are posted at the consolidation unit level rather than at the group level. In the real world, you might still want to post some entries at the consolidation unit level in SAP S/4HANA Finance for group reporting to cater to some last-minute adjustments. You can post these entries using the Post General Journal Entries app. Figure 4.50 shows the details of the app, including the following fields (fields marked with an asterisk are mandatory):

- **Journal Entry Date**
  The date on which you're posting the journal.

- **Posting Date**
  The date the journal reflects in the financials. Figure 4.50 shows the posting date as **14.05.2020**, which means the journal entry is posted in period 5, and the values in this journal are reflected in the financial statement of consolidation unit FT03 in period 5.

- **Journal Entry Type**
  The document type of the journal entry.

- **Company Code**
  The consolidation unit to which you're posting your journal entry.

- **Translation Currency**
  The currency in which the consolidation unit transacts.

- **G/L Account**
  The general ledger account to which you're posting the balances.

- **Debit**
  On side of a balanced journal entry.

- **Credit**
  The other side of a balanced journal entry.

A few points to remember when posting a journal entry are that balance sheet accounts might need a profit center, income statement accounts might need a cost center or functional area, and a journal entry should be balanced. When you're done, click the **Post** button.

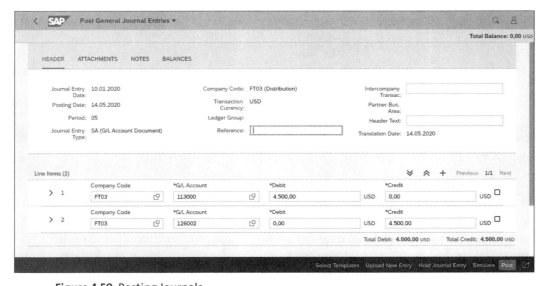

Figure 4.50 Posting Journals

After you post the entry, it will take you to the **Manage Journal Entries** screen shown in Figure 4.51, where you validate your entry before posting it into the system by clicking **Post** again. Figure 4.52 shows you the status of your posted journal entry.

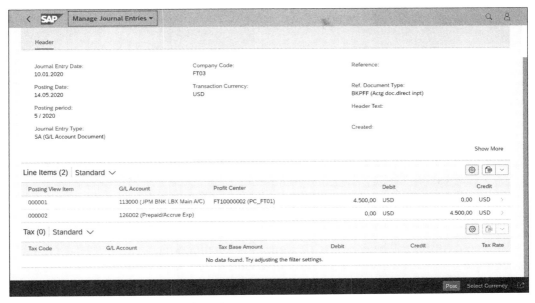

Figure 4.51 Manage General Journal Entries

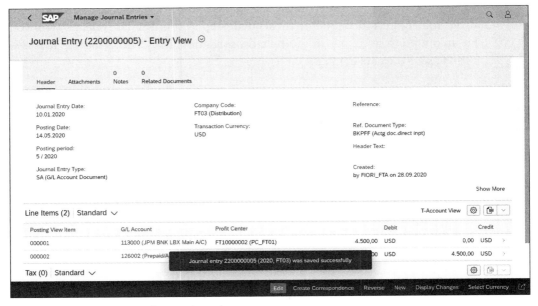

Figure 4.52 Posting General Journal Entries

You can then go to table ACDOCA or any data analysis app at the consolidation unit level and validate the posted journal entry. Figure 4.53 shows the entry in table ACDOCA.

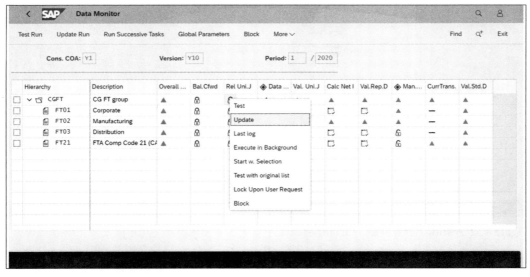

Figure 4.53 Validating Posted Journal Entries

4.8.3   Release Universal Journal Task

These entries will be posted to the consolidation unit, which will be reflected in table ACDOCA. Next, you need to release them to table ACDOCU, which is done by triggering the **Rel.Uni.J** task in the Data Monitor. We've covered this task in a detail in Section 4.3; here, we're just emphasizing task execution, which would release the journals you've posted in earlier steps from table ACDOCA to table ACDOCU.

Figure 4.54 shows the execution of the task in the Data Monitor by clicking the **Update** button, and Figure 4.55 shows the subsequent step to confirm data release. Here you have an option to select one or multiple consolidation units before clicking the **Save** button to save the data in table ACDOCU.

Figure 4.54 Release Universal Journal Task

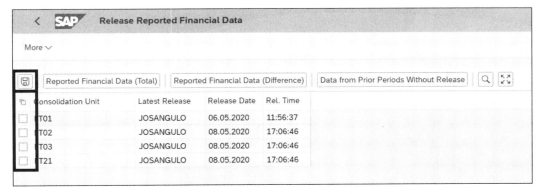

Figure 4.55 Release the Journals to Table ACDOCU

Figure 4.56 shows the expected success message after your posting. Click the **Continue** button to confirm the data release.

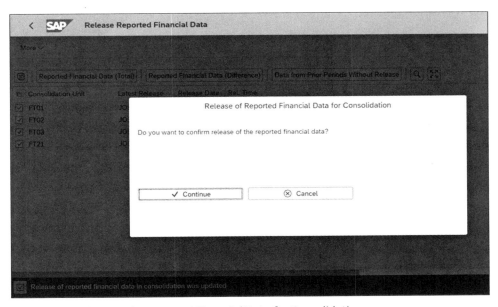

Figure 4.56 Releasing the Reported Financial Data for Consolidation

4.8.4 Validate Universal Journal Task

Now that you have the reported financial data in the Universal Journal (table ACDOCU), you need to validate the data before you proceed with performing consolidations. This is one of the key data validation steps in the Data Monitor, but this only applies to those consolidation units that have the data transfer method set as **Read from Universal Document**. We've discussed the assignment of data transfer method to a consolidation unit in Section 4.3. Now let's look at the execution of this task in the Data Monitor.

Figure 4.57 shows you the execution steps of the task in the Data Monitor. Right-click on the task, and select **Update** to view and validate the journal entries.

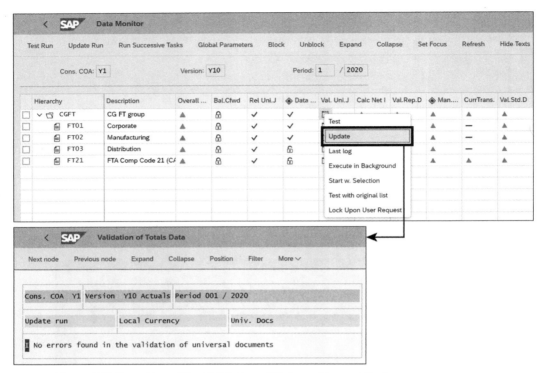

Figure 4.57 Execution of the Validation of Universal Journal Task

This task gives you details of errors, if any, related to missing or incorrect subassignments for FS items where a subassignment is required. Based on this, you can do necessary corrections in the FS item subassignments.

4.9   Summary

In this chapter, we've focused on preparing for consolidations, where we've extensively discussed the data collection process of SAP S/4HANA Finance for group reporting. We started with setting up the Data Monitor with the necessary tasks, then moved on to discuss various ways to upload the data related to SAP and non-SAP entities into group reporting, carrying forward the prior year's end balances, having the opening balance sheet ready in group reporting, performing net income calculation, and having your data ready to start validations. After we performed validations, we moved on to post adjustments to the reported financial data both at the consolidation unit level as well as the consolidation group level, and finally we validated the data in the Universal Journal.

We'll now move on to our next topic, currency translations, where you'll learn about the process of translating the local currency of a consolidation unit to the group currency of the consolidation group to produce group financial statements with which you'll complete the preparations for month-end consolidation activities.

4

Chapter 5
Currency Translation

In this chapter, we'll discuss currency translation, exchange rate types, and configuration of currency translation methods in group reporting in detail, followed by execution of the currency translation task in the Data Monitor and validating the results.

In the data collection phase of preparing for consolidations, currency translation is an important step in which you translate local currencies to the group currency so that the consolidation unit's financial data that is reported in local currency can be included in the group financial statements after consolidations.

We'll begin this chapter with a discussion of core currency translation concepts. Then, we'll move on to the step-by-step configuration of currency translation in SAP S/4HANA Finance for group reporting. We'll close with the steps to translate reported currency and report your results.

5.1 What Is Currency Translation?

Currency translation is a process in which an organization translates the financial data of its foreign subsidiaries from their transaction currency into the group currency of an organization so that subsidiaries' financials can be recorded in group financial statements. The foreign subsidiaries still report their financials in their corresponding transaction or local currencies.

Let's discuss an example to better understand the currency translation process. An organization that operates in multiple countries will have financials in multiple currencies as a result of business operations in different companies. For consolidation purposes, you need to have financials in the organization's group currency; this is the primary reason you need to perform currency translation. In the scenario that we're discussing in this chapter, holding company FT01 reports in USD, which is also the group currency for your consolidations and its subsidiary FT21, which reports in Canadian dollars for its transaction currency. In this chapter, we'll discuss how to translate FT21's reported financial data from Canadian dollars to USD to consolidate the financials at the group level.

Currency translation makes it easier to analyze the financials at the group level for the executive team of an organization; otherwise, it would be very hard to analyze the organizational performance in more than one currency.

In the following sections, we'll introduce key currency translation concepts and functionality in SAP S/4HANA Finance for group reporting.

5.1.1   Currency Translation Basics

Currency translation can be a very complex issue due to various factors. Following are two major factors that may impact the reported financial data:

- Exchange rate fluctuations
- Inflation rates

For example, consider a subsidiary that is in a country whose currency is weak compared to the parent. As you perform currency conversion using year-end rates to convert its assets into group currency, there is a risk of understating the subsidiaries' asset values as their depreciation might not be proportional with the local currency of the subsidiary. However, due to inflation, the fixed assets of the subsidiary aren't impacted much because they are worth more in the subsidiaries' local currency. Typically, these two scenarios offset each other, so there is greater probability that assets of the subsidiary are pretty much stable in parent companies' books. But this isn't the same case with the inventories, receivables, and liabilities, as their value is directly proportional to the subsidiaries' currency, which means irrespective of their maturity, they all depreciate with the local currency. On the other hand, if the subsidiaries' local currency is stronger than that of the parent, the implications are reversed, but the situation is still the same. Because of this, you need to consider the following points to accurately capture the developments related to the foreign subsidiary:

- What is the impact on the consolidated results due to the translation of the subsidiary's local currency into the parent company's group currency?
- What adjustments will arise due to the translation of a subsidiary's assets?

The answer to these questions comes from using currency translation methods and capturing the translating differences that arise due to these translations. Following are the two most common methods used:

- **Closing rate method**
  This is used when a subsidiary is financially independent of its parent (most common case). In this method, the currency translation differences are recorded under the shareholders' equity. All assets and liabilities are translated at this rate, which is essentially the rate of exchange at the balance sheet date.

  Revenues and expenses are translated using the average rate, which is the average exchange rate for the period.

- **Temporal rate method**

  This is used when a subsidiary isn't financially independent of its parent. In this method, the difference between the net income on the balance sheet and the net income on the income statement is recorded on the income statement as foreign exchange gains and losses. The following rates are relevant:

  - Closing rate: Monetary items such as cash, receivables, and payables are converted into group currency using the closing rate.

  - Historical rate: Nonmonetary items such as fixed assets, depreciation, amortization, goodwill, inventories, prepayments, and shareholders' equity are converted using the historical rates.

  - Average rate: Income and expenses are converted.

Now let's discuss currency translation adjustment (CTA). CTA is an entry that is recorded in the balance sheet in the Accumulated Other Comprehensive Income section. This helps you analyze the gains and losses that result from dynamic exchange rates. This entry helps investors of an organization understand actual operating gains and losses versus the gains and losses generated by currency conversion. Organizations with foreign subsidiaries make sure that CTAs are an integral part of their financial statements. The CTA balance accumulated over the years is recorded in the accumulated other comprehensive income, which is a component of equity.

Let's discuss an example. In this scenario, FTO1 invested USD $100 million in the foreign subsidiary FT21. Let's assume that this investment has appreciated to USD $110 million due to the foreign exchange, so you need to understand how to record this unrealized gain of USD $10 million.

The following is the journal entry that you would post to record the gains due to foreign exchange fluctuations:

- Debit: Investment (increase in foreign assets) USD $10 M
- Credit: CTA account USD $10 M

When you liquidate FT21, you would record the transactions as follows:

- Debit: CTA account USD $10 M
- Credit: Income statement USD $10 M

Let's discuss a practical example of currency conversion and booking CTA. Table 5.1 shows the retained earnings of your foreign subsidiary FT21 at the beginning of fiscal year 2019, which is translated from local currency to group currency by historical rates. It also shows the net income at the end of the FY 2019, which has been translated using the average method and has been rolled forward to the retained earnings. Finally, you have year-end values for retained earnings, which are recorded in FT21's balance sheet.

	FT21 (Pre-Currency Conversion)	Rate	Method	FT21 (Post-Currency Conversion)
Retained earnings (1/1/2019)	2,700,000.00	1.51	Historical	4,077,000.00
Net income (12/31/2019)	1,100,000.00	1.54	Average	1,694,000.00
Retained earnings (12/31/2019)	3,800,000.00	-	-	5,771,000.00

Table 5.1 Calculation of Retained Earnings

Now that the retained earnings are calculated at the FY 2019 year end, the balance sheet of FT21 will be carried forward to FY 2020. Table 5.2 shows the trial balance of FT21 pre-currency conversion and post-currency conversion and the calculation of CTA. It describes the trial balance of FT21 in Canadian currency and how each balance sheet item and profit and loss (P&L) statement is calculated. Balance sheet items such as cash, accounts receivable, inventory, plant and equipment, accounts payable, and long-term debt are translated using closing or end rates, whereas other balance sheet items such as common stock are translated based on historical rates.

	FT21 (Canadian Subsidiary)	Rate	Method	FT01 (US Holding Company)
Cash	600,000.00	1.53	Closing/end	918,000.00
Accounts receivables	2,700,000.00	1.53	Closing/end	4,131,000.00
Inventory	9,000,000.00	1.53	Closing/end	13,770,000.00
Plant and equipment	17,200,000.00	1.53	Closing/end	26,316,000.00
Account payables	(500,000.00)	1.53	Closing/end	(765,000.00)
Long-term debt	(2,000,000.00)	1.53	Closing/end	(3,060,000.00)
Common stock	(20,000,000.00)	1.51	Closing/end	(30,200,000.00)
Retained earnings (1/1/2020)	(3,800,000.00)	-		(5,771,000.00)
Sales	(13,900,000.00)	1.55	Average	(21,545,000.00)
Cost of goods sold (COGS)	8,100,000.00	1.55	Average	12,555,000.00

Table 5.2 Calculating CTA

	FT21 (Canadian Subsidiary)	Rate	Method	FT01 (US Holding Company)
Depreciation expenses	900,000.00	1.55	Average	1,395,000.00
Other expenses	950,000.00	1.55	Average	1,472,500.00
Dividends payables	750,000.00	1.58	Historical	1,185,000.00
CTA	-	-	-	(401,500.00)

Table 5.2 Calculating CTA (Cont.)

Retained earnings have been carried forward from the prior year as is, whereas income statement items such as sales, COGS, depreciation expenses, and other expenses are calculated per average rates, and dividends declared are recorded per the exchange rate when they were declared.

After the entire trial balance is converted to group currency, which is USD, you aggregate the values to derive the CTA, which is presented in the Accumulated Other Comprehensive Income section of the company's translated balance sheet. As you can see in this example, the CTA of FT21 in USD after conversion gives you a picture of gains and losses that happened due to foreign currency exchange rate fluctuations over fiscal periods. Recording CTA separately helps you identify actual operational gains and losses versus gains and losses that result from currency exchange gains and losses.

5.1.2 Currency Translation in SAP S/4HANA

Currency translation is done in the corporate close process using SAP S/4HANA Finance for group reporting. It's very common for an organization to have multiple subsidiaries in other countries that report in their local currencies at the month end when the corporation is consolidating its financials. The company consumes the subsidiaries' financials in local currency, translates them into group currency, and finally uses the values in the group currency to generate group financial statements during the period close.

The following are some key terms that you need to know to understand the currency translation process in SAP S/4HANA Finance for group reporting:

- **Exchange rates**
  Exchange rates are maintained in SAP S/4HANA Finance for group reporting to perform currency translation (e.g., period average rates or monthly rates).

- **Posting level**
  OT is the posting level for standardized and consolidated data, which is used in rounding from currency translation.

- **Methods**

  The following are the predefined methods in SAP S/4HANA for group reporting:

  - Y0901: Standard method in group reporting for YTD values.

  - Y0902: Keep group currency values from SAP S/4HANA (table ACDOCA) and balance sheet retranslate at the closing rate.

  - S0901, S0902: These methods can be both YTD as well as periodic, but they are also dependent on the period of acquisition.

  - S0903: Standard method for periodic values that you generally use for income statement values.

- **Selection object**

  In the currency translation method, you use this indicator to specify how you determine the source data region, such as opening balance of current asset accounts. If you select **Selection Object**, it allows for the use of a previously defined selection object; if you didn't select it, then the source data region becomes method specific.

- **Financial statement (FS) items**

  While defining the FS items, you can select currency translation and define conditions in the Define FS Items app.

- **Measures**

  You can define reports with specific measures, which can be defined with one of the following values:

  - **Local Currency (LC)**

  - **Group Currency (GC)**

  - **Transaction Currency (TC)**

- **Currency fields**

  Currency fields in both table ACDOCA and table ACDOCU are used to hold details about the currency values. Currency fields in table ACDOCA are as follows:

  - WSL: Transaction currency.

  - HSL: Local currency.

  - KSL: Group currency amount.

  - TSL: Transaction currency (documents that are posted in period 000).

  Currency fields used in table ACDOCU are as follows:

  - WSL: Forms a union between the WSL field in universal journal and the TSL field in the consolidation journal.

  - HSL and KSL: Uses ledger-dependent data sender currency fields of the consolidation unit to decide which amount fields are read from the Universal Journal as local currency and group currency.

Before getting started with currency translation with SAP S/4HANA Finance for group reporting, there are two prerequisites that you need to take care of to run currency translation:

- **Maintaining exchange rates**
  Maintain the rates in the system so that they can be applied to the foreign subsidiaries' data and convert that data from the subsidiary's local currency to the group currency.

- **Assigning the method**
  Assign a currency translation method to the consolidation unit whose currency you want to translate from the local currency to group currency.

5.2 Configuring Currency Translation

In this section, we'll review the currency translation configuration in SAP S/4HANA Finance for group reporting with which you'll perform the currency translation before you start consolidating the financials. We'll start with discussing the various exchange rate types and how they are used in translating a trial balance by balance sheet or by income statement from local to group currency. We'll then review the exchange rate indicators you'll use to trigger exchange rates, followed by discussing the currency translation methods offered by SAP S/4HANA Finance for group reporting. We'll then move on to assigning a currency translation method to a consolidation unit so that the consolidation unit is automatically translated using the assigned method. Finally, we'll review the FS items used in currency translation because, at the end of the translation, you'll still look at group financial statements that are read by FS items.

5.2.1 Exchange Rate Types

An exchange rate type is a value/field that's used to define exchange rates in the system. Each currency pair needs to be defined with exchange rates. You need different exchange rates for many purposes such as valuation, conversion, translation, and planning. These exchange rates are identified using exchange rate types. A few examples of exchange rate types are as follows:

- **Buying rate**
  Rate at which foreign currency is bought.

- **Selling rate**
  Rate at which foreign currency is sold for local currency.

- **Average rate**
  Monthly average rates.

- **Historical rate**
  Exchange rate at which an asset or a liability is acquired.

In the following sections, we'll walk through creating exchange rate types, using translation ratios, and maintaining exchange rates.

Create Exchange Rate Types

To view exchange rate types, execute Transaction OB07 to arrive at the screen shown in Figure 5.1. You can create a new exchange rate type by clicking **New Entries**.

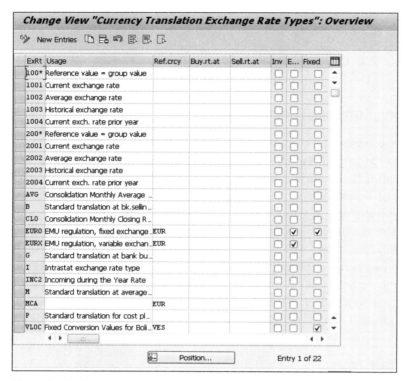

Figure 5.1 Exchange Rate Types

Figure 5.2 shows how you can create a new exchange rate type based on your requirements after clicking the **New Entries** button. You can enter the following values:

- **ExRt**
  This field contains the exchange rate type.

- **Usage**
  This field specifies the exchange rate usage.

- **Ref.crcy**
  Using this field for reference currency, you can maintain the exchange rates. With the help of the exchange rates, you can manage the currency translation, which is critical for an organization that operates in many different currencies. The exchange rates are maintained against the exchange rate type and the reference currency combination.

- **Buy.rt.at**
  This field for the buying rate is optional; you can specify the buying exchange rate here.

- **Sell.rt.at**

  This field for the selling rate is optional; you can specify the selling exchange rate here.

- **Inverter Exchange Rate**

  This field helps you create an inverted exchange rate for a currency pair as the exchange rate. For example, if an exchange rate USD/EUR isn't maintained in the system, and you've selected this option, then the system will consider the exchange rate for EUR/USD.

- **EMU**

  This field is used when you have a requirement to meet European Monetary Union (EMU) statutory guidelines. If you're using this option, you also need to select a reference currency per the EMU guidelines.

- **Fixed**

  This field is used to calculate the exchange rates from the manually entered currency.

After you create a new rate type, click **Save**.

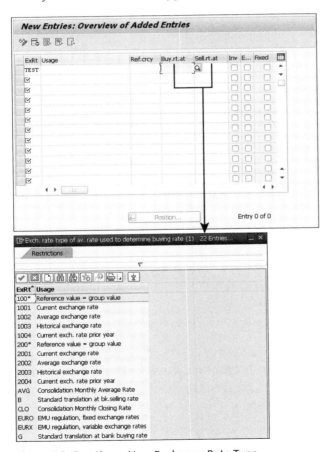

Figure 5.2 Creating a New Exchange Rate Type

Specify Translation Ratios

After you've maintained exchange rates, you need to specify translation ratios. For each combination of the exchange rate, you can specify the translation ratios. The combination of exchange rate includes a source currency and a target currency, which are subjected to translation. Translation ratios are extremely helpful to control the number of decimal places that are used for the exchange rates. There are predefined translation ratios in the system by default. You need to maintain translation ratios for every currency exchange pair.

Figure 5.3 shows the currency translation ratios you can access by executing Transaction CXE9N, expanding **Currency Translation for Consolidation**, and selecting **Specify Translation Ratios**. Here you maintain exchange rate type **ExRt**, specify the currency pair that tells you **From** and **To** currencies that have been translated, and update the alternate exchange rate **Alt.ERT**.

You can also create new entries by selecting **New Entries** and entering the following values:

- **ExRt**
  Enter an exchange rate type in this field.

- **From**
  This field indicates the currency you want to translate, which is generally the foreign currency.

- **To**
  This field indicates what will be the local/translated currency.

- **Valid from**
  This field indicates the date from which you want the ratio to be valid.

- **Ratio(from)**
  This field indicates the ratio at which the foreign currency value is translated.

- **Ratio (to)**
  This field indicates the ratio at which the local currency values are calculated during the currency translation.

- **Alt. ERT**
  If needed, specify the alternative exchange rate types that the government regulatory bodies allow to be used in this field.

When you're done, click **Save**.

Let's consider an example of updating the ratios: 1 CAD = 0.74 USD. In this example, the **From** currency is **CAD** and the **To** currency is **USD**. This would make the **Ratio(from)** : **Ratio (to)** equal to 1:1, which can be understood as 1 CAD = 0.74 * 1 USD, where 0.74 is the exchange rate that is maintained in the system.

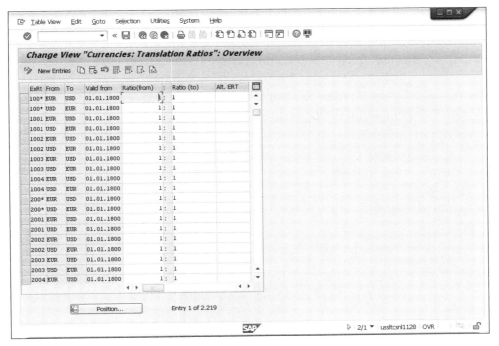

Figure 5.3 Specifying Translation Ratios

Maintain Exchange Rates

For an organization, exchange rates are required to convert from one currency to another based on the translation date for financial transactions. In addition, it's essential to convert from local currency to group currency to produce consolidated group financials. You can access the screen to maintain exchange rates by using Transaction OB08 or by going to the IMG and choosing **Currency Translation for Consolidation • Maintain Exchange Rates**.

Here you encounter two new fields: **Indir.quot** (indirect quotation) and **Dir.quot** (direct quotation), which are used to manage the exchange rates. The type of quotation that you need to use depends on the market standards, as follows:

- **Indirect quotation**
  This is widely used for exchange rates with the euro and resulted from the start of the dual currency phase of the EMU. Here the cost of one unit of local currency is given in units of foreign currency.

- **Direct quotation**
  When the cost of one unit of foreign currency is given in units of local currency, it's called a direct quotation.

For example, when your local currency is USD, this is what direct and indirect rates look like:

- Direct exchange rate: 1 CAD = 0.74 USD
- Indirect exchange rate: 1 USD = 1.36 CAD

Figure 5.4 shows the screen where you can maintain the exchange rates, which you can access by executing Transaction CXE9N, expanding **Currency Translation for Consolidation**, and selecting **Maintain Exchange Rates**. You can create new rates by selecting the **New Entries** option and entering the following fields:

- **ExRt**
  Enter the exchange rate you want to use, for example, historical, average, or closing rates.

- **ValidFrom**
  Specify the date from which you want this rate to be valid.

- **Indir.quot**
  Specify whether you have any indirectly quoted exchange rate.

- **Ratio(from)**
  Indicate the ratio at which the foreign currency value is translated.

- **From**
  Specify your from currency/foreign currency.

- **Dir.quot**
  Specify directly quoted exchange rates here.

Change View "Currency Exchange Rates": Overview

New Entries

ExRt	ValidFrom	Indir.quot	X	Ratio(from)	From	=	Dir.quot.	X	Ratio (to)	To
100*	01.01.2001		X		1 EUR	=	0,94000	X		1 USD
100*	01.01.2001	0,94000	X		1 USD	=		X		1 EUR
1001	01.01.2001		X		1 EUR	=	0,94000	X		1 USD
1001	01.01.2001	0,94000	X		1 USD	=		X		1 EUR
1002	01.01.2001		X		1 EUR	=	0,94000	X		1 USD
1002	01.01.2001	0,94000	X		1 USD	=		X		1 EUR
1003	01.01.2001		X		1 EUR	=	0,94000	X		1 USD
1003	01.01.2001	0,94000	X		1 USD	=		X		1 EUR
1004	01.01.2001		X		1 EUR	=	0,94000	X		1 USD
1004	01.01.2001	0,94000	X		1 USD	=		X		1 EUR
200*	01.01.2001		X		1 EUR	=	0,94000	X		1 USD
200*	01.01.2001	0,94000	X		1 USD	=		X		1 EUR
2001	01.01.2001		X		1 EUR	=	0,94000	X		1 USD
2001	01.01.2001	0,94000	X		1 USD	=		X		1 EUR
2002	01.01.2001		X		1 EUR	=	0,94000	X		1 USD
2002	01.01.2001	0,94000	X		1 USD	=		X		1 EUR
2003	01.01.2001		X		1 EUR	=	0,94000	X		1 USD
2003	01.01.2001	0,94000	X		1 USD	=		X		1 EUR
2004	01.01.2001		X		1 EUR	=	0,94000	X		1 USD

Position...   Entry 1 of 12.054

Figure 5.4 Maintaining Exchange Rates

- **Ratio (to)**

  Indicate the ratio at which the local currency values are calculated during the currency translation.

- **To**

  Specify your "To" currency here, which is basically translated values in local currency or group currency in consolidations.

Instead of automatically updating this table manually, you can also provision an automatic feed of exchange rates to this table; that is, you can schedule the jobs so that these exchange rates are fed to the SAP S/4HANA system daily. For this, you need a third-party exchange rate feed. Some examples of third-party providers are Bloomberg, Data Scope, and Reuters. These third-party suppliers can provide feeds per business need, and they don't need instruments such as a currency pair (e.g., USD/CAD). These suppliers sell the instruments in packages.

Let's consider an example in which a third-party supplier is selling 100 instruments for an amount of $1,000 every hour for a period of one month. Connections from the client SAP system to the third-party supplier can be checked by executing program RSHTTP05 using Transaction SE38, as shown in Figure 5.5 **1**.

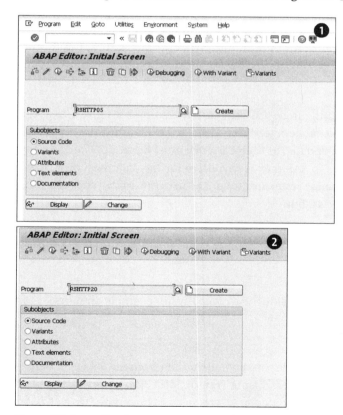

Figure 5.5 Executing Programs to Set Up the Connection URL

After the agreement between the client and the third-party investment supplier is established and you set up the connection, it's time to get the feed from the provider. The third-party feed providers provide their URL and credentials so that the client can connect to their servers. After you have the details of the URL, you need to save them in the system, which can be done using program RSHTTP20 from Transaction SE38. Figure 5.5 ❷ shows how to execute the program for updating the URL.

When you execute program RSHTTP20, the screen shown in Figure 5.6 opens. Here you update the **URI** of the third-party provider that feeds the exchange rates. If you want to restrict the editing/updating of the URL, you can use the **User** and **Password** feature. **RFC Destination** reflects the receiver details, which, in this case, is an SAP system. By entering these details, you authorize the system to connect to the URL of the third-party provider.

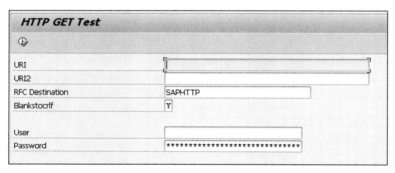

Figure 5.6 Setting Up the URL

The system also needs to be configured with each currency pair for the given data feed so that you can update the exchange rate. It's essential to check which exchange rate types per currency need to be updated as each currency must be set up. The following are predefined exchange rates in SAP that are available for the data feed logic. These values aren't available for selection in the frontend; SAP uses these rate types while the exchange rates are fed into the system:

- **G type**
  This bank buying rate type is used for when the bank is buying from the company for exports.
- **B type**
  This rate is used when the bank is selling to a company, for example, imports.
- **M type**
  This is the average exchange rate.

After each currency setup is configured, you can pull the data from the data feed. Figure 5.7 shows the screen of the data feed run. Using Transaction TBD4, you can trigger the data feed request for the current market data. All you need to do is enter the details in this screen, as follows:

- **Market Data Class**
  Select which type of market data you want to request. A laundry list of options are available that cover all the financial data available in the market.

- **Market Data Selection**
  Based on the type of market data class selected in the preceding, you select the appropriate option here as a notation of the master data.

- **Datafeed**
  This is the name of the third-party firm from which you're getting the data feed.

- **Output Control**
  Here you specify how you want the market data to be saved.

> **Note**
>
> This transaction can be automated to run as a batch job in the background in Transaction SM37. Based on your business needs, this job can be set to run hourly, daily, weekly, and so on.

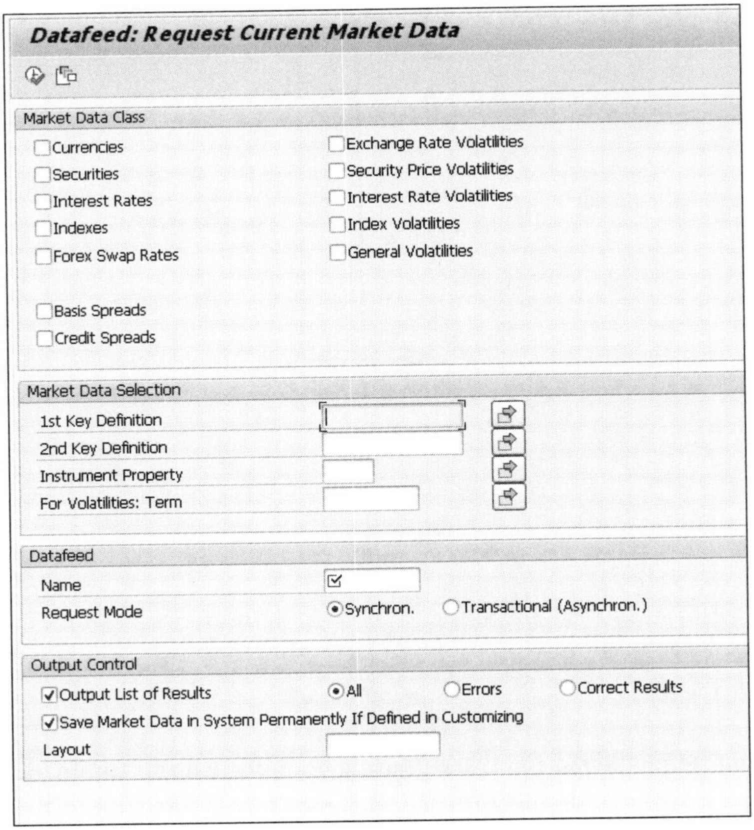

Figure 5.7 Data Feed from the Third-Party Provider

Now it's time to validate the currency feed. For this, go to Transaction SE16N or Transaction SE16, enter the **Table** name as "TCURR" (**Exchange Rates**), and click the **Execute** icon, as shown in Figure 5.8. You can also check using Transaction OB08 and see the exchange rate updated automatically. In this transaction, you can also maintain the exchange rates manually.

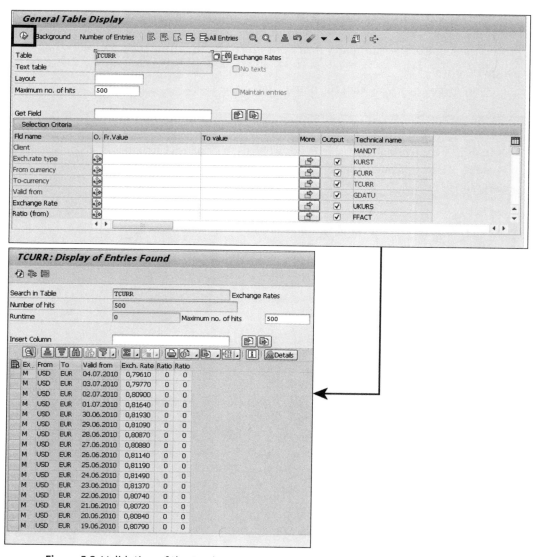

Figure 5.8 Validation of the Feed

So far, you've seen uploading the rates in SAP GUI using both manual and automatic feed options. Now let's look at the SAP Fiori app that you can use to upload the exchange rates to the SAP S/4HANA Finance for group reporting system.

The SAP Fiori Import Foreign Exchange Rates app, found in the SAP Fiori launchpad, allows you to input all the most updated foreign exchange rates into a template that can be downloaded from the same screen. After all the data is in the template, you can upload the data and import the template. The most updated foreign exchange rate will be imported into the system in this way. Figure 5.9 shows the screen you use to download the template by selecting the **Download Template** button, updating the exchange rates, and clicking the **Browse** option to upload the rates back to the system.

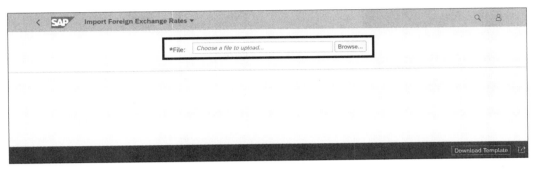

Figure 5.9 Import Foreign Exchange Rates App

5.2.2   Exchange Rate Indicators

Before defining the currency translation methods, we need to look into exchange rate indicators. Exchange rate indicators are centrally maintained in the system. In this step, you define the exchange rate indicators for a specific time and version and use them for consolidations.

Exchange rate indicators for the current rate, average rate, historical rate, and current rate for the prior year are predefined in the standard system, along with the exchange rate types for consolidation (discussed in Section 5.2.1).

The following are the high-level steps to define the exchange rate indicators:

1. Create the exchange rate indicators per your requirement.

2. Assign them to the exchange rate types.

Figure 5.10 shows the predefined exchange rate indicators, which you can access by executing Transaction CXE9N, expanding **Currency Translation for Consolidations**, and selecting **Define Exchange Rate Indicators**. Each of these exchange rate indicators are mapped to version- and time-dependent exchange rate types.

To create a new exchange rate indicator, click the **New Entries** button, and the screen shown in Figure 5.11 opens. You can provide the following details:

- **Exch. rate ind.**
  Define the exchange rates during currency translation.

- **Description**
  Enter a description of the exchange rate indicator.

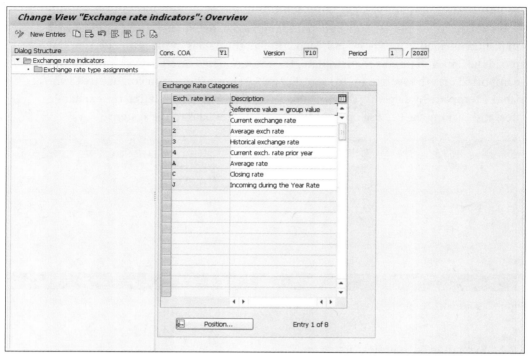

Figure 5.10 Exchange Rate Indicators

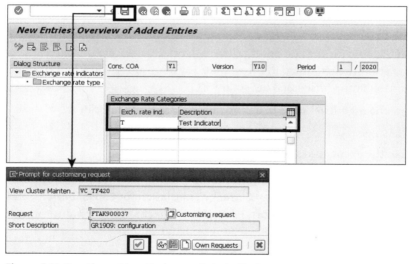

Figure 5.11 Creating a New Exchange Rate Indicator

After you've entered these details, click on **Save**, and approve the customizing request.

If asked for transport, enter the details and proceed further by clicking the green check-mark.

Figure 5.12 shows the assignment of the rate types, which you can navigate to by clicking the **Exchange rate type assignments** folder in the **Dialog Structure**. You enter the following values:

- **Start Year**
  Indicates from when you want to use the exchange rate indicator.

- **Period eff**
  Indicates from which period you want this exchange rate type to be active.

- **ER type**
  Indicates the exchange rate type. The most widely used exchange rates are **AVG** (average) and **CLO** (monthly closing rate).

- **Usage**
  Indicates the usage of the exchange rate type; this is auto populated as you enter the exchange rate type.

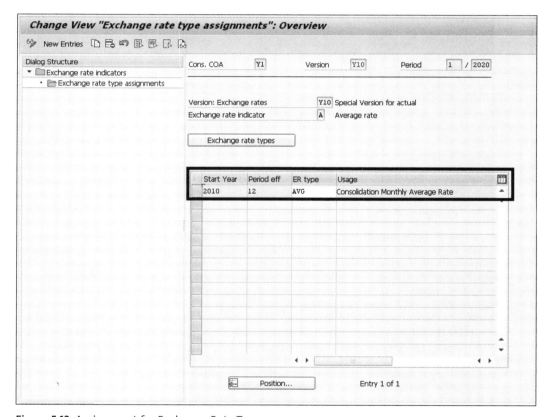

Figure 5.12 Assignment for Exchange Rate Types

Alternatively, you can create the currency exchange rates using the SAP Fiori Currency Exchange Rates app. This app gives you the ability to create, change, and delete exchange rates. You can indicate validity periods for specific exchange rates, view and monitor all exchange rates, and perform amount conversions using the **Quick Calculate** option. Using **Currency Exchange Rate Trend**, you can view the exchange rate trend for a currency pair over the past 7 days, 30 days, or 12 months. Figure 5.13 shows the SAP Fiori app screen where you can create, modify, or delete exchange rates. To create a new rate type, click **Create**, and enter the following:

- **Exchange rate type**
  Enter the exchange rate type you want to use ("CLO" or "AVG").

- **Valid From**
  Enter the date from which you want to have this exchange rate valid.

- **Currency Pair**
  Instead of from and to currencies, enter the currency pair, which indicates the foreign and local currencies.

- **Rate 1:1**
  This is the ratio of conversion; in SAP GUI, you'll see **Ratio From** and **Ratio To**.

Figure 5.13 Currency Exchange Rates

5.2.3   Currency Translation Methods

Now let's discuss the currency translation methods, which are essential in the currency translation process. A currency translation method is used to specify the reference exchange rate such as average rate, closing rate, or historical rate. The following points are key to note:

- Methods consist of sequences. Each sequence is used to translate sets of FS items and transaction types, such as nonhistorical balance sheet movements at average.

- Differences between the two amounts are currency translation differences.

- Currency translation methods are assigned to consolidation units.

The currency translation method communicates to the system about how it must process and post currency translations, including accounting for any translation or rounding differences. You can check the predefined translation methods and define a new one if needed.

Before setting up the currency translation process, organizations should determine the following:

- Which translation methods might be required
- How rounding needs to be done
- How to translate balance sheet, income statement, and statistical items
- How to post CTA

When you have a strong understanding of these tasks, you can go ahead with the following configuration steps in SAP S/4HANA Finance for group reporting.

You can maintain or create consolidation unit master data individually if the local currency is different from the group currency. The translation method determines the exchange rate used for specific FS items and how translation and rounding differences are posted. Figure 5.14 shows the predefined methods in the system, which you can access by executing Transaction CXE9N, expanding **Currency Translation for Consolidation**, and selecting **Define Currency Translation Methods.**

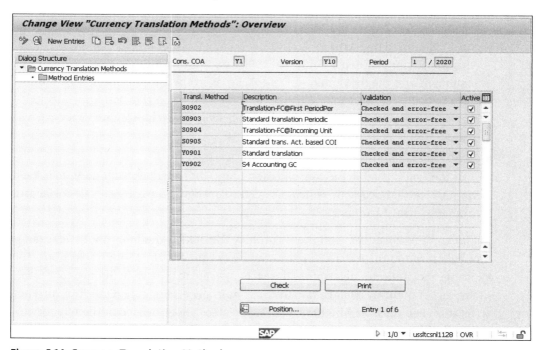

Figure 5.14 Currency Translation Methods

As part of SAP Best Practices, SAP predelivers the following currency translation methods that you can use:

- **S0902 (Translation-FC@First PeriodPer)**
  This method can be assigned to a consolidation unit that is included in the group

195

starting from the first period of the fiscal year. The FS items in the P&L statement and the movement-related FS items in the balance sheet are translated to periodic values at the exchange rates for their respective periods using this method.

- **S0903 (Standard translation Periodic)**
  This method can be used to translates values for all FS items at the monthly average exchange rate for each period.

- **S0904 (Translation-FC@Incoming Unit)**
  This method is helpful to translate the incoming units at a specific rate that is specially maintained for the incoming units. You use the exchange rate indicator "J" for this purpose.

- **S0905 (Standard trans. Act. based COI)**
  This currency translation method is useful when you have a requirement to use the task for automatic consolidation of investments in the Consolidation Monitor. You need to maintain the reported financial data of the consolidation unit for investment and equity items in both local currency and group currency. This method uses the **No Retranslation of Existing Group Currency Value** translation key for investment and equity to fix the group currency values to the historical rate.

- **Y0901 (Standard translation)**
  This translation method is similar to S0903, except that for the FS items in the P&L statement and the movement-related FS items in the balance sheet, S0903 translates periodic values at the exchange rates for their respective periods while Y0901 translates cumulative values at the monthly average exchange rate of the current period.

- **Y0902 (S4 Accounting GC)**
  This method is used in the consolidation units whose data transfer method is **Read from Universal Document**, which means the consolidation unit reads financial data from universal documents.

The main differences between these currency translation methods are the exchange rate indicator and the translation key that are assigned to the FS item selections. The exchange rate indicator determines the exchange rate to be used in the currency translation, either monthly average rate (**AVG**) or monthly closing rate (**CLO**). The currency translation key controls whether cumulative values are translated at the rate for current period (**YTD**) or periodic values are translated at the rates for their respective periods (**PER**). Table 5.3 displays the detailed settings for each method.

Method	Description	P&L, Balance Sheet Movements		Opening Balances in Balance Sheet*		Balance Sheet FS Items – Incoming Units		Investments and Equity in Balance Sheet*	
		Exchange rate indicator	Currency type key	Exchange rate indicator	Currency type key	Exchange rate indicator	Currency type key	Exchange rate indicator	Currency type key
S0902	Translation-FC@First PeriodPer	AVG	PER	AVG	PER	CLO	PER	AVG	PER
S0903	Standard translation Periodic	AVG	PER	AVG	PER	AVG	PER	AVG	PER
S0904	Translation-FC@Incoming Unit	AVG	PER	AVG	PER	INC2	PER	AVG	PER
S0905	Standard trans. Act. based COI	AVG	PER	AVG	PER	AVG	PER	Existing group currency values aren't retranslated.	
Y0901	Standard translation	AVG	PER	AVG	PER	AVG	PER	AVG	PER
Y0902	S4 Accounting GC	Existing group currency values aren't retranslated.							

*Because the opening balance is stored on period 000, the amount in the group currency is kept at its original value.

Table 5.3 Currency Translation Method Settings

When an FS item isn't included in any rule, the reference exchange rate defined in the methods will apply.

When the translation results in rounding differences, these differences are posted in the group currency on the following FS items:

- Balance sheet rounding difference is posted on FS item 314800.
- Annual net income – balance sheet, P&L rounding difference is posted on FS item 799000.
- P&L rounding difference is posted on FS item 604000.

Figure 5.15 shows the process to create a new method after clicking the **New Entries** button:

1. Click **Translation Method**, and select the methods from the popup.

2. Select **Ref.ex.rate ind.** to open the popup to choose the exchange rate indicator.

3. Select the **Validation** method with one of the following three predefined validations:

    – **Unchecked**: Do not execute the validations of the method.

    – **Checked and error-free**: Validate the method and specify that the method should be error free.

    – **Checked and with errors**: Complete validations with errors.

When you're finished with these steps, click **Save**.

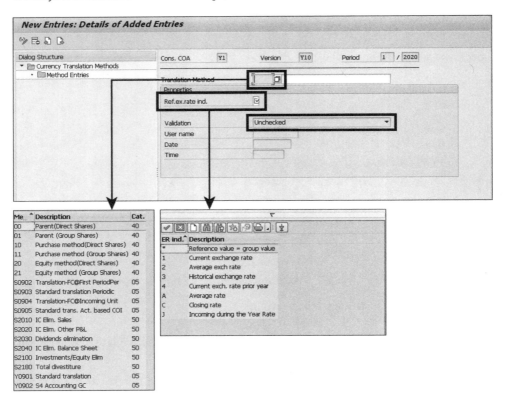

Figure 5.15 Creation of a New Translation Method

After you create a new translation method, you need to assign the method's entries. Figure 5.16 shows the predefined method entries in the system, which you can access by navigating to the **Method Entries** folder in the **Dialog Structure**. However, you can create a new method entry based on your requirements by selecting **New Entries**.

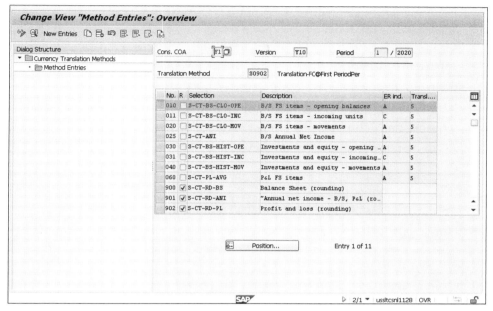

Figure 5.16 Method Entries

Figure 5.17 shows the screen where you can create a new method entry by filling in the following fields:

- **Seq.Number**
  Uniquely identifies a translation/rounding step (a step represents a combination of currency translation key and exchange rate type). The number doesn't impact the sequence of processing.

- **Rounding entry**
  Uses the sequence for rounding.

- **Selection**
  Determines the range of FS items and subitems that are applicable to the translation step.

- **Exch. rate ind.**
  Determines the appropriate exchange rate types and exchange rates needed from the currency translation rate tables.

- **Prior yr ER**
  Selects the prior year closing rate, which, for example, can be used to translate balance sheet opening balances.

- **Translation key**
  Determines the base currency (i.e., local or transactional) and type of exchange rate to be used. The following values are available (1, 5, and 6 are typically used in implementations):

- **1**: Translation of cumulative local values at the current period rate (generally applied to balance statement item balances).
- **5**: Translation of each period at the applicable rate for each period (generally applied to P&L items and balance statement movements).
- **6**: No retranslation of existing group currency values.
- **0**: Translation resulting in group currency value of zero.
- **9**: Translation of transaction currency values (like 1).
- **A**: Translation of transaction currency values (like 5).

Note

The following characteristics of the translation keys are important to note:

- Translation keys 0, 1, 5, and 6 use local currency as the base. Translation keys 9 and A use translation currency as the base. Only translation keys 1 and 5 allow posting to the initiating item.
- For translation key 6, there is no retranslation of existing global currency for balance sheet and P&L items. It's used on consolidation units where the local currency <> global currency, but you don't want anything retranslated for global currency. This is an important integration feature.
- The exchange rate indicator * (reference value = group value) is used to allow the use of existing values in group currency to determine the translation differences instead of a reference rate. This is new as of SAP S/4HANA 1909.

- **Translation differences**
  Gives you the ability to separately store in the database any temporal differences incurred during currency translation. This uses currency translation indicator 3 to capture the period value in group currency for the temporal difference with respect to the delta between the group currency value and the reference currency value.

  Available when translation key 1 is used, **Does not affect earnings** is used to notify whether the posting of a translation difference with a debit balance impacts net income. Used in a situation when you have an income statement differential item with balance sheet selection object, **Debit - Item Role** and **Credit - Item Role** are FS items where you want the CTA to be posted.

- **Account Assignment**
  This is the **FS Item** (and related subitems) where translation differences between the exchange rate and the reference rate are posted. In the preceding example, the FS item won't change from the source selection, but the transaction type 980 is used to capture the CTA for both debit and credit values. When you specify an FS item, the screen will add another field's subject to the breakdown category assigned to it. You can add fields using the **Add Characteristic** icon.

New Entries: Details of Added Entries

Dialog Structure		
▼ ☐ Currency Translation Methods		
• 📂 Method Entries		

Cons. COA [Y1]   Version [Y10]   Period [1] / [2020]

Transl. Method [S0902]   Translation-FC@First PeriodPer
Seq.Number [ ]   ☐ Rounding entry

Selection

Selection [▼] [Edit]

Type of translation

Exch. rate ind. [ ]
☐ Prior yr ER
Translation key [ ]

Translation differences

☐ Does not affect earnings

Debit - Item Role   Credit - Item Role
[ ]   [ ]
[ ]   [ ]

Account Assignment

🗐 Characteri...	Debit	Credit	Default
🗐 FS Item			

Figure 5.17 Creation of New Method Entries

5.2.4 Consolidation Unit Method Assignment

You need to assign a currency translation method to a consolidation unit to perform currency translation tasks on that consolidation unit and translate its reported financial data from the local currency to the group currency. Figure 5.18 shows the SAP Fiori Consolidation Unit Change app, where you can perform this assignment by entering a **Consolidation Unit** ("FT21", in this example).

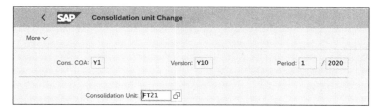

Figure 5.18 Change Consolidation Unit App

After providing the consolidation unit, press [Enter], and the system will take you to a screen where you can perform the configuration, as shown in Figure 5.19. In the **Methods** tab, you choose the method from the list of existing methods in the system. Figure 5.20 shows you a list of existing currency translation methods in the system, which is populated by selecting the **Translation Method** under the **Currency translation** area shown in Figure 5.19. When you're done, click the **Save** button.

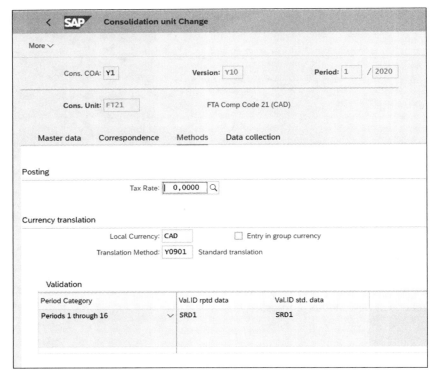

Figure 5.19 Method Assignment to the Consolidation Unit

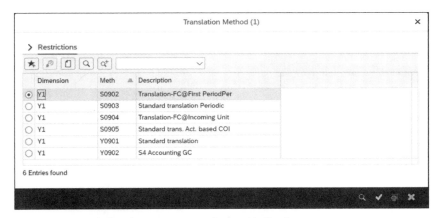

Figure 5.20 Predefined Currency Translation Methods

5.2.5   Financial Statement Item Currency Translation Attribute

An FS item selection attribute is a classification that you assign to FS items. This way, all FS items that share the same attribute value can be selected to be treated in the same way. In this section, we'll look into the currency translation selection attribute.

We mentioned that FS items that are assigned with the same attribute value are treated in the same way in currency translation; that is, they share the same currency translation settings in a specific translation method, for example, whether translated by the monthly average rate or the monthly closing rate. In Figure 5.21, you can see the Define FS Items app, which enables you to assign a currency translation selection attribute to an FS item. Select the FS item to be assigned with a selection attribute, and review the screen shown in Figure 5.22 that provides FS item **79900D** as an example. The selected FS item doesn't have any currency translation selection attribute assigned. Select this and assign an attribute by clicking the **Go** button.

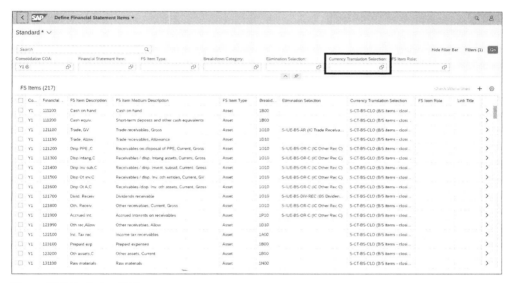

Figure 5.21 Defining FS Items

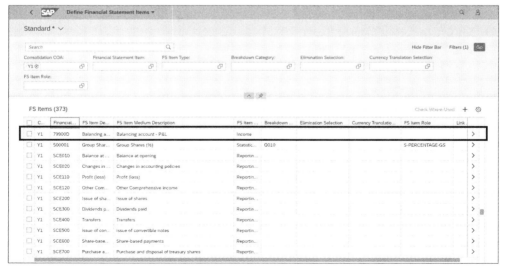

Figure 5.22 Selecting an FS Item

Navigate to the **Attributes for Processing** tab, and click the **Edit** button, as shown in Figure 5.23.

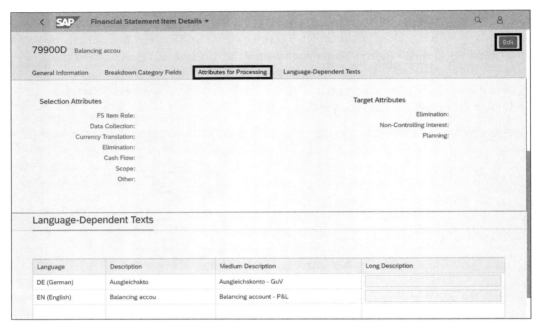

Figure 5.23 Assigning an Attribute to an FS Item

You'll arrive at the screen shown in Figure 5.24 for the assignment of the attribute to FS item 79900D. In the **Selection Attributes** area, you'll see the **Currency Translation** dropdown, from which you can choose one of the following predelivered attributes:

- **S-CT-ANI-BS (Net Income)**
  Post annual net income (balance sheet).

- **S-CT-ANI-PL (Net Income/Loss)**
  Post annual net income (P&L).

- **S-CT-BS-CLO (B/S items - closing rate)**
  Post to balance sheet items at closing rate.

- **S-CT-BS-HIST (B/S items - historical conv)**
  Post to balance sheet items at historical conversion rate.

- **S-CT-BS-HIST-OPE (B/S items - hist conv, OPE)**
  Post to balance sheet items at historical opening rates.

- **S-CT-NCI-NI (NCI-Net Income)**
  Post noncontrolling interest (NCI).

- **S-CT-PL-AVG (P&L items- average rate)**
  Post to P&L items at average rates.

By assigning these to FS items, the FS item now automatically posts based on the attribute selected. Figure 5.25 shows you the selected attribute value, which is **S-CT-ANI-PL (Net Income/Loss)** in this example. Click the **Save** button when you're finished. In this example, we've assigned the currency translation attribute **S-CT-ANI-PL** to FS item **79900D**.

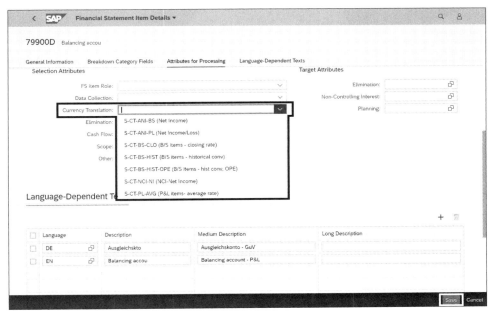

Figure 5.24 Attribute Selection

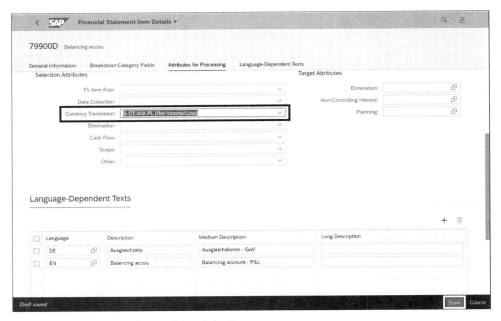

Figure 5.25 Processing the Attribute Selection

You can now go to the Define FS Items app and review the values assigned to the FS item. Figure 5.26 shows you the screen displaying the currency translation attribute assigned to your FS item.

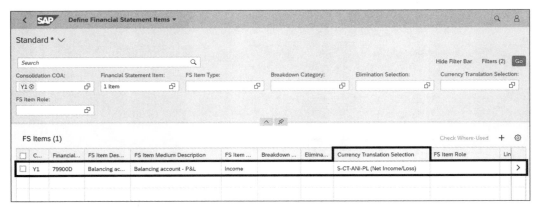

Figure 5.26 Attribute Assigned to FS Item

5.3   Translating Reported Currency

In this section, we'll look at the execution process of currency translation. Before executing the currency translation, let's review the activities that are prerequisites for currency translation in SAP S/4HANA Finance for group reporting that we've discussed so far in this chapter:

- Maintaining the exchange rates
- Assigning a currency translation method to the consolidation unit
- Assigning a currency translation attribute to the FS item

We'll walk through the execution process in the Data Monitor in this section and discuss how to validate the execution and report your results.

5.3.1   Execution in the Data Monitor

Now it's time to execute the currency translation task in the Data Monitor. The task can be easily executed using the Data Monitor app in SAP Fiori as well as in SAP GUI by executing Transaction CXCD. The currency translation method is configured while setting up the Data Monitor (see Chapter 4).

Figure 5.27 shows you the details of running the task by clicking the **Update** button in the **CurrTrans.** column.

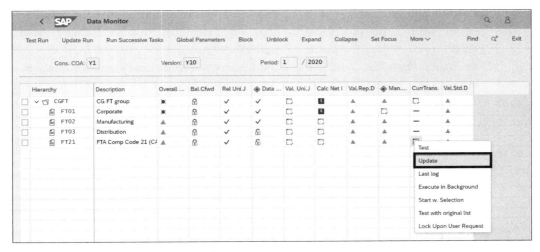

Figure 5.27 Execution in the Data Monitor

5.3.2   Validating the Execution

Figure 5.28 shows you the validation of the currency translation task that you just executed via the SAP Fiori Task Logs app. This app can be searched for in the SAP Fiori app directory. The highlighted columns in Figure 5.28 shows you the values in local currency (**LC Amount**) and translated group currency (**GC Amount**).

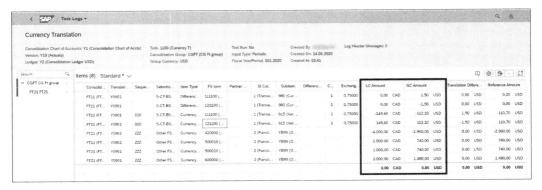

Figure 5.28 Validation of Currency Translation

5.3.3   Reporting

Now that you've run the currency translation task and validated the results, let's look at various apps that SAP delivers to analyze the results:

- **Currency Translation Difference Analysis – Accessible**
  As we discussed in the earlier sections, while performing the consolidations, if you have subsidiaries on a holding company in a foreign company, you'll perform

currency conversion to convert the local currency of the subsidiary to the group currency. During this process, you encounter differences for all the balance sheet accounts caused by the currency conversion as you work with different types of exchange rates. Figure 5.29 shows the Currency Translation Difference Analysis – Accessible app, which provides a multidimensional view of the value differences for all the balance sheet accounts.

> **Note**
>
> The Currency Translation Difference Analysis – Accessible app should be run before the Currency Translation Difference Analysis app, which we'll discuss later in this section and provides multidimensional view of data.

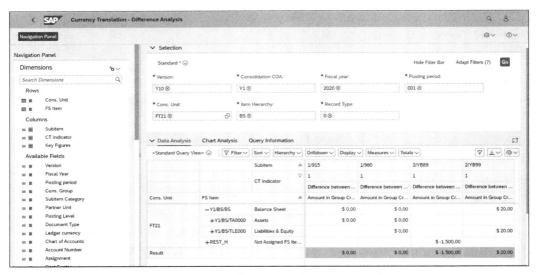

Figure 5.29 Currency Translation Difference Analysis – Accessible App

This app also provides the currency translation difference analysis in the form of a chart. Figure 5.30 shows the difference analysis in a chart form within the **Chart Analysis** tab. This app also gives you the backend query details in the **Query Information** option, which is shown in Figure 5.31.

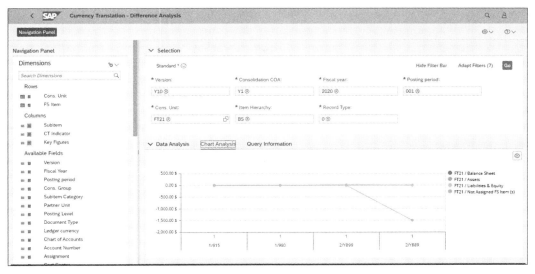

Figure 5.30 Currency Translation Chart Analysis

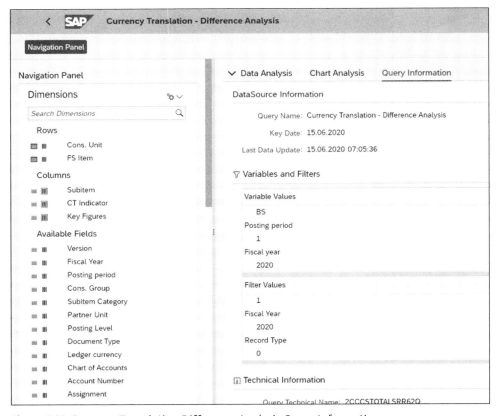

Figure 5.31 Currency Translation Difference Analysis Query Information

- **Currency Translation Difference Analysis**

  This app displays currency translation difference amounts of all the balance sheet accounts, as shown in Figure 5.32. The difference is determined by comparing translated group currency values between values calculated using the reference rate and based on the fiscal year, posting period, and consolidation group that you select. The calculation logic is indicated by **CT Indicator** (currency translation key) **1**.

> **Note**
>
> Currency Translation Difference Analysis is the successor of the Currency Translation Difference Analysis – Accessible app. This app provides you the two-dimensional view of data so that businesses can quickly check the currency translation differences by subitems.

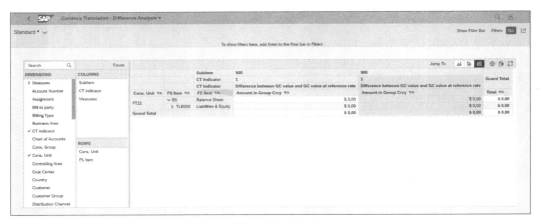

Figure 5.32 Currency Translation Difference Analysis

- **Currency Translation Reserve Analysis – Accessible**

  This app enables you to view value differences for all balance sheet items, such as assets, liabilities, and equity accounts, which are caused due to exchange rates raised due to currency translation. This gives you a view of all consolidation units of a consolidation group.

> **Note**
>
> The Currency Translation Reserve Analysis – Accessible app should be executed before the Currency Translation Reserve Analysis app. It provides a multidimensional view of reserves.

Figure 5.33 gives you the view of all balance sheet items of all consolidation units of consolidation groups.

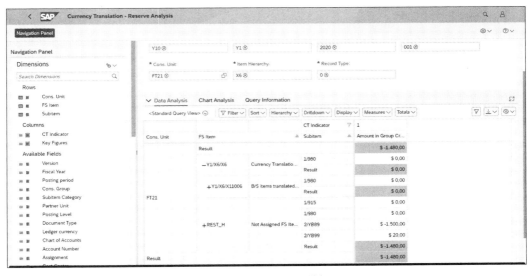

Figure 5.33 Currency Translation Reserve Analysis – Accessible

This app also enables you to look at the currency translation reserve analysis in the form of a chart. Figure 5.34 shows you the chart in the **Chart Analysis** tab with which you can do the reserve analysis. In this app, you can also look at the backend **Query Information**, which can be seen in Figure 5.35.

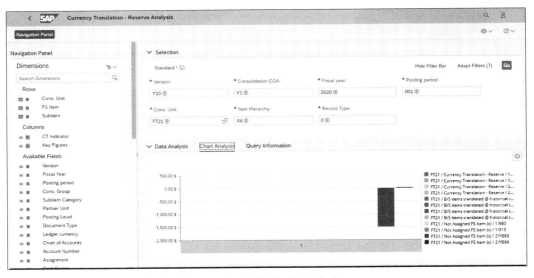

Figure 5.34 Currency Translation Reserve Analysis Chart Analysis

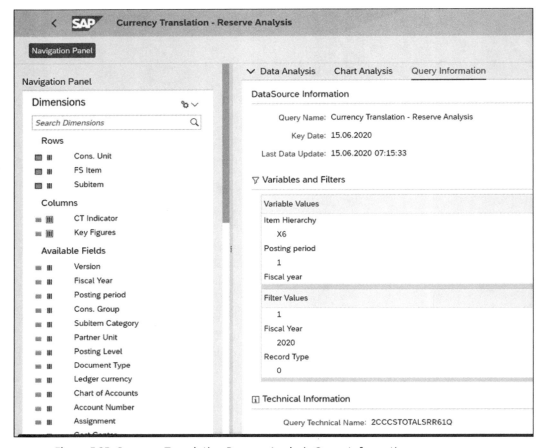

Figure 5.35 Currency Translation Reserve Analysis Query Information

- **Currency Translation Reserve Analysis**
  This app gives you the ability to look at reserves and do analysis per each different dimensionality. Figure 5.36 shows you the details of this app with which you can understand the reserves and perform analysis based on subitems (mainly transaction types).

Note

The Currency Translation Reserve Analysis app is the successor of the Currency Translation Reserve Analysis – Accessible app, which provides the two-dimensional view of data so businesses can quickly check the currency translation reserves by subitems.

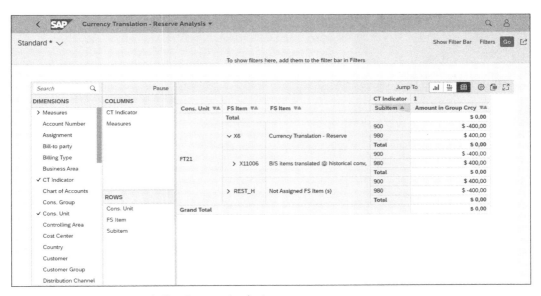

Figure 5.36 Currency Translation Reserve Analysis

5.4   Summary

In this chapter, we reviewed the currency translation process concepts, configuration, execution, and reporting in SAP S/4HANA Finance for group reporting. After an overview of currency translation, you now understand why organizations need currency translation and how to set up group reporting for the currency translation, including a detailed look at the configuration.

We also covered the importance of currency translation adjustments. SAP S/4HANA Finance for group reporting allows for seamless currency translation and provides an integrated process in the Data Monitor, which serves as a centralized location to run all the data collection tasks and gives you more flexibility to run the task as well as keep track of the overall data collection process. We've looked into currency translation methods and their assignments to consolidation units, assigning currency translation attributes to the FS items updating the translation ratios, and maintaining exchange rates manually as well as automatically.

Finally, you executed the task in the Data Monitor and reported results using various apps that are predelivered by SAP S/4HANA Finance for group reporting.

In the next chapter, we'll move on to configuring and performing intercompany eliminations with SAP S/4HANA Finance for group reporting.

Chapter 6
Intercompany Elimination

In this chapter, we'll discuss one of the most vital aspects of consolidations: intercompany eliminations. You'll learn about what an intercompany elimination is and how it will help you consolidate various entities at the group level, as well as the advanced features of SAP S/4HANA Finance for group reporting to perform intercompany eliminations.

Intercompany elimination is a key step in the consolidation process that helps in the creation of consolidated financials, which represent an organization's assets, liabilities, equity, revenue, and expenses. Intercompany elimination helps organizations report financial statements accurately by not inflating the balance sheet and profit and loss (P&L) due to transactions within the consolidation units of a consolidated group. In simple terms, the consolidated financials would only contain the transactions with third parties but not among the consolidation units of a group. Table 6.1 shows the high-level process flow; in this chapter, we're discussing the third step where you perform consolidations and prepare financial statements that will be audited as well as reported both internally and externally.

Some of the most common types of interunit transactions are as follows:

- **Interunit revenue and expenses**
  Elimination of sales and corresponding cost of goods sold (COGS) between consolidation units of a consolidation group.

- **Interunit loans and borrowings**
  Loans, deposits, and their corresponding payables between consolidation units of a consolidation group and their resulting expenses and revenues.

- **Interunit dividends**
  Elimination of dividends paid and received between consolidation units.

Prerequisites for Consolidations	Preparing for Consolidations	Performing Consolidations
■ Setting up the system by defining global parameters ■ Setting up master data ■ Data validations	■ Carry forward balances ■ Currency conversions ■ Data validations	■ Performing intercompany eliminations ■ Consolidation of investments ■ Manual journal entries

Table 6.1 Consolidation Process Flow

215

In this chapter, we'll explain intercompany elimination concepts, walk through the Consolidation Monitor and how to set it up, discuss how to configure intercompany elimination, and finally execute intercompany eliminations in the Consolidation Monitor.

6.1   What Is Intercompany Elimination?

Consolidated financial results of an organization must be presented as if the group of legal entities is a single unit. The impact caused by transactions on the reported financials of legal entities within the scope of consolidation must be completely or partially eliminated from the consolidated results, depending on whether the related entity is in the scope of consolidation requirements. However, the transactions with unrelated entities don't require an elimination.

The intercompany transactions are recorded by both the parties that are involved in the transaction. Together with the other company, they are recorded as trading partners on their books, and this data is reported as is at the group level. If the data from both entities involved in the transaction is made proportional at 100%, then the full amount must be eliminated; if the data is made proportional by any of the entities to less than 100%, then you only eliminate the amount that's controlled in common.

In this section, we'll discuss the importance of intercompany elimination from an organization standpoint. The accounting and finance departments of any organization connect all other departments of an organization, and one of the main reasons is that key members of each department will eventually look at the accounting and financial aspects of their respective departments. An organization has two types of reporting requirements: financial reporting and management reporting. Consolidation of entities at the group level is essential for financial reporting for various requirements of an organization such as statutory reporting, regulatory requirements, and corporate governance, which mainly is used to disclose financial information to various stakeholders about the financial performance of an organization.

6.1.1   Reporting and Financial Statements

The International Accounting Standard Board (IASB) has defined the objective of financial reporting as "to provide information about the financial position, performance, and changes in financial position of an enterprise that is useful to a wide range of users in making economic decisions." The financial reporting department in an organization is important as it does the following:

- Provides key information to leadership that will help in financial planning and analysis
- Provides information to investors, promoters, debt providers, and creditors to help them make rational and prudent decisions regarding investments, credits, and so on

- Provides information to shareholders if the organization is listed
- Represents changes in resources based on macro- and micro economic factors, for example, assets, liabilities, and owner's equity
- Represents the ethical aspects, fiduciary duties and responsibilities, and facilitates audits

To keep track of their responsibilities, the financial reporting division of an organization owns one of the most critical documents—financial statements—which play a crucial role in making strategic decisions. These statements are used by various stakeholders of the organizations and as part of audits. For companies that are publicly traded, these statements are used in filing their financial accounting activity with the US Securities and Exchange Commission (SEC). The following is an overview of these statements:

- **Form 10-K**
  Provides a detailed overview of the financial activities of an organization over the past year. This is audited by external auditors and is filed within 60 days of year end for larger organizations and 90 days of year end for smaller organizations.

- **Form 10-Q**
  Provides a detailed overview of the financial activities of an organization on a quarterly basis. This is filed within 40 days of year end for larger organizations and 45 days of year end for smaller organizations.

Both these forms include details of four key financial statements and footnotes of management reporting.

After you perform consolidations, validate results, and post adjustment entries, you validate financials, which are the end products of consolidations. A key point to remember is that intercompany transactions are eliminated, and you'll only consider transactions with third parties. Next, we'll discuss the financial statements that are a result of intercompany eliminations.

The *balance sheet* is one of the most important financial statements of an organization as it gives an overview of an organization's financial position. A balance sheet in its simplest description details what you own (assets) and what you owe (liabilities). After performing consolidations, you get to see the consolidated balance sheet, which is generally used in an organization with multiple subsidiaries and ownership calculations between these consolidation units. The parent organization performs consolidation of all these entities and derives a consolidated view of the balance sheet for corporate managers. The rule of thumb for balance sheet is *Assets = Liabilities + Equity*. In the following, we'll break it down into simple terms.

There are two ways to classify assets, and each of them has a corresponding claim that will help you derive the preceding equation:

- **Raising capital through shareholders**
  The shareholders' claim on these assets is also known as owners' *equity*.

- **Raising capital through lenders (banks, creditors, etc.)**
  The debts raised due to borrowing from lenders is known as *liabilities*.

This breakdown of assets, liabilities, and equity shows how the accounting equation is derived and how the balance sheet is viewed.

The *income statement* is also one of the crucial financial statements for an organization. With the help of this statement, you can determine the net income of the organization for a given time period. Net income is derived based on revenue and expenses, which are the components of an income statement. Revenue is also known as sales, and expenses are also known as cost of goods sold (COGS). Expenses are recorded after the revenue in the income statement. The main objective of an income statement is to derive the net income, which we've simplified as a two-step process:

1. Derive gross profit:
   Gross profit = Revenue – Expense

2. Derive net profit:
   Net profit = Gross profit – Other expenses (income tax, etc.)

The *statement of equity* gives the management of an organization a view of changes in the equity of the organization's business for a given time period. Various types of equity are recorded with the opening balances, equity transactions (e.g., shares issued, dividends, etc.) during that period, and ending balance. This is generally prepared after preparing the income statement. This statement mainly contains the following details:

- **Contributed/share capital**
  Contributed capital (share capital) refers to amounts received by the reporting company from transactions with shareholders. Companies can generally issue either common shares or preferred shares. Common shares represent residual ownership in a company, and, in the event of liquidation or dividend payments, common shares can only receive payments after preferred shareholders have been paid first.

  The reporting consolidation unit records the transactions with the shareholders. This capital is further divided into two: common stock and preferred stock. Common stock is announced as part of a public offering and entitle the shareholders to dividends; however, dividends are paid based on the performance of the company. Preferred stock is similar, but it entitles the holder to fixed dividends and generally has priority over the common stock dividends.

- **Retained earnings**
  This section of equity refers to the profits generated by the organization that isn't distributed to shareholders. However, these profits are consumed by the organization so that they can be used for investments (purchase of fixed assets, working capital, etc.) into their businesses.

- **Dividends**

  Payments are paid to the shareholders solely at the discretion of an organization.

The *statement of cash flow* gives management the ability to view the changes to the organization's cash balance for a given period. This statement provides the details on the cash inflows and outflows from various activities, such as operations, investments, and so on.

In SAP S/4HANA Finance for group reporting, the intercompany elimination process starts after you collect the reported financial data by individual consolidation units and standardize the data by various tasks like currency conversion, net income calculation and so on. One of the interesting features of group reporting is that you can review the intercompany elimination process by checking out-of-the-box reconciliation reports, data analysis reports, and other reports as you perform the reclassification process. Last but not the least, you need to verify the master data of the consolidation units and financial statement (FS) items.

SAP S/4HANA Finance for group reporting uses the reclassification methods for intercompany eliminations. It's a best practice to review intercompany differences before you run the reclassification methods to perform intercompany eliminations.

6.1.2   Sales and COGS Elimination

One of the most common intercompany transactions is one consolidation unit selling some goods to another consolidation unit. When this happens, you need to eliminate that sale and the corresponding COGS.

Let's assume FT01 purchases goods from FT02. This becomes an intercompany transaction; when financial statements of consolidation units are consolidated, such sales become transfer of goods within a consolidated group, and these intercompany sales must be eliminated to avoid double counting. Most importantly, no profit can be realized on an intercompany sale until the profit is realized by a sale to an outside party.

Generally, when there is an intercompany sale, it also involves accounts receivable (AR) and accounts payable (AP) because mostly the sale will be on credit, which is considered internal debt and must be eliminated as well. Table 6.2 shows how the elimination happens.

Company	Account	Amount
FT02	Sales	($1,000)
FT02	AR	$1,000
FT01	COGS	$1,000
FT01	AP	($1,000)

Table 6.2 Sample Sale and COGS Elimination

In many cases, the seller consolidation unit will record the sale, but the buyer consolidation unit either records partial COGS or, in some cases, doesn't record an offset at all. It's in these scenarios that you would want to perform *one-sided elimination* based on sale values. You'll see how SAP S/4HANA Finance for group reporting helps you perform one-sided elimination in upcoming sections.

6.1.3   Inventory Elimination

Inventory refers to the goods that are available to sell or to the available raw materials to manufacture or produce finished goods that are then sold. Income is generated by the sale of goods, so inventory is one of the key aspects of any organization. Inventory is classified as a current asset of an organization's balance sheet; corresponding COGS is recorded on the income statement. On the other hand, holding inventory for any organization might add up to additional costs such as storage and so on. Basically, inventory is classified into raw materials, work-in-progress materials, and finished goods. Many consolidation units hold inventory and sell to other consolidation units in a consolidation group; therefore, eliminating the intercompany transactions is commonly done in organizations. Let's discuss an example and then cover the configuration in SAP S/4HANA for group reporting in later sections.

In this example, manufacturing entity FTO2 purchases inventory and sells it to distribution segment FTO1, which in turn sells the goods to a third party. This is the only transaction that's recorded at the consolidated group level. However, the transactions between FTO2 and FTO1 need to be eliminated at the consolidated group level.

While preparing consolidated income statements, the elimination process of intercompany inventory transactions involves the complete elimination of all revenue and expenses recorded by consolidation units, and any profits and losses are deferred until the inventory is sold to a third party. On the other hand, while preparing consolidated balance sheets, only the historical cost associated to the inventory is eliminated. If the inventory is still on hand, then the cost associated with inventory is charged in the period when the sale is made to a third party.

Let's analyze how the transactions are recorded in each entity's books and how they are eliminated. In Table 6.3, FTO2 has recorded inventory of $10,000, sale to FTO1, and cost of the inventory. Correspondingly, FTO2 records inventory purchase and cost of goods after the sale happens to the third party.

FTO2	FTO1
Purchases an inventory of $10,000	Buys inventory from FTO2 for $15,000
Sells the inventory to distribution segment FTO1 for $15,000	Sells the inventory to a third party for $20,000

Table 6.3 Inventory Sale Example

While preparing consolidated statements, profits are recorded. An intercompany inventory sale is only recognized when the sale happens to a third party outside the consolidation group. Sales recorded in FTO2's books and COGS recorded in FTO1 are eliminated. Table 6.4 shows how inventory is recorded throughout the process until a profit is realized.

FTO2 Financials		FTO1 Financials	
Inventory	$10,000	Inventory	$15,000
Cash	($10,000)	Cash	($15,000)
Cash	$15,000	Cash	$20,000
Sale to intercompany	($15,000)	Sale to third party	($20,000)
COGS	$10,000	COGS	$15,000
Inventory	($10,000)	Inventory	($15,000)

Table 6.4 Inventory Flow between Consolidation Units

If inventory is held for more than one period before the sale happens with the third party, then you need to consider dividends from intercompany, income from subsidiary, retained earnings, and appropriate adjustments. This allows you to prepare consolidated financial statements in the period of the intercompany sale as well as in the periods when the inventory is held till the inventory is sold to a nonaffiliate and profit is recorded.

6.1.4   Expense Elimination

When a consolidation unit purchases goods or manufactures goods, the associated costs are capitalized as inventory, and these costs are treated as expenses when a profit is realized with the sale of these goods. Expenses include purchase cost, storage cost, material cost, labor cost, and other overhead costs. These expenses should be matched with the revenue by recording the expenses in the time period when these expenses are used to generate revenue. Together the revenue and expenses are aggregated to derive gross profit, which is the profit before deducting overhead, payroll, tax, and other expenses, such as interest payments. You derive net income by removing the operating expenses and taxes from the gross profit. Expenses are divided into two types:

- **Operating expenses**
  These are the day-to-day expenses required to run a business, for example, administrative costs, sales costs, and so on.

- **Nonoperating expenses**
  These are expenses related to capital expenditure such as developing existing production plant equipment, acquiring a long-term asset, and so on.

Following are some common expenses that an organization incurs and how they are eliminated:

- **Rent/lease expenses**
  When FTO2 and FTO1 consolidation units record the lease income/expenses as operating lease, then FTO2 (let's assume is a lessee) will record lease payments as intercompany rent expenses, whereas FTO1 records lease payments received as intercompany revenue. This intercompany transaction is eliminated by offsetting intercompany rent expenses with intercompany revenue from rent.

- **Service expenses**
  There will be situations when one consolidation unit will render services to another consolidation unit. For example, FTO2 needs a technician who can service some production equipment and requests a technician from FTO1. In this case, FTO1 charges an intercompany management fee to FTO2, and FTO2 records intercompany service expenses on its books.

- **Income tax expenses**
  As intercompany revenue and expenses are eliminated, there is no effect of income tax. However, both FTO1 and FTO2 can file their taxes separately or at the consolidation group.

- **Depreciation expenses**
  Depreciation is a process in which expenses related to an asset are distributed to its entire useful life. The depreciation expense account that appears on the income statement is debited, and the accumulated depreciation account on the balance sheet is credited, which will go on until the accumulated depreciation is equal to the original cost of the asset. Let's consider a scenario where FTO1 sells equipment to FTO2. In this case, you need to eliminate the gain on sale and accumulated depreciation from FTO1 with depreciation expenses and equipment from FTO2.

6.2   What Is the Consolidation Monitor?

The Consolidation Monitor is a layout that lists consolidation groups, subgroups, and various consolidation-related tasks that you would perform on them. This layout also provides you the ability to update the global parameters, if required. The purpose of the Consolidation Monitor is to perform intercompany eliminations and post data at the consolidated group level. All the tasks are predefined and ready to use, but you can also have customized tasks. Each task must be configured and sequenced in the order of execution in the process. You'll open the period and execute the tasks on the consolidation groups. After the task is successfully executed, you need to block the task and move to the next task.

The Consolidation Monitor can be accessed using both the SAP GUI by executing Transaction CX20 and by accessing the SAP Fiori Consolidation Monitor app. In the following sections, we'll explore the layout and the various tasks that are available.

6.2.1   Layout

You'll perform all the consolidation-related tasks in the Consolidation Monitor, which is similar to the Data Monitor (discussed in Chapter 4). The Consolidation Monitor gives you a view of a consolidation group and all the tasks that you'll be performing on this group to consolidate the consolidation units within the group. Figure 6.1 shows the layout of the Consolidation Monitor, and the following lists describes a few more options you can use in the Consolidation Monitor:

- **Test**
  Allows you to simulate the task.

- **Update Run**
  Allows you to change the task status and generates documents.

- **Run successive tasks**
  Allows you to run multiple tasks at the same time.

- **Run successive tasks w/o stop**
  Allows you to run multiple tasks at the same time but doesn't stop at milestone tasks.

- **Data Monitor**
  Allows you to go to the Data Monitor if you need to check any process.

- **Save user layout**
  Allows you to save the layout and retain it when you log off and log back in.

Hierarchy		Description	Status	Error	Warnings	Date	Time	Last cha...	
⌄ ⛶ CGFT		Corporate Group	●	0	0	09/09/2020	13:35:07	FIORI_FTA	
	⚙ 2011	IC Elim. Sales	▲	0	0	09/09/2020	13:35:07	FIORI_FTA	
	⚙ 2021	IC Elim. Other Income/Expense	▲	0	0	09/09/2020	13:35:07	FIORI_FTA	
	⚙ 2031	Dividends Elimination	▲	0	0	09/09/2020	13:35:07	FIORI_FTA	
	⚙ 2041	IC Elim. Balance Sheet	▲	0	0	09/09/2020	13:35:07	FIORI_FTA	
	◆ 2050	Manual Eliminations (PL20)	✖	0	0				
	⚙ 2060	Preparation Cons Group Change	▲	0	0	09/09/2020	13:35:07	FIORI_FTA	
	⚙ 2141	Calculate Group Shares (PL 30)	▲	0	0	09/09/2020	13:35:07	FIORI_FTA	
	◆ 2140	Enter Group Shares (PL30)	▲	0	0	09/09/2020	13:35:07	FIORI_FTA	
	⚙ 2100	Investments / Equity elimin.	▲	0	0	09/09/2020	13:35:07	FIORI_FTA	
	◆ 2150	Manual Eliminations (PL30)	✖	0	0				
	⚙ 2180	Total Divestiture	▲	0	0	09/09/2020	13:35:07	FIORI_FTA	
	⚙ 2980	Consolidated Data Validation	▲	0	0	09/09/2020	13:35:07	FIORI_FTA	

Figure 6.1 Consolidation Monitor Layout

Table 6.5 shows and describes the various icons that you'll encounter while performing consolidations. It's essential for you to have a thorough understanding of the layout to navigate easily. The Consolidation Monitor also shows you a time stamp along with the ID of the person who has run each consolidation task.

Icon	Description
	Consolidation group
	Consolidation tasks
	Milestone task
	Errors in overall status of consolidations
	Open consolidations
	Successful completion of consolidations
	Initial stage of the consolidation process (default status when performing consolidations for a period for the first time)
	Incomplete Data Monitor
	Task has errors
	Task is incomplete
	Preceding task is pending
	Task is error free
	Task is blocked
	Task is unblocked
	Task is blocked on request
	Task is unblocked on request
	Task isn't required/is irrelevant
	Task is in initial stage
Green bar	Consolidation process completed successfully

Table 6.5 Understanding Icons in the Consolidation Monitor

6.2.2   Tasks

Like the Data Monitor, the Consolidation Monitor consists of several tasks, as shown previously in Figure 6.1. Let's walk through them:

- **IC Elim. Sales**
  This task enables you to eliminate interunit sales in a consolidation group.

- **IC Elim. Other Income/Expense**
  This task enables you to eliminate other income and expenses in a P&L statement.

- **Dividends Elimination**

  This task enables you to eliminate the dividends received from a consolidation unit that belongs to the same consolidated group.

- **IC Elim. Balance Sheet**

  This task enables you to eliminate intercompany transactions that are recorded on a balance sheet.

- **Manual Eliminations (PL20)**

  This task enables you to perform intercompany eliminations on data that has been posted manually; posting level 20 specifies the intercompany elimination.

- **Preparation Cons Group Change**

  This task enables you to adjust the data when a new consolidation unit is acquired or divested from a consolidation group during the fiscal year. This allows the data during the time period when the consolidation unit is part of the consolidation group to be populated in group financial statements.

- **Enter Group Shares (PL30)**

  This task enables you to post the group share values that can be used during consolidation of investments.

- **Investments / Equity elimin.**

  This task gives you the ability to perform elimination of investments made by a consolidation unit in another consolidation unit of the same consolidation group and equity. This would essentially include equity items such as noncontrolling interest (NCI) and dividends.

- **Manual Eliminations (PL30)**

  This task enables you to perform consolidation of investments on the data that has been posted manually.

- **Total Divestiture**

  This task enables you to adjust consolidated financial data when a consolidation unit is divested from a consolidation group during the year. After this data is adjusted, the financial statements contain only the data that arose during the time the consolidation unit was part of the consolidation group.

- **Consolidated Data Validation**

  This task gives you the ability to perform validation checks on the consolidated data; you'll generally perform this last to make sure that your consolidated data is successfully validated.

- **Integration of Transaction Data into Cons Group**

  This task gives you the ability to read the data, apply the reporting logic, and post the results to the consolidation groups. However, this task is only applicable if the client has initially implemented group reporting with a release earlier than 1909 and has activated the new reporting logic.

Table 6.6 lists these predefined consolidation tasks. As we discussed earlier, these tasks are predefined and ready to use.

Task ID	Description	Posting Level	Reclassification Method	Document Type
2011	IC Elim. Sales	20	S2010	2E
2021	IC Elim. Other Income/Expense	20	S2020	2F
2031	Dividends Elimination	20	S2030	2H
2041	IC Elim. Balance Sheet	20	S2040	2G
2050	Manual Eliminations (PL20)	-	-	21,22
2060	Preparation Cons Group Change	-	-	2Z
2140	Enter Group Shares (PL30)	-	-	39
2100	Investments / Equity elimin.	30	S2100	3A
2150	Manual Eliminations (PL30)	-	-	32, 31
2180	Total Divestiture	30	S2180	3Z
2900	Integration of Transaction Data into Cons Group	-	-	-
2980	Consolidated Data Validation	-	-	-

Table 6.6 Consolidation Tasks

We'll discuss these consolidation tasks and their corresponding methods and document types further in Section 6.3.

The following document types and posting levels are used for these tasks:

- Document types 2E, 2F, 2G, 2H, and 2Z are all related to interunit eliminations and have a posting level of 20; the currency used in posting is group currency. Posting level 20 is used to reclassify the data of intercompany eliminations.

- Document types 3A and 3Z are related to consolidation of investments with a posting level of 30 and the currency used in posting is group currency. Posting level 30 is used to reclassify the data of investment consolidations.

- Document types 21 and 22 are related to manual eliminations that are posted for correction of interunit payables and receivables. They use posting level 20, and the currency used in posting is group currency.

- Document types 31 and 32 are related to manual consolidation adjustments 30, and the currency used in posting is group currency.

- Document type 39 is used in posting group shares, and the posting level is 30. Quantity is used in posting.

We'll discuss the assigned reclassification methods in the next section.

6.3   Configuring the Consolidation Monitor

In this section, you'll learn how to configure the Consolidation Monitor as we discuss all the predefined methods, assigning the methods to tasks, assigning the tasks to task groups, and preparing for consolidation group changes.

6.3.1   Reclassification Methods

A *reclassification method* uses triggers to reclassify data from source to destination accounts/FS items. Here you specify which FS item values are to be reclassified. Each reclassification method must define the trigger, source, and destination values.

Figure 6.2 gives a view of predelivered reclassification methods that you can use to perform your intercompany eliminations. To access predefined task groups, execute Transaction CXE9N, open **Reclassification**, and select the **Define Reclassification Method** option.

Consider the predefined method **S2010** to understand the various components that are required to set up a method, how the method is used in interunit eliminations, and how it's integrated to the tasks in the Consolidation Monitor.

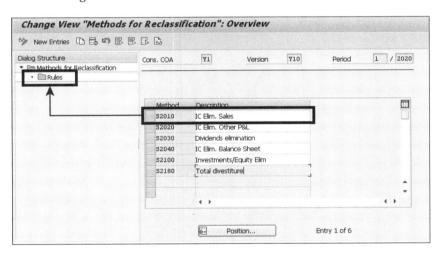

Figure 6.2 Predefined Reclassification Methods

For a method, you need to define rules. After you select the **S2010** method, you can navigate to the **Rules** folder in the **Dialog Structure**. Figure 6.3 shows a view of rule details that you need to set up to use a reclassification method.

Let's define the settings by starting with the **Periodic Activities** and **Document Settings** sections, which contains the following fields:

- **Periodic reclassification**
  This option enables you to reclassify the value of periods that are in the current range of the consolidation frequency but not the entire item value.

- **Cons Frequency**

  This option enables you to select your consolidation frequency; sample values include **Monthly**, **Quarterly**, and so on.

- **Cumul. document**

  This option enables you to generate cumulative documents rather than one document for each triggering item.

- **Post to partner uni**

  This option indicates how the elimination entries will be posted. You can post the elimination entry to the triggering consolidation unit, you can post the source or destination items to the partner unit (refer to master data section for FS item attribute value details), post an elimination entry completely to the partner unit, and post the elimination entry to any consolidation unit.

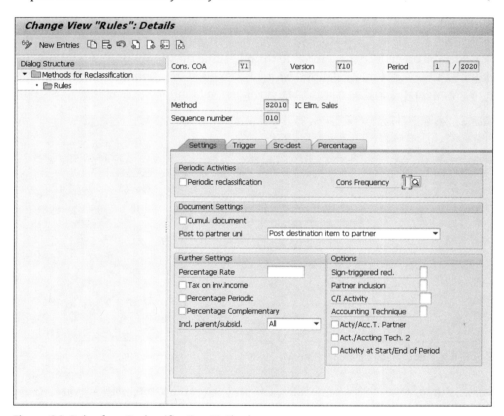

Figure 6.3 Rules for a Reclassification Method

Next, the **Further Settings** section contains the following fields:

- **Percentage Rate**

  This option enables you to input a rate at which you want the values to be reclassified.

- **Tax on inv.income**
  This option enables you to select the tax rate for the investment income of the triggering consolidation unit instead of some fixed rates.

- **Percentage Periodic**
  This option enables you to run reclassification on values of the periods within the current range of consolidation frequency.

- **Percentage Complementary**
  This option enables you to use the reclassification at a hundredth percentage rather than a percentage determined from master or transaction data.

- **Incl. parent/subsid.**
  This option enables you to include all consolidation units, only parent units, or only subsidiary units.

Finally, the following fields are available within the **Options** section:

- **Sign-triggered recl.**
  This option gives you the ability to select the debit/credit signage for the balances during the reclassification process.

- **Partner inclusion**
  This option enables you to select partners at posting level 30. Blank indicates all the partners are selected, **1** indicates that only partners in the group are selected, and **2** indicates that partners outside the group are selected.

- **C/I Activity**
  This option enables you to set consolidation of investment activity that can impact the reclassification.

- **Accounting Technique**
  This option enables you to set the accounting technique for reclassification by specifying whether the method is purchase or equity.

- **Acty/Acc.T. Partner**
  Using this checkbox enables you to use the accounting technique of the partner unit.

- **Act./Accting Tech. 2**
  Using this checkbox enables you to use the accounting technique of both the consolidation unit and partner unit.

- **Activity at Start/End of Period**
  Using this checkbox enables you to check the divestiture accounting at the beginning of the period and first consolidation at the end of the period of a reclassification method.

Now let's discuss the other parameters of a method. The additional tabs, as listed here, contain the following configuration fields:

- **Trigger**

  Here a triggering selection is entered (see Figure 6.4) that triggers the reclassification from the source account assignment to the destination account assignment; the debit/credit sign of the value of the triggering selection determines whether reclassification occurs. We'll discuss how to configure the trigger later in this section.

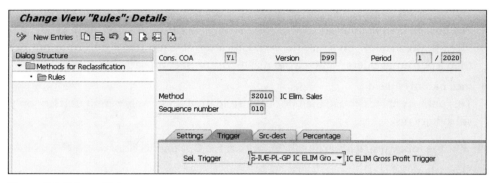

Figure 6.4 Trigger Tab

- **Src-dest**

  Using **Target Attr. for Src** and **Target Attr. for Dest**, you can use the target attributes of FS items, which you define in FS item master data (see Figure 6.5). You generally use this if you don't want to specify the **Source Item Role/Dest. Item Role**. It's also easy to use as you only have one target attribute for elimination, NCI, and planning.

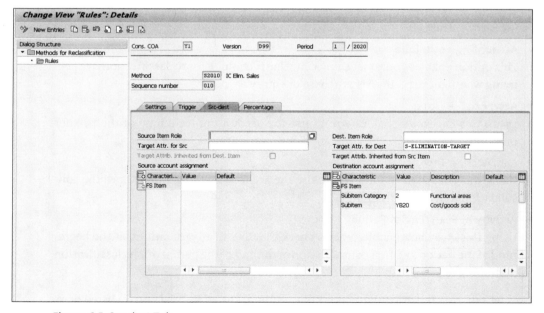

Figure 6.5 Src-dest Tab

If **Target Attrib. Inherited from Src Item** is checked, then the system inherits the target from the source item. Otherwise, it's inherited from the trigger item. Source **FS item** is the source for the reclassification, and destination **FS Item** is the target to which the value is posted as a result of reclassification. You can enter the source and destination FS items or leave one or both blank. If they are left blank, the triggering item is used as both source and destination. Both source and destination FS items are mandatory if the reclassification is triggered by the debit/credit sign, which you generally use in one-sided eliminations.

- **Percentage**
  When specified in the tab shown in Figure 6.6, the system selects the transaction data for determining the percentage for the reclassification method. If you're selecting this, you need to make sure that the reclassification of investment income tax indicator (**Tax on inv.income** field) on the **Settings** tab is blank.

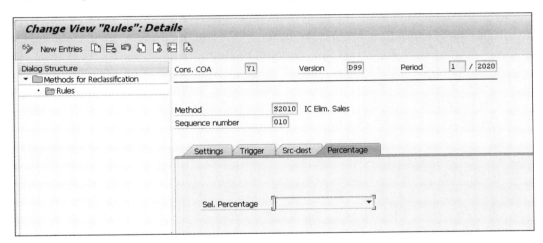

Figure 6.6 Percentage Tab

The trigger is configured in the SAP Fiori Define Selections app, as shown in Figure 6.7. Let's see the trigger that method S2010 uses, which is **S-IUE-PL-GP** (shown on the left-hand side). After you select that trigger, details are displayed where you can check the conditions in the **Selection Expression** pane. Here you specify values and attributes of master data that you want to consider for this trigger.

For example, in Figure 6.7, you can see that **SubItemCategory** is defined as **2**, so only those subitems are considered. **Show Value List** contains all the master data and its attributes as selected in the **Selection Expression** pane. The trigger is applied only on the data that is on the intersection of the master data that's defined in the trigger; in other words, you're explicitly directing the system to perform consolidation tasks on the transaction data that is against these master data values.

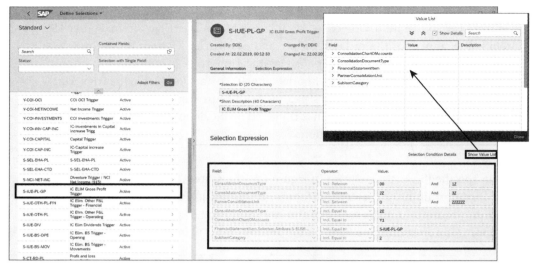

Figure 6.7 Defining a Selection for a Trigger

A trigger can also be assigned to an FS item so that you can apply the selection attributes on these FS items. Go to the Define FS Items app and check which FS items have this selection attribute. Figure 6.8 shows the FS item **411100** has the **Elimination Selection** attribute as **S-IUE-PL-GP**.

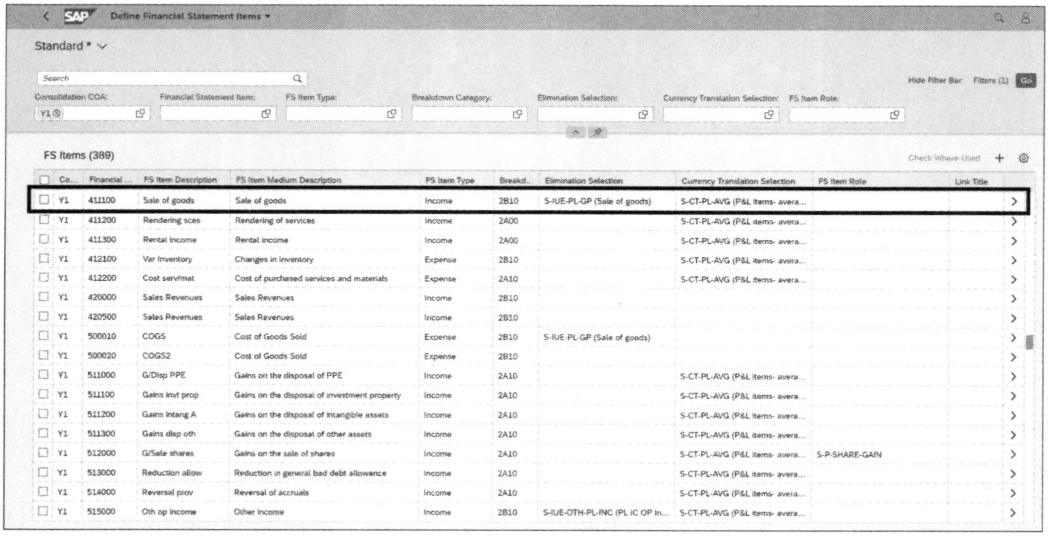

Figure 6.8 Defining Selection Attributes for an FS Item

When you select that FS item and click **Go** to get into the details, you can see the attributes, as shown in Figure 6.9. Here you can see your trigger under the selection attributes as well as the target attribute, which is **41200D**. This means when you run the task that's assigned to method S2010, the selection trigger will execute and eliminate the value in FS item 411100 and post an offset to the 41200D account.

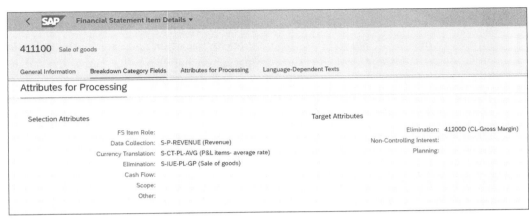

Figure 6.9 Selection Attributes of an FS Item

6.3.2   Tasks and Task Groups

In this section, we'll review the consolidation tasks and their assignments to methods and document types. We'll then assign the tasks to the task group that you want to use and finally assign the consolidation group to the dimension.

As the first step, let's look at the tasks. Figure 6.10 gives you a view of consolidation tasks, which you can access by executing Transaction CXE9N, opening **Reclassification**, and selecting the **Define Reclassification Method** option.

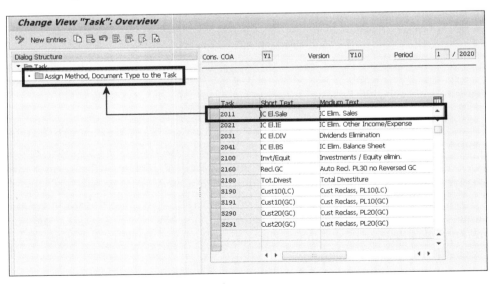

Figure 6.10 Predefined Consolidation Tasks

This screen shows the tasks and their corresponding **Short Text** and **Medium Text**. You can also create a new task by selecting **New Entries**. These are the tasks that would eventually show up in the Consolidation Monitor and enable you to perform intercompany eliminations.

Now you need to assign the task to a method so that when you execute the task, the method executes and generates the elimination entries. Figure 6.11 shows the screen where you do the assignments, which you can navigate to by selecting a task (**IC Elim. Sales**, in this example) and clicking the **Assign Method, Document Type to the Task** folder in the **Dialog Structure**. Here you enter the year (**Start Year**); **Period eff**, which specifies the year and period that you want to use this task; the reclassification **Method** that you want to assign this task to; and finally the **Document Type**.

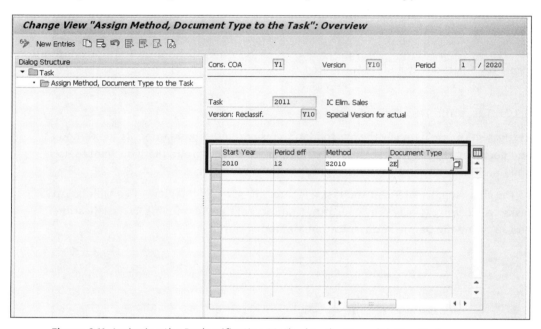

Figure 6.11 Assigning the Reclassification Method to the Consolidation Task

The next step in the process is assigning the tasks that you want to execute to the task group. To do so, go to Transaction CXE9N, expand **Reclassification**, execute **Define Reclassification**, select a task, and click on **Assign Method, Document Type.** After this step, you now need to assign this task to the task group by going to Transaction CXE9N, expanding **Configuration for Consolidation Processing**, and selecting **Define Task Group** to arrive at the screen shown in Figure 6.12. Here you define the task group for the Consolidation Monitor; in this task group, you assign the tasks that you want to be executed in the Consolidation Monitor.

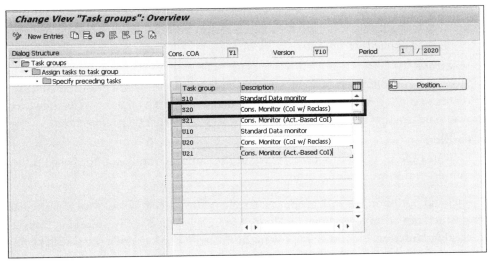

Figure 6.12 Task Groups

Let's look at the **S20** task group from Figure 6.12, which you can select and then choose **Assign tasks to task group** in the **Dialog Structure** to display the available tasks for the assignment (see Figure 6.13). The following are some details of this screen that you need to provide:

- **Task/Short Text**
  Provides the basic details of a task. The preceding example uses SAP-delivered tasks, but you can create custom tasks and assign them to your task group.

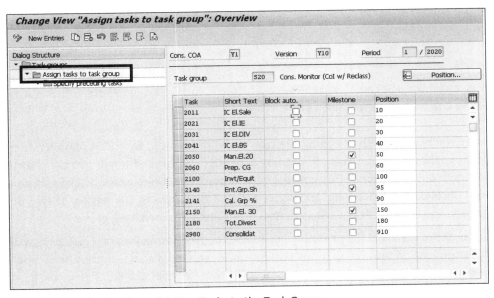

Figure 6.13 Assigning Consolidation Tasks to the Task Group

- **Block auto.**

  Blocks a task automatically after it's successfully executed; however, a task can also be blocked explicitly from the Data Monitor.

- **Milestone**

  Stops the consolidation process, which is very helpful especially during the automated execution of Data Monitor tasks. When you select a task as a milestone task, you're instructing the system to stop the process after that task is executed.

- **Position**

  Indicates the position of a certain task in the Consolidation Monitor based on its numeric value in ascending order.

The second option in the task groups is to specify the preceding tasks for a particular task, which can be done as shown in Figure 6.14 by selecting **Specify preceding tasks** in the **Dialog Structure**. Press the F4 key in the **Preceding task** to open the task list from where you can select the **Preceding task** and arrange your tasks in the task group.

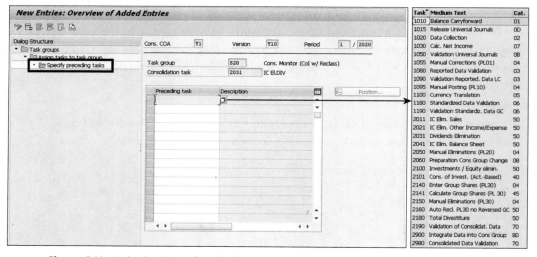

Figure 6.14 Assigning Preceding Tasks

After you're done with assigning the task to the task group, you need to assign that group to the dimension that you're going to use in the consolidation process, as shown in Figure 6.15. To arrive at this screen, go to Transaction CXE9N, expand **Configuration for Consolidation Processing**, and select **Assign Task Group to Dimension**. Then, you need to enter a **Start Year**, **Period eff**, **Period cat.**, and **Cons mon. task group**.

So far, we've reviewed the predefined tasks and their assignment to task groups as well as assigning that task group to the dimension. Next, we'll discuss an important topic: document types to complete the Consolidation Monitor configuration.

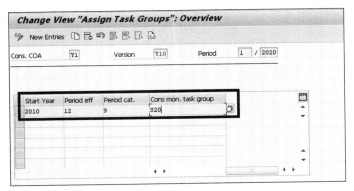

Figure 6.15 Assign the Task to the Dimension

6.3.3 Defining Document Types

In this section, we'll discuss the document types for reclassification and changing consolidation groups in the Consolidation Monitor. Let's first look into document types for reclassification.

Document Types for Reclassification

You need document types to post journal entries. It's best practice to use one document type for every automatic consolidation task; the system also contains document types for various posting levels. Figure 6.16 shows the predefined document types, which you can access by using Transaction CXE9N, expanding **Reclassification**, and executing **Define Document Types for Reclassification in Consolidation Monitor**. You can also create new document types by selecting the **New Entries** option.

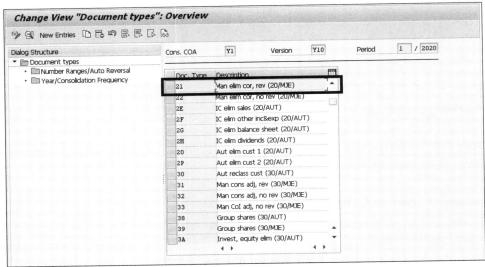

Figure 6.16 Defining Document Types for Reclassification in the Consolidation Monitor

Figure 6.17 shows the following options or assignments for the document types found under the **Dialog Structure**:

- **Number Ranges/Auto Reversal**
  Shown on the left-hand side of Figure 6.17, this pane enables you to enter the number range for allocating the document numbers. Using the **Auto reversal** checkbox, you can indicate if the document should be reversed automatically in the next period as well as the following year.

- **Year/Consolidation Frequency**
  Shown on the right-hand side of Figure 6.17, this pane determines the posting period for automatic reversals. Specify the consolidation frequency that determines the posting period for automatic reversals. Consolidation frequency can be monthly, quarterly, semi-annually, or annually. For example, if the consolidation frequency is monthly, the system determines next month as the posting period for automatic reversals. It's generally a best practice to only create a consolidation frequency for those document types that post the automatic reversals to the next period. Here you specify the version that you want the document type to be used in as well as the date from which you want this document type to be active.

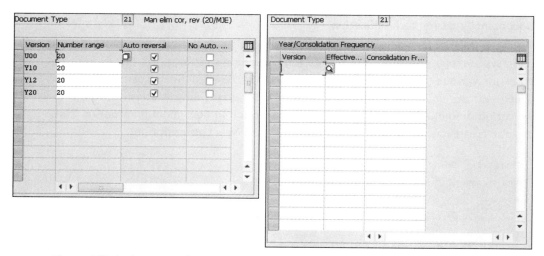

Figure 6.17 Assignments for Document Types for Reclassification

After you finish entering the number ranges and consolidation frequencies, click the **Save** button to finish the setup.

Document Types for Consolidation Group Changes

Similar to assigning document types for reclassification, you also assign document types for consolidation group changes. Figure 6.18 gives you a view of the document types for consolidation group changes, which can be accessed by executing Transaction CXE9N. Open **Preparation for Changes in the Consolidation Group**, and select

Define Document Types for Cons. Group Change in Consolidation Monitor. The default document type for preparing for consolidation group change is **2Z**, which is predefined in this screen. Here you specify the following:

- **Posting Level**
  Enter the posting level; the default is two-sided elimination with reporting logic and without reporting logic. Reporting logic is a new feature in SAP S/4HANA Finance for group reporting, which enables you to seamlessly slice and dice data. This is covered in Chapter 11.

- **Posting**
  Select whether the posting type is **Manual** or **Automatic** (default is **Automatic**). Automatic posting happens when you're getting the data from the source systems, whereas manual postings are related to manual journal entries that you enter in table ACDOCU.

- **Currencies**
  Specify in which currency the documents are to be posted under the **Currencies** section. In almost all cases, you post the values in group currency at the group level. In some cases, you might need to consolidate financials in multiple currencies. For example, a corporation has subsidiaries in Mexico, and there is a requirement that you need to consolidate the Mexico entities and report financials in pesos to the Mexican government. In those cases, you try to post in the local currency, which is the peso. Similarly, when there are intercompany transactions between two Mexican consolidation units, you can also consume data in the transaction currency that these consolidation units transact and perform eliminations.

- **Deferred Income Taxes**
  Specify whether you want to credit or debit the tax based on the consolidation group changes.

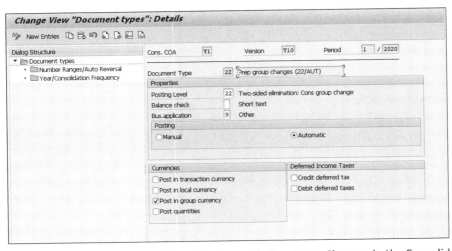

Figure 6.18 Define Document Types for Consolidation Group Changes in the Consolidation Monitor

Figure 6.19 shows the **Number Ranges/Auto Reversal** and **Year/Consolidation Frequency** screens for document types for group changes. The settings here are similar to what we discussed for reclassification.

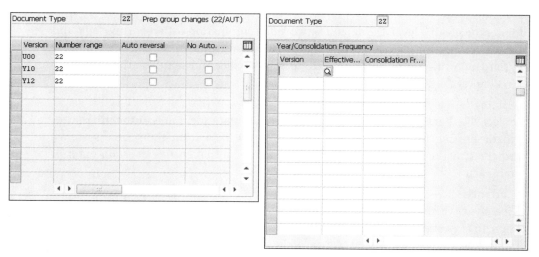

Figure 6.19 Assignment for Document Types for Group Changes

6.4   Configuring Intercompany Elimination

In this section, we'll discuss how to configure intercompany eliminations in SAP S/4HANA Finance for group reporting. We'll review how to create a new method, task, and document type, as well as cover some predefined configuration. Configuring intercompany eliminations in group reporting is totally different from earlier versions of the SAP consolidation tool, and SAP has provided you with a variety of master data attributes that can automate the elimination process in organizations very efficiently. In addition, intersections such as posting levels, document types, and so on make analysis of data very easy.

6.4.1   Business Rules

In this section, we'll discuss how to create a new method and a new task, how to assign that method to the new task, and finally how to assign the task to the Consolidation Monitor task group. With these steps, you'll see how to create a new custom elimination business rule per your requirement. Let's look at the step-by-step procedure at a high-level:

1. Create a new document type.
2. Create a new method.
3. Create a new trigger.

4. Create a custom task, and assign a method and document type.

5. Assign the task to the task group.

Create a New Document Type

You'll start with creating a new document type. To do so, execute Transaction CXE9N, and expand **Reclassification**. From there, select **Define Document Types for Reclassification in Consolidation Monitor**, and click the **New Entries** button. Enter the **Document Type** as "ZZ" and perform the following configurations, as shown in Figure 6.20:

- Set the **Posting Level** as **20** for two-sided elimination.
- Under **Posting**, choose **Automatic** because the data is posted by triggering the reclassification method through tasks in the Consolidation Monitor.
- Under **Currencies**, choose **Post in group currency**.
- Enter values for the **Properties**, **Posting**, and **Currencies** sections per your requirements, as explained in Section 6.3.3.

Click **Save** when finished.

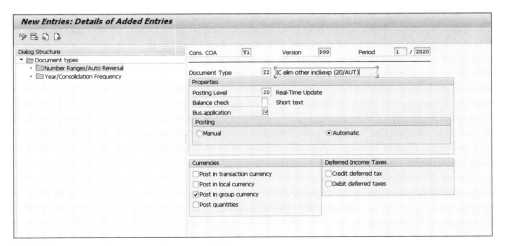

Figure 6.20 Creating a New Document Type

Now you need to assign **Number Ranges/Auto Reversal** and **Year/Consolidation Frequency** as explained in Section 6.3.3.

Create a New Method

Now you have a new document type created that is a prerequisite for creating a task. Next, let's discuss creating a new method.

Apart from rule-based predefined methods that for balance sheet, P&L, and consolidation of investments reclassification methods, you'll now create a new method. Let's consider an example to understand the configuration of intercompany eliminations.

The FTO1 corporate division of a consolidation group receives interest from its subsidiary FTO2 based on the money that FTO1 has lent/invested in FTO2. Interest is calculated by multiplying the principal amount by the interest rate applied, considering the time the money is lent. So FTO1 records this interest income from FTO2, and FTO2 records the interest expense on its books.

To create a new method, access Transaction CXE9N. Expand **Reclassification**, and select **Define Reclassification Methods**. Now select **New Entries**, and enter the new **Method** "ZIIIE" and its **Description**, as shown in Figure 6.21.

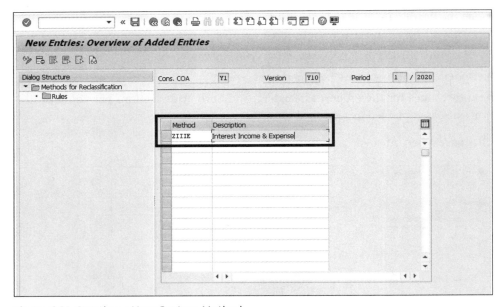

Figure 6.21 Creating a New Custom Method

With the new method now defined, you need to assign rules to it as shown in Figure 6.22 and Figure 6.23. Select **Rules** in the **Dialog Structure**, and you'll see four familiar tabs: **Settings**, **Trigger**, **Scr-dest**, and **Percentage**. Figure 6.22 shows **Settings**, which we discussed extensively in Section 6.3.1.

Now let's look at configuring the method based on your requirements. You're passing values for a few important parameters that will help you in this rule, as follows:

❶ **Periodic reclassification**
  Activate the periodic treatment for this method by selecting the checkbox.

❷ **Cons Frequency**
  Enter "9" (monthly) as the consolidation frequency.

❸ **Post to partner uni**
  Specify the system to post the reclassification value to the triggering unit.

❹ **Incl. parent/subsid.**
  Specify the system to consider both the parent and the subsidiary.

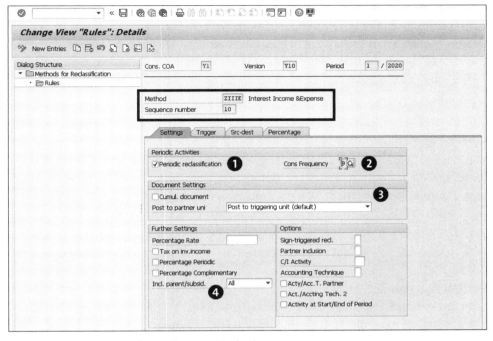

Figure 6.22 Assigning Rules to the New Method

Figure 6.23 shows the other tabs in the **Rules** screen. In this example, in the **Trigger** tab, a custom selection trigger has been created to assign to the custom method, which will be discussed next. For now, however, the selection trigger "Z_IUE_IIIE" needs to be assigned, which triggers the reclassification activity from the source account assignment to the destination account assignment.

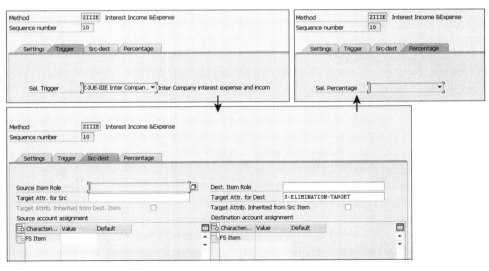

Figure 6.23 Assigning Rules

In the **Src-dest** tab of the rule, the target attributes have been configured for the destination item instead of the FS item. In this example, **S-ELIMINATION-TARGET** has been chosen. **Percentage** is the last tab in the rules screen, which has been left blank for this example to eliminate 100% of the values of the intercompany transactions.

Click **Save** to complete the setup. Next, you'll create the new selection trigger to use in the method.

Create a New Trigger

You can configure the new selection trigger using SAP Fiori in SAP S/4HANA Finance for group reporting by accessing the **Define Selections** tile and selecting **Create Selection**. Figure 6.24 shows the screen on which you can define the trigger based on your requirements:

- **Selection ID**
  In this mandatory field ❶, enter a unique name for your trigger (in this example, "Z_IUE_IIIE").

- **Short Description**
  In this mandatory field ❷, enter any description that's appropriate for your requirement; in this example, "Inter Company interest expense and income" is used.

- **Selection Expression/Show Value List**
  In the **Selection Expression** tab of this screen, define various parameters for your trigger in the **Show Value List** ❸. The code format is given in the **Selection Condition Details** view.

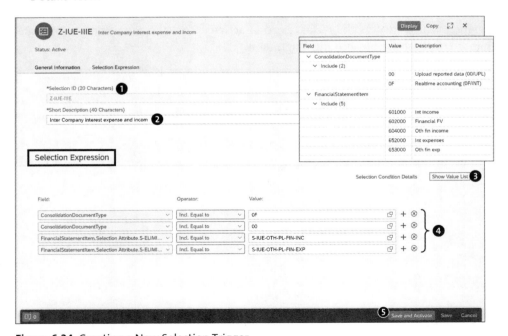

Figure 6.24 Creating a New Selection Trigger

There are three parts to the selection expression ❹, as shown in Figure 6.25:

- **Field**: Select various fields available in table ACDOCU for creating filters on which your triggering item applies; in this example, document type and FS item are selected. Apart from the fields, you can also select attributes, as shown in Figure 6.25.

- **Operator**: Choose **Include** or **Exclude** as the operator.

- **Value**: Select the values for the fields.

In this example, the **Document Type** is set as "ZZ" for the document type that was created. Document type "OO" is set as a default document type for source data. The predefined selection attribute is **S-IUE-OTH-PL-FIN-INC** for interest income and **S-IUE-OTH-PL-FIN-EXP** for interest expense FS items. Therefore, the system considers only data against these values and performs eliminations.

■ **Save and Activate**

When you're done with the configuration of the selection trigger, save and activate it by clicking this button ❺ in Figure 6.24.

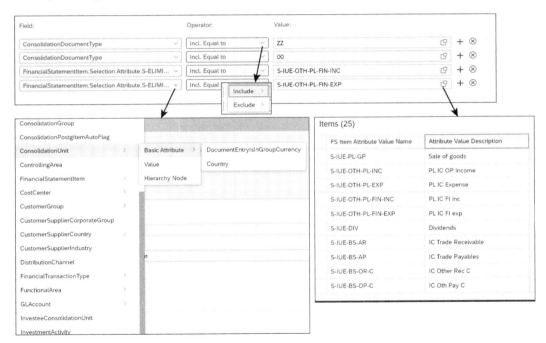

Figure 6.25 Updating the Selection Expression

Create a New Task

You've now created a method, defined rules for the method, created a selection trigger, and assigned it to the method. By doing these activities, you're now a couple of steps closer to completing the creation of your custom business rule, which you can use per your requirements. Next, you'll create a task that you would ultimately add to the Consolidation Monitor.

Figure 6.26 shows the screen to add a new task, which you can access by executing Transaction CXE9N, expanding **Reclassification**, and selecting **Define Reclassification Task**. Now you need to select **New Entries** to add a new custom task. Enter the following information:

❶ Create a task by adding a new **Task** ID and **Medium Text**.

❷ Click on **Assign Method, Document Type to the Task** in the **Dialog Structure** to assign a reclassification method and a document type.

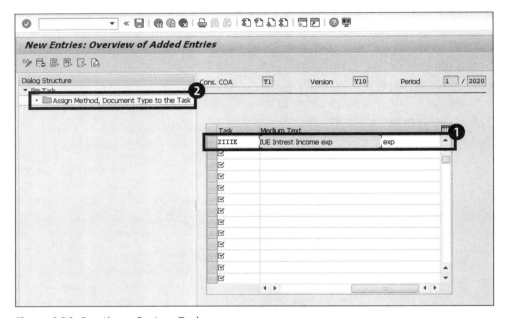

Figure 6.26 Creating a Custom Task

Figure 6.27 shows the screen where you assign a method and document type to the task. In this screen, you can see the task name and the following details:

❶ **Start Year**
The start year indicates the year that you'll be using this task.

❷ **Period eff**
Period effective is the period from which this task can be actively used in the Consolidation Monitor.

❸ **Method**
This is the method that you want to assign to this task. In this example, the method is "ZIIIE".

❹ **Document Type**
You can update any document type that you want to use in this task; in this example, the document type created is "ZZ".

After you're done with these steps, click the **Save** icon.

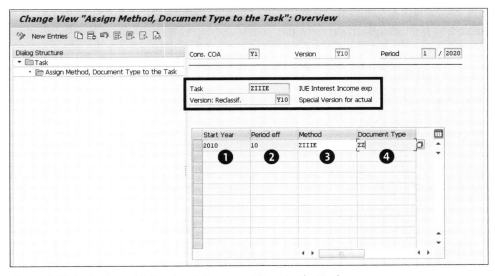

Figure 6.27 Assigning a Method and Document Type to the Task

Assign Tasks to Task Groups

The last step is to assign the task to the task group, as shown in Figure 6.28. To access this screen, execute Transaction CXE9N, expand **Configuration for Consolidation Processing**, and select **Define Task Group**. Now select a task group ❶ (in this example, the **S20** task group, which is for the Consolidation Monitor).

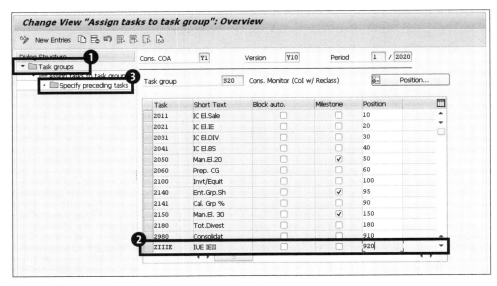

Figure 6.28 Assigning a New Task to Task Group

Select **Assign tasks to task group** next from the **Dialog Structure**, and then select the task that you want to assign to the task group (in this example, the **ZIIIE** task ❷). Finally, you can navigate to the **Specify preceding tasks** folder in the **Dialog Structure** to select preceding tasks ❸, but this is optional.

6.4.2   Predefined Configurations

You can use various predefined configurations in your projects, from methods to tasks to selection triggers. As we've covered these extensively in Section 6.3, in this section, we'll discuss the overall predefined configuration available for intercompany eliminations. To access predefined configuration, execute Transaction CXE9N and expand **Reclassification**. The following are the predefined configuration options available in SAP S/4HANA Finance for group reporting for reclassification:

- **Define Reclassification Methods**
  Review all the predefined content for reclassification methods that SAP S/4HANA Finance for group reporting offers, including balance sheet eliminations, sales and COGS elimination, and rule-based consolidation of investments elimination methods. In addition, you need to set rules in which you can use a predefined selection trigger or create a new trigger.

- **Define Reclassification Task**
  Review all the predefined content for the reclassification task that SAP S/4HANA Finance for group reporting offers. These are in turn tagged to a reclassification method to enable you to perform interunit eliminations.

- **Define Document Types for Reclassification in Consolidation Monitor**
  Review all the predefined content for document types that SAP S/4HANA Finance for group reporting offers. These are in turn tagged to a task to enable you to use the task to perform interunit eliminations.

In addition, under **Configuration for Consolidation Processing**, you'll find the following predefined configurations:

- **Define Task Group**
  Assign your tasks to the task group. Task groups are mirrors of the Consolidation Monitor or the Data Monitor.

- **Assign Task Group to Dimension**
  Assign the task group to the dimension that you've set up in global parameters so that you can use the Consolidation Monitor or the Data Monitor.

- **Maintain Log Archiving Settings for Tasks**
  Maintain the settings for the archiving log for tasks that have been executed in the Data Monitor and the Consolidation Monitor. When you're selecting the indicator, you're storing the log to display later, which happens during the update run. Figure 6.29 gives you a glimpse of the predefined log, which can be modified based on your requirements.

Display View "Log Archiving": Overview

Cons. COA [Y1]   Version [Y10]   Period [1] / [2020]

Log Archiving

Task	Medium Text	Task category	Archive log	Log
1010	Balance Carryforward	Balance Carryforw… ▼	☑	☑
1015	Release Universal Journals	Release of Report… ▼	☐	☑
1020	Data Collection	Data Collection ▼	☑	☑
1030	Calc. Net Income	Item Substitution… ▼	☑	☑
1050	Validation Universal Journals	Validation of Uni… ▼	☑	☑
1055	Manual Corrections (PL01)	Manual Posting ▼	☐	☑
1080	Reported Data Validation	Reported Data Val… ▼	☐	☑
1090	Validation Reported. Data LC	Reported Data Val… ▼	☑	☑
1095	Manual Posting (PL10)	Manual Posting ▼	☐	☑
1100	Currency Translation	Currency Translat… ▼	☑	☑
1180	Standardized Data Validation	Standardized Data… ▼	☐	☑
1190	Validation Standardiz. Data GC	Standardized Data… ▼	☑	☑
2011	IC Elim. Sales	Reclassification ▼	☑	☑
2021	IC Elim. Other Income/Expense	Reclassification ▼	☑	☑
2031	Dividends Elimination	Reclassification ▼	☑	☑
2041	IC Elim. Balance Sheet	Reclassification ▼	☑	☑
2050	Manual Eliminations (PL20)	Manual Posting ▼	☐	☑
2060	Preparation Cons Group Change	Preparation for C… ▼	☐	☑
2100	Investments / Equity elimin.	Reclassification ▼	☑	☑
2101	Cons. of Invest. (Act.-Based)	Consolidation of … ▼	☑	☑
2140	Enter Group Shares (PL30)	Manual Posting ▼	☐	☑
2141	Calculate Group Shares (PL 30)	Posting of Group … ▼	☐	☑
2150	Manual Eliminations (PL30)	Manual Posting ▼	☐	☑

Figure 6.29 Maintaining the Log

6.5   Eliminating Intercompany Transactions

So far, we've discussed the predefined configurations related to intercompany eliminations and their usage, and we've reviewed the creation of an elimination task, which is a method to configure a custom reclassification rule. In this section, we'll execute the method in the Consolidation Monitor and validate the results. In addition, we'll use this as an opportunity to review the custom reclassification rule and its functionality.

6.5.1   Execution in the Consolidation Monitor

Before executing a task in the Consolidation Monitor, let's look at the global parameters and make sure that you have the right parameters set for the month-end activity. You can either user SAP Fiori or SAP GUI via Transaction CX20 to run eliminations using the Consolidation Monitor. SAP Fiori is preferred due to its look and feel, ease of use, and simple navigation to other SAP Fiori apps that you'll need while running the intercompany elimination processes.

In the SAP Fiori Consolidation Monitor app, select the **Global parameters** option, and make sure that your consolidation group, consolidation chart of accounts, version, and period are properly set. Right-click on the **Status** of your custom task to see the following options, as shown in Figure 6.30:

- **Test**
  Enables you to simulate the task.

- **Update run**
  Enables you to change the task status and generate documents.

- **Last log**
  Provides you the details of the log that was generated the last time when the task was executed.

- **Execute in Background**
  Provides the flexibility of running a task in the background while performing other duties.

- **Lock Upon User Request**
  Enables you to lock the task.

- **Test with original list**
  Provides you with the details of the first time the task was executed.

- **Start w. Selection**
  Enables you to select details such as consolidation unit, consolidation group, version, and so on, similar to global settings.

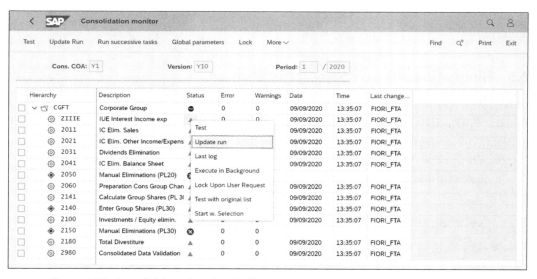

Figure 6.30 Consolidation Monitor Options

Select **Update run**. After the task is successfully run, you get a success message, and the icon changes to success, as shown in Figure 6.31.

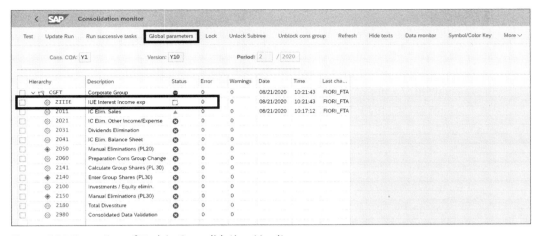

Figure 6.31 Execution of Task in Consolidation Monitor

6.5.2   Validating Eliminations and Reclassifications

After the task is executed successfully, the system takes you to the **Task logs** screen, as shown in Figure 6.32. Let's discuss each item in detail for **CGFT Corporate Group**, which is your consolidation group that includes consolidation units FTO1 and FTO2:

- **Reclass**
  Your custom method "ZIIIE".

- **Sequence**
  Sequence of your task.

- **Item Type**
  The entry is a journal entry or a triggering entry that has been generated using your custom method and custom task.

- **Journal Entry**
  Journal entry number.

- **Consolidation Unit**
  The consolidation unit that books the interest income and interest expenses on its books (in this case, FTO1 and FTO2).

- **Partner Unit**
  The consolidation unit that transacts with another consolidation unit with a group.

- **FS Item**
  FS item that holds journal entry values and that you want to eliminate using your reclassification method and task.

- **Subitem**
  Transaction type, functional area, or any other subitem that you need for this transaction.

- **SI Category**
  Subitem category that your selected subitem falls in.

- **Triggering Amount in GC**
  Amount generated by the reclassification method.

- **Journal Entry Amount in GC**
  Amount posted in table ACODCU.

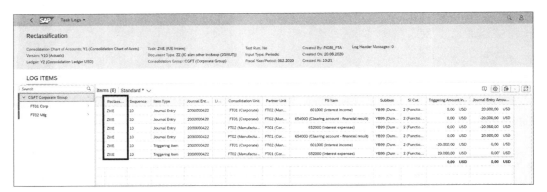

Figure 6.32 Task Logs Screen

Figure 6.33 shows a further breakdown by consolidation unit. This gives you a clear picture of the posting of each consolidation unit, which is extremely helpful in analyzing how the data has been reported and how it got reclassified. In Figure 6.33, you can see that FTO1 has recorded interest income from partner unit FTO2, and FTO2 has recorded an income expense with the partner unit FTO1 via a journal entry. As your reclassification task is executed, the elimination entry is posted in the clearing account, and the triggering amount is posted to balance the original journal entry transaction.

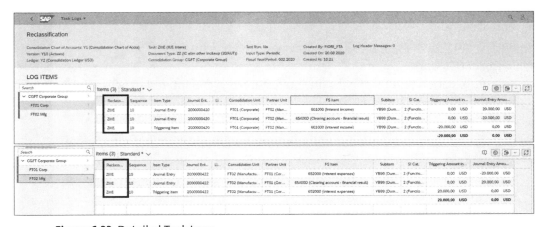

Figure 6.33 Detailed Task Logs

6.5.3 Reporting

Now that you've executed the task in the Consolidation Monitor and validated the result in the task logs, it's time to run a report and see the data generated. SAP S/4HANA Finance for group reporting provides an out-of-the-box app called Group Data Analysis. Using this app, you can slice and dice the data whichever way you want. Let's look at a few interesting points in Figure 6.34, which shows the data generated by your custom task:

- **Posting Level**
  Posting level 00 indicates the data that is reported by the entity. Posting level 20 indicates the elimination entry generated, and here you can recollect from earlier sections that posting level 20 is used for two-sided elimination entries.

- **Document Type**
  Document type ZZ is the document that you've created and assigned to the task. When the task is executed, the reclassification entries are posted to this document type.

Apart from these fields, you may add other fields as well for your analysis by selecting the dimensions from the list and dragging and dropping them into either rows or columns based on your requirements.

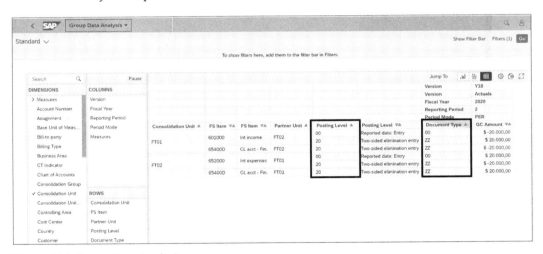

Figure 6.34 Group Data Analysis

This app is extremely helpful for business users to analyze the data, as well as helpful for the project teams to look at data as reclassification happens and validate the configuration.

Let's look at an example predefined elimination task. Table 6.7 provides the details of the predefined configuration.

Task ID	Description	Posting Level	Assigned Method	Document Type
2011	IC Elim. Sales	20	S2010	2E

Table 6.7 Predefined Sales and COGS Elimination

Table 6.8 shows a sample data set that you're going to use for the sales elimination. The following example demonstrates that FT01 has recorded a sale of $20,000 to its partner unit FT02, and FT02 has recorded a cost of sale on its books with the partner unit as FT01.

Cons Unit	Partner Unit	FS Item	Posting level	Amount
FT01	FT02	411100 (Sales)	00	($20,000)
FT02	FT01	500010 (COGS)	00	$20,000

Table 6.8 Sample Data Set for Sales Elimination

Now let's validate the results. Figure 6.35 gives you the details of the reclassification results. As this is a two-sided elimination, which means both the transacting consolidation units record transactions on their books, you should look for values generated at posting level 20. For the task 2011, which is **IC. Elim Sales**, the predefined document type is 2E. This is the document type to which the reclassification entries are posted, which is shown in Figure 6.35. In simple terms, the reported data of the consolidation units is with document type "00", and after the reclassification happens, the data gets reclassified to "2E" per the configuration.

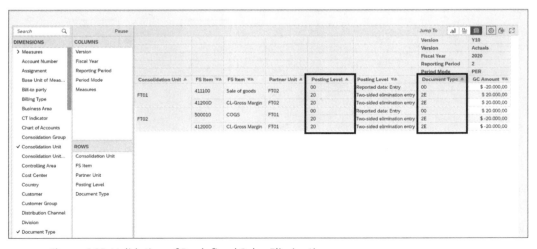

Figure 6.35 Validation of Predefined Sales Elimination

6.6   Summary

In this chapter, we've focused on performing tasks for consolidations. We've extensively discussed the consolidation process, including intercompany eliminations and generation of consolidated financial statements in SAP S/4HANA Finance for group reporting.

Before we started, we made sure the reported financial data for each consolidation unit of the consolidation group was up to date and closed in SAP S/4HANA. We also consumed this reported data into group reporting and performed data collection tasks in the Data Monitor. After all of this, we began performing consolidations.

Performing consolidations starts with setting up the Consolidation Monitor with the tasks you need. We discussed the various reclassification methods that are predelivered as part of the group reporting 1909 solution, and we covered the reclassification tasks and document types required for these reclassification tasks. We reviewed balance sheet, P&L eliminations, and topside entries that result in generating financial statements such as consolidated balance sheet, consolidated P&L, consolidated statement of equity, and consolidated statement of cash flow. Apart from reviewing the predefined content, we also created a custom method and task and then assigned them to the Consolidation Monitor task group. After this, we executed this task and showed the results in task logs as well as the SAP Fiori Group Data Analysis app. We also looked into various configuration items and reviewed the predefined content, executed the intercompany eliminations, and validated the results.

In the next chapter, we'll discuss the consolidation of investments, where we'll focus on the investments made by one consolidation unit in another consolidation unit, dividends that will be paid as part of that investment, and subsequent postings in retained earnings and NCI.

Chapter 7
Consolidation of Investments

In this chapter, we'll discuss the various methods and both rule-based and activity-based consolidation of investments. We'll walk through its predefined configuration in SAP S/4HANA Finance for group reporting, look at some customizations, review the execution process, and validate the results.

Consolidation of investments and minority interest calculations is the process of eliminating the investments held by the parent company in its subsidiaries. The holding company records investment in the subsidiary, whereas the subsidiary records equity. Here, the investment in the subsidiary means investment for equity of the subsidiary company, which includes share capital plus reserves on acquisition of the subsidiary. The holding company's balance in the investment in the subaccount is eliminated by the equity value in the subsidiary's books.

Two concepts are key to consolidation of investments:

- **Goodwill**
  When a business is acquired, the acquisition cost is generally higher than the physical or tangible assets because the intangible assets (e.g., patents, brand name, etc.) are also considered in the acquisition cost. This intangible portion of assets is known as goodwill. If the investment is more than the equity value, then the goodwill is positive; if the investment is less than the equity, then the goodwill is negative. For example, FTO1 invests $100,000 in its subsidiary FTO2 for 80% of its equity, whereas FTO2's equity on the date when this investment occurred is $150,000, 80% of which is $120,000. It's clear here that investment is less than the equity, so the goodwill recorded will be negative.

- **Minority interest**
  In the purchase method of consolidations, minority interest is calculated to record residual ownership excluding the holding company's ownership in the subsidiaries of equity. In this example, FTO1 owns 80% of FTO2, so the minority interest in subsidiaries equity is 20%. Generally, minority interest values include the minority share of equity in the subsidiary, minority share of pre-acquisition and post-acquisition revenues, and balances such as dividends earned, and so on.

Now, let's dive deeper into the consolidation of investments, starting with the basics. We'll then walk through configuration steps and running equity pickup.

7.1   What Is Consolidation of Investments?

Consolidation of investments is a process during the preparation of the consolidated financials that eliminates the investment on investors' books and eliminates the equity on its subsidiary's books. In SAP S/4HANA Finance for group reporting, the system uses the reported financials of the investor and investee consolidation units along with group-dependent investment share percentages to calculate the noncontrolling interests (NCI) of the eliminated investment and equity. It then reclassifies the minority portion of profit and loss (P&L) that is reported by the investee consolidation unit.

SAP S/4HANA Finance for group reporting offers the following two approaches for consolidation of investments:

- **Rule-based**

    In Chapter 6, we discussed in detail the delivered reclassification rules by SAP for consolidations. Rule-based consolidation of investment uses the reclassification steps you define in the reclassification methods and then executes the reclassification task via the Consolidation Monitor. It also uses the document types for group-dependent postings.

    Task group S20 contains reclassification tasks 2100 and 2180 for rule-based consolidation of investments.

- **Activity-based**

    The results of activity-based consolidation are defined by activities that impact various business transactions. These activities are predefined by SAP S/4HANA Finance for group reporting so that they are readily available for customers to use. Some examples of these business transactions are first consolidation, subsequent consolidation, change in capitalization, and total divestiture. The system processes the task of category consolidation of investment and performs consolidation of investment calculations.

    In activity-based consolidation, you assign consolidation of investments methods to consolidation units in the Manage Group Structure app. Task group S21 contains automatic posting task 2101 for activity-based consolidation of investment.

Let's discuss both types of consolidation of investments in detail.

7.1.1   Rule-Based Consolidation of Investments

The rule-based consolidation of investments consists of the investments/equity elimination, the total divestiture, and the dividends elimination tasks that are predelivered. The following are the activities that consolidation of investment can perform for consolidation units using the purchase method:

- **First consolidation**

    This activity performs the elimination of investments, elimination of capital, retained earnings, and other comprehensive income accounts and then calculates the group share and NCI for the retained earnings financial statement (FS) items. You need to do the following as part of first consolidation:

– Post the group shares in the previous task for each consolidation group for the first consolidation. After the first consolidation, you only need to post changes in group shares.

– Maintain the period for which you perform the first consolidation and for divestiture in the master data of the respective consolidation group.

- **Subsequent consolidation**
  This activity calculates the group share, NCI for your net income, other comprehensive income, and retained earnings FS items.

- **Share changes**
  This activity calculates the group share changes, based on which you would calculate the NCI for the other comprehensive income and retained earnings. Here, you might adjust the allocation of net income, which, in many companies, is done using a journal entry.

- **Increase in capital**
  This activity eliminates changes in investment and capital value with no change in the group share.

- **Total divestiture**
  This activity reverses the consolidation of investment postings.

Table 7.1 shows the methods that are part of the predelivered content.

Method	Description	Task	Posting Level	Document Type
S2100	Investment/equity elimination	2100	30	3A
S2180	Total divestiture	2180	30	3Z
S2030	Dividends elimination	2031	20	2H

Table 7.1 Consolidation of Investments: Rule-Based Methods

These methods are configured using rules, which we discussed in Chapter 6. The following reiterates the rules that are critical for reclassifying consolidation of investments:

- **Percentages**
  Maintaining periodic percentages helps you calculate the periodic value of FS items starting when these percentages are recorded. On the other hand, maintaining complementary percentages enables you to use the complemented percentage that is recorded against an FS item; for example, here the complementary percentage is 100.

- **Activity**

  The reclassification steps are determined based on the activities assigned to consolidation unit, such as first consolidation or subsequent consolidation and first consolidation period/year and last consolidation period or year. Figure 7.1 shows the Manage Consolidation Group Structure app that's gives more details on these assignments to consolidation group **CGFT**. These activities determine the execution of reclassifications based on the activity of a consolidation unit and its group.

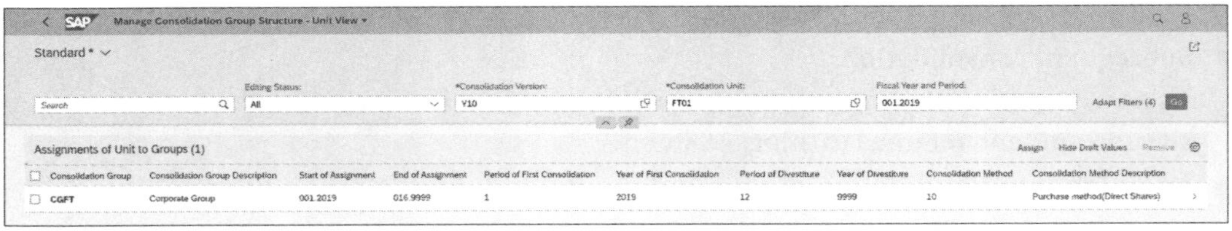

Figure 7.1 Assignments to the Consolidation Unit

- **Accounting technique**

  This is a critical step because reclassification steps only apply when the accounting technique in the step definition is identical to that of the reclassification method assigned to the consolidation unit. Similar to the consolidation unit, an accounting technique is also applied to the partner unit.

Let's consider an example to understand the concept of rule-based elimination in SAP S/4HANA Finance for group reporting. In this example, FT01 holds an investment of 80%. Table 7.2 shows the initial elimination of the investment made by FT01 in FT02 to own 80% of FT02's equity. Method S100 (investment/equity elimination) is used here.

Consolidation Unit	Partner Unit	FS Item	Value	Posting Level
FT01	FT02	172100 Investments	$500,000.00	10
FT01	FT02	172100 Investments	($500,000.00)	30
FT01	FT02	17210C Elim Investment	$500,000.00	30
FT02	FT01	1721HC Elim of Investment Held	($500,000.00)	30
FT02	FT01	311600 Retained Earnings	$500,000.00	30
FT02	FT01	311000 Issued Capital	($450,000.00)	10
FT02	FT01	311000 Issued Capital	$450,000.00	30
FT02	FT01	311600 Retained Earnings	($90,000.00)	30

Table 7.2 Consolidation of Investments Activity: First Consolidation

Consolidation Unit	Partner Unit	FS Item	Value	Posting Level
FT02	FT01	314000 Surplus before Tax	$40,000.00	10
FT02	FT01	314000 Surplus before Tax	$40,000.00	30
FT02	FT01	316000 Retained Earnings	($8,000.00)	30

Table 7.2 Consolidation of Investments Activity: First Consolidation (Cont.)

Table 7.3 shows how dividends that are recorded by FT02 are eliminated using reclassification method S2030.

Consolidation Unit	Partner Unit	FS Item	Value	Posting Level
FT02	FT01	601000 Interest Income	($100,000.00)	10
FT02	FT01	601000 Interest Income	$100,000.00	20
FT02	FT01	316000 Retained Earnings	($100,000.00)	20
FT02	FT01	317000 Net Income	($100,000.00)	20
FT02	FT01	799000 Net Income	$100,000.00	20

Table 7.3 Consolidation of Investments Activity: Dividends Elimination

Table 7.4 shows how the net income, NCI, and retained earnings are eliminated.

Consolidation Unit	Partner Unit	FS Item	Value	Posting Level
FT02		317000 Net Income	($90,000)	10
FT02		317000 Net Income	$18,000	30
FT02		792000 Net Income – NCI	($18,000)	30
FT02		317000 Net Income	($200,000)	10
FT02		317000 Net Income	$40,000	30
FT02		792000 Net Income – NCI	($40,000)	30
FT02		314000 Surplus before Tax	($50,000)	10
FT02		314000 Surplus before Tax	$10,000	10

Table 7.4 Consolidation of Investments Activity: Subsequent Consolidation

Consolida-tion Unit	Partner Unit	FS Item	Value	Posting Level
FT02		321001 Surplus before Tax – NCI	($10,000)	30
FT02		316000 Retained Earnings	($30,000)	10
FT02		316000 Retained Earnings	$6,000	30
FT02		316000 Retained Earnings	$100,000.00	10
FT02		316000 Retained Earnings	$20,000.00	30
FT02		321100 NCI Reserves and RE	($6,000)	30
FT02		321100 NCI Reserves and RE	($20,000.00)	30

Table 7.4 Consolidation of Investments Activity: Subsequent Consolidation (Cont.)

7.1.2   Activity-Based Consolidation of Investments

When you perform consolidation of investments with SAP S/4HANA Finance for group reporting, you can do postings for first consolidation, subsequent consolidation, changes in investee's equity, and divestitures automatically with posting level 30. For divestures, you may need postings from previous activities as well, and generally this information is recorded in statistical FS items. These statistical items don't depend on the accounting technique; for example, if a consolidation unit is consolidated using a purchase method on top of these postings, the system also posts to these statistical FS items as if the consolidation unit is consolidated using the equity method.

The sequence of execution of consolidation of investment activities is key in the postings of consolidation of investments. The sequence is mainly dependent on the sequencing of activities and the sequence in which the consolidation units of the investment hierarchy are processed.

Let's discuss the activities that drive activity-based consolidation of investments. When a company acquires another company, and you want to include the acquired company in the group financial statements, you need to perform the following activities:

- **First consolidation**
  When a consolidation unit joins for the first time in a consolidation group as a result of an acquisition, that is first consolidation, as discussed in the previous section. This activity is used to eliminate the entire investment that has been reported and its corresponding equity. In a group where there has been an acquisition, first consolidation is mandatory to proceed to the next steps in the consolidation process. You need to assign the consolidation method to the acquired unit in the group structure, enter the date of first consolidation for the investee in the group structure, and

specify whether the first consolidation needs to be executed at the start of the period or at the end of the period.

- **Step acquisition**
  After you perform the first consolidation of the consolidation units, you'll use this activity to eliminate the increase in investment data that has been reported. This activity maps the increase of shares in the consolidation unit (i.e., investor) to the consolidation unit (i.e., investee).

- **Change in capitalization**
  This activity is used when there is an increase or decrease in capitalization so that the changes in the equity of the consolidation unit that holds investments (investee) can be tracked. To perform this activity, you need to make sure that the consolidation unit's (investor's) book value is changed without modifying the ownership percentages. Then, you must increase the percentage of ownership elimination of investment. Equity happens when there is no change in ownership percentage as a result of the capitalization. When it's noted that the percentage of ownership is increased, then you consider the step acquisition activity. On the other hand, if the percentage of ownership has fallen, the partial divestiture activity is performed.

- **Subsequent consolidation**
  You use this activity to report the NCI for the equity section of the balance sheet on the books of the consolidation unit that holds the investment (investee). Because this is equity data, it may or may not affect the net income. You need to make sure that the consolidation unit that is reporting the NCI has gone through the first consolidation.

- **Divestiture**
  When a consolidation unit that is an investee leaves the consolidation group completely, then you consider the activity of total divestiture. When a consolidation unit (i.e., an investor) reduces its ownership in a consolidation unit (i.e., an investee), and you already performed the activity of first consolidation, then you consider the activity of partial divestiture.

  Partial divestiture generates a reduction of shares of the holding company in its subsidiary. Partial divestiture results in a reduction of group share, NCI, and investment book value while using a purchase method. On the other hand, a partial divestiture could just be an adjustment entry when using an equity method of consolidations.

  Alternatively, the *total divestiture* activity is used to invert all the data that was previously posted as part of consolidation of investments for the divested consolidation unit (i.e., an investee). Some key points to remember are that you need to maintain the date of divestiture for the consolidation unit in the group structure, and you should also indicate if you want to perform the divestiture at the end of the period or at the beginning. If the total divestiture occurs at the beginning of the period, it reverses the totals records of all prior periods, and no further activity is needed. On the other hand, if the total divestiture activity occurs at the end of the period, it reverses the totals records of all the prior periods as well as the total records generated by the activities in the divestiture period.

- **Indirect activity**
  Increases or decreases in indirect investments are activities that the system generates to post adjustments related to consolidation of investments made to the new group shares. This is a result of some indirect activities such as change in ownership percentages due to some acquisitions or divestitures that have an impact on increased/decreased group share. An increase in indirect investment is generated by the step acquisition, and a decrease in indirect investment is generated by the partial or total divestiture.

- **Treatment of goodwill**
  Goodwill activity eliminates a positive differential amount (positive goodwill) on a capital reserves account and writes off a negative differential amount (negative goodwill) into the P&L statement. You perform the disclosure of goodwill and impairment postings via manual journal entries.

7.2   Configuring Consolidation of Investments

In this section, we'll review the configuration of consolidation of investments and go through different settings that you need to configure to perform the tasks from the task monitor related to consolidation of investments. We'll discuss the consolidation methods and their configuration, the consolidation group structure, and modifying the predefined configuration.

7.2.1   Reviewing Consolidation Methods

In this section, we'll walk through the steps to define the consolidation of investment methods. We'll review the various methods, provide some examples, and take a look at predefined configuration content.

Method Configuration

Figure 7.2 shows the predefined configuration of consolidation of investment methods. You can access this screen by executing Transaction CXE9N, expanding **Consolidation of Investments**, and selecting **Define Methods**.

You need one method for each accounting technique; for example, if you're using both the purchase method and the equity method, you need to define one method for each technique. By default, you use method **00** for **Parent Unit**, which is a full consolidation.

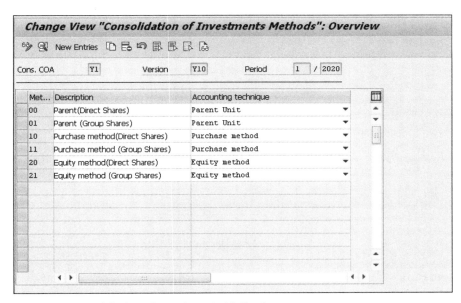

Figure 7.2 Consolidation of Investments Methods

If you want to use only one method, it can be either of the following:

- **Equity method**
  The equity method is used to record revenue earned from investments of one consolidation unit in other consolidation units based on the ownership. For example, if FTO1 buys 1 million shares for FTO2 at $10 per share, FTO1 will record investment as 10 million during the first period after the investment has been made, and this investment is impacted by gains and losses related to it down the line.

- **Proportionate method**
  This method is used when the percentage of ownership is directly proportionate to the reported data. For example, if FTO1 owns 50% of FTO2, then FTO1 will record 50% of FTO2's assets, liabilities, revenues, and expenses.

Similar to intercompany eliminations, after you have a method, you'll create a task. To check the preexisting configuration and to create a new task, execute Transaction CXE9N, expand **Consolidation of Investments**, and select **Define Tasks**.

You can create a new task by selecting **New Entries**, or you can select the preexisting task, (2101 consolidation of investments [activity-based]). You now need to assign the task to activities and accounting techniques, as shown in Figure 7.3. You can select any of the options and click the **Save** button.

C/I activity	Short Descript.
00	All activities
01	First consolidation
02	Subsequent consolidation
03	Amortization of goodwill
04	Amortization of hidden reserves/FVA
05	Increase in capitalization
06	Reduction in capitalization
07	Step acquisition
08	Partial transfer
09	Total transfer
10	Partial divestiture
11	Total divestiture
12	Liquidation
13	Reclassification of treasury stock
14	Investment amortization
15	Investment writeup
16	Horizontal business combination
17	Vertical business combination
18	Distribution of dividends
19	Capitalization of manual goodwill
20	Increase in indirect investment
21	Reduction in indirect investment
22	Indirect transfer
23	Currency translation of goodwill
32	Purchase -> Proportional
33	Purchase -> Equity
34	Purchase -> Mutual stock
42	Proportional -> Purchase
45	Proportional -> Equity
46	Proportional -> Mutual stock
48	Equity -> Purchase
50	Equity -> Proportional
52	Equity -> Mutual stock
54	Mutual stock -> Purchase
56	Mutual stock -> Proportional
57	Mutual stock -> Equity
58	Method change
38	History

Activity	Accounting technique

Accounting technique	Short Descript.
0	All accounting techniques
1	Purchase method
2	Pooling of interest method
3	Proportional consolidation
4	Equity method
5	Mutual stock method
6	Cost method

Figure 7.3 Defining Activities for Consolidation of Investments Tasks

Another important step in configuration is creating document types. Table 7.5 clearly lists the document types that are predefined for SAP S/4HANA Finance for group reporting. To configure document types, execute Transaction CXE9N, expand **Consolidation of Investments**, and select **Define Document Types for Consolidation of Investments**. Just like other document types, you also need to update the details of the document type, such as **Number Ranges/Auto Reversal** and **Year/Consolidation Frequency** (refer to the discussion in Chapter 6, Section 6.3.3).

Document Type	Description
30	Aut reclass cust (30/AUT)
31	Man cons adj, rev (30/MJE)

Table 7.5 Predefined Document Types for Consolidation of Investments

Document Type	Description
32	Man cons adj, no rev (30/MJE)
33	Man Col adj, no rev (30/MJE)
38	Group shares (30/AUT)
39	Group shares (30/MJE)
3A	Invest, equity elim (30/AUT)
3B	Auto Col adj. (30/AUT)
3Z	Total divestiture (30/AUT)

Table 7.5 Predefined Document Types for Consolidation of Investments (Cont.)

With this, you've completed reviewing the consolidation methods.

Method Examples

Now let's discuss an example of activity-based consolidation of investments using the purchase method. A purchase method in consolidation of investments indicates that 100% of the subsidiaries' fully consolidated balances are included in consolidated group financial statements.

To start, you need to maintain the ownership data, that is, direct shares and group shares. For this example, FT01 invested $100,000 in FT02, and FT01 owns 80% of FT02.

With the purchase method, investment in FT01's books is eliminated, as shown in Table 7.6.

Consolidation Unit	Partner Unit	Group	FS Item	Amount
FT01	FT02		172100 (Inv in sub)	$100,000
FT01	FT02	CGFT	172100 (Inv in sub)	($100,000)

Table 7.6 Elimination of the Investment in the Subsidiary

Meanwhile, equity in FT02's books is eliminated, as shown in Table 7.7.

Consolidation Unit	Partner Unit	Group	FS Item	Amount
FT02	FT01		311000 (Issues Capital)	($25,000)
FT02	FT01		312000 (Share Premium)	($10,000)

Table 7.7 Elimination of Equity

Consolidation Unit	Partner Unit	Group	FS Item	Amount
FT02	FT01		313000 (Treasury Shares)	($5,000)
FT02	FT01		316000 (Ret. Earnings)	($30,000)
FT02	FT01	CGFT	311000 (Issues Capital)	$25,000
FT02	FT01	CGFT	312000 (Share Premium)	$10,000
FT02	FT01	CGFT	313000 (Treasury Shares)	$5,000
FT02	FT01	CGFT	316000 (Ret. Earnings)	$30,000

Table 7.7 Elimination of Equity (Cont.)

Now you need to calculate the NCI on FT02's books for the 20% that's not owned by FT01, as shown in Table 7.8.

Consolidation Unit	Partner Unit	Group	FS Item	Amount
FT02	FT01	CGFT	321100 (NCI – RE)	$5,000
FT02	FT01	CGFT	321100 (NCI – RE)	$2,000
FT02	FT01	CGFT	321700 (NCI Treasury Shares)	$1,000
FT02	FT01	CGFT	321100 (NCI – RE)	$6,000

Table 7.8 Eliminating NCI

Total retained earnings is $56,000 based on this calculation: *Noncontrolling interests + Other retained earnings items.* The remainder of the investment, $44,000, is posted in the goodwill account on FT02's books.

Next, let's look at an example of consolidation of investments using the equity method, as shown in Table 7.9.

FS Item	FT01	FT02	Reclassification Entries	Group View
Goodwill		$8,000		$8,000
Cash	$80,000	$60,000	($60,000)	$80,000
Investments	$20,000		($8,000)	$12,000
Common stock	$40,000	$60,000	($60,000)	$40,000
Retained earnings	$60,000			$60,000

Table 7.9 Equity-Based Consolidation of Investment

The equity method is used when ownership is less than 50%. This is an accounting technique used for consolidating affiliates, subsidiaries, and joint ventures. Here the subsidiary's (FTO2) cash and equity won't appear on the investor's (FTO1) book because FTO1 doesn't have significant ownership in FTO2. In this example, FTO1 has purchased 20% of FTO2 for $20,000 and records that amount as an investment. FTO2 has an equity of $60,000 because you're using the equity method, and FTO1 owns only 20% of FTO2; therefore, 20% of FTO2's equity belongs to FTO1, which is $12,000 (60,000 × 0.2). Because FTO1 has invested in FTO2 for $20,000, FTO1's equity held by FTO2 is classified as goodwill. The net effect will be to debit goodwill for $8,000 and credit the investment account by $8,000.

7.2.2   Configuring Consolidation Groups

Now that you understand methods, let's look at one of the most important configuration items—group structure. A consolidation group is a consolidation point of all the subsidiaries that fall under the group. you'll have multiple consolidation groups based on line of business, location, and so on. Configuring consolidation groups basically is setting up a parent-subsidiary relationship and defining the relationship based on the methods (i.e., purchase, proportionate, or equity). Figure 7.4 shows the SAP Fiori Manage Consolidation Group Structure – Group View app, where you can configure your consolidation group.

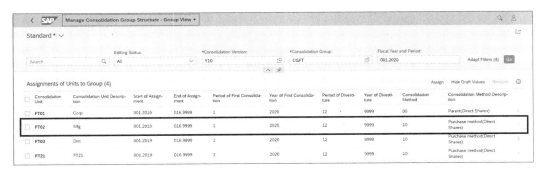

Figure 7.4 Manage Consolidation Group Structure

Following are the configuration details of this screen:

- **Consolidation Unit**
  Consolidation units that you want to be assigned to the group. Additional consolidation units can be assigned by selecting the **Assign** button.

- **Consolidation Unit Description**
  Text description of your consolidation unit.

- **Start of Assignment**
  Period from which a particular consolidation unit is assigned to the group.

- **End of Assignment**
  Period until which a particular consolidation unit is assigned to the group.
- **Period of First Consolidation**
  Period when a consolidation unit is consolidated for the first time in the group.
- **Year of First Consolidation**
  Year when a consolidation unit is consolidated for the first time in the group.
- **Period of Divestiture**
  Period when a consolidation unit is leaving the consolidation group.
- **Year of Divestiture**
  Year when a consolidation unit is leaving the consolidation group.
- **Consolidation Method**
  Consolidation method that is applied to a particular consolidation unit when consolidations are executed.
- **Consolidation Method Description**
  Description of the consolidation method that is applied to a consolidation unit.

All these details can be assigned to a consolidation unit. To do so, select FT02 and click **Go** to go to the screen shown in Figure 7.5. Here you can fill in the details under **First Consolidation**, **Divestiture**, and **Consolidation Method**, and then click the **Save** button.

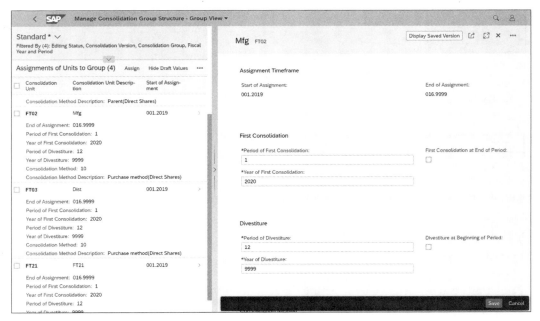

Figure 7.5 Assignment of Activities

After you've set up your group structure, you need to review ownership percentages. You can upload the ownership percentages of the holding company in its subsidiary using a flat file to direct shares, group shared FS items using the Flexible Upload of Reported Financial Data app, and review them in the Group Data Analysis app (see Figure 7.6), which we discussed in Chapter 6, Section 6.5.3. You should be looking at **Document Type 39** to see the ownership data. The task used to execute this is 2140 in the Consolidation Monitor.

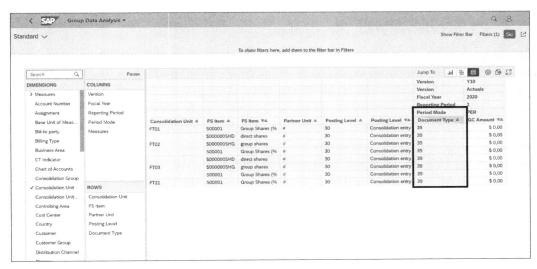

Figure 7.6 Review Ownership Percentages

7.2.3   Modifying Predefined Configuration

Now let's go over some predefined configurations and see how to modify them based on the predefined parameters or any custom parameters that you can create. In this section, we'll review various consolidation of investment configuration items.

Goodwill Settings

Figure 7.7 shows the system utilization screen, which has settings for goodwill. This screen can be accessed by executing Transaction CXE9N and opening **Consolidation of Investments** and then **Determine System Utilization for C/I**.

The following options are available:

- **Extraordinary Amortization of Goodwill**
  This option capitalizes and then applies extraordinary amortization to the goodwill that's incurred during consolidation of investments.

- **Direct Writeoff of Goodwill**
  This option writes off total goodwill that is incurred during consolidation of investments rather than capitalizing.

- **Direct Elimination of Goodwill**

  This option eliminates the goodwill that has been incurred during the consolidation of investment against the retained earnings.

- **Extraord. Amortization of Neg. Goodwill**

  This option is used when you identify that the fair value is less than the book value and while manually checking the goodwill for impairment.

- **Direct Writeoff of Negative Goodwill**

  This option writes off any negative goodwill incurred during the consolidation of investments.

- **Direct Elimination of Negative Goodwill**

  This option writes off any negative goodwill that is incurred during the consolidation of investments.

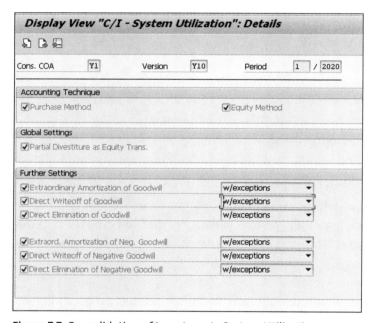

Figure 7.7 Consolidation of Investments System Utilization

In these settings, you can select you the following options:

- **Global**

  Enables the setting for all methods.

- **w/exceptions**

  Enables the setting for all methods, but you'll be able to allow exceptions for some methods when necessary. You can select this option if you need to define any exceptions for any consolidation units in a consolidation group.

- **per methods**
  Enables the setting for each method individually.

Define Global Goodwill Items

In this section, we'll define the FS item roles and subitems for posting goodwill, which can be consumed across all consolidation of investments methods. You specify the roles as FS item attribute value names in the master data (refer to Chapter 3 more information on this assignment). To access the screen to do this, execute Transaction CXE9N, expand **Consolidation of Investments**, and select **Define Global Goodwill Items**. Here you specify **Amortization of Goodwill**, **Direct Elimination of Goodwill**, **Amortization of Negative Goodwill**, and **Direct Elimination of Negative Goodwill**.

As a prerequisite, you need to set up system utilization details for consolidation of investments to define the global goodwill. Figure 7.8 shows the predefined configuration of goodwill items and how you can edit the predefined configuration:

- **Amortization of goodwill**
  Amortization of goodwill is the process of writing the initial cost of goodwill (which is an asset on the balance sheet). To do that in SAP S/4HANA Finance for group reporting, you specify item roles and subitems that help you define amortization of goodwill. Here you have details of acquisition, offsetting of original cost, accumulated amortization, amortization expenses, writeup items, and any statistical FS items if you want to use them. This level of detail provides you with a complete end-to-end picture on how goodwill is amortized in an organization.

- **Direct elimination of goodwill**
  In some instances, organizations will want to clear out the incurred goodwill (reduce it to zero) during the acquisition. This is when you can use this setting and eliminate goodwill completely. Because you're not amortizing, you only use details of acquisition, offset of original cost, and any statistical items.

- **Amortization of negative goodwill**
  In some instances, organizations do come across negative goodwill; in this case, goodwill is recorded as a gain on the purchaser's income statement. Here you use the same item roles and subitems as amortization of positive goodwill.

- **Direct elimination of negative goodwill**
  When you need to clear the negative goodwill, you use this setting, and you have same items and subitems as direct elimination of positive goodwill.

On each role item, if you press [F4], you get a list of FS item attributes from which you'll be selecting those related to goodwill (highlighted in Figure 7.8). If you have a requirement where the existing configuration isn't sufficient, you can create a new global goodwill item by selecting **New Entries** and specifying the item roles and subitems for posting positive and negative goodwill.

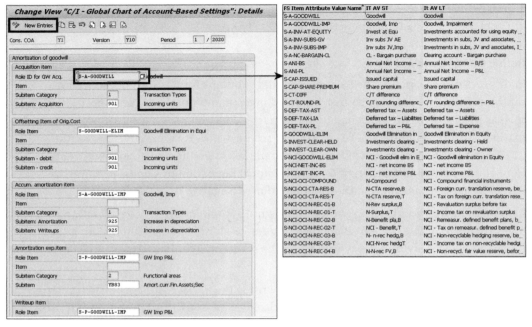

Figure 7.8 Defining Global Goodwill Items

Specify Equity Items and Items for Statistical Equity Postings

When you're setting up consolidation of investments in this step, the system displays all equity FS items and the statistical equity FS items assigned to them. These statistical items are used to record the group share in the equity values. To execute activity-based consolidations, these statistical entries are used. To understand this better, let's consider an example in activity-based consolidation of investments following these steps:

1. The first consolidation process clears the equity that's included in the consolidations.

2. The minority interest is then transferred to equity.

3. Now the group share is eliminated against earnings of the subsidiary.

4. Finally, the goodwill is posted.

To view equity items, execute Transaction CXE9N, expand **Consolidation of Investments**, and select **Specify Equity Items and Items for Statistical Equity Postings** (which you define in equity FS item master data as discussed next).

Equity items are defined in **Specify Miscellaneous Special Items**. To access this, execute Transaction CXE9N, expand **Consolidation of Investments**, and select **Specify Miscellaneous Special Items**. You'll arrive at the screen shown Figure 7.9, where you specify the item roles and subitems for automatic consolidation of investment postings. You can provide the following details:

- **Special items for the purchase method**

  Details of FS items and FS item roles before performing consolidations, during first consolidations, and during partial divestiture.

- **Minority interest in annual net income**

  Details of FS items and FS item roles that hold values for minority interest of a parent/investor company in annual net income.

- **Divestiture**

  FS items that contain values such as gain from divestiture on the parent consolidation units' books when a company is divested from a consolidation group.

- **Investment and Equity**

  Item roles of investment and equity.

- **Statistical Items**

  All offsetting and adjustments FS items.

- **Group Share Items**

  FS items that hold group share and direct share values.

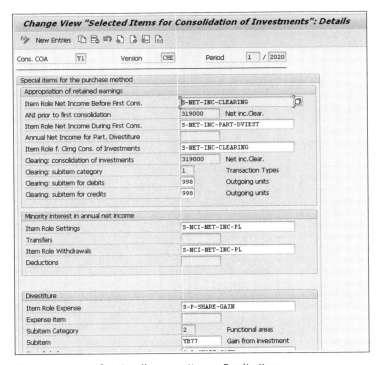

Figure 7.9 Specify Miscellaneous Items: Equity Item

Specify Minority Interest Items

When you're setting up consolidation of investments in this step, the system enables you to transfer the minority interest in investments and equity capital to the corresponding minority interest items. Essentially, the minority interest is considered only when the group share is less than 100%. You need to define the minority interest as a target attribute in the equity FS item master data. For example, in the **Capital Stock FS Item**, specify **Minorities in Capital Stock** as a target attribute.

To access the screen, expand **Consolidation of Investments**, and select **Specify Minority Interest**, as shown in Figure 7.10.

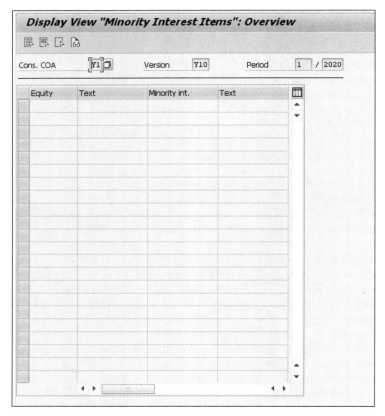

Figure 7.10 Minority Interest Items

Here you'll be able to see the equity items (**Equity**) as well as the items to which the system posts minority interest (**Minority int**).

Equity Holdings Adjustments

Equity holdings adjustments are needed for processing activity-based consolidation using the equity method. Here you'll specify the selections for the reported financial data that's required for the equity holdings adjustments to the consolidation unit. The selections for reported financial data of a consolidation unit for equity holdings adjustments must contain distinct values for FS items.

To access the screen for equity holdings adjustments, execute Transaction CXE9N, expand **Consolidation of Investments**, and select **Specify Reported Items for Equity Holdings Adjustments**. Figure 7.11 shows the screen where you can define the selections for reported items for equity holding adjustments. If a consolidation unit is using the equity method, then during the subsequent consolidations, you need to update the equity in the earnings of the affiliate. This happens automatically whenever one of the following events occurs:

- Recording of annual net income
- Payment of dividends
- Payment of bonuses
- Currency translation differences
- Goodwill elimination in the consolidation group to which the consolidation unit belongs
- Any adjustments made to the earnings in prior periods

These events can be selected in the **Extent** column of data by pressing [F4].

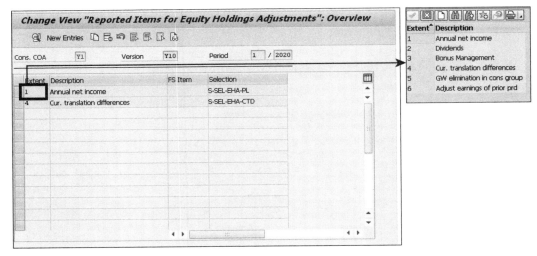

Figure 7.11 Reported Items for Equity

Treatment of Goodwill in Acquisitions of Investments

In the process of acquisitions, you need to define a valuation allowance procedure that you can use in calculating goodwill. Values should be specified in system utilization for consolidation of investments. You need to specify goodwill calculations in the following real-time scenarios:

- Direct acquisitions (step acquisitions, increases/reductions in capitalization)
- Indirect acquisitions (increases in indirect investment)

This setting enables the system to post a positive differential incurred in these acquisitions, irrespective of the goodwill treatment defined in the consolidation of investment method.

To access the screen for defining goodwill treatment for acquisitions, execute Transaction CXE9N, expand **Consolidation of Investments**, and select **Define Goodwill Treatment for Acquisitions**. Figure 7.12 show some details of the predefined configuration, which can also be edited or changed by selecting the dropdown button in each column:

- **Activity**
  Specify the activities of a consolidation unit in consolidation of investments.

- **Goodwill**
  Specify how you want the goodwill to be treated; in most cases, you eliminate it by selecting **Direct elimination**. Other possible options are **Extraordinary Amortization**, which is used in capitalization and valuation allowances while goodwill is calculated, and **Direct Writeoff**, which is used when a debt can't be recovered.

- **Neg. GW**
  Specify how you want the negative goodwill to be treated; in most cases, you write it off by selecting **Direct Writeoff**. Other possible options are **Extraordinary Amortization** and **Direct Elimination**.

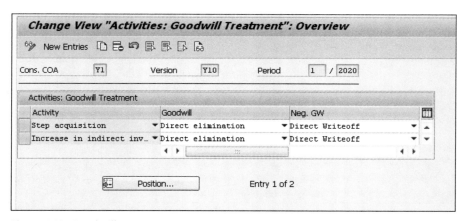

Figure 7.12 Goodwill Treatment

Listing the Customizing Consolidation of Investments

Here you can display the settings of consolidation of investment in an overview. Figure 7.13 shows the screen where you can specify your **Consolidation COA**, **Version**, and **Method** (consolidation of investment method). To access the screen, execute Transaction CXE9N, expand **Consolidation of Investments**, and select **Listing Customizing Consolidation of Investments**. Enter the values in the following fields:

- **Consolidation COA**

  Automatically shows up from the global parameter values.

- **Version**

  Automatically shows up from the global parameter values.

- **Method**

  Press F4 in the field, and select a consolidation method.

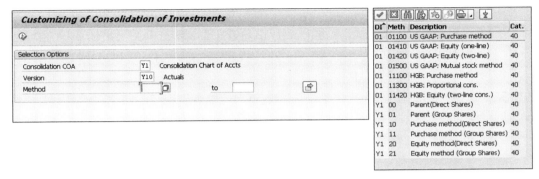

Figure 7.13 Customizing Consolidation of Investments

7.3 Running Equity Pickup

In this section, we'll discuss execution of the equity pickup and validating the results. You can run rule-based as well as activity-based consolidations. We'll start with reviewing the task in the Consolidation Monitor and then execute and validate it.

7.3.1 Execution in the Consolidation Monitor

Now that you understand the consolidation of investments concepts, we can execute a consolidation of investment task from the Consolidation Monitor and validate the results. To do that, let's consider a simple example:

- FT01 records investment in the subsidiary.
- FT02 records equity in its books.

You just eliminate the investment from FT01's books and equity from FT02's books using a predefined method and validate the document type and posting level to which the reclassification entry is posted. Table 7.10 provides the details of the predefined task that you'll use.

279

Task ID	Description	Posting Level	Assigned Method	Document type
2100	Investments/Equity elimin.	30	S2100	3A

Table 7.10 Predefined Task Used in This Example

Figure 7.14 shows the execution process of the task in the Consolidation Monitor. You need to make sure that the global parameters are set properly, so check for your consolidation group, consolidation unit, period, version, ledger, and chart of accounts. Then, select **Update run** from the list of options to execute the investment and equity elimination.

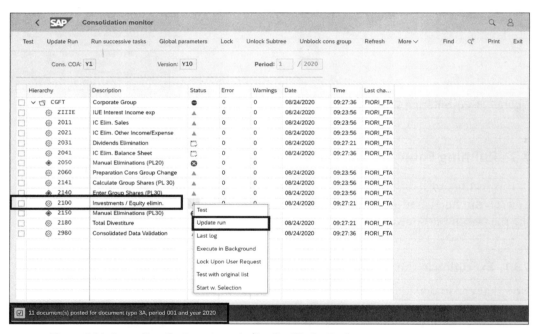

Figure 7.14 Executing the Investments/Equity Elimin. Task

You can see the message that pops up after the postings are completed successfully.

7.3.2   Validating Consolidation of Investments

After you execute the task successfully in the Consolidation Monitor, it takes you to the task log where you can see the details of the data posted. Here, you look for reclassification methods, FS items, and amounts. It's similar to how you checked after executing the interunit elimination process in Chapter 6, Section 6.5.2. Figure 7.15 shows the **Tasks Logs** screen.

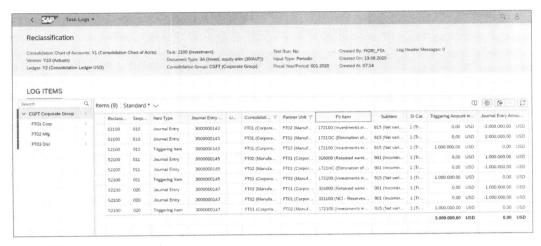

Figure 7.15 Validation in Task Log

7.3.3   Reporting

The final step in the process is to validate the data in the SAP Fiori Group Data Analysis app, as discussed in Chapter 6, Section 6.5.3. Figure 7.16 shows the screen of this app, where you can start to analyze the posting that happened as a result of executing on investment/equity elimination.

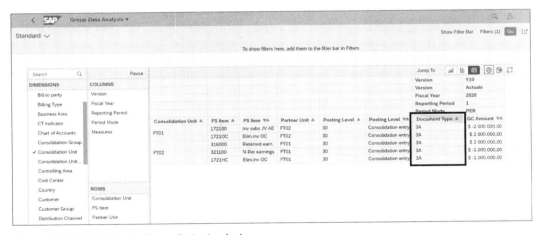

Figure 7.16 Validation in Group Data Analysis

The following points are key to note:

- **Posting Level 00** indicates the data that is reported by the entity.
- **Posting Level 30** indicates the consolidation of investment posting for which the posting level is 30.

- **Document Type 3A** is the document assigned to task 2100. When the task is executed, the reclassification entries are posted to this document type.

Apart from these fields, you may add other fields as well for your analysis, which we described in Chapter 6, Section 6.5.3.

Businesses can use this app to analyze the data via the slice-and-dice mechanism on various dimensions.

7.4   Summary

In this chapter, we've extensively reviewed consolidation of investments. We started with getting a general idea about consolidation of investments and then we looked at a few examples to understand the concept better. We then moved on to analyze the consolidation of investment capabilities in SAP S/4HANA for group reporting and reviewed both rule-based and activity-based consolidations in detail.

We also covered the core purpose of consolidation of investments and the benefits it provides to automate the investments in a consolidation group. With this understanding, we reviewed the predefined configuration of consolidation of investments in SAP S/4HANA Finance for group reporting, and also discussed the process of modifying the predefined configuration. Finally, we successfully executed the task in Consolidation Monitor and validated the results.

In the next chapter, we'll move on to consolidation entries for corporate adjustments.

Chapter 8
Consolidation Entries

This chapter discusses consolidation entries, including manual reclassifications, standard adjustments, and corporate adjustments using journals in group reporting. You'll learn how journal entries are posted in the solution and the configuration necessary for updating the layout of journals based on user requirements.

Consolidation entries, also referred to as topside entries in the consolidation process, support the adjusting of financial data to fulfill group-level reporting requirements. In an ideal scenario, adjustments to data should be done in the source system for ease of reconciliation, although there are cases where it's not always feasible to adjust the data at the source or the adjustment is at a group level and not at an entity level. Another requirement for topside entries arises when there is no automated process of reclassifying a subset of data, and it becomes imperative to include a manual entry for reporting the financials.

The nature of any journal posting in group reporting is determined by the dimensions within group reporting, such as posting level and document type. In this chapter, we'll begin with the most common consolidation entries used in a consolidation process. We'll then move on to configuring the journal entry template and making consolidation entries.

8.1 Common Consolidation Entries

Consolidation pro forma entries include late adjustments, Generally Accepted Accounting Principles (GAAP) adjustments, and other corporate group adjustments. Let's take a closer look at each:

- **Late journal adjustments**
  In a standard consolidation environment, the financial data source is the general ledger. The general ledger also follows a period close process and any data adjustments during the period are allowed as long as the period is open. The following scenarios best describe late journal adjustments and are depicted in Figure 8.1:

  - **During the year late adjustments**
    Journal entries in the consolidation solution are done during the period in the event of a closed period in the general ledger and are reversed in the next period.

The general ledger, however, brings in the same adjustment in the subsequent period.

– **End of the year late adjustments**
During year-end close, the source general ledger uses the special periods (e.g., 13–16) for capturing the financial data. Standard consolidation solutions consider the data alignment from special periods to the last period of the fiscal year. Such late entries in the consolidation solution ensure an audit trail. These entries also ensure that the opening balances in the new fiscal year in the consolidation solution align with the opening balances of the source ledger.

When late adjustments are posted in the consolidation system, you need to keep a few basic principles in mind as best practices and maintain transparency regarding adjustments made to the financial data. The entries should be easy to track and trace all the way to the financial general ledger data source while also maintaining an audit trail. A typical adjustment should be as follows:

– At the legal entity level
– In the local currency
– In the local GAAP
– Before eliminations

		P10	P11	P12	P13	New Year P01
General Ledger	Opening Balance	250	250	250	250	580
	Movements	90	100	80	0	15
	Late Journal Entry	0	10	0	50	0
	Closing Balance	340	450	530	580	595

		P10	P11	P12	P13	New Year P01
Consolidations	Opening Balance	250	250	250		580
	Movements	90	100	80		15
	Late Journal Entry	10	-10+10=0	50		0
	Closing Balance	350	450	580		595

Month-end scenario
• Reversal in next period

Year-end scenario
• No reversal in next period
• No data movement beyond P12

Figure 8.1 Late Journal Adjustments Scenario

■ **Adjustment journals**
GAAP adjustment entries or other adjustment entries are done to prepare local entity financial statements in line with group accounting policies prevailing in the region of operations or where they are being reported to legal authorities. Depending on the reporting requirements and based on the governing laws of the region where the consolidated results are being published, adjustments using journals are required to report financials.

Let's consider an example that involves journals posting. An investee is a publicly traded entity, so it's required to reverse the equity pickup entry that is created for US GAAP at the legal entity financial statements level. However, this has to be reposted by the consolidation of investments process in consolidations. Such adjustments are pro forma in nature, don't affect entity financial statements, and don't need to be performed in the entity book of records. This is distinct from late journal entries. Adjustments can be either manual, one-time journal entries to prepare reports, or they can be automatic on a recurring basis. Adjustment journals are also posted for group currency adjustments, fair value adjustments, and manual reclassifications.

Group reporting provides two standard methods of posting consolidation entries: standard Excel-based templates that are filled and imported, and a web interface to post individual journals manually to the system. The details on each of these methods are provided in the next section.

Before we dive into configuration, a few key considerations regarding journal entries are as follows:

- Strict controls should be enabled to keep journal entries at a minimum, and any requirement of frequent late entries is an indication of an adjustment to the close process or to automate the entry using automatic reclassifications.

- As of the time of writing (fall 2020), group reporting currently follows the K4 fiscal variant, which allows 12 periods (customers can remove this restriction with SAP's support) and 4 special periods only. Data release from SAP S/4HANA for group reporting is only possible for 12 periods. A special period is a concept that subdivides the last posting period into several periods for creating supplementary financial statements.

- Journal entries in group reporting are version- and ledger-specific and can't be posted across multiple versions.

In addition, note the following SAP Fiori apps that are used for consolidation entries:

- **Post Group Journal Entries**
  Used for posting individual journals.

- **Import Group Journal Entries**
  Used to mass-import group journals.

- **Display Group Journal Entries**
  Used to manage and display the journals already posted.

8.2   Journal Entry Template

In this section, we'll dive into templates for consolidation entries. We'll explore the different journal entry templates that are available to business users for posting adjustments, before walking through configuration steps and seeing how to make the consolidation entries.

8.2.1 Getting Started

We'll begin with the SAP Fiori Import Group Journal Entries app. Group reporting by default provides three journal entry templates out of the box for adjusting or correcting the data at multiple levels, which we'll discuss in this section. To start, open the Import Group Journal Entries app, choose a template (see Figure 8.2), and click the **Download** button to access the Excel-based template.

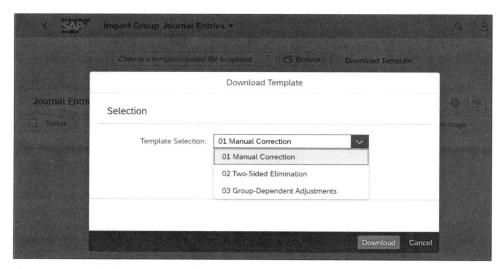

Figure 8.2 Standard Group Journal Import Templates

Each template has two sections, **Header Data** and **Line Item**, with fields assigned to them. Depending on the type of template, the fields can be mandatory or optional.

Let's walk through the **Header Data** fields first, which are common to all three types of templates:

- ***Journal Entry ID (10)**
  A unique numeric identifier based on the header data that is used for identifying the journal entry when being uploaded. The ID doesn't represent the document number that is generated by the system after the journal is posted successfully.

- ***Document Type (2)**
  Consolidation master data two-digit alphanumeric ID. This mandatory field selection should be filled with a value based on the type of entry, as explained in Chapter 3, that provides the details on possible value types.

- ***Ledger (2)**
  Consolidation master data two-digit alphanumeric ID for the consolidation ledger value that also specifies the group currency of the journal entry.

- ***Consolidation Chart of Accounts (2)**
  Consolidation master data two-digit alphanumeric ID as defined in the consolidation master data settings.

- ***Consolidation Version (3)**
  Consolidation master data three-digit alphanumeric ID for the version that provides the data category where the journal is being posted.

- ***Fiscal Year (4)**
  Consolidation master data four-digit fiscal year ID for the year specific to the journal entry to be posted.

- ***Posting period (3)**
  Consolidation master data three-digit fiscal period ID for the posting period of the journal entry where the data correction is being done.

- ***Consolidation Unit (18)**
  Consolidation master data for legal entity ID for the legal entity entered for the specific journal to be posted.

- **Remarks (50)**
  Meaningful text information to add context/comment for the journal posting. This provides additional details for easy understanding and tracking the data for audits.

Next, let's walk through the **Line Item** fields:

- ***Line Item (6)**
  Six-digit numeric ID providing uniqueness to each line of the journal. This creates individual line items for the entire journal entry.

- ***Financial Statement Item (10)**
  Consolidation master data 10-digit alphanumeric ID for the financial statement (FS) item as in the master data for the consolidation chart of accounts.

- ***Value in Local Currency**
  Amount in legal entity currency.

- ***Value in Group Currency**
  Amount in consolidation ledger currency.

These are the standard fields for each of the three template options we mentioned at the beginning of this section (refer to Figure 8.2). These actually provide the exact data context where the amount is being posted for data adjustment. One template can be used to post multiple journal entries in one go. Now, let's walk through the differences between the three available template options:

- **Consolidation unit-level adjustments**
  Template **01 Manual Correction** is used for any adjustments or standardization of reported data, as shown in Figure 8.3. Posting level 10 is the predominant posting level where the data is posted using this template. Other posting levels used for capturing corrections in reported data are 0C and 01. Additional details pertaining to the usage of these posting levels are covered in Chapter 3.

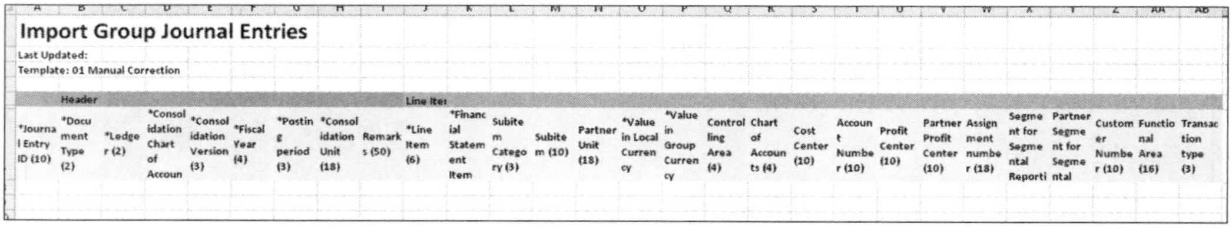

Figure 8.3 Journal Template: Unit-Dependent Adjustments

- **Consolidation unit pair-level adjustment**
  Template **02 Two-Sided Elimination** is used for posting two-sided eliminating entries for the consolidation and partner unit pair, as shown in Figure 8.4. Posting level 20 is the identification for any two-sided elimination entries. The **Line Item** section contains the ***Partner Unit (18)** mandatory field in this template. Partner unit identifies the trading partner entity in the two-sided transaction in this template.

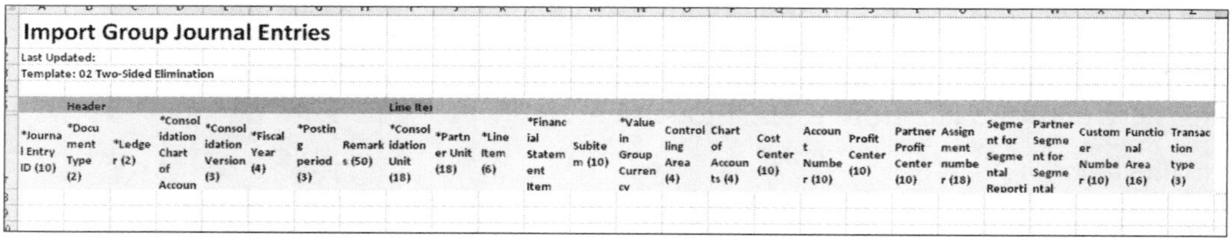

Figure 8.4 Journal Template: Two-Sided Adjustments

- **Consolidation group-level adjustment**
  Template **03 Group-Dependent Adjustments** is used to post group elimination entries or adjustments at the consolidation group level, as shown in Figure 8.5. Such entries are identified using posting level 30. ***Consolidation Group (18)** is set as an additional mandatory **Header** item in this template. This provides an option to adjust the data at the consolidation group level.

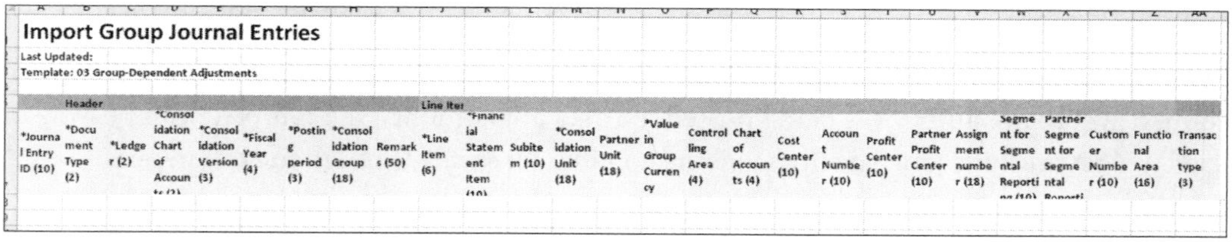

Figure 8.5 Journal Template: Group-Dependent Adjustments

8.2.2 Configuring the Journal Entry Template

Journal templates for importing the manual postings are delivered as standard, and you can't update the static structure of the import templates. Any custom field addition or removal doesn't have any effect on the structure of the template.

288

The standard SAP Fiori Post Group Journal Entries app, however, should be used for extensibility and modifications per your requirements. As explained in Chapter 3, master data configuration needs modification to include or exclude the additional fields.

Customer-specific enhancements to extend the consolidation Universal Journal (table ACDOCU) are supported via the standard code block extension and use the SAP Fiori Custom Field and Logic app. Custom fields are then available as described in two scenarios that we'll discuss in this section with an example.

Enable Fields

Let's begin with the first scenario, in which the **BillingDocumentType** field is enabled for inputs in the IMG path **SAP S/4HANA for Group Reporting • Master Data • Define Consolidation Master Data Fields**, as shown in Figure 8.6.

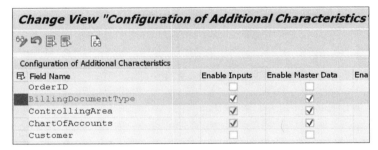

Figure 8.6 Scenario 1: Billing Type Enabled

Figure 8.7 confirms that the field is available for entry in the SAP Fiori Post Group Journal Entries app, displayed as **Billing Type** in the **Additional Data** tab.

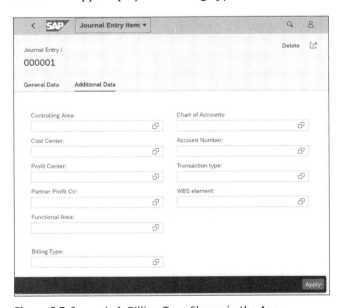

Figure 8.7 Scenario 1: Billing Type Shows in the App

Disable Fields

Next, let's consider a second scenario, where the **BillingDocumentType** field is disabled for inputs in the IMG path **SAP S/4HANA for Group Reporting • Master Data • Define Consolidation Master Data Fields**, as shown in Figure 8.8.

Figure 8.9 confirms that the field isn't available for entry in the SAP Fiori Post Group Journal Entries app, as it's not present in the **Additional Data** tab.

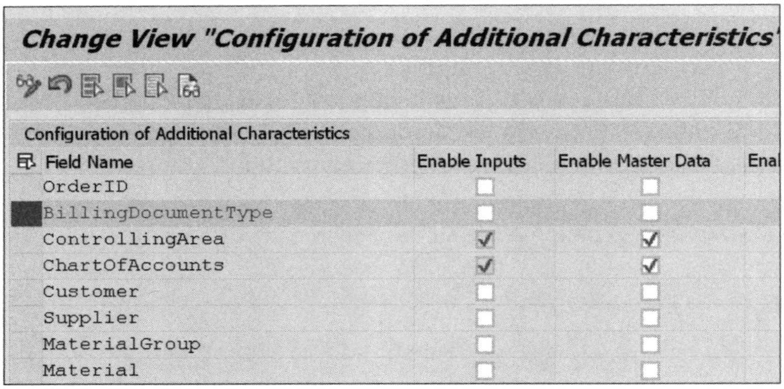

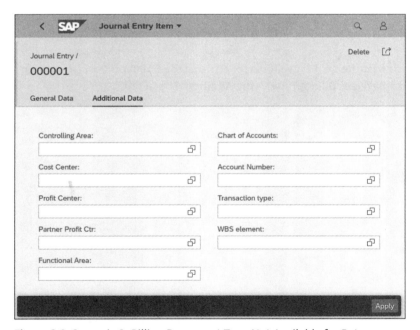

Figure 8.8 Scenario 2: Billing Document Type Unchecked

Figure 8.9 Scenario 2: Billing Document Type Not Available for Entry

8.2.3   Making Consolidation Entries

As explained in the previous section, manual postings are done either by posting individual documents using the standard SAP Fiori Post Group Journal Entries app or importing them in bulk using one of the import templates within group reporting (Import Group Journal Entries). To understand it better, in this section, we'll go through an example of manual posting using both scenarios.

Figure 8.10 and Figure 8.11, for example, provide the posting information for the individual posting scenario. They provide information regarding postings to be done on **Document Type 32**, a consolidation entry done at **Posting Level 30**, which needs to be done in group currency. The entry won't be reversed in the next period based on the setting in Figure 8.11.

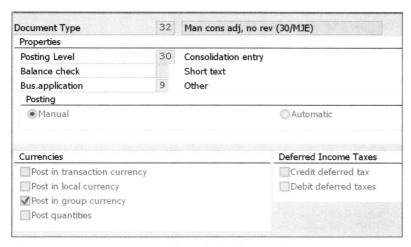

Figure 8.10 Document Type 32 for Individual Journal Entry

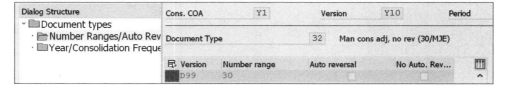

Figure 8.11 Document Type 32 Standard Reversal Settings

Figure 8.12 and Figure 8.13 provide information regarding the journal entries done using a template. Document types **16** and **18** are shown and both provide the ability to post the journals at the local and group currency levels. Both document types will post at level **10** (standardizing entry) and aren't going to be reversed in the next period.

Document Type	18	Man std GC, no DT/rev (10/MJE)	
Properties			
Posting Level	10	Standardizing entry	
Balance check	0	Error if balance is not zero	
Bus.application	9	Other	
☐ Translate to group crcy			
Posting			
⦿ Manual		○ Automatic	

Currencies	**Deferred Income Taxes**
☑ Post in transaction currency	☐ Credit deferred tax
☑ Post in local currency	☐ Debit deferred taxes
☑ Post in group currency	
☐ Post quantities	

Document Type	16	Man std GC, DT, no rev(10/MJE)	
Properties			
Posting Level	10	Standardizing entry	
Balance check	0	Error if balance is not zero	
Bus.application	9	Other	
☐ Translate to group crcy			
Posting			
⦿ Manual		○ Automatic	

Currencies	**Deferred Income Taxes**
☐ Post in transaction currency	☑ Credit deferred tax
☑ Post in local currency	☑ Debit deferred taxes
☑ Post in group currency	
☐ Post quantities	

Figure 8.12 Document Types 16 and 18

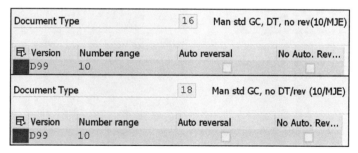

Document Type		16	Man std GC, DT, no rev(10/MJE)	
🖩 Version	Number range	Auto reversal		No Auto. Rev...
⬛ D99	10	☐		☐
Document Type		18	Man std GC, no DT/rev (10/MJE)	
🖩 Version	Number range	Auto reversal		No Auto. Rev...
⬛ D99	10	☐		☐

Figure 8.13 Reversal Settings for Document Types 16 and 18

Individual Journal Entry

In our first scenario, a model group LEGAL requires manual journals to be posted for tax reporting. Indirect costs such as salaries and benefits need reclassification to cost of material. This journal entry will contain two line items with an adjustment amount of $224,131.00 posted with debit/credit to each of the FS items as follows:

- Debit FS item: 412200 – Cost of purchased services and materials
- Credit FS item: 560000 – Salaries and other benefits

As this is a consolidation group adjustment, document type 32 is selected for the posting. Document type 32 determines that the posting is for the current period only and doesn't reverse in the next period. You use the Post Group Journal Entries app to post this single entry. To do so, open the Post Group Journal Entries app and click **Create**, as shown in Figure 8.14.

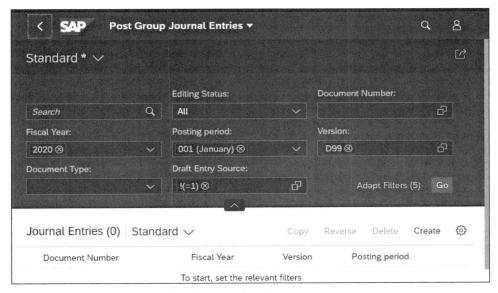

Figure 8.14 Post Group Journal Entries App: Create

Fill in the details on the **General Data** tab and **Line Items** tab, as shown in Figure 8.15:

- **Ledger**
  Consolidation ledger value that also specifies the group currency of the journal entry. Value **Y2** is used in this example.

- **Consolidation COA**
  As defined in the consolidation master data settings. Value **Y1** is used here.

- **Version**
  The version is the data category where the journal is to be posted. **D99** is used here.

- **Document Type**
  This mandatory field selection should be filled with a value based on the type of entry, as explained in Chapter 3, providing the details on possible value types. Numeric value **32** is used here.

- ***Fiscal Year**
  Year specific to the journal entry to be posted. Value **2020** is used here.

- ***Posting period**
  Posting period of the journal entry where the data correction is being done. Value **1** (January) is used here.

- ***Consolidation Group**
  The consolidation group used. Value **LEGAL** is used here.

- **Consolidation Unit**
  Legal entity entered for the specific journal to be posted. Value **FT01** is used here.

- **Text**
  Meaningful text information to add context/comments for the journal posting. This provides additional details for easy understanding and tracking the data for audits. Value **Indirect Costs** is used here.

- **Financial Statement Item**
  The FS item ID as in the master data for the consolidation chart of accounts specific to the scenario.

- **Value in Group Currency**
  Amount in the consolidation ledger currency. Value **$224,131.00** is used here.

- **Subitem**
  For the subitem, value **YB99** is the default value.

With each step, the system automatically saves a draft version of the journal.

After the entry details are filled, click **Check** to verify that there are no errors. Click **Post** to post the journal. A number in the subsequent screen, as shown in Figure 8.16, confirms that a document is generated.

Figure 8.15 Post Group Journal Entry

Figure 8.16 Successful Posting with Generated Document Number

Group Journal Entries

In the second scenario, a model group LEGAL requires multiple manual journals to be posted for a Canadian entity FT21. The following details provide the specifics of the journal entries:

- Entry 1: Royalty cash paid for the period, containing the following debit/credit items:
  - Debit FS item: 211800 – Other payables, current
  - Credit FS item: 111100 – Cash on hand
- Entry 2: Adjustments to fair value reserve before tax, containing the following debit/credit items:
  - Debit FS item: 314800 – Foreign currency translation reserve, before tax
  - Credit FS item: 314600 – Recyclable fair value reserve, before tax

You use the journal entry template **01 Manual Correction** for this posting and document types **16** and **18**, which allow posting only in group currency and no reversal in subsequent periods.

Open the Import Group Journal Entries app, and select the **Download Template** link to access the journal entry template, as shown in Figure 8.17.

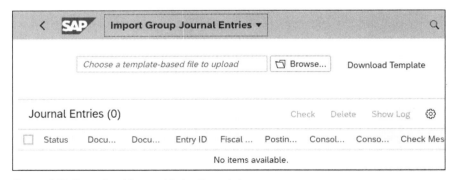

Figure 8.17 Download Journal Entry Template

Choose template **01 Manual Correction** as listed earlier in Figure 8.2. After the template is downloaded, fill in the details as shown in Figure 8.18, which we described in Section 8.2.1.

295

Import Group Journal Entries

Last Updated:
Template: 01 Manual Correction

*Journal Entry ID (10)	Header Data		*Consolidation Chart of Accounts (2)	*Consolidation Version (3)	*Fiscal Year (4)	*Posting period (3)	*Consolidation Unit (18)	Remarks (50)	Line Item		Subitem Category (3)	Subitem (10)	Partner Unit (18)	*Value in Local Currency	*Value in Group Currency
	*Document Type (2)	*Ledger (2)							*Line Item (6)	*Financial Statement Item (10)					
1000000100	16 Man std GC, DT, no	Y2 Consolidation	Y1 Consolidatic	D99	2020	1	FT21		000001	211800	1	915		0	14200
1000000100	16 Man std GC, DT, no	Y2 Consolidation	Y1 Consolidatic	D99	2020	1	FT21		000002	111100	1	915		0	-14200
1000000101	18 Man std GC, no DT,	Y2 Consolidation	Y1 Consolidatic	D99	2020	1	FT21		000001	314800	1	915		0	-12052
1000000101	18 Man std GC, no DT,	Y2 Consolidation	Y1 Consolidatic	D99	2020	1	FT21		000002	314600	1	915		0	12052

Figure 8.18 Manual Journal with Entries

As shown in Figure 8.18, a journal template allows multiple entries to multiple document types. This can be particularly helpful for postings across versions to reduce repetitive effort when the same entry needs posting to multiple versions. Based on the document type selected, the local or group currency amounts are expected. In the current scenario (document type 16 and 18), the amounts are posted in group currencies. In addition to all the dimensions of the group reporting consolidation model that are available in the template, there are additional steps that we'll walk through next.

After the template is ready, select **Browse** from the Import Group Journal Entries app as shown earlier in Figure 8.17, and upload the template with journal entries.

Figure 8.19 shows the journals in **Draft** state. They can be validated for any errors using the **Check** option.

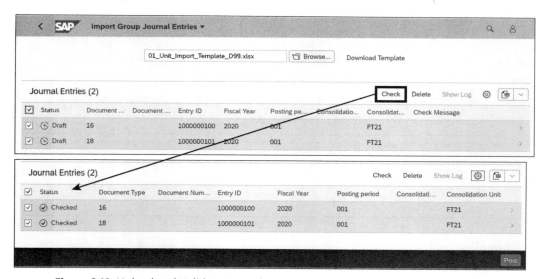

Figure 8.19 Upload and Validate Journals

If you're satisfied with the result, you can click on **Post** to post the journals. After the journals are posted successfully, a unique document number is generated, as shown in Figure 8.20.

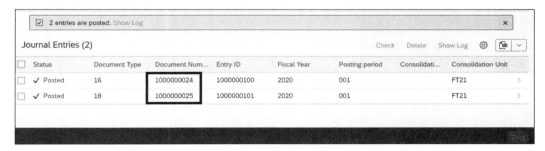

Figure 8.20 Successful Posting of Journals

8.3   Summary

You should now have an understanding of the most common consolidation journal entries. This chapter explained how SAP S/4HANA Finance for group reporting handles multiple type of journal entries in specific business scenarios. You should now be able to understand the significance of additional master data fields and how these fields are modified to enhance the journal entry web interface for usage. Journal posting in group reporting is driven by the document type master data, and you should now have an understanding of the usage of document types with the nature of journals to be posted.

Now, we'll move on to a new consolidation topic, matrix consolidation, in the next chapter.

Chapter 9
Matrix Consolidation

This chapter explains matrix consolidation, which uses the profit center as the dimension by which management wants to understand consolidations. It covers how to configure matrix consolidation and report on it for management purposes.

Many companies want to perform both legal and management consolidations but have been limited, until now, to performing management consolidations at ease. With SAP S/4HANA Finance for group reporting 1909, the functionality to perform full management consolidations, specifically matrix consolidation, without heavy customization and manual processes is finally a possibility.

In this chapter, we'll walk through the matrix consolidation process in SAP S/4HANA Finance for group reporting. We'll begin by providing you with an overview of the key concepts underlying matrix consolidation, before showing you how to configure and run it in your system.

9.1 What Is Matrix Consolidation?

Matrix consolidation is a type of management consolidation for management-oriented organizational units, such as profit centers, cost centers, and business segments. Matrix consolidation differs from your standard legal consolidation in that matrix consolidation uses the standard legal entity dimension but also these management-oriented dimensions, and, in our case, profit center or business segment. The purpose of matrix consolidation is to satisfy management requirements to analyze and understand internal performance that may not be reported to the street.

As consolidations are performed, the eliminations that occur for matrix consolidation will be performed virtually, in the case of group reporting, showing intercompany transactions across profit centers or business segments.

To help illustrate, let's walk through an example in which there is a profit center, Diet Cream Soda, from the legal entity, Natural Soda NA, performing an intercompany transaction with another profit center, Black Cherry Cola, within the same legal entity, as shown in Figure 9.1.

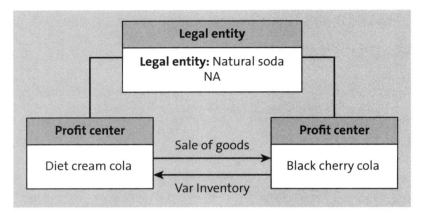

Figure 9.1 Illustration of Intercompany Transactions between Two Profit Centers

In this example, the Diet Cream Soda profit center sells goods to the Black Cherry Cola profit center as part of the same legal entity, Natural Soda NA. The Black Cherry Cola profit center delivers inventory to the Diet Cream Soda profit center via the Var Inventory account in exchange for their purchase of goods. However, from management's point of view, this is an intercompany transaction between two profit centers that they want to eliminate to show true profitability at the profit center level. In doing so, they would need to perform matrix consolidation.

Matrix consolidation follows the normal process steps undertaken during your standard consolidation:

1. Collect and prepare the data.
2. Perform balance carryforward.
3. Perform consolidations that include execution of currency translation, running intercompany eliminations, and running consolidation of investments.

Matrix consolidation will occur during this third step, and we'll dig into more detail in Section 9.3. But first, let's understand how to set up matrix consolidation.

9.2   Configuring Matrix Consolidation

Configuring matrix consolidation is a simple task because it occurs virtually and requires a defined hierarchy of consolidation units, profit centers, and segments to display properly as it's eliminated.

In this section, we'll walk through the configuration steps for matrix consolidation master data and business rules.

9.2.1   Parameters and Master Data

You need to make the relevant configuration settings in your backend system by entering Transaction SPRO and accessing the Customizing activities under the IMG. In the overall IMG structure to define the consolidation master data fields, choose **SAP S/4HANA for Group Reporting • Master Data • Define Consolidation Master Data Fields**, as shown in Figure 9.2.

Figure 9.2 Define Consolidation Master Data Fields

Once there, the **Change View "Configuration of Additional Characteristics": Overview** screen allows you to configure the additional characteristics for the profit center, as shown in Figure 9.3. This configuration is critical to successful execution of matrix consolidation. The two characteristics that need to be enabled are as follows:

- **Enable Hierarchy**
  Multidimensional reporting is supported when data is organized in a tree structure through hierarchies by showing data with multiple set of levels; for instance, costs may be grouped with costs as the parent, and many subcosts may be grouped as children of that parent. This allows for hierarchy reporting to occur and to understand pre- and post-matrix consolidation transactions.

- **Enable Hierarchical Elimination**

  This allows for virtual elimination, by profit center, during hierarchy reporting.

Following the configuration, make sure to save using the **Save** icon.

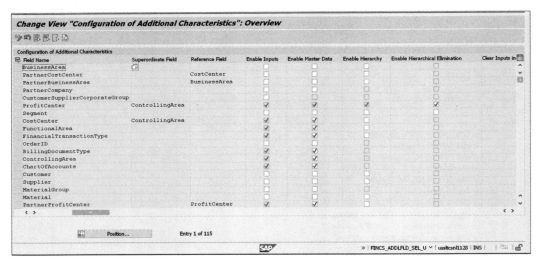

Figure 9.3 Configuration of Additional Characteristics

Note

In addition to profit centers, other dimensions, such as cost center or segment, can have **Enable Hierarchy** and **Enable Hierarchical Elimination** turned on to facilitate elimination across those dimensions as well, should the business wish to do so.

After both hierarchy and hierarchy elimination have been enabled, you're ready to check your business rules to ensure the right rules are in place to perform matrix consolidation.

9.2.2   Business Rules

Matrix consolidation uses the same intercompany rules that were configured and discussed in Chapter 6. But, as a reminder, you must update the necessary configuration settings in your backend system by entering Transaction SPRO and accessing the Customizing activities under the IMG. Once there, you'll navigate to **SAP S/4HANA for Group Reporting • Reclassification • Define Reclassification Methods**.

You'll arrive at the screen shown in Figure 9.4, which highlights the different methods, or business rules, used for reclassification. This nomenclature can be misleading because this is also where users can define a new method or update an existing method, which matrix consolidation uses when it's run.

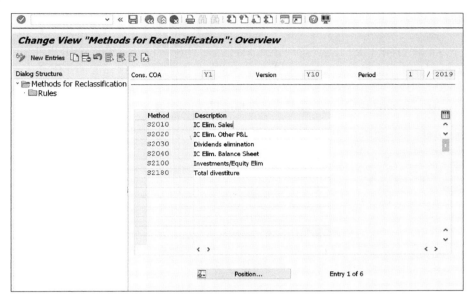

Figure 9.4 Methods for Reclassification

In this example, we'll use **Method S2010** to look at the rule that was defined in a little bit more detail. When you open **Method S2010**, **IC Elims Sales**, you'll see the following four tabs, highlighted in Figure 9.5:

- **Settings**
  The first tab contains various settings that are covered in Chapter 6 during the discussion of intercompany eliminations.

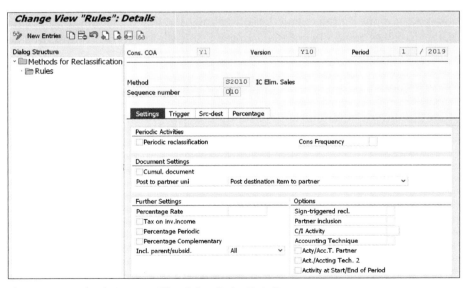

Figure 9.5 Method S2010, IC Elim. Sales: Rules Details

- **Trigger**

  This tab, as shown in Figure 9.6, shows the specific trigger associated with the method. As a reminder, the trigger that is selected should be updated in the account master data for the specific accounts that will use this business rule. The trigger is used to reclassify data from source to destination accounts/financial statement (FS) items. You'll select the trigger that was defined for this reclassification rule.

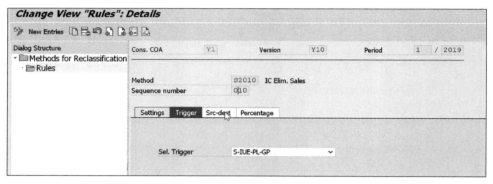

Figure 9.6 Select Trigger for S2010 Method

- **Src-dest**

  The source destination tab shows the target attribution for the destination of **S-ELIM-INATION-TARGET**, which is the destination of the elimination (see Figure 9.7). If **Target Attrib. Inherited from Src Item** is checked, then the system inherits the target from the source item. Otherwise, it's inherited from the trigger. Source account assignment **FS Item** is the source for the reclassification, and destination account assignment **FS Item** is the target to which the value is posted as a result of reclassification. You have the option to end the source and destination FS items or leave one or both blank. But remember, if they are left blank, the triggering item is used as both source and destination.

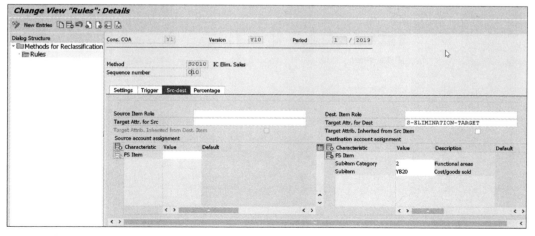

Figure 9.7 Source Destination Details

> **Note**
>
> Use IMG menu **SAP S/4HANA for Group Reporting • Consolidation FS Item Configuration • FS Item Attribute • Values Attribute • Attribute Value** to create new attribute values for elimination rules.

- **Percentage**

  The system uses the percentage defined in this tab to determine the percentage to be applied to the reclassification. This isn't required as part of matrix consolidation and typically is only relevant for consolidation of investments, covered in Chapter 7.

Now that you've confirmed the right business rules and matrix consolidation configurations are in place, you're ready to run matrix consolidation.

9.3   Running Matrix Consolidation

Matrix consolidation requires a simple configuration, but most of the magic that happens is in the running and reporting of matrix consolidation. In fact, it's through the use of global accounting hierarchies that you can easily define and run through reports. We'll walk through tasks related to running matrix consolidation in the following sections, including managing global accounting hierarchies and reporting.

9.3.1   Managing Global Accounting Hierarchies

Before running matrix consolidation, you must confirm there are defined hierarchies for consolidation units and profit centers because eliminations will consolidate and display hierarchically. Using the SAP Fiori frontend, select the **Manage Global Accounting Hierarchies** tile shown in Figure 9.8.

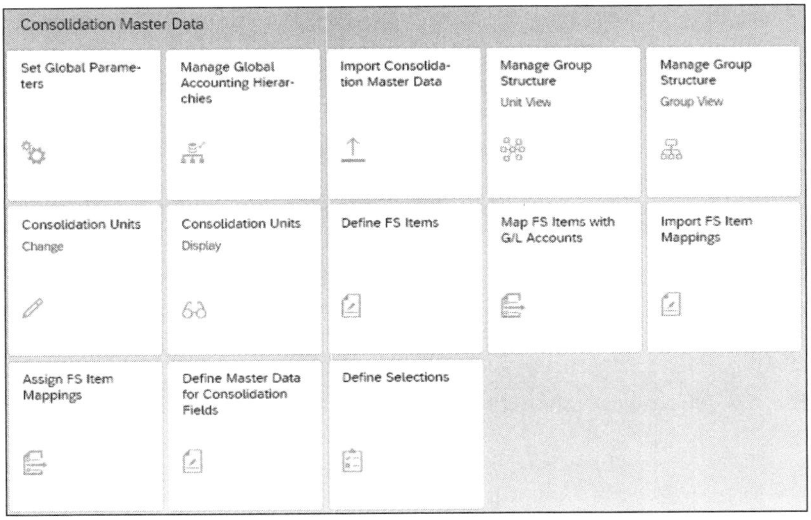

Figure 9.8 Manage Global Accounting Hierarchies Tile

Once there, you'll see all defined hierarchies available, as shown in Figure 9.9.

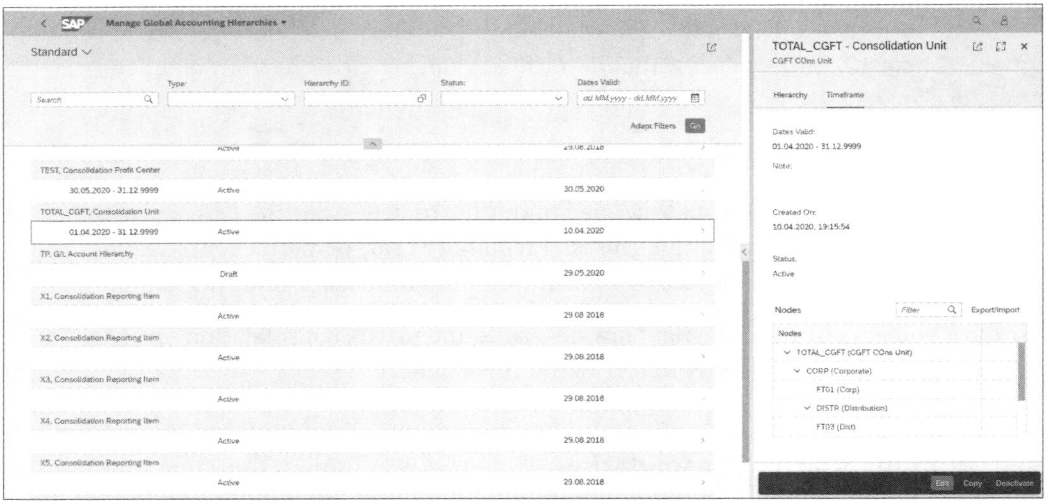

Figure 9.9 Display of All Global Accounting Hierarchies

Within the Manage Global Accounting Hierarchies app, you can create and edit hierarchies and their respective time frames (covered in detail in Chapter 3, Section 3.2.3). The hierarchies are defined, so you can double-click the hierarchy you want to view, which are the following two hierarchies: **TOTAL_CGFT – Consolidation Unit**, as shown in Figure 9.10, and **PFCTR – Consolidation Profit Center**, as shown in Figure 9.11.

Figure 9.10 TOTAL_CGFT: Consolidation Unit Hierarchy

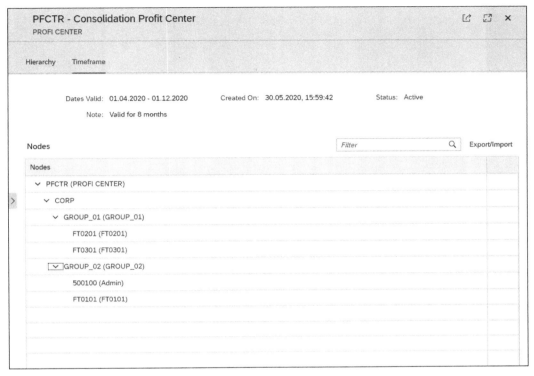

Figure 9.11 PFCTR: Consolidation Profit Center Hierarchy

In the consolidation unit hierarchy, you'll notice legal entities roll up to groups, which roll up to a parent consolidation unit.

Take note of the entities rolling up to each group node. For instance, **FT03 (Dist)** rolls up to **DISTR (Distribution)** but not **MANF (Manufacturing)**.

In the consolidation profit center hierarchies, you'll notice profit centers roll up to parent profit centers. For instance, **FT0101** rolls up to **Group_02** but **FT0201** and **FT0301** roll up to **Group_01**. This is important to understanding where the eliminations will occur as part of matrix consolidation.

9.3.2   Reporting

To analyze the data in the matrix consolidation, navigate to **Group Reports • Group Data Analysis** using the SAP Fiori frontend, as shown in Figure 9.12.

307

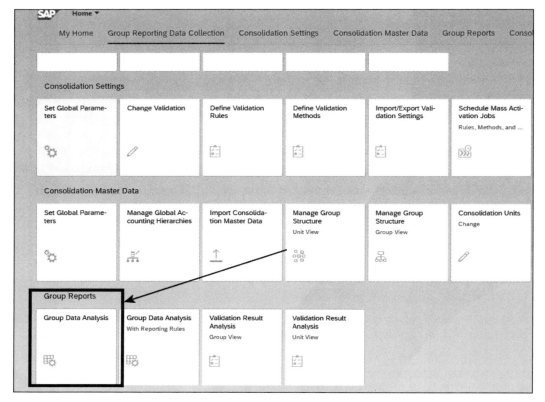

Figure 9.12 Group Data Analysis Tile

Double-click the tile to open the Group Data Analysis app. From here, you'll need to populate the necessary parameters for which you want to analyze the data. As you'll see in Figure 9.13, there are several fields to update, but only the fields with a red asterisk are required fields:

- **Version**
  Represents the data set version, such as **D99** for **Actuals**.

- **Ledger**
  Represents the ledger for which data is being analyzed, which is **Y2**, consolidation ledger, in this example.

- **Consolidation COA**
  Represents the version chart of accounts to be used, which is typically just one version of a consolidation chart of accounts. Value **Y1** is used in this example.

- **Period/Year**
  The period and year for which analysis will be run, which is January 2020 in this example.

- **Period Mode**
  You can show periodic (**PER**) or year-to-date (**YTD**) aggregated values for each measure. **PER** is chosen in this example.

- **Consolidation Group**
  With multiple consolidation groups to choose, this selection determines the consolidation group to run the report on.

- **Consolidation Unit Hierarchy**
  Represents the appropriate organizational unit hierarchy of which elimination members are derived at runtime for the consolidation unit. Value **CS17** is chosen in this example, which means the matrix consolidation will derive at that level of the consolidation unit hierarchy.

- **Profit Center Hierarchy**
  Similar to consolidation unit hierarchy, this represents the appropriate level at which elimination members will be derived at runtime for the profit center. In this example, they will be derived at **CS04**.

- **Segment Hierarchy**
  Similar to the profit center and consolidation unit hierarchies, this represents the appropriate level at which elimination members will be derived at runtime for the segment.

- **Hierarchy Valid On**
  Applicable to consolidation unit, profit center, and segment hierarchies, this represents that they are valid within the periods selected.

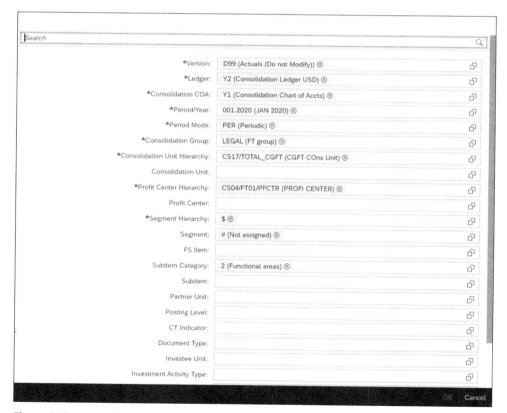

Figure 9.13 Group Data Analysis Parameters

> **Note**
>
> Ensure that you have the right date for the **Hierarchy Valid On** field. This is the date the hierarchy is valid for and sometimes can be overlooked and be the reason why a report doesn't contain data after all parameters are updated.

After you've updated all your parameters, click **OK**, and the report will execute. In this example, you'll see the **Consolidation Unit Hierarchy** and **Profit Center Hierarchy** are selected that we reviewed earlier. The results of the Group Data Analysis are presented in Figure 9.14.

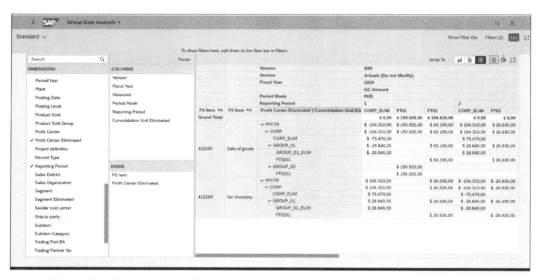

Figure 9.14 Group Data Analysis Results

You've done it! You now have results for a matrix consolidation. As you can see in Figure 9.14, eliminations have been made across two accounts: **Sales of goods** and **Var Inventory**.

For **Sale of goods**, you can see there is a –$75,470.00 elimination appearing in the **CORP_ELIM** elimination profit center and the offsetting $75,470.00 appearing in the **Var Inventory** account on the **CORP_ELIM** elimination profit center.

This report is configurable through drag and drop. For instance, you can drag and drop dimensions from the left to the columns or rows area if you want to visually see this differently. We'll cover more details on reporting in Chapter 11.

9.4   Summary

Matrix consolidation functionality, included as part of group reporting, will reduce added complexities and manual effort for many companies who have done matrix consolidation using manual, time-intensive processes. With its easy, one-time configuration, companies will have the ability to set up matrix consolidation business rules and easily run their reports on a monthly basis to get the matrix consolidation view they require.

Our next chapter will walk through the financial close process, including the importance of the ledger close, the details of the group close, and how group reporting can be used to facilitate continuous accounting.

9

Chapter 10
Financial Close

This chapter walks through the typical ledger and group close processes that accounting and finance teams perform each month. While the focus of this chapter is on the group close, it outlines activities that must happen during ledger close to complete group close properly. Finally, the chapter introduces the continuous accounting concept that facilitates a faster close.

In this chapter, we'll explore financial close in general and group close in particular. Although the group close is dependent on the ledger close, you can run the group consolidation process before the ledger is closed. That will happen, but it won't be final until the starting point for the group close is a closed ledger.

As a result, we'll dig into the ledger close, specifically the period-end close, first. Then, we'll walk through the group period-end close, including dependencies and continuous accounting.

10.1 Ledger Close

Each month, a company must close the ledger, which maintains a complete record of all financial transactions (e.g., credits and debits) that are done throughout the month. The *ledger close* is where accounting has completed its month-end activities related to the general ledger and is prepared to close it for the month.

> **Note**
> In SAP S/4HANA, you have to define one ledger as the leading ledger, and the leading ledger in the standard system is 0L. The leading ledger gets assigned to all company codes and contains currency, fiscal year variant, and posting period variant settings that apply to the company code.

Keep in mind that the ledger close focuses on closing the ledger by entity. Some companies may have only a handful of entities, whereas others may have hundreds or thousands. But either way, the ledger close breaks down into two simple steps that must be completed before starting the group close:

1. All revenue accounts are closed by entity.
2. All expense accounts are closed by entity.

While those two steps may sound easy, they are actually quite complex for many companies. Figure 10.1 shows the following four cycles that make up the financial close at a high level:

- **Processing cycles**
  Consists of transactions happening throughout the month such as accounts payable (AP) transactions, accounts receivable transactions, and payroll transactions. These may flow in automatically or require posting journal entries to the ledger and adjusting journal entries throughout the month.

- **Ledger close cycle**
  Reconciliation of all account balances to ensure the general ledger can be closed, the period is closed so no further transactions can occur, and accruals are properly entered.

- **Group close cycle**
  Follows the standard consolidation process, including data collection, carrying forward the ending balance from the prior year to the beginning balance of the current fiscal year, executing currency translation, moving net income to retained earnings, eliminating intercompany balances, eliminating investment in subsidiaries, and executing topside adjustments

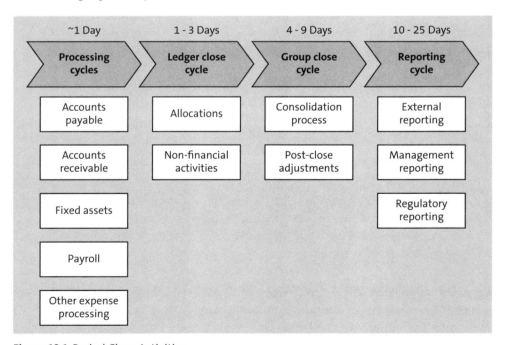

Figure 10.1 Period Close Activities

- **Reporting cycle**
  Execution of month-end, quarter-end, or year-end financial statements to parties outside of the reporting entity, which include investors, creditors, and lenders who require the reporting information to evaluate the financial condition of the company. Also includes the execution of management reporting for parties within the reporting entity, including executive leadership, board members, and other management team members. Finally, this also includes any required regulatory reporting that may or may not be applicable for all companies.

As we dig a little bit deeper, you see that the ledger close process usually takes between one and three days and involves quite a few processes. On day 1, the following processes typically occur and can last up to two or three days depending on a company's ability to standardize, automate, and integrate:

- **Accounts payable**
  This process is about settling up all the money that was paid by the business to its vendors or suppliers and is shown as a liability on the company's balance sheet.

- **Accounts receivable**
  These are all the receivable payments that are owed to the company for services or goods provided. What makes them a receivable is that customers have placed an order for a good but have not yet paid for it. At month end, these are all accounted for and settled up where appropriate.

- **Fixed assets**
  At month end, finance must account for all known tangible assets such as property, plant, or equipment that can't be easily converted into cash.

- **Payroll**
  Just like it sounds, this is accounting for the expense to pay all employees for the month.

- **Other expense processing**
  Expense processing is a general process but really means accounting for any other expenses that impact a company's bottom line and fall into the category of expense, such as rent expenses, travel expenses, and so on.

Following these activities, the allocation process will be run. As part of the allocation process, certain methods are chosen to allocate overhead costs to business segments, profit centers, and/or companies. For example, the overhead cost of finance and HR may be allocated to three different business segments of a soda producer. One-third of the cost may go to the distributing company, one-third to the bottling company, and one-third to the international company because finance and HR are distributed evenly to those businesses that use it. Similarly, if you're a manufacturer of goods, distribution of the factory overhead costs is critical to understanding your true production cost. An allocation methodology is typically designed to do just that.

Following allocations, some nonfinancial activities may occur as well as working with controls and compliance to ensure the numbers are accurate. At that point, the ledger will be locked to prevent any journal entries or other entries from changing the numbers, and the group close cycle can begin.

10.2   Group Close

Group close is the process following the ledger close and includes execution of all consolidation activities and post-close adjustments that occur following consolidation activities. In this section, we'll discuss period-end close and the consolidation activities in additional detail, before moving on to a summary of dependencies on ledger close and a deep dive into continuous accounting using group reporting.

10.2.1   Period-End Close

After the leading ledger is closed for the month, the group close process can begin. The consolidation ledger determines the reference SAP S/4HANA ledger (typically the leading ledger, OL) and group currency. Two consolidation ledgers are delivered with group reporting:

- **Y1 consolidation ledger EUR**
  Delivered with group reporting best practice content where the group currency is set to EUR and valuation must be defined to integrate to an accounting reference ledger.

- **Y2 consolidation ledger USD**
  Delivered with group reporting best practice content where the group currency is set to USD and valuation must be defined to integrate to an accounting reference ledger. Typically, you'll only define integration to one source ledger of the Universal Journal.

The consolidation ledgers serve two purposes:

1. Define the group currency.
2. Define the valuation.

In this second step, an accounting reference ledger is assigned to a consolidation ledger. While this configuration is covered in Chapter 3, Section 3.2.1, it's a helpful reminder to highlight the dependency on the accounting ledger, especially from an integration perspective.

The group close follows the consolidation process discussed in Chapter 1 and focuses on two basic areas, data collection and execution/reporting, as reviewed in Figure 10.2 and discussed in the following sections.

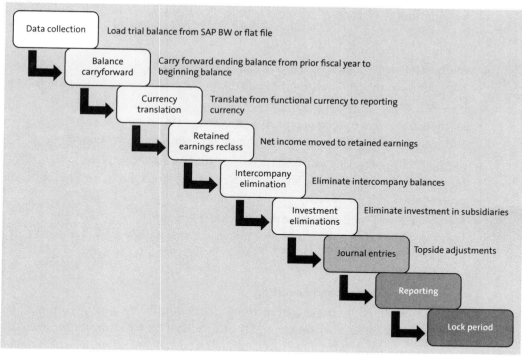

Figure 10.2 Consolidation Process for Group Close

Collecting and Preparing the Data

Using the Data Monitor, you can run the tasks needed to prepare data prior to running the consolidations and eliminations, as shown in Figure 10.3 (we discussed this configuration of the Data Monitor in Chapter 4, Section 4.2). As a reminder, you can access the Data Monitor via the tile on the SAP Fiori launchpad.

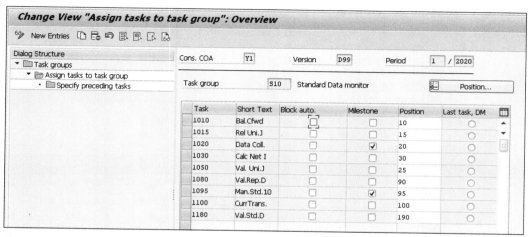

Figure 10.3 Data Monitor Used to Prepare Data for the Group Close

The following are various options for loading data from table ACDOCA (leading ledger table) to table ACDOCU (consolidation table). As part of collecting and preparing the data, any or all of these methods can be used:

- **Method 1: Release data from table ACDOCA to table ACDOCU**
  Integrate accounting data from SAP S/4HANA table ACDOCA to consolidation table ACDOCU.

- **Method 2: Flexible upload of reporting financial data**
  Manually upload data for one or many periods to consolidation table ACDOCU.

- **Method 3: Import group journal entries (via standard SAP template)**
  Manually import journal entries, in group currency, directly into the consolidation process via the standard SAP journal entry template.

- **Method 4: Post group journal entries (via SAP Fiori app)**
  Post topside journal entries, post-consolidation, using the standard Journal Entry SAP Fiori app.

Executing Consolidations and Reporting

Executing consolidations consists of currency translation, intercompany eliminations, investment eliminations, and reporting. The Consolidation Monitor, shown in Figure 10.4, can be used to perform these tasks, excluding currency translation, which can be executed using the Data Monitor (refer to Chapter 5).

Hierarchy		Description	Status	Error	Warnings	Date	Time	Last changed by
☑ ∨ 🗁 CGFT		Corporate Group	◐	0	0			
☐	⚙ ZIIIE	IUE Interest Income exp	✕	0	0			
☐	⚙ 2011	IC Elim. Sales	✕	0	0			
☐	⚙ 2021	IC Elim. Other Income/Expense	✕	0	0			
☐	⚙ 2031	Dividends Elimination	✕	0	0			
☐	⚙ 2041	IC Elim. Balance Sheet	✕	0	0			
☐	◆ 2050	Manual Eliminations (PL20)	✕	0	0			
☐	⚙ 2060	Preparation Cons Group Change	✕	0	0			
☐	⚙ 2141	Calculate Group Shares (PL 30)	✕	0	0			
☐	◆ 2140	Enter Group Shares (PL30)	✕	0	0			
☐	⚙ 2100	Investments / Equity elimin.	✕	0	0			
☐	◆ 2150	Manual Eliminations (PL30)	✕	0	0			
☐	⚙ 2180	Total Divestiture	✕	0	0			
☐	⚙ 2980	Consolidated Data Validation	✕	0	0			

Figure 10.4 Consolidation Monitor Used to Run Consolidations

When using the Consolidation Monitor, you have the ability to monitor the overall status of the consolidation task, such as **Open**, **Initial Stage**, **Error**, or **Completed**. Additionally, you can add milestones for each consolidation task to allow users to monitor and validate each task when executing the group close, as discussed in Chapter 6.

> **Note**
>
> The Consolidation Monitor only completes tasks for consolidation groups, as consolidation units aren't visible in the monitor.

After all the tasks are completed successfully as part of the Consolidation Monitor, it's time to perform validations on reported financial data. Most of the details as it relates to running consolidated reporting will be covered in Chapter 11. But for purposes of this chapter, the group close is complete after data has been collected and prepared, run through consolidations, and properly validated.

10.2.2   Dependencies on Ledger Close

Entities must be closed, with no further accounting activity occurring, before the group close can begin. In other words, revenue and expense accounts must be closed for each entity before the group close can start.

However, in most companies, there are always going to be late journal entries that come in after the fact, usually driven by certain business scenarios that require some flexibility in the close process. Typically, the external reporting team will work with the accounting team to ensure all late journal entries have been accounted for in the process and are included as part of the group close. It may mean running through the consolidation another time or reloading table ACDOCU to include any late journal entries.

10.2.3   Continuous Accounting Using Group Reporting

SAP S/4HANA Finance for group reporting, when implemented correctly, offers the opportunity for some companies to perform continuous accounting. But before understanding how this is possible, it's important to understand what continuous accounting is.

Continuous accounting is an approach that allows finance to perform real-time financial analysis, empowers finance to be a better business partner, and enables finance to serve a more strategic function in the corporation. Quite simply, it focuses on real-time processing that delivers in-depth analysis resulting in a more efficient close and more accurate financials.

Figure 10.5 shows an illustration of where continuous accounting activities can take place to allow for real-time or near real-time financial analysis starting with the ledger close.

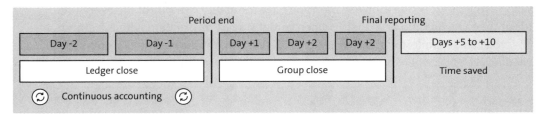

Figure 10.5 Saving Time through Continuous Accounting

To effectively deliver continuous accounting, there are five areas of focus that can help you get started:

- **Automation**
  Automation plays an integral part in the ledger close process. Identifying opportunities to automate manual processes (e.g., manual journal entries) will save time, such as removing all manual journal entries from the ledger close and ensuring they are fully automated, in real time, so management can view them at any point in the process.

- **Real-time data processing**
  Real-time data processing allows for instant insights, immediate reconciliation, and automatic review of the details, removing any time delay to wait for data to be processed or shared. For example, you might remove any batch data processing so transactions are posted in the ledger in real time and not processed nightly or weekly, which would delay management's ability to view transactions anytime they want.

- **Elevate your talent**
  Elevate your talent to ensure your finance organization has the necessary skills to transform from task takers and executors to analyzers of information. For example, by removing manual journal entries and the time required to add them to the system, your team's time can be repurposed to report on information throughout the month rather than waiting until month end.

- **Monitor metrics and results**
  Monitor metrics and results by measuring existing and updated processes against automation benchmarks to understand where improvement remains. For example, consider identifying monthly baselines, a revenue baseline, or an expense baseline, and measure against it throughout the month.

- **Review your progress**
  Review your progress as you navigate your continuous accounting journey, and identify process gaps and bottlenecks to seek continued improvement. For example, what bottlenecks are preventing you from seeing information in real time across your company's books? Do you have a bottom-up approach where subsidiaries may not complete their entries until day 1 or 2?

10.3 Summary

You should now have a good understanding of the unique differences between ledger close and group close and how continuous accounting can shorten your close cycle. And while it may sound simple, the close process can actually be quite complex.

Group reporting with the Data Monitor and Consolidation Monitor provide real-time visibility into all the processes that go into executing the group close, and these monitors help immensely with understanding all the tasks being executed and the status of each task to ensure a successful group close.

In the next chapter, we'll journey further into the reporting functionality with SAP S/4HANA Finance for group reporting.

10

Chapter 11
Consolidation Reporting

You've learned all about group reporting, including how to set up the configuration and execute the consolidation process. In this chapter, we'll focus on the different reporting options available for group reporting.

This chapter discusses the reporting options available in SAP S/4HANA Finance for group reporting. Several SAP-delivered reports are available as well as additional reporting tools to meet the reporting requirements. In this chapter, we'll explain the steps to use SAP Analysis for Microsoft Office, SAP Analytics Cloud, SAP Fiori, and reporting rules to create a custom report.

11.1 Predefined Reports

With SAP S/4HANA Finance for group reporting, predelivered financial reports are available to standardize reporting using SAP Fiori. These reports can be categorized as *local reports* that provide data visualization at the legal entity level prior to consolidation rules processing, and *group reports* that support statutory group-level reporting after the consolidation rules are applied. These reports are supplied with a predefined default structure when opened but support visualization capabilities such as data filtering, dimensionality changes, and drill through to line item level details. A built-in feature to choose between grid design and charts for visual interpretation is also supported.

In the following sections, we'll provide more details on the various delivered reports and their usage.

11.1.1 Local (Preconsolidation) Reports

As mentioned, local reports support data analysis at the consolidation unit level primarily for activities such as root cause identification and drilldown to transaction-level details analysis. The following local reports are delivered via SAP Fiori:

- **Validation Results Analysis – Unit View**
  Provides validation results for tasks performed at various steps in the consolidation process. The report offers a combination of charts and table views by consolidation

version, ledger, fiscal period, and task types (including reported data validations and standardized data validations). Reported data validation is a task that gives you the ability to validate reported financial data of a consolidation unit in its local currency per the assigned validations in the **Methods** tab of the consolidation unit. Standardized data validation is a task that gives you the ability to validate the financial data of a consolidation unit in its group currency per the assigned validations in the **Methods** tab of the consolidation unit.

- **Balance Sheet**
  Provides balance sheet data results by consolidation unit, by movements or transaction types, and by yearly comparison analysis, as shown in Figure 11.1. The reports provide results in both local and group currency values.

Figure 11.1 Balance Sheet Standard SAP Fiori Tiles

- **P&L Statement by Nature of Expense**
  Provides results for profit and loss (P&L) data by consolidation unit, by functional area or subitem category 2, and by yearly comparative analysis, as shown in Figure 11.2.

Figure 11.2 Standard P&L by Nature of Expense SAP Fiori Tiles

11.1.2   Group (Consolidated) Reports

Group reports provide a view of data after all consolidation processes are executed and financial statements are ready for analysis. The following reports are provided as part of the standard delivery via SAP Fiori:

- **Validation Results Analysis – Group View**
  Provides validation results for tasks performed at various steps in the consolidation

process. The report provides a combination of charts and table views by consolidation version, ledger, fiscal period, consolidation group, and task types (including standardized data validations and consolidated data validations).

- **Consolidated Balance Sheet**
  Provides balance sheet data results by consolidation group, by movements or transaction types, and by yearly comparison analysis, as shown in Figure 11.3. The report provides results in group currency values.

Figure 11.3 Consolidated Balance Sheet SAP Fiori Tiles

- **Consolidation P&L Statements by Nature of Expense**
  Provides consolidated data results for P&L using a standard layout for consolidation group, functional area, consolidation subgroup, and yearly comparison, as shown in Figure 11.4. The data can be viewed in group currency only.

Figure 11.4 Consolidated P&L Standard SAP Fiori Tiles

In addition, the following rule-based group reports are available (which we'll discuss further in Section 11.3):

- **Consolidated P&L Statements by Function of Expense**
  This report provides the data results when P&L statement items are defined using the reporting rules. Standard delivered hierarchy X4 is used for reporting on consolidation group, consolidation subgroup, or comparative year analysis of data, as shown in Figure 11.5.

Figure 11.5 Consolidated P&L by Function of Expense

- **Cash Flow Statement**
  This report provides the data results for the cash flow statement; the line items for this are defined using the reporting rules. Standard delivered hierarchy X2 is used for reporting.

- **Statement of Comprehensive Income**
  This report provides the data results for statement of comprehensive income; the line items for this are defined using the reporting rules. Standard delivered hierarchy X3 is used for reporting.

- **Statement of Changes in Equity**
  This report provides the data results for financial statement of changes in equity; the line items for this are defined using the reporting rules. Standard delivered hierarchy X1 is used for reporting.

- **IC Reconciliation**
  This is a standard report providing the reconciliation amounts and differences in the group and local currencies for intercompany scenarios for a selected consolidation unit and trading partners. The report can provide data on an entity level or group level, depending on the selected tile view. The report generates a more manageable view of intercompany transactions based on creating the unit trading partner pairs on the fly, leveraging the standard delivered hierarchy X5.

11.2   Drill-Through to Transaction Data

The dynamic display of journal entries, such as analyzing the details of the adjustment entries for revenue expenses, is often a common requirement of business users. The high-value piece of information should be available to the user in the right form without having to know how to pull data from table ACDOCU. The out-of-the-box functionality of group reporting allows users to drill through from a report to the details of the journal entry.

Figure 11.6 shows the Trial Balance consolidation report, from which you can get the details of the journal entry.

		Version	Y10
		Version	Actuals
		Fiscal Year	2019
		Reporting Period	12
		Period Mode	PER
FS Item ▲	FS Item ▽▲		LC Amount ▽▲
121800	Oth. Receiv.		3.040,00 EUR
211100	Tra pay L.,NC		-22.240,00 EUR
121100	Trade, GV		$ 27.000,00
131600	Oth inventories		$ -383,95
211100	Tra pay L.,NC		$ -271.965,30
283100	Oth liab, NC		$ 0,00
412100	Var Inventory		$ -243.578,00
585000	Oth op.expenses		$ -15.000,00
586000	Op. FV losses		$ 1.599,80

Figure 11.6 Consolidation Report

Let's walk through the steps to drill-through to the transaction data:

1. After the report is displayed in the SAP Fiori app, select the row for which you want to look at the details.

2. Right-click on the row, click **Jump To**, and select **Display Journal Entries With Reporting Logic**, as shown in Figure 11.7.

Figure 11.7 List of Journal Entries

3. The report will display all the journal entries associated with the row. In this example, there are three journal entries displayed with a hyperlink for each document and line item. You can click the hyperlink to get the details of each journal entry.

327

11.3 Data Analysis Using Reporting Rules

Group Data Analysis is a predelivered SAP Fiori app that allows you to look at the consolidated data based on a hierarchical view of consolidation groups. We've explored this app in specific scenarios in Chapter 6 for intercompany eliminations and Chapter 7 for the consolidation of investments. Now, let's dive into this app on a more general level.

There are five predelivered reports based on the hierarchies (X) and reporting rules, which we introduced in Section 11.1.2:

- Statement of Changes in Equity (X1)
- Statement of Cash Flow (X2)
- Statement of Comprehensive Income (X3)
- P&L by Function of Expense (X4)
- IC Reconciliation (X5)

The reporting rule provides flexible options for users to create their own reporting rules based on business requirements. For example, if you're using a standard cash flow report at the consolidated level, the report will show only the loan balance. If you need to see the details of what the loan borrowed and the repaid amount at the consolidated level, it might be a bit tricky to get the data. However, you can use the reporting rule to create the report.

There are three main steps to create a new report using reporting rules:

1. Define a reporting item hierarchy.
2. Define a reporting rule.
3. Assign the reporting rule to the consolidation version with a validity period.

Let's walk through this process. In this example, we'll create a reporting rule to display the cash flow reporting data at a detailed level (operating, investment, and financing). Follow these steps:

1. Launch the SAP Fiori Manage Global Accounting Hierarchies app under the **Consolidation Master Data** SAP Fiori group to arrive at the screen shown in Figure 11.8. It's easier to copy an existing delivered hierarchy. In this scenario, we'll search for the X2 hierarchy and copy it into our custom CFR hierarchy.

2. On the right-side panel at the bottom, you have the option to **Edit**, **Copy**, and **Deactivate** a hierarchy. In this example, make a copy of the hierarchy by clicking the **Copy** button.

   Figure 11.9 shows the screen after you copy the hierarchy. Now, you can click **Edit** on the right-side panel at the bottom, and by clicking **+**, you can add/remove nodes or financial statement (FS) items within the nodes.

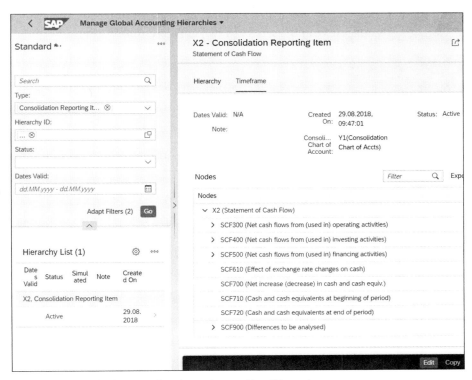

Figure 11.8 SAP Fiori App to Create an Accounting Hierarchy

Figure 11.9 Modify Reporting Hierarchy

3. Launch the SAP Fiori Define Reporting Rules app from the **Consolidation Settings** SAP Fiori group. You'll arrive at the screen shown in Figure 11.10.

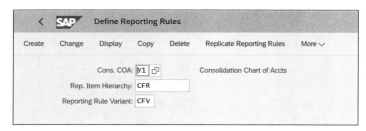

Figure 11.10 SAP Fiori Reporting Rules App

4. Select the consolidation chart of accounts in the **Cons. COA** field (**Y1**, in this example), select the reporting item hierarchy (**Rep. Item Hierarchy**) created in step 1 (**CFR**, in this example), and enter a name for the reporting rule variant ("CFV", in this example), as shown in Figure 11.11.

Reporting Rules: Change

Display <-> Change   More ∨

Cons. COA: Y1   Chart Chart of Accounts
Rep. Item Hierarchy: CFR
Reporting Rule Variant: CFV   Description: Cash Flow Reporting Variant

Rep. Item	Attribute Name	Attribute Desc.	Attribute Valu...	Value Descri...	Item Hier.	Node	FS Item From	FS Item To	SI Cat.	Subitem From	Subitem To
SCF100	S-CASH-FLO∨	Cash Flow	S-CF-EQU-E8	Retained earnin					1	915	915
SCF201	S-CASH-FLO∨	Cash Flow	S-CF-TAX-P1	Income tax exp					2	YB00	YBZZ
SCF202	S-CASH-FLO∨	Cash Flow	S-CF-INT-P1	Interest income					2	YB00	YBZZ
SCF202	S-CASH-FLO∨	Cash Flow	S-CF-INT-P2	Interest expens					2	YB00	YBZZ
SCF211	S-CASH-FLO∨	Cash Flow	S-CF-INVE-A1	Inventories & b					1	915	915
SCF211	S-CASH-FLO∨	Cash Flow	S-CF-INVE-A1	Inventories & b					1	925	925
SCF211	S-CASH-FLO∨	Cash Flow	S-CF-INVE-A1	Inventories & b					1	935	935
SCF212	S-CASH-FLO∨	Cash Flow	S-CF-REC-A1	Trade receivabl					1	915	915
SCF212	S-CASH-FLO∨	Cash Flow	S-CF-REC-A2	Allowances on t					1	925	925
SCF212	S-CASH-FLO∨	Cash Flow	S-CF-REC-A2	Allowances on t					1	935	935
SCF213	S-CASH-FLO∨	Cash Flow	S-CF-REC-A3	Prepaid expens					1	915	915
SCF214	S-CASH-FLO∨	Cash Flow	S-CF-PAY-L1	Trade payables					1	915	915
SCF215	S-CASH-FLO∨	Cash Flow	S-CF-PAY-L2	Other payables					1	915	915
SCF221	S-CASH-FLO∨	Cash Flow	S-CF-DEP-A1	Depreciation on					1	925	925
SCF221	S-CASH-FLO∨	Cash Flow	S-CF-DEP-A2	Depreciation on					1	925	925
SCF221	S-CASH-FLO∨	Cash Flow	S-CF-AMT-A1	Amortization int					1	925	925

Figure 11.11 Maintain Reporting Rule

5. Click **Create** in the menu bar. Now you can add the reporting items, attribute name, item hierarchy, range of FS item, subitem category, subitems, document types, and consolidation unit. You can also download an existing predelivered reporting rule and modify the FS items and upload them to the SAP Fiori app from the buttons above the data grid.

6. Launch the SAP Fiori Assign Reporting Rules to Versions app from the **Consolidation Settings** SAP Fiori group. You'll arrive at the screen shown in Figure 11.12.

7. Select the **Report Rule Version (Y10)** checkbox, and click **Save** at the bottom of the screen.

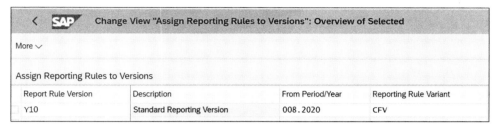

	Change View "Assign Reporting Rules to Versions": Overview of Selected

More ∨

Assign Reporting Rules to Versions

Report Rule Version	Description	From Period/Year	Reporting Rule Variant
Y10	Standard Reporting Version	008.2020	CFV

Figure 11.12 SAP Fiori Assign Reporting Rules to Versions App

8. Now that you've assigned the rules, open the SAP Fiori Group Data Analysis app. Enter the following selection parameters as shown in Figure 11.13, and click **OK**:

- **Version**
  A consolidation version that holds actual financial data. You can also use a plan or budget version of you're working on management consolidation.
- **Ledger**
  A consolidation ledger from one of the SAP S/4HANA ledgers, such as OL.
- **Consolidation COA**
  Consolidation chart of accounts that contains FS items on which you want to run your consolidation.
- **Period/Year**
  Month and year for which you're running the report.
- **Period Mode**
  In which mode you want to see the financials of a period (periodic or year to date).
- **Consolidation Group**
  Consolidation group you want to see the consolidated balances for.
- **Consolidation Unit Hierarchy**
  Consolidation units for which you want the financials to be displayed for the consolidation group chosen.
- **Profit Center Hierarchy**
  Financials on the profit centers that intersect with the selected consolidation chart of accounts and consolidation unit.
- **Segment Hierarchy**
  Financials of the business segment that intersect with selected consolidation chart of accounts and consolidation unit.
- **Rep. Item Hierarchy**
  A reporting item hierarchy assigned to FS items for the rule-based report.
- **Reporting Rule Var.**
  The reporting rule variant that has been defined using a reporting item.

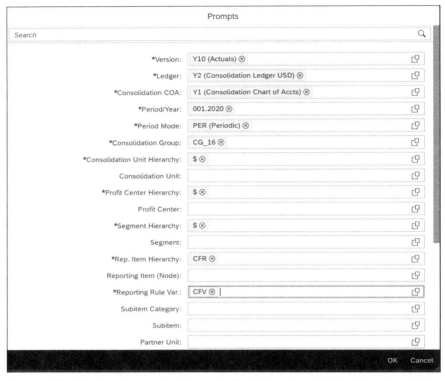

Figure 11.13 Selection Parameter Values for Cash Flow Report Using Reporting Rules

9. The cash flow report will be displayed based on the custom reporting rule, as shown in Figure 11.14.

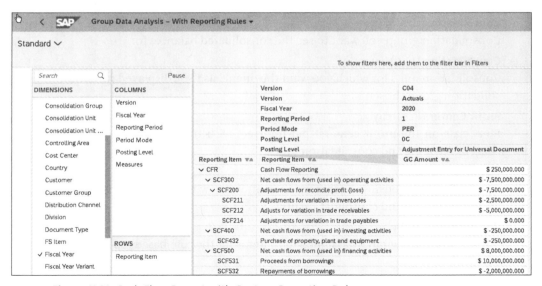

Figure 11.14 Cash Flow Report with Custom Reporting Rules

11.4   Additional Reporting Tools

In the previous sections, we explained the standard delivered reports and also created reports using reporting rules. Now, we'll look into other reporting tools, such as SAP Analysis for Microsoft Office, SAP Analytics Cloud, and SAP Fiori, as well as how to create a report using the tools.

11.4.1   SAP Analysis for Microsoft Office

In Chapter 2, Section 2.2.2, we introduced SAP Analysis for Microsoft Office. In this chapter, we'll do a deep dive into the features of this tool and walk you through an example of creating an SAP Analysis for Microsoft Office report.

Getting Started

An SAP Analysis for Microsoft Office page open with an interface similar to an Excel spreadsheet. Click on **File** on the top-left corner of the sheet, and then click **Analysis**, as shown in Figure 11.15.

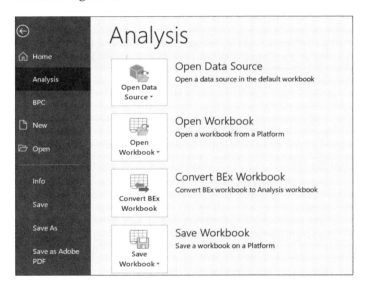

Figure 11.15 SAP Analysis for Microsoft Office Launch Page

The following options are available:

- **Open Data Source**
  Use a default workbook to open a data source.
- **Open Workbook**
  Open a workbook from a SAP Business Objects Business Intelligence (SAP Business-Objects BI) platform or SAP Business Warehouse (SAP BW) platform.

- **Convert BEx Workbook**
  Convert a SAP Business Explorer (SAP BEx) workbook to SAP Analysis for Microsoft Office formulas.

- **Save Workbook**
  Save a workbook to an SAP Business Objects BI platform or SAP BW platform.

For our purposes, select the **Open Workbook** dropdown, and select **Open Workbook from the SAP Platform**.

Analysis Ribbon

In Microsoft Excel, **Analysis** is available as a separate tab in the Microsoft Office ribbon. The ribbon is part of the Microsoft Office user interface of the main work area that presents commands and options.

There are two tabs as part of the **Analysis** office toolbar:

- **Analysis Ribbon**
  This tab is directly related to the analysis, such as adding data sources and configuring filters, measures, and hierarchies.

- **Analysis Design**
  This tab contains the formatting features that can used for design of the workbook. Here you can show the charts and info fields as well as format the tables and cells.

Figure 11.16 shows different ways to add a data source to create an SAP Analysis for Microsoft Office report:

- **Insert Data Source**
  Data sources can be opened in a formula-optimized mode. This allows creation of highly flexible and formatted reports. When working in this mode, no cross-tab is displayed.

- **Refresh All**
  Refresh data for all reports in one workbook. **Refresh Data Source** button helps you refresh only one report in a workbook. **Reset Data Source** is used to remove all table design rules manually.

- **Undo/Redo**
  These buttons function similarly to the way they do in a normal Excel workbook. Changes or updates made to the report via the other functions will allow you to revert back to previous views.

  Note that unlike Excel, $\boxed{\text{Ctrl}}$+$\boxed{\text{Z}}$ and $\boxed{\text{Ctrl}}$+$\boxed{\text{Y}}$ aren't keyboard shortcuts for this function.

- **Messages**
  Shows the error, warning, or information messages regarding the report in use.

- **Prompts**

  Prompts for the workbook will initiate the popup screen to change and select inputs. After you select the inputs, the variable selections will be applied to all the tabs in the report or input form. Prompt for the data source is used for refreshing data for a single query/data source and not the entire workbook.

Figure 11.16 Methods to Add a Data Source

Filters

When analyzing the data in the report, it's very common to restrict the data on the report to see a subset of the data. In SAP Analysis for Microsoft Office, you can restrict the data using filters.

Figure 11.17 shows the different options to filter the data such as **Filter By Member**, **Filter By Range**, or **Filter by Measure**.

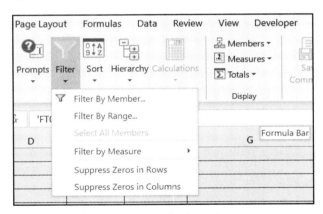

Figure 11.17 Filter Options on the Report

The **Filter • Filter By Member** selection (or the **Filter** icon) will initiate a popup screen. You may select **Individual Selection** or **Range Selection**. **Individual Selection** places a filter on a specific member. **Range Selection** applies a filter on a range of members. The **Filter • Filter By Measure • All Dimensions Independently • Edit** selection will initiate the **Filter by Measure** popup screen.

The **Filter • Suppress Zeros in Rows** and **Suppress Zeros in Columns** will remove any rows and columns that have null value.

Sort

To conduct a regular sort on a column, click any cell in the column of interest. Then, go to **Sort** and choose either **Sort Ascending** or **Sort Descending**. Based on the column selected, data in the cross-tab will be sorted. A cross-tab in a report is the data section where the report data is shown in rows and columns.

Selecting **Sort • More Sort Options** opens a popup that gives you the option to sort on the rows and columns (or measures).

Calculations

Figure 11.18 shows the **Calculations** button that becomes available when the column header cell of interest is selected. This option provides many precalculated functions that can be selected via the dropdown list.

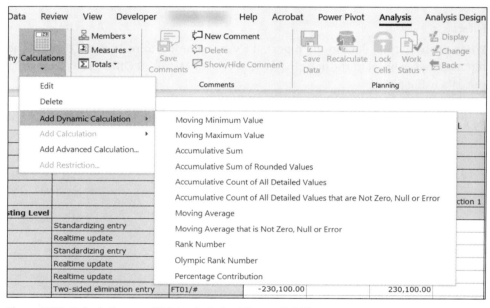

Figure 11.18 Calculations on SAP Analysis for Microsoft Office

Choose the calculation required, and a new column will appear to the right of the original column (source of the calculation).

Select **Calculations • Add Advanced Calculations**, and enter a formula for the new measure in the **Calculation** area.

Figure 11.19 shows that there are two options to add calculation: **Insert Member** or **Insert Function** (mathematical, +, -, %, etc.).

With **Insert Member**, you can select the measures of the data source as operands. With **Insert Function**, you can select the operator for the calculation. The new calculated measure is added to the cross-tab and the design panel.

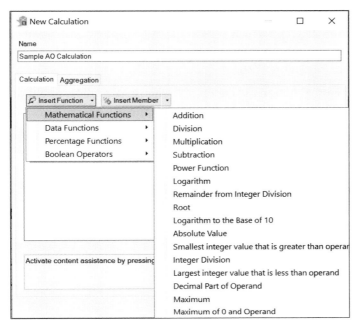

Figure 11.19 Advance Calculation Options

Members

Members can be displayed as key, text, or both. For texts, you can define which text should be displayed.

The **Members** button will give a dropdown of selections in which to display the selected attribute in the rows and/or columns, as shown in Figure 11.20. Select the row or column attribute in which to change the view.

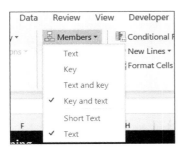

Figure 11.20 Members Dropdown

Select **Members** and choose the text to be displayed: **Text** (text name), **Key** (technical name), or both. The definition of the member display doesn't affect the totals and subtotals in your analysis.

Measures

Measure are numerical values in a report such as sales quantity, product cost, number of employees, etc. Let's walk through the steps to format, scale, add totals, and add calculations using the measure (see Figure 11.21):

1. The **Measures • Number Format** option can be selected when a data cell for a column of interest is selected.

2. The **Scaling Factor** popup screen summarizes the data cell values into powers of 10. The **Decimal Places** will display the data cell values in the desired number of decimals. Checking off the **Display Scaling Factor and Units in the Header for all Measures** option will summarize the unit and scaling factor in the header. Note the default selection in a scaling factor is 1 and 2 decimal places.

3. The **Measures • General Format** option allows you to select how negative values and zeros are to be displayed. For example, the original displayed negative values as **-X** and zero values as **0.00**; the settings will change the report to display negative values as **(X)** and zero values as -.

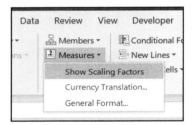

Figure 11.21 Measures Dropdown

Totals

To select how totals are displayed in the rows, click on any cell for the row attribute of interest. The first two options in the **Totals** dropdown are used to show or hide totals (see Figure 11.22). To hide totals where there is only one member, choose **Totals • Hide Totals**.

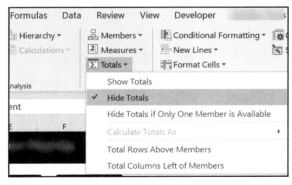

Figure 11.22 Totals Dropdown

In the default display, totals are displayed below and to the right of the members. You have the following options to change the display when you select a cross-tab cell:

- Choose **Totals • Total Rows Above Members** for totals to be displayed above the members.
- Choose **Totals • Total Columns Left of Members** for totals to be displayed left of the members.
- The user can choose how the total is calculated by selecting the column header of interest and going to **Totals • Calculate Totals As**. The default selection is to calculate totals according to the query definition. There are several other methods to calculate the total such as minimum, maximum, sum, average, and median.
- The options for commenting a data cell are available in the **Comments** group in the ribbon. You can use the **New Comment** tab to add a comment on a cell.

Design Panel

To access the design panel, go to **Display • Display Design Panel**, and open the dialog box for analysis, as shown in Figure 11.23.

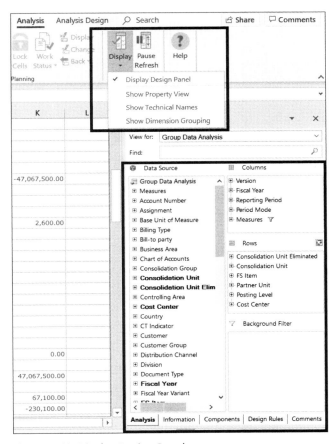

Figure 11.23 Display Design Panel

On the **Analysis** tab, you can see the available fields for a single data source and the fields currently used to display the data in a cross-tab in columns and rows. If you use multiple data sources in your analysis, select a cross-tab cell of the required data source to specify which data source information should be displayed.

The **Analysis** tab contains the following sections:

- **Find**
  Finds the data source if more than one is used in the report.

- **Data Source**
  Displays all the fields (characteristics) from the source SAP BW query or core data services (CDS) views.

- **Columns**
  Displays all the fields displayed in the column on the report. You can drag and drop any field from the data source into either column or rows. A common practice is to drag the key figures or measures into columns.

- **Rows**
  Displays all the fields displayed in rows on the report.

- **Background Filter**
  Applies any filters to the data source, for example, controlling area.

On the **Information** tab, you can see detailed information about a data source or the complete workbook. You can also find information on filters and variables on this tab. The general information is displayed as text elements.

On the **Components** tab, you have options to control the workbook data refresh.

The **Pause Refresh** button pauses all refreshes and updates until the button is clicked again. When clicked, the button will highlight, and all refreshes stop. When you're making several changes, such as adding more data elements to the rows or columns and adding calculations, it's recommended to click the **Pause Refresh** button and then refresh after the report format is in the desired state.

Create a Report Using the Standard CDS View

Now that you're familiar with the SAP Analysis for Microsoft Office tools and options, you can build your first SAP Analysis for Microsoft Office report based on the delivered standard CDS view. Follow these steps:

1. In the SAP Fiori Group Data Analysis app, click **Settings** on the top right of the application, and the technical name of the CDS view is displayed.

2. Open a blank Excel sheet, and from the **Analysis** tab, click **Insert Data Source • Select Data Source for Analysis** (see Figure 11.24), and search for the CDS view "2CCSRPT3OQ – Group Data Analysis".

Figure 11.24 SAP Analysis for Microsoft Office: Select Data Source for Analysis

3. After you select the CDS view, the SAP Analysis for Microsoft Office report will prompt for filters to display the data. Input the values for the prompts, and click **OK**.

The initial SAP Analysis for Microsoft Office report based on the definition of the CDS view is placed into the spreadsheet. Figure 11.25 is created based on the standard SAP Fiori Group Data Analysis app underlying the CDS view.

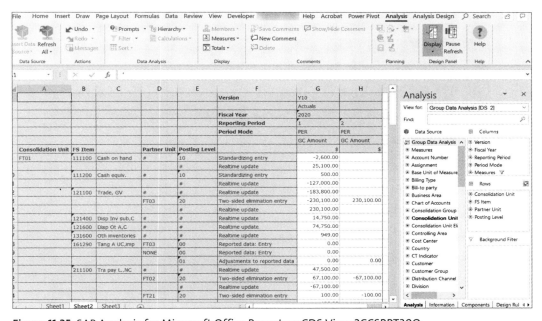

Figure 11.25 SAP Analysis for Microsoft Office Report on CDS View 2CCSRPT30Q

After you've created your first SAP Analysis for Microsoft Office report, you can rearrange the fields by dragging and dropping from the **Analysis** panel and adding additional fields and calculations. You can use the features we covered in the previous sections.

11.4.2   SAP Analytics Cloud

Chapter 2, Section 2.2.2, provided an introduction to SAP Analytics Cloud, and in this section, you'll learn the components of SAP Analytics Cloud and the steps to create an SAP Analytics Cloud report. SAP Analytics Cloud is a software-as-a-service (SaaS) business intelligence (BI) platform built on SAP Cloud Platform and enhanced with the power of predictive analytics and machine learning technology to provide all analytics capabilities in a single product.

SAP Analytics Cloud stands out as unique from the other BI platforms because it allows data analysts and business decision-makers to visualize, plan, and predict in a single, cloud-based platform. SAP Analytics Cloud clusters predictive analysis, BI, enterprise planning, and digital boardroom capabilities into one unit to perform data analysis from all SAP and non-SAP data sources.

Home Page Navigation

After you log in to SAP Analytics Cloud, you'll land in the home page navigation, as shown in Figure 11.26.

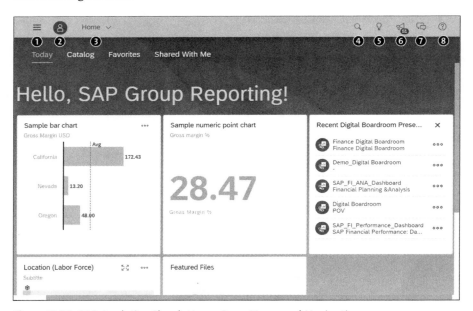

Figure 11.26 SAP Analytics Cloud: Home Page Menu and Navigation

The following components are presented:

❶ **Menu**
The main menu helps you navigate across the SAP Analytics Cloud environment.

❷ **Profile Settings**
These are the system settings, language preference, time, number formatting, and other user preferences. Users can also request roles from this menu.

❸ Note

Add a new note and edit the order of the **Home** tiles.

❹ Search

Search stores, files, and models.

❺ Search to Insight

Search using simple English phrases to find key insights in your data. For example, what is the gross margin for 2020?

❻ Notification

Any alerts on information such as collaboration with other users, system messages, and statuses of a file download, progress, and connection.

❼ Collaboration

Use the discussion features in SAP Analytics Cloud to collaborate with other users in real time and through notifications.

❽ Help

Links to documentation and videos, for sending feedback, to explore new features, and other help-related links can be accessed from here.

Features

We provided an overview of SAP Analytics Cloud in the previous section. Now, we'll explain the key capabilities of SAP Analytics Cloud:

- Cloud deployment
- Lower infrastructure costs
- Integration with other cloud solutions
- Centralize data storage versus Excel workbooks
- Integration with SAP, which includes the following:
  - SAP Business Planning and Consolidation (SAP BPC)
  - SAP BW
  - SAP HANA
  - SAP S/4HANA
  - SAP cloud applications
- Dynamic visualizations from many sources, including the following types:
  - Variance analysis
  - Predictive forecasting
- Collaboration with colleagues, including the following options:
  - Calendar with tasks and processes
  - Sharing stories, files, and templates
  - Adding comments to story items
  - Creating discussion topics

Data Connections

Live models can be created from data sources in on-premise or cloud systems. Stories can be built and online analysis performed based on these models without data replication, which allows for scenarios where data can't be moved into the cloud for security or privacy reasons, or where data already exists on a different cloud system.

Data acquisition models can also be created where data is imported (copied) to the SAP Analytics Cloud SAP HANA in-memory database, and changes made to the data in the source system don't affect the imported data. However, import jobs can be executed manually or scheduled with the desired frequency to pull the latest data from the source system. Similarly, data can also be exported from the SAP Analytics Cloud model to the source system. Furthermore, SAP Analytics Cloud provides Security Assertion Markup Language (SAML) capabilities to enable single sign-on (SSO), simplifying authentication to SAP Analytics Cloud and also to connected data sources.

Figure 11.27 shows a live connection architecture with the following parts:

- SAP Analytics Cloud delivers the business logic and builds the queries required to see data in the browser.
- As you can see, the cloud data source can be any data source that is in the cloud (e.g., SAP S/4HANA Cloud, essentials edition, or the SAP HANA database in SAP Cloud Platform).
- Cross-origin resource sharing (CORS) is used for the live connection. Since 2018, this has been the only method to establish the live connection, as a reverse proxy is no longer supported. Setup is more straightforward with this option as there is no additional software to install or manage.
- Reverse proxy is used for the import connect, and it involves additional software that the client has to maintain. However, SAP Web Dispatcher can be leveraged as a simple reverse proxy if the client already has it in their landscape.

Figure 11.27 shows the two options to connect data sources (on-premise or cloud-hosted on an infrastructure-as-a-service [IaaS]) to SAP Analytics Cloud. The recommended option is CORS in order to have a live connection to SAP Analytics Cloud. The data only persists in the source system and is aggregated to the SAP Analytics Cloud layer at runtime. For most scenarios, this is the preferred option, as you don't have to manage and maintain data in both SAP Analytics Cloud and the source system.

The other option is to create an import connection using a reverse proxy. The option has near real-time replication from the data sources, and data is persisted both in SAP Analytics Cloud as well as in the data source. This option comes in handy when dealing with massive data sets, where having a direct connection could cause performance issues. That said, the majority of the use cases should leverage the CORS connection.

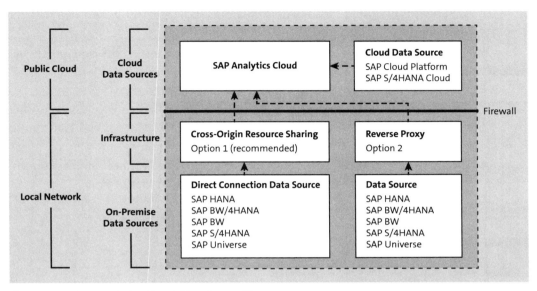

Figure 11.27 SAP Analytics Cloud: Live Connection

For any analytical application, the first step is to connect to the data source. SAP Analytics Cloud can connect to almost any data source available in the market today. SAP Analytics Cloud can work with live or imported data connections. Additionally, models can also be built within SAP Analytics Cloud without connecting to a source system and uploading data via Excel files. Let's examine the differences between live and imported data connections:

- **Live data connections**
  - Doesn't replicate data in SAP Analytics Cloud
  - No need to refresh
  - Always current and real time
- **Import data connections**
  - Replicates data in SAP Analytics Cloud
  - Need to refresh manually or schedule

Figure 11.28 shows the import data connection architecture in which SAP Analytics Cloud acquires the source data and stores it locally within the SAP Analytics Cloud platform. The following are the parts of the architecture:

- Open connector is a service offered by SAP on SAP Cloud Platform that's part of their integration suite (SAP Cloud Platform Integration). The service has prebuilt adapters and application programming interfaces (APIs) to more than 180+ non-SAP cloud providers. As an example, if you need to connect an Azure data lake, then you can use open connectors to read data from Azure and aggregate it with SAP data for reporting.

- Cloud applications include all applications that are hosted on the cloud, both SAP and non-SAP.

- The cloud connector is a proxy that connects the client's landscape to the cloud. The cloud connector is managed and maintained by the client and typically sits on a small virtual machine. It's essentially the glue that allows SAP Cloud Platform to receive and send data from the landscape.

- The SAP Analytics Cloud agent only supports the import connection from the client's source systems to SAP Analytics Cloud in SAP Cloud Platform.

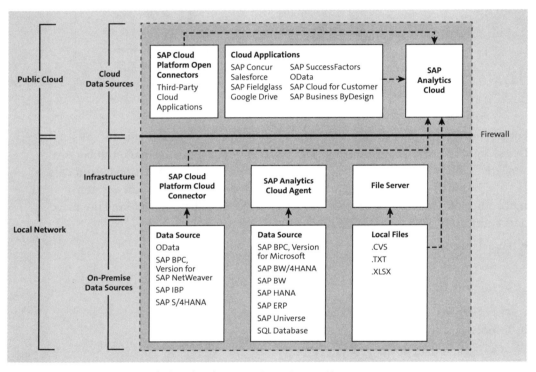

Figure 11.28 SAP Analytics Cloud: Import Data Connection

The choice to use a live or imported connection should be based on your user requirements. However, connections to cloud-based data sources are the simplest and fastest to configure. The browser, in turn, sends those queries through the reverse proxy and down or through a direct live connection to the on-premise database.

The results of those queries are returned to the browser, where visualizations are rendered. SAP Analytics Cloud stores only the metadata and allows the query to rebuild on its own. Still, the actual data isn't saved within the cloud environment, and the metadata is transferred to the browser and encrypted in memory.

Models

To create an SAP Analytics Cloud dashboard, report, or digital boardroom, you first need to create a model. Models are the basis for all of your analysis in SAP Analytics Cloud to evaluate the performance of your organization. It's a high-level design that exposes the analytic requirements of end users. You can create planning, analytics, and predictive models based on both the cloud and on-premise data sources.

There are two different models available within SAP Analytics Cloud. Analytical models are more straightforward, flexible, and primarily used for reporting and data analytics. Planning models are full-featured models for business analysts and finance professionals to quickly and easily build connected models to analyze and plan data. The models built in SAP Analytics Cloud are preconfigured with time and version dimensions. Planning models can be linked to rate tables to support multicurrency translations and enable planning in multiple currencies. The model also has security features at a more granular level, both at the model and dimension levels.

Both models are built based on two foundational elements: dimensions and measures. *Dimensions* are data objects that represent categorical data in a data set such as product and company code. A *measure* is a data object that represents transaction data and mostly represents a numerical value such as revenue and travel expenses.

To choose your connection, from the home page, access the **Connection** tab, as shown in Figure 11.29. SAP Analytics Cloud will display a list of all available connections. You can either use an existing connection or click the **+** icon on the right side of the page, which will display all **Connection Types** to choose from. After you select the connection, then enter the **Name** and **Description** to create the connection.

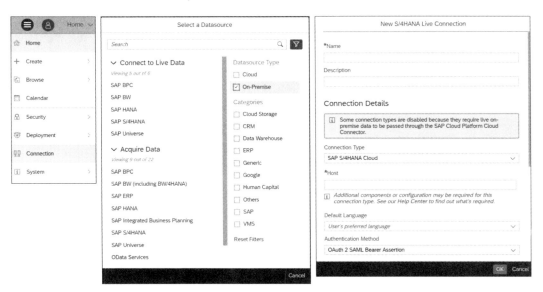

Figure 11.29 Set Up an SAP Analytics Cloud Connection

After you choose the connection, either live or import, the next step is to create a model.

Figure 11.30 shows how to access the model settings from the home page by going to **Create • Model**. After you initiate a new model, there are three options to build the model:

- Start with a blank model.
- Import a file from your local system, and use it as the metadata structure for the model.
- Get data from a data source to create the model.

Figure 11.30 Create a Model

After you create a model, if you go to **Model** settings and switch the planning capabilities toggle to off, it will automatically turn the model into an analytical model. Additional dimensions such as time, organization type, and any generic type of dimensions can be added based on your requirements. After the dimensions are added, you can map the dimensions to the source.

Now, let's create a story with this model. Stories are dashboards where you can explore, visualize, and analyze your data for reporting. Each story can have multiple pages.

There are three page types:

- **Responsive pages**
  - Creates lanes to section the page content into groups
  - Content reflows based on the resolution
  - Suitable when the story is viewed on multiple devices
  - Ideal for the SAP Digital Boardroom experience
- **Grid pages**
  - Used to work with numbers and formulas
  - Can be built using a model or without a model
  - Whole page acts like a spreadsheet
  - Allows text and cell formatting, flexibility to freeze column and rows
- **Canvas pages**
  - Ideal for advanced, pixel-perfect layouts
  - Allows to set exact canvas and object size
  - Group two or more objects
  - Supports overlay objects and bringing objects to front/back

Stories can be created from an existing model, a file, or a data source. Figure 11.31 shows how to navigate the main menu to create a story by going to **Create • Story**. For this example, also select **Add a Grid Page**.

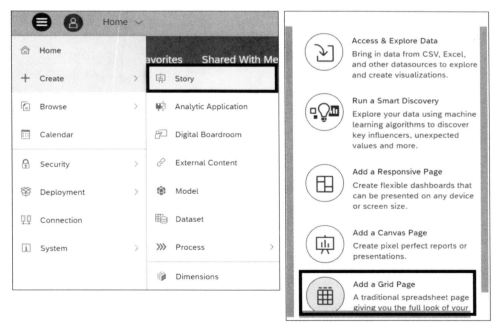

Figure 11.31 Create an SAP Analytics Cloud Story: Grid

After you get into the design screen, click **Insert**, and search for the model created in the previous step, as shown in Figure 11.32 ❶. All the dimensions will be shown on the right side design panel ❷. Drag and drop the dimensions to the report, and save the story.

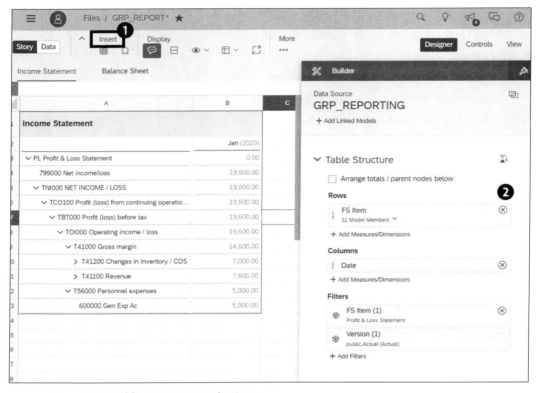

Figure 11.32 Adding a Report to the Story

11.4.3   SAP Fiori

Chapter 2, Section 2.1.2, provided an introduction to SAP Fiori, and in this section, you'll learn to create a simple SAP Fiori app to consume the consolidation data. Follow these steps to do so:

1. Log on to the SAP Web IDE from *https://account.hanatrial.ondemand.com/cockpit* to create an SAP Fiori app.

2. After you log in, from the **Services** tab, select the **SAP Web IDE** option, and click **Go to Service**.

3. When you arrive at the SAP Web IDE home page, click **Open my workspace**.

4. In the screen shown in Figure 11.33, select **File • New • Project from Template**.

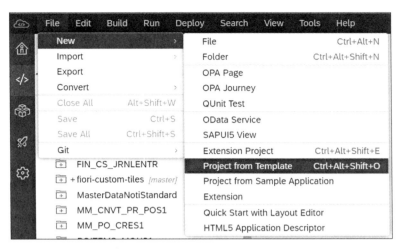

Figure 11.33 SAP Web IDE

5. From the **Template Selection** tab, select **SAP Fiori Elements** as the **Category**, and select **List Report Application** from the template (see Figure 11.34). Click **Next**.

Figure 11.34 SAP Web IDE Template Selection

6. In the next tab, **Basic Information**, shown in Figure 11.35, enter the details for **Project Name**, **Title**, **Namespace**, and **Description**. Click **Next**.

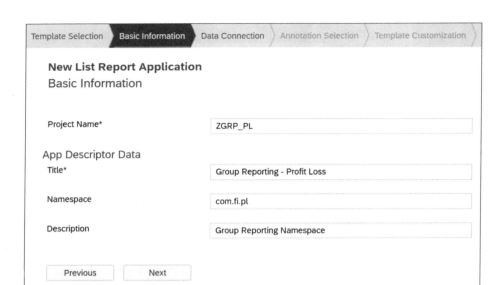

Figure 11.35 SAP Web IDE: SAP Fiori App Information

7. From the **Data Connection** tab, select the group reporting **System** and the **Services** (CDS view) from the dropdown, as shown in Figure 11.36. Click **Next**.

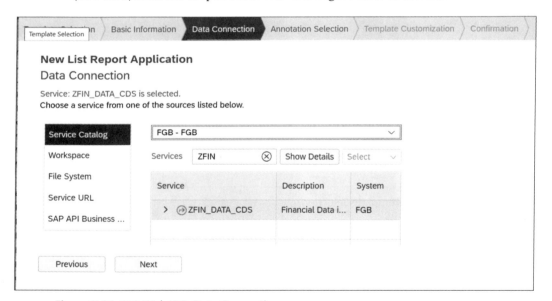

Figure 11.36 SAP Web IDE: Data Connection

8. The OData service ZFIN_DATA_CDS provides two annotation files to store the meta-data and the catalog service. From the **Annotation** tab, select both services by clicking the checkboxes, as shown in Figure 11.37.

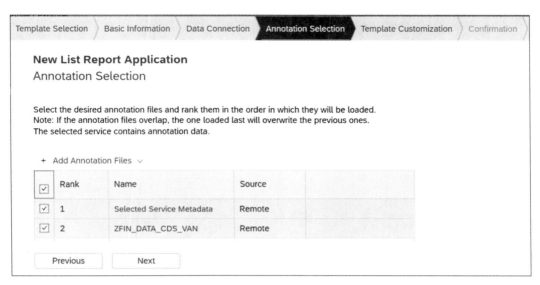

Figure 11.37 SAP Web IDE: Annotation

9. From the **Template Customization** tab, click the **OData Collection** dropdown, select the data model, and click **Finish**, as shown in Figure 11.38.

Figure 11.38 SAP Web IDE: Template Customization

10. The new SAP Fiori app is now created. From the main menu in SAP Web IDE, select the new SAP Fiori app (**ZGRP_PLS**, in this example), and right-click **Run • Run as Web Application**, as shown in Figure 11.39. This step will display the SAP Fiori app in the SAP Fiori home page as shown in Figure 11.40. After you click the SAP Fiori app, it will execute and show the data in a list view.

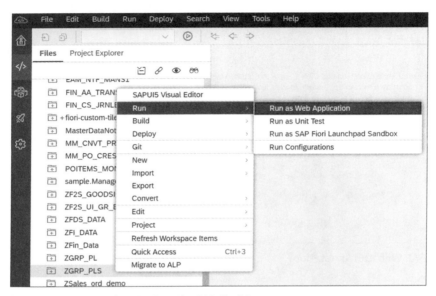

Figure 11.39 SAP Web IDE – Run the SAP Fiori App

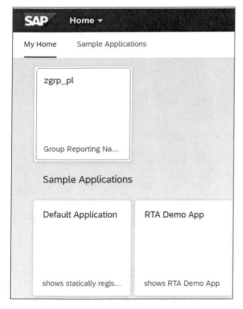

Figure 11.40 Custom SAP Fiori App

11. Now you can publish the SAP Fiori app to the roles for the users to consume the report.

11.5   Summary

In this chapter, you learned about the predelivered local and group reports. We also went into details on other reporting options and provided instructions to create an advanced SAP Analysis for Microsoft Office report, SAP Analytics for Cloud report, and SAP Fiori report. You also learned to drill through to Universal Journal details from the SAP Fiori report.

In the next chapter, we'll conclude and recap all the chapters on group reporting.

11

Chapter 12
Conclusion

This chapter reflects the content covered in the book, outlines a few considerations for group reporting projects, and identifies five key takeaways from the authors' experience.

You've made it to the end of our journey through consolidation with SAP S/4HANA Finance for group reporting! Whether this is an introduction to financial consolidation or you're a seasoned vet, hopefully you've learned something along the way.

Let's recap what you've learned, before we finish off with some considerations and key takeaways.

12.1   Book Summary

We started our journey by introducing financial consolidations and understanding the difference between legal and management consolidations, while also discussing some of the consolidation regulations.

From there, we walked through the on-premise and cloud architecture of group reporting in SAP S/4HANA with a focus on the data model and predelivered content. A thorough in-depth analysis of master data, specifically, group reporting configuration's dependencies on global settings and a set of specific master data elements was discussed. It's important to remember that your group reporting configuration is dependent on certain master data being configured and set up correctly. We highly recommend earmarking Chapter 3 as you'll likely revisit this chapter often throughout your group reporting work.

Following a discussion on master data, we dove into the different approaches to integrating financial transaction data into your consolidation. This is one of the key takeaways we'll discuss later in this chapter. Transaction data integration covered three main areas:

- Universal ledger
- Flexible upload
- Application programming interface (API) integration (cloud only)

These three areas are important parts of group reporting's value proposition for large multinational companies choosing to implement group reporting as they help with near real-time analysis and supporting a soft close, if configured and architected correctly.

After our discussion of transaction data, it was time to dive into the critical steps of the consolidation process, starting with currency translation. Each of the critical consolidation activities began with a brief overview of the process, discussed the configuration, and explained how to execute the process. If you'll take one thing away, pay close attention to the detailed configuration steps as they are a great reference for understanding not only the process but also how it can be set up to work for your organization.

Each of the consolidation steps were reviewed in detail, and, while they all are equally important in their own ways, the two that we find ourselves going back to are currency translation and consolidation of investments. Most every company performs both, but more than any other process, they require accurate, detailed information to be used by external reporting teams.

Matrix consolidation is a new feature in SAP S/4HANA Finance for group reporting 1909 that many companies will find incredibly useful. Understanding what a matrix is, how to configure it, and how to run and verify it are all covered in detail in Chapter 9.

This book came to an end by discussing the financial close (i.e., the typical ledger and group close processes that accounting and finance perform each month) and providing an in-depth look at consolidation reporting with a focus on reporting architecture and predefined reports.

12.2   Considerations for Your Group Reporting Journey

After finishing this book, you're ready to embark on your own group reporting journey. But before doing so, there are five areas to consider:

- **Enterprise reporting strategy**
  You should consider integrating the group reporting tool into the enterprise reporting strategy. Most notably, you may choose to integrate group reporting across user data needs, types of reports being produced and the problems they are solving, and a deliberate purpose and approach to designing reports to support specific reporting requirements. Additionally, reporting should take into consideration performance needs of users, which is another key consideration we'll cover.

- **Acquisition and divestiture strategy**
  As you're designing your group reporting solution, you'll want to consider the role your enterprise's acquisition and divestiture strategy plays in the overall design. For instance, if you acquire a company, how do you plan to integrate that company into the consolidation process? Would it be a high-level journal entry, or would you upload a flat file to table ACDOCU to be used as part of consolidations? If a divestiture

occurs, how is it handled as part of your consolidation of investments? Is it seam-lessly integrated, or does it require some manual intervention?

You'll also want to consider testing various acquisition and divestiture scenarios as you go through your integration test cycles to ensure the solution you've designed and built supports any potential acquisitions or divestitures.

- **Performance**

  Performance is an important consideration that must be kept in mind from the very start. We've seen far too many examples of companies not considering performance in their data model design and reporting architecture.

  This is why it's so important to consider the role performance plays as part of your group reporting design. Starting from data model design, it's good to understand the number of dimensions required in your data model. Consolidation data models typically keep their dimensions between 12 and 15, depending on the reporting requirements set forth by the business. You should also consider the number of monthly financial transactions that will need to be consolidated. Large, multina-tional companies typically have millions if not billions of transactions each month that require thoughtful architecture design to ensure that a job such as currency translation doesn't take too long to run.

  And, finally, understand the business's reporting service-level agreements (SLAs) so you can properly design a solution that meets their performance needs. This can typically be accomplished through data model and architecture design.

- **Security**

  Similar to performance, security must be considered from the very start of group reporting prep and design. We recommend bringing in a security expert or two who can share insights into how to integrate security design to support effective use of the group reporting tool. How will users be administrated? How will users be authenticated? These are things that should be a part of those initial security discus-sions.

  Typically, a role-based security approach is used to restrict system access to autho-rized users. Role-based security includes role permissions (e.g., ability to view a set of profit centers or legal entities) and user-role relationships.

- **Change management and user adoption approach**

  A group reporting design and implementation would not be complete without care-ful consideration given to how users will be trained and adopt the new solution, which is why we recommend considering your company's change management and user adoption approach and strategy. How many users will be impacted by the change? When is a good time to introduce new functionality and processes to users so they can be successful in using the tool? Paying close attention to the scope of training, timing of training, delivery of training, and measuring the success of user adoption are critical components to ensuring the organization and its users are ready to take on the new tool and all the benefits that come with it.

12.3   Five Key Takeaways

As we conclude, we want to leave you with five key takeaways to remember on your group reporting journey:

1. **Understanding master data is a fundamental concept that is critical to successfully implementing and running group reporting**

   As discussed in Chapter 3 and shown in Table 12.1, we've highlighted several different master data items that are critical to implementing group reporting and running a successful financial consolidation:

   – Financial statement (FS) items, such as charts of accounts, must be properly set up and governed to effectively run a consolidation. For example, the business rules for intercompany eliminations depend on the right accounts being set up.

   – Subitem categories classify the subassignments of FS items. Two that are critical to the consolidation process are transaction types, a movement type associated with the balance sheet, and functional areas, an organizational unit that classifies an expense typically associated with the profit and loss (P&L) statement.

   – Consolidation units and consolidation groups are required for integration with the accounting functional area and form the basis for consolidation, with consolidation units integrating to existing SAP S/4HANA companies.

   – Additional characteristics, such as profit center, may be need to be configured as part of your company's consolidation process requirements.

   – Finally, reporting items used in reporting rules can be configured. For example, master data for income statement by function, cash flow statement, statement of changes in equity, and others may all require reporting items to be configured to properly support reporting requirements.

Master Data	Description
FS items	▪ Chart of accounts ▪ Functions controlled through attributes
Subitems (transaction types)	▪ All balance sheet accounts ▪ Integration with accounting consolidation type
Subitems (functional areas)	▪ All P&L accounts for purpose income statement by function ▪ Integration with accounting functional area
Consolidation units, partner units, consolidation groups	▪ All P&L accounts for purpose income statement by function ▪ Integration with accounting functional area
Additional characteristics	▪ Sample master data
Reporting items	▪ Master data for income statement by function, cash flow, statement of changes in equity, etc.

Table 12.1 Group Reporting Master Data

2. **Group reporting's unique architecture supports three different types of data integration**
   As you read in Chapter 4, table ACDOCU stores data integration across the following three areas:
   - First, it stores data coming from table ACDOCA as part of the data release.
   - Second, it stores data coming in as part of the flexible upload process (e.g., flat file upload).
   - Third, it stores consolidation calculation results such as opening balances, retained earnings, intercompany elimination data, and so on.

3. **Use the consolidation process to lead your design, your build, and your testing**
   The consolidation process and its associated activities serve as the map you should be following for design, build, and testing phases during your implementation journey. For instance, you may choose to set up design sessions around currency translation, reporting, balance carryforward, intercompany eliminations, and so on. In addition, when you build the solution, you'll build according to the process. Most consolidation processes are the same for different companies with a few exceptions or modifications to each activity. For example, not all companies will translate from local currency to group currency, but most will. Having a deep understanding of each consolidation activity, the requirements and configuration needed to support it, and any exceptions will be key to implementation and execution success.

4. **Your analytics strategy impacts finance performance management capabilities**
   The enterprise data warehouse/analytics strategy directly impacts consolidation and reporting functionality. Transforming the external reporting capability from one focused on "insights" to one focused on "foresights" is enabled by a company's analytics strategy and integrating that strategy into their consolidation and reporting processes to provide leading-edge reporting capabilities and get the most out of group reporting.

5. **SAP S/4HANA Finance for group reporting is the consolidation tool of the future**
   SAP has invested significant time and money into ensuring that it's creating a product that supports most, if not all, large multinational global companies' desires to close the books in a timely manner without much manual intervention. With this investment comes new features on a quarterly basis (for cloud solutions) and annual basis (for on-premise solutions). Having an understanding of group reporting architecture, data integration, and processes will be important as new features are released.

The Authors

Eric Ryan is an expert in the enterprise performance management (EPM) space with more than 15 years of experience. He's delivered multiple FP&A and consolidation projects using SAP consolidation solutions and is a market leader in the consolidation space, who provides thought leadership to clients' controllers and CFOs. Eric participated in group reporting beta testing with the SAP S/4HANA group reporting product team in Germany. He sits on Deloitte's Global CTO council, driving innovation and transformation strategy globally.

Thiagu Bala is the solution owner for several next-generation consolidation solutions for Deloitte, where he leverages the modern digital finance architecture. He has worked in the SAP space for more than 20 years. During this time, he has led several SAP-enabled large-scale global finance transformations focusing on business intelligence and EPM. A recognized leader in next-generation technologies like SAP S/4HANA, business intelligence, and business planning and consolidation, he is a sought-after speaker at various external events, including SAP Radio, SAPPHIRE, and SAP Financials.

Satyendra Raghav is a specialist in the finance and EPM practice at Deloitte. An expert in modeling the architecture for financial consolidations, he has worked with major clients in life sciences and healthcare, chemicals, and retail. He has more than 11 years of experience with SAP and has been involved with implementations of SAP financial planning and consolidation solutions throughout his entire career.

Azharuddin Mohammed is a team lead in the finance practice at Deloitte and a solution architect with expertise in FP&A, financial consolidations, and financial reporting applications. With more than 9 years of experience with SAP, he has solved numerous complex business problems for his clients. He has also conducted multiple training sessions on SAP S/4HANA Finance for group reporting within Deloitte.

Index

A

Account assignments 200
Account dimension 60, 79
Accounting reference ledger 316
Accounting technique 229
Accounts payable 315
Accounts receivable 315
Acquisitions 277
Activities 260, 262
Activity-based consolidation 258, 262, 267
   activities 262
   statistical entries 274
Adjustment journals 284
Adjustments 284
   templates 287
Alerts 47
Allocation 315
Amortization of goodwill 273
Analytical apps 32, 36
Analytical engine 33
Analytical models 347
Analytics 38
   CDS views 40
   embedded 39
   strategy 361
Application logs 54
Application programming interfaces
  (APIs) 30, 38
   data integration 138
   set up connection 138
Architecture 31, 361
   cloud 37
   embedded analytics 39
   import data connections 345
   on-premise 32, 37
   SAP Analytics Cloud 344
Archiving log 248
Assign FS Items Mappings app 60
Assign Reporting Rules to Versions app 330
Assignment of Financial Statement Items
  app 106
Attributes 83
   create 83
   predelivered 84
   SAP S/4HANA Cloud 106
   versions 104
Audit trails 108, 284

B

Authorization 67
Auto reversal 238, 240
Automatic postings 147–148, 239
Automation 320
Average rate 177, 181

B type 188
Balance carryforward 101, 123, 140
   configure 140
   execute 145
   FS items 141
   general ledger accounts 143
   output 146
   subitems 143
Balance check 112
Balance Sheet report 324
Balance sheets 149, 217
   account differences 208
   inventory 220
   item value differences 210
   results 324–325
Balancing adjustments 147
Best practices 66
Breakdown categories 72, 81, 92, 97
   changes 93
   characteristics 92
   create 92
   types 93
Bulk uploads 75, 78
Business catalogs 67
Business roles 67
Business rules 240
   matrix consolidation 302
Buying rate 181

C

Calculation of net income 123, 147
   automatic entries 148
   configure 147
   execute 150
   validate 150
Calculations 336
Canvas pages 349
Capitalization 263
Cash Flow Statement report 326

Cash flows 82
   report 332
Categories 103
   source 104
Change management 359
Chart of accounts 71, 79
   create 80
   custom 83
Check Correct Breakdowns of Transaction
   Data app 93
Closing rate 177
   method 176
Cloud 30
Cloud connector 346
Combined view 65
Common stock 178, 218
CompositeProviders 43
Compounded characteristics 120
Conditions 152
Configuration
   balance carryforward 140
   calculation of net income 147
   consolidation groups 269
   Consolidation Monitor 227
   consolidation of investments 264
   currency translation 181
   Data Monitor 124
   data validation 152
   global settings 69
   intercompany elimination 240
   journal entries 164
   journal entry templates 288
   master data 69, 72
   matrix consolidation 300
   methods 264
   modify 271
   selections 118
Consistency Check of Setting for FI
   Integration app 51
Consistency checks 51, 79
   errors 52
   results 51
Consolidated accounting 17
Consolidated Balance Sheet report 325
Consolidated P&L Statements by Function
   of Expense report 325
Consolidation 17
   entities 72
   evolution 23
   frequency 228, 238
   key concepts 20
   ledgers 72, 316

Consolidation (Cont.)
   management 299
   matrix 299
   methods 264
   modes 70
   motivation 22
   process flow 215
   reporting 323
   steps 18
   types 17, 72
   versions 103
Consolidation chart of accounts 79, 81
   transport 82
Consolidation entries 283
   create 291
   SAP Fiori apps 285
Consolidation groups 59, 76, 269, 360
   adjustment 293
   assign units 78
   attributes 77
   changes 123
   configure 269
   create 76
   currency 79
   Data Monitor 122
   document types for changes 238
   hierarchies 79
   structure 59
   versions 105
Consolidation Groups Create & Change
   app 76
Consolidation Monitor 63, 222
   configure 227
   consolidation of investments 279
   document types 237
   eliminate intercompany transactions 249
   group close 318
   icons 223
   layout 223
   options 64
   ownership data 271
   tasks 63, 116, 224
   validate eliminations and reclassifications ...
      251
Consolidation of investments 21, 257
   activity-based 258, 262
   configure 264
   consolidation groups 269
   display settings 278
   modify predefined configurations 271
   reporting 281
   rule-based 258

Consolidation of investments (Cont.)
   rules 259
   run equity pickup 279
   validate 280
Consolidation P&L Statements by Nature
  of Expense report 325
Consolidation Unit Change app 201
Consolidation units 59, 72, 360
   assign methods 201
   assign to groups 59, 77–78
   attributes 74
   configure 270
   create 73
   data collection 131
   flexible upload 134
   hierarchies 307
   input template 75
   task logs 252
Consolidation Units – Change View app 131
Continuous accounting 30, 319–320
Contributed capital 218
Control 23
Copy Totals Records app 52
Core data services (CDS) views 33
   architecture 40
   SAP Analysis for Microsoft Office 340
Cost method 22
Cost of goods sold (COGS) 218
   eliminate 219
Cross-origin resource sharing (CORS) 344
Cumulative settings 53
Currencies 113, 175, 239
Currency Exchange Rates app 51, 193
Currency feed 187
   trigger request 188
   validate 190
Currency fields 180
Currency pairs 188
Currency translation 18, 20, 123, 175, 358
   assign method to consolidation unit 201
   basics 176
   configure 181
   example 177
   execute 206
   FS items 202
   methods 194
   predefined methods 195
   predelivered attributes 204
   prerequisites 180
   reporting 207
   reserve analysis 211
   SAP S/4HANA 179
   validate 207

Currency translation adjustment (CTA) 177
   calculate 178
Currency Translation Difference Analysis –
  Accessible app 207
Currency Translation Difference Analysis
  app 208, 210
Currency Translation Reserve Analysis –
  Accessible app 210
Currency Translation Reserve Analysis
  app 210, 212
Custom Field and Logic app 289
Customizing 69

D

Data acquisition models 344
Data collection 18, 25, 27, 74, 121,
  123, 131, 175
   methods 38
Data connections 344
   import 344
   live 344
   SAP Fiori apps 352
   select 347
Data consistency 92
Data integration 130
   APIs 138
   plan data 139
Data loads 131
Data modeling 27, 33
Data Monitor 49, 62, 121
   assign preceding tasks 129
   assign task groups to dimensions 128
   balance carryforward 145
   calculation of net income 147, 150
   configure 124
   create task groups 127
   define tasks 125
   execute currency translation 206
   flexible upload task 136
   group close 317
   layout 122
   options 122
   reported data validation 161
   standardized data validation 163
   task groups 125
   task settings 127
   tasks 49, 116, 121, 123–124
   Universal Journal release task 131, 170
   Universal Journal validate task 171

Data preparation 51
Data trails 107
Data transfer methods 75, 131, 134
   read from universal document 171
Data validation 123–124, 152
   execute 161
   import/export 160
   methods 156
   reported 161, 324
   results 162, 164
   rules 152
   standardized 163, 324
Data Validation app 152
Data Validations Methods app 157
Data versions 103
Deferred taxes 150, 239
Define FS Items app 60, 81, 180, 203, 206, 232
Define Master Data for Consolidation Fields app 102
Define Reporting Rules app 330
Define Selections app 118, 231, 244
Define Validation Methods app 157
Depreciation 222
   expenses 222
Dimensions 103, 128, 347
   assign task groups 236
Direct acquisitions 277
Direct quotations 185
Display Breakdown Categories app 92
Display Group Journal Entries app 58, 285
Divestiture 262–263
   strategy 358
Dividends 219
Document types 62, 107, 117, 253
   balance carryforward 141
   consolidation group changes 238
   Consolidation Monitor 226, 237
   consolidation of investments 266
   create 112, 117, 241
   define 237
   number ranges 112, 114
   post journal entries 291
   predefined 237
   predelivered 62, 108–109
   reclassification 237
   reclassification tasks 115
Drilldowns 34
Dynamic eliminations 102

E

Elimination 59, 257, 267
   dynamic 102
   enable 101
   expense 221
   goodwill 272–273
   intercompany 215
   intercompany transactions 249
   inventory 220
   post entries 228
   rule-based 260
   sales and COGS 219
   validate 251
Embedded analytics 39
Enterprise Controlling – Consolidation System (EC-CS) 24
Enterprise Performance Management (EPM) 27
Entity dimension 72
Equity 218, 263
   automatic update 277
   define 274
   method 21–22, 262, 265, 268, 276
   ownership 21
   pickup 21, 279
Equity holdings adjustments 276
European Monetary Union (EMU) statutory guidelines 183
Events 277
Exchange rate indicators 106, 191, 196, 200
   create 191
   predefined 191
Exchange rate types 181, 188
   assignments 193
   create 182
Exchange rates 50, 179
   automatic feed 187
   connection URL 188
   create 186, 193
   fluctuations 176
   inverted 183
   maintain 185
   specify translation ratios 184
   upload 190
Expenses 218, 222
   eliminate 221
   processing 315
Extraordinary amortization 271

F

Fact sheet apps 32, 37
File upload 78
File-driven methods 135
Filters 335
Financial accounting 17
Financial Accounting – Legal Consolidation
   (FI-LC) 24
Financial Accounting Standards Board
   (FASB) 22
Financial close 313, 358
   cycles 314
   group close 316
   ledger close 313
Financial consolidation 17
Financial planning and analysis (FP&A) 65
Financial reporting 216
Financial statement (FS) items 60, 79,
   82, 180, 360
   assign attributes 204
   assign trigger 232
   attributes 83
   automatic postings 147
   balance carryforward 141–142
   create 80
   currency translation 203
   goodwill 273
   hierarchies 61
   import template 80
   map to general ledger accounts 106
   properties 81
   review attributes 206
   roles 150
   selection attributes 202
   statistical 262, 274
   types 81
   versions 103
Financial statements 215–216
Fiscal year variant 75
Fixed assets 176, 315
Flexible upload 133
   execute task 136
   methods 134
   prepare files 135
   Reported Financial Data app 136
   template 135
Flexible Upload of Reported Financial
   Data app 133, 137, 271
Formulas 155
Functional areas 93, 100, 149, 360

G

G type 188
General journal entries 167
   post 168
General ledger 283
General ledger accounts 60
   balance carryforward 143
   mapping 106
Generally Accepted Accounting Principles
   (GAAP) 17, 23, 283
Global settings 69–70, 122, 250
   global parameters 70
Goodwill 257, 264
   amortization 273
   calculate for acquisitions 277
   define global items 273
   elimination 273
   settings 271
Grid pages 349
Group close 313, 316
   continuous accounting 319
   cycle 314
   data loading 318
   dependencies on ledger close 319
   execute consolidations 318
   prepare data 317
Group consolidation view 65
Group currency 175, 179, 207
   rounding differences 197
Group Data Analysis app 65–66, 253,
   271, 281, 307, 328, 331, 340
   calculation of net income 150
   parameters 308
   results 310
Group journal entries 164
   post 167
Group journal templates 101
Group reporting 29, 37
   architecture 37
   best practices 66
   considerations 358
   consolidation entries 283
   consolidation of investments 258
   currency translation 175
   data collection 38
   financial close 313
   key takeaways 360
   master data 69, 72
   matrix consolidation 299
   predelivered content 48
   reporting 323

Group reports 323–324
   rule-based 325
Group-dependent adjustments 164, 288

H

Hierarchical consolidation view 65
Hierarchies 25, 83, 87, 91
   add 88
   add members/nodes 90
   consolidation groups 79
   copy 328
   enable eliminations 102
   export/import 91
   FS items 61
   matrix consolidation 301, 305
   predelivered 87
   reporting rules 66
   selections 120
   statuses 91
   types 88
   valid on 310
Historical rate 177, 181

I

IC Reconciliation report 326
Identity Authentication service 37
Identity providers 37
Implementation Guide (IMG) 69
Import Consolidation Master Data app 75,
   78, 83
Import data connections 345
Import Foreign Exchange Rates app 50, 191
Import FS Item Mappings app 60
Import Group Journal Entries app 56, 164,
   167, 285–286, 291, 295–296
Import Master Data for Consolidation Fields
   app 97, 99
Import/Export Validation Settings app 160
Income statements 218
   inventory 220
Income tax expenses 222
Indirect acquisitions 277
Indirect activity 264
Indirect investments 264
Indirect quotations 185
Inflation rates 176
Initialization settings 70
Intercompany elimination 19–20, 215–216
   configure 240
   eliminate intercompany transactions 249

Intercompany elimination (Cont.)
   predefined configurations 248
   reporting 253
Intercompany inventory sales 221
Intercompany transactions 20, 216
   eliminate 249
International Accounting Standards
   Board (IASB) 22, 216
International Financial Reporting
   Standards (IFRS) 17, 22
   principles 23
Interunit dividends 215
Interunit loans and borrowings 215
Interunit revenue and expenses 215
Interunit transactions 215
Inventory 220
   elimination 220
   handling 23
Investment elimination methods 21
Investor/investee relationship 23
Item roles 150

J

Journal entries 19, 164, 285
   adjustments 283
   configure templates 288
   dynamic display 326
   general 167
   group 164, 295
   import 56
   individual 292
   manual correction 166
   post 57, 167, 294, 296
   release from Universal Journal 170
   templates 56–57, 285
   validate 170
Journal Entry app 318
Journals posting 285

K

K4 fiscal variant 285
Key performance indicators (KPIs) 34

L

Leading ledgers 313
Ledger close 313, 319
   processes 315
Ledgers 71–72
   consolidation 316

Ledgers (Cont.)
  source 104
  versions 105
Legal consolidation 17, 24, 299
Liabilities 218
Live data connections 345
Local currency 74, 207
Local reports 323
Lock period 19
Logical ports 138

M

M type 188
Manage Consolidation Group Structure – Group
  View app 269
Manage Data Validation Tasks app 161, 163
Manage Global Accounting Hierarchies app ......
  87–88, 90, 102, 305–306, 328
Manage Group Structure app 59, 258
  Group View app 77
Management consolidation 17, 299
Management reporting 216
Manual postings 123, 239, 288, 291
Map FS Items with G/L Accounts app 60
Market data 188
Mass activation 161
Mass Reversal app 58
Master data 59, 69, 72, 357, 360
  additional fields 100, 103
  attributes 83
  breakdown categories 92
  consolidation groups 76
  consolidation units 72
  document types 107
  FS items 79, 83
  global settings 69
  hierarchies 87
  initialization settings 70
  matrix consolidation 301
  predefined 62
  selections 118
  subitems 93
Matrix consolidation 25, 299, 358
  business rules 302
  configure 300
  hierarchies 301, 307
  master data 301
  methods 302
  process steps 300
  reporting 307
  results 310
  run 305

Matrix eliminations 91
Measures 180, 338, 347
Members 90, 118, 337
Metadata 69
Methods 180, 194, 264
  assign rules 242
  assign tasks 234
  assign to consolidation unit 201
  configure 264
  create 198, 241
  currency translation 176, 194
  define rules 227
  examples 267
  matrix consolidation 302
  parameters 229
  predefined 195
  reclassification 227
  rule-based 259
Milestone tasks 127, 236
Minority interest 82
  specify 275
Mobile reporting 47
Models 347
  create 348
Month-end close 54
Monthly average rate 196
Monthly closing rate 196
Multidimensional reporting 301

N

Negative goodwill 273
Net income 147
  calculation 148
  derive 218
Nodes 90–91
Noncontrolling interest (NCI) 82
  calculate 268
Nonoperating expenses 221
Number ranges 114, 238, 240

O

Object versions 103, 105
OData services 32, 353
One-sided eliminations 220, 231
On-premise 32
Open connector 345
Opening balances 140
Operands 156
Operating expenses 221
Operational reporting 47

Operators 245
Organizational units 122
OutlookSoft 26
Ownership 20, 22, 76
   elimination 263
   maintain data 267
   review percentages 270

P

P&L Statement by Nature of Expense report 324
Parent companies 17, 20, 22, 38, 257
Parent units 79
Partial divestiture 263
Partner units 92
Payroll 315
Percentages 231, 244, 259
   matrix consolidation 305
   review 270
Performance 359
Period categories 128
   create 128
Period-end close 316
Periodic reclassification 227
Plan data 103
   integration 139
   version 104
Planning 82
   models 347
Post General Journal Entries app 168
Post Group Journal Entries app 285, 289–291, 293
Post Journal Entries app 57
Posting levels 107, 117, 239, 253
   Consolidation Monitor 226
Posting types 164
Preceding tasks 129, 236
Predefined reports 323
Predelivered content 48
   reports 328
   roles 67
   rule-based methods 259
Preferred stock 218
Profit and loss (P&L) statements 149
Profit center hierarchies 309, 331
Program RSHTTP20 188
Prompts 335
Proportional method 21
Purchase method 21, 258, 267

Q

Query Browser 40
Quotations 185

R

Real-Time Consolidation (RTC) 28
   challenges 29
   features 28
Real-time data processing 320
Reclassification methods 227
   create new method 242
   further settings 228
   options 229
   periodic activities 227
Reclassifications 106, 115
   consolidation of investments 259
   create new document type 241
   document types 237
   matrix consolidation 302
   methods 115
   predefined configurations 248
   rules 258
   validate 251, 254
Record copies 52
Reference currency 182
Rent/lease expenses 222
Report jump 47
Reported data validation 161, 324
Reported Financial Data for Group Reporting – Bulk Import and Update API 138
Reported Financial Data for Group Reporting – Receive Confirmation API 138
Reporting 19, 26–27, 41, 44, 323
   additional tools 333
   consolidation of investments 281
   currency translation 207
   cycle 315
   data analysis using reporting rules 328
   decision tree 45
   drill-through to transaction data 326
   financial 216
   intercompany elimination 253
   matrix consolidation 307
   predelivered reports 323, 328
   rule hierarchies 66
   SAP Analysis for Microsoft Office 333
   SAP Analytics Cloud 342
   SAP Fiori 350
   strategy 358
   tool comparison 46

Reporting item hierarchies 66, 87
Reporting logic 239
Reporting rules 87, 328, 360
    create 328
    create a new report 328
    maintain 330
Responsive pages 349
Retained earnings 140, 142, 147, 179, 268
    calculate 177
    reclass 19
Revenue 218
Reverse proxy 344
Role-based design 36
Roles 67
Rounding differences 197
Rule expressions 153
Rule-based consolidation 258
    configure 155
    example 260

S

SAP Analysis for Microsoft Office 29, 42,
    46, 333
    add data source 334
    capabilities 42
    sample report 43, 341
    standard CDS views 340
SAP Analytics Cloud 30, 41, 46, 131, 342
    agent 346
    create models 348
    data connections 344, 347
    features 41, 343
    home page 342
    live connection 344
    models 347
    plan data integration 139
SAP Best Practices 67, 79
SAP BPC optimized for SAP S/4HANA 26
SAP BPC, version for Microsoft 26
SAP BPC, version for SAP NetWeaver 26
SAP Business Planning and Consolidation
    (SAP BPC) 26
SAP Business Planning and Consolidation
    (SAP BPC)
    standard features 27
SAP Business Warehouse (SAP BW) 24, 26
SAP BusinessObjects Business Intelligence ....
    26, 44
SAP BusinessObjects Web Intelligence ... 44, 46
    features 44

SAP Cloud Platform 37, 342, 345
SAP Cloud Platform Integration 345
SAP ERP 24, 27
SAP Fiori 32, 34, 36, 46, 350
    apps 32, 34, 36–37, 67
    catalog 36
    create apps 350
    predelivered content 36, 48
    reporting 323
    run apps 354
SAP Fiori launchpad 32, 34
SAP Gateway 32
SAP HANA 32, 40, 344
SAP Landscape Transformation Replication
    Server 38
SAP NetWeaver 26
SAP R/3 23–24
SAP S/4HANA 28–29
    architecture 31
    currency translation 179
    data integration 139
    embedded analytics 39
    ledgers 313
    on-premise 32
    predelivered content 48
SAP S/4HANA Cloud 37
    APIs 138
    attributes 106
SAP S/4HANA Cloud SDK 37
SAP S/4HANA Finance 31, 37
SAP S/4HANA Finance for group
    reporting 29, 361
SAP S/4HANA Finance for group reporting
    architecture 31
    consolidation of investments 258
    currency translation 175
    data integration 130
    intercompany elimination 219
    master data 69
    matrix consolidation 299
    predefined reports 323
SAP Strategic Enterprise Management – Business
    Consolidation System (SEM-BCS) 25
SAP Web Dispatcher 344
SAP Web IDE 350, 354
Scaling factor 338
Scheduling 47
Scripting 27
Security 359
Security Assertion Markup Language
    (SAML) 344
Segment hierarchies 309, 331

Selections 118–119
   attributes 202, 204
   create 118
   expression 118, 244
   objects 72, 180
Self-service reporting 46
Selling rate 181
Service expenses 222
Service-level agreements (SLAs) 359
Set Global Parameters app 70
Share capital 218
Share changes 259
Single sign-on (SSO) 344
Source destination 230, 244
   matrix consolidation 304
Special fields 105
Special periods 284–285
Special versions 105
   create 107
Standard upload template 75, 80, 83
Standardized data validation 163, 324
Statement of cash flow 219
Statement of Changes in Equity report 326
Statement of Comprehensive Income report 326
Statement of equity 218
Step acquisition 263
Stories 344, 348
   create 349
   page types 348
Subassignments 150, 172
Subitems 62, 93, 99
   balance carryforward 143
   categories 93, 100, 144, 360
   create 97
   goodwill 273
   mass upload 98
   predelivered 93
Subsidiaries 17, 20, 22, 38, 257
   currency translation 175
   legal 20
Superordinate characteristics 88

T

Table ACDOCA 28, 32, 39, 56, 62, 104, 130, 139, 170, 180, 318, 361
Table ACDOCC 28
Table ACDOCP 104
Table ACDOCU 62, 71, 100, 121, 131, 133, 170, 180, 318, 361
Table TCURR 50

Task groups 125, 233
   assign tasks 234, 247
   assign to dimension 128, 236
   Consolidation Monitor 234
   custom 127
   define 125
   predefined 227
Task logs 54, 248, 280
   consolidation units 252
Task Logs app 54, 207
Tasks 115, 117, 233
   assign 116
   assign preceding tasks 129
   assign to group 125
   assign to method 234
   assign to task groups 234, 247
   block 145
   Consolidation Monitor 224, 234
   consolidation of investments 265
   create 234, 245
   Data Monitor 121, 123
   define 125
   preceding 236
   predefined 225
   sequencing 129
   settings 127
   statuses 122
   versions 107
Tax rates 74, 229
Templates 91, 99
   configure 288
   customize 353
   disable fields 290
   enable fields 289
   exchange rates 191
   header data 286
   journal entries 285
   line item fields 287
   options 287
   types 164
Temporal rate method 177
Test run 70, 122
Third-party exchange rate feed 187
   connect to URL 188
Topside entries 283
Total divestiture 259, 263
Totals 338
Trading partners 59, 92
Transaction
   CX10 80
   CX1I4 92
   CX1M 73

Transaction (Cont.)
   CX1N 73
   CX1O 73
   CX1P 76
   CX1Q 76
   CX1R 76
   CX1S4 97
   CX2O 222, 249
   CX53 112
   CX8ITAVC 83
   CXB1 .... 104, 107
   CXCD 121, 206
   CXD1 106
   CXDCPV 103
   CXE1 112
   CXE9N 66, 69, 125, 127–129, 138,
      141, 143, 147, 184, 186, 191, 195, 227, 233–
      234, 236–238, 241–242, 246–248, 264, 266,
      271, 273–274, 277–278
   CXEG 117
   CXEH 117
   CXEJ 117
   CXEK 117
   CXER 117
   CXGP 70
   FINCS_ADDLFLD_SEL_U 100
   FINCS_RRULE 87
   OBO7 182
   OBO8 .... 185, 190
   SE16N 190
   SE38 187
   SM37 189
   SOAMANAGER 138
   SPRO 301–302
   SUO1 36
   TBD4 188
Transaction currency 175
Transaction data 121, 357
   drill-through reporting 326
   integrate 130
Transaction types 93, 100, 144, 360
Transactional apps 36
Transactional logic 33
Translation differences 200
   analysis 208
Translation keys 196, 199
Translation methods 74, 106
Translation ratios 184
   create 184
Trial Balance report 326

Trigger 230, 243
   assign to FS items 232
   configure 231
   create 244
   matrix consolidation 304
Two-sided adjustments 288
Two-sided eliminations 56, 164, 239,
   254, 288

U

Unit-dependent adjustments 164, 287, 295
Universal Journal ... 28–29, 32, 38, 104, 121, 139
   data integration 130
   release 123, 131, 170
   validate 123, 171
Universal ledger 131
User adoption 359
User experience (UX) 34
User-defined fields 103

V

Validation methods 72, 74, 156
   create 158
   predelivered 157
Validation Results Analysis – Group View
   report 324
Validation Results Analysis – Unit View
   report 323
Validation rules 152
   assign to method 158
   create 154
   predelivered 153
Valuation allowance procedure 277
Versioning 25
Versions 70, 103, 107, 331
   attributes 104
   create 103
   predelivered 103
   special 105
   tasks 107
Virtual data models (VDMs) 33, 36, 39–40
Virtual data providers 43
Visualizations 34, 46, 346
   dashboard 48
   dynamic 343

W

Wildcards 120